Kessinger Publishing's
Rare Mystical Reprints

THOUSANDS OF SCARCE BOOKS
ON THESE AND OTHER SUBJECTS:

Freemasonry * Akashic * Alchemy * Alternative Health * Ancient Civilizations * Anthroposophy * Astrology * Astronomy * Aura * Bible Study * Cabalah * Cartomancy * Chakras * Clairvoyance * Comparative Religions * Divination * Druids * Eastern Thought * Egyptology * Esoterism * Essenes * Etheric * ESP * Gnosticism * Great White Brotherhood * Hermetics * Kabalah * Karma * Knights Templar * Kundalini * Magic * Meditation * Mediumship * Mesmerism * Metaphysics * Mithraism * Mystery Schools * Mysticism * Mythology * Numerology * Occultism * Palmistry * Pantheism * Parapsychology * Philosophy * Prosperity * Psychokinesis * Psychology * Pyramids * Qabalah * Reincarnation * Rosicrucian * Sacred Geometry * Secret Rituals * Secret Societies * Spiritism * Symbolism * Tarot * Telepathy * Theosophy * Transcendentalism * Upanishads * Vedanta * Wisdom * Yoga * *Plus Much More!*

DOWNLOAD A FREE CATALOG
AND
SEARCH OUR TITLES AT:

www.kessinger.net

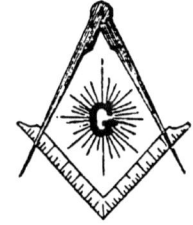

Frontispiece   *A recent photograph*

"CHEIRO"
(pronounced Ki-ro)

CONFESSIONS: MEMOIRS OF A MODERN SEER

INCLUDING REMINISCENCES OF AND INTERVIEWS WITH

KING EDWARD VII; QUEEN ALEXANDRA; HIS HOLINESS POPE LEO XIII; THE CZAR OF RUSSIA; KING LEOPOLD OF BELGIUM; KING HUMBERT OF ITALY; HIS EMINENCE CARDINAL SARTO; THE SHAH OF PERSIA; LOUIS PHILIPPE, DUKE OF ORLEANS; THE INFANTA EULALIE OF SPAIN; PRINCESS DE MONTGLYON; PRINCE ALEXIS KARAGEORGEVITCH OF SERVIA; THE PRESIDENT AND MRS. GROVER CLEVELAND; THE RIGHT HONBLE. W. E. GLADSTONE; LORD KITCHENER OF KHARTOUM; THE RIGHT HONBLE. JOSEPH CHAMBERLAIN; SIR AUSTEN CHAMBERLAIN; LORD BALFOUR; LORD RANDOLPH CHURCHILL; SIR H. M. STANLEY, *the Explorer*; CECIL RHODES; SIR LIONEL PHILLIPS; THE DUKE OF NEWCASTLE; LORD PIRIE; THE BISHOP OF BIRMINGHAM; THE REV. FATHER VAUGHAN, S.J.; "BOSS" CROKER *of Tammany Hall*; BARON VON BISSING; SIR ERNEST SHACKLETON *the Explorer*; FLAMMARION *the Astronomer*; LORD RUSSELL OF KILLOWEN, *Lord Chief Justice of England*; SIR EDWARD MARSHALL-HALL, K.C.; SARAH BERNHARDT; DUSE; OSCAR WILDE; W. T. STEAD; CHARLES STEWART PARNELL; MARK TWAIN; BLANCHE ROOSEVELT; ELLA WHEELER WILCOX; JULIA WARD HOWE; LILLIE LANGTRY; MELBA; NORDICA; CALVÉ; LILLIAN RUSSELL; WHITTAKER WRIGHT; PHILIP ARMOUR OF CHICAGO; JOE LEITER; H. GORDON SELFRIDGE; GABY DESLYS; MATA HARI; RASPUTIN; ETC. ETC.

By

"CHEIRO"

(Count Louis Hamon)

FORTY-ONE REPRODUCTIONS OF AUTOGRAPHS AND PHOTOGRAPHS

JARROLDS *Publishers* LONDON
Limited, 34 Paternoster Row, E.C.4
MCMXXXII

Printed in Great Britain at
The Mayflower Press, Plymouth. William Brendon & Son, Ltd.

CONTENTS

	PAGE
FOREWORD	13
INTRODUCTION	15

CHAPTER I

THE "MAKING OF A SEER." SOMETHING ABOUT MY EARLY LIFE AND MY REASON FOR ADOPTING SUCH AN UNUSUAL CAREER . . . 21

CHAPTER II

CURIOUS FACTS ABOUT THE HAND NOT GENERALLY KNOWN. I GET ON BOARD A TRAMP STEAMER IN ORDER TO SEE THE WORLD . . 26

CHAPTER III

I MAKE MYSELF USEFUL ON BOARD SHIP. THE ROUGH SAILORS BECOME MY FRIENDS. MY STUDY OF HANDS IS THE KEY THAT UNLOCKS THEIR HEARTS 29

CHAPTER IV

THE MAGIC OF INDIA. AGAIN MY STUDY OF HANDS BRINGS ME FRIENDS 32

CHAPTER V

INTERVIEWS WITH KING EDWARD VII. I READ HIS HANDS BEHIND CURTAINS. HIS "FADIC NUMBERS" GIVE DATE OF HIS DEATH . 39

CHAPTER VI

KING EDWARD'S VISIT TO PARIS. MY SERVICES TOWARDS THE "ENTENTE CORDIALE." I LAUNCH A NEWSPAPER IN THE INTERESTS OF PEACE . 43

CHAPTER VII

THE REASON "THE LAW" DID NOT INTERFERE WITH ME. HOW I CONVERTED SIR GEORGE LEWIS 50

CHAPTER VIII

KING LEOPOLD OF BELGIUM HELPS ME WITH AN "IRISH STEW." THE INFLUENCE OF GABY DESLYS OVER TWO KINGS 53

CHAPTER IX

INTERVIEWS WITH THE CZAR OF RUSSIA. HOW I FORETOLD HIS FATE. I MEET RASPUTIN AND PREDICT HIS DEATH 62

CHAPTER X

THE REAL STORY OF RASPUTIN. HIS INFLUENCE OVER THE CZARINA. THE TRUE CAUSE OF RUSSIA'S DOWNFALL 72

CHAPTER XI

STRANGE EXPERIENCES IN RUSSIA. THE "ANGEL OF THE REVOLUTION." THE CZAR'S EFFORTS FOR A WORLD-WIDE PEACE. I AM FORCED TO WITNESS AN EXECUTION IN THE FORTRESS OF ST. PETER AND ST. PAUL 82

CHAPTER XII

THE GREAT CATHEDRAL OF KIEFF. THE HOLY PICTURE ON HUMAN SKIN IS LOWERED FOR ME TO KISS 89

CHAPTER XIII

TIFLIS AND THE WONDERFUL KASPECK MOUNTAIN. I AM GIVEN A CONCESSION WORTH A FORTUNE, BUT AM MADE PRISONER BY BANDITS ON THE ROUTE OF GEORGIA 92

CHAPTER XIV

HOW I MET LORD KITCHENER. THE ONLY IMPRESSION OF HIS HAND THAT WAS EVER OBTAINED. HOW I PREDICTED HIS EXACT DATE OF DEATH 97

CHAPTER XV

I AM RECEIVED BY HIS HOLINESS POPE LEO XIII. CONVERSATION ON THE SUBJECT OF "FADIC NUMBERS." HIS HOLINESS PRESENTS ME TO CARDINAL SARTO, FATED TO FOLLOW HIM ON "THE THRONE OF ST. PETER" 102

CHAPTER XVI

AN EXTRAORDINARY INTERVIEW WITH KING HUMBERT OF ITALY. HIS ONLY QUESTION, "WHEN SHALL I DIE?" 108

CHAPTER XVII

HOW I MET MUZAFFER-ED-DIN, THE SHAH OF PERSIA, AND WHY HE GAVE ME THE DECORATION OF "THE LION AND THE SUN" . . . 113

CHAPTER XVIII

SIR H. M. STANLEY, THE FAMOUS EXPLORER, INTRODUCES ME TO GLADSTONE 117

CHAPTER XIX

A STRANGE STORY OF PRE-NATAL INFLUENCE 120

CHAPTER XX

MORE INTERVIEWS WITH FAMOUS PERSONALITIES. LORD RANDOLPH CHURCHILL. CECIL RHODES. JOSEPH CHAMBERLAIN—MY PREDICTIONS FOR HIS SON, NOW SIR AUSTEN. LORD BALFOUR. SIR LIONEL PHILLIPS. THE BISHOP OF BIRMINGHAM. THE REVEREND FATHER VAUGHAN. THE DUKE OF NEWCASTLE. LORD PIRIE AND "BOSS" CROKER OF TAMMANY HALL 123

CHAPTER XXI

A DINNER WITH LOUIS PHILIPPE, DUKE OF ORLEANS AND PRETENDER TO THE THRONE OF FRANCE. I MEET BARON VON BISSING, THE INFANTA EULALIE OF SPAIN AND PRINCE ALEXIS KARAGEORGEVITCH OF SERVIA 129

CONTENTS

CHAPTER XXII

An amusing Experience with Sir Ernest Shackleton, the Explorer. A Night with Flammarion, the celebrated Astronomer, in the Observatory at Juvisy 132

CHAPTER XXIII

How I met the late Sir Edward Marshall Hall, Q.C. I am nearly made a Co-respondent in the Divorce Court. A curious Example of Clairvoyance 135

CHAPTER XXIV

Why the Lord Chief Justice of England, Lord Russell of Killowen, gave me signed Impressions of his Hands 145

CHAPTER XXV

Sarah Bernhardt—an Interview under strange Conditions . . 147

CHAPTER XXVI

Blanche Roosevelt's Party and Oscar Wilde. A Startling Prediction and its Fulfilment 151

CHAPTER XXVII

A curious Instance of Prevision 155

CHAPTER XXVIII

Lillie Langtry's Acknowledgment. Melba, Nordica, Perugini, Lillian Russell, Calvé, The Great Duse and Janotha, Court Pianist to the Emperor of Germany 158

CHAPTER XXIX

Interviews with W. T. Stead—his tragic End on the ill-fated "Titanic" foretold. Mark Twain, Ella Wheeler Wilcox, the famous American Poetess, Mary Leiter, who became Vicereine of India 166

CHAPTER XXX

Some notable Experiences in the United States. My first Lecture in Boston. I meet Julia Ward Howe, the Authoress of the "Battle Hymn," and other interesting People . . . 172

CHAPTER XXXI

A Lecture at Syracuse that nearly spelt—Failure . . . 177

CHAPTER XXXII

How the Vanity of one Man nearly broke my Career . . . 179

CHAPTER XXXIII

A VISIT TO DETROIT AND CHICAGO. I MEET MR. ARMOUR, MARSHALL FIELD, H. G. SELFRIDGE, JOE LEITER, MAJOR LOGAN, AND A PREDICTION FULFILLED TO THE EXACT DATE 184

CHAPTER XXXIV

VISIT TO SALEM WHERE THE LAST WITCH IN THE UNITED STATES WAS BURNED AT THE STAKE. A BEAUTIFUL WOMAN SENT TO TRAP ME . 191

CHAPTER XXXV

AN EXTRAORDINARY GAMBLE. THE SHARES OF A METALLURGICAL COMPANY THAT ACTUALLY MADE GOLD 195

CHAPTER XXXVI

AN INVITATION TO A CHATAUQUA. A METHODIST ASSEMBLY IN FLORIDA AND SOME CURIOUS EXPERIENCES 203

CHAPTER XXXVII

I VISIT WASHINGTON. INTERVIEWS WITH PRESIDENT AND MRS. CLEVELAND, ADMIRAL DEWEY AND MEMBERS OF THE GOVERNMENT . 210

CHAPTER XXXVIII

THE MAN WITH THE "DOUBLE LINE OF HEAD" . . . 213

CHAPTER XXXIX

SOME GAMBLERS WHO CONSULTED ME. LORD CLANRICARDE AND HIS "SHILLING BETS." HOW I HELPED ARTHUR DE COURCY BOWER TO "BREAK THE BANK" AT MONTE CARLO 235

CHAPTER XL

CRIME HAS A PECULIAR FASCINATION OF ITS OWN. HOW WHITTAKER WRIGHT MET HIS WATERLOO 244

CHAPTER XLI

MATA HARI, THE FAMOUS WOMAN SPY. SHE TELLS ME THE STORY OF HER LIFE 248

CHAPTER XLII

I VISIT MONTE CARLO TO PROVE MY SYSTEM OF NUMBERS. ITS ASTROLOGICAL FOUNDATION 258

CHAPTER XLIII

THE LEGEND OF MONTE CARLO. THE SECRET THAT BECAME LOST . 262

CHAPTER XLIV

A Deal in a South African Mine. A Lady pays her Hundred Pound Bet. I am outwitted by a French Adventuress . . 272

CHAPTER XLV

Strange Fatalities of the Great War. How I predicted a Violent Death for Lena Guilbert Ford, Authoress of the famous song, "Keep the home fires burning" 279

CHAPTER XLVI

How Captain Lionel Bowles won the Victoria Cross, to be killed by a bomb in a London Street 282

CHAPTER XLVII

The Strange Story of the Duchess d'Avaray, Princess de Montglyon 286

CHAPTER XLVIII

How I married—and Why 293

Conclusion 297

Index 299

LIST OF ILLUSTRATIONS

"Cheiro"	*Frontispiece*
	FACING PAGE
H.M. the Queen at the Time of her Marriage to the King	36
X-Ray Photograph of the Hand of H.R.H. the Prince of Wales given to "Cheiro" at the Interview in Marlborough House	40
King Edward VII	46
The late King Leopold of Belgium at Wiesbaden . . .	58
The last Photograph of Nicholas II as Czar	84
Autographed Impression of the Hand of Lord Kitchener of Khartoum	98
Lord Kitchener of Khartoum	100
The late King Humbert of Italy	110
Muzaffer-ed-Din, the Shah of Persia	114
Sir H. M. Stanley, the African Explorer	116
Gladstone	118
"Cheiro" in 1897, before the "Thought Machine" which he demonstrated to Gladstone	120
Hands of Joseph Chamberlain and his Son, Sir Austen Chamberlain	124
A Candid Expression from Sir Lionel Phillips, the South African Millionaire	126
A Page from "Cheiro's" Visitors' Book: "Mark Twain" and the Rev. H. Russell Wakefield	128
What the Rev. Bernard Vaughan, S.J., wrote in the Visitors' Book	130
In "Cheiro's" Visitors' Book: Sir H. Drummond Wolff and Melton Prior	132
Sir Edward Marshall Hall at sixty-nine	142
Autographed Impression of the Right Hand of Lord Russell of Killowen, the famous Lord Chief Justice	146
What Sarah Bernhardt wrote after her Interview with "Cheiro"	148
The Right Hand of Sarah Bernhardt	152
Oscar Wilde in the Visitors' Book	154
Lillie Langtry (Lady de Bathe)	160
Madame Melba	162

LIST OF ILLUSTRATIONS

	FACING PAGE
LILLIAN RUSSELL AND SIGNOR PERUGINI	164
THE RIGHT HAND OF "MARK TWAIN"	166
"MARK TWAIN"	168
LADY ARTHUR PAGET	170
LADY ARTHUR PAGET'S OPINION	174
A STRIKING TESTIMONY FROM LILLIE LANGTRY (LADY DE BATHE)	192
MADAME MELBA'S WORDS IN "CHEIRO'S" VISITORS' BOOK	224
TESTIMONY FROM ELLA WHEELER WILCOX	240
THE RIGHT HAND OF MATA HARI, THE FAMOUS WOMAN SPY	254
LUCILE (LADY DUFF-GORDON), THE FAMOUS COSTUMIÈRE, AND THE REV. J. PAGE HOPPS	276
COUNTESS HAMON	294

FOREWORD

IN the course of my long professional career as " Cheiro," I have received innumerable letters from persons in all classes and conditions of life, requesting me to publish my reminiscences and experiences. In looking over these letters I have been much struck by the fact that it is what I myself call " the human " or more purely personal side of interviews with my various clients that appealed to my correspondents the most.

It is for this reason, in offering this volume of reminiscences to the public, that I determined they should take more the form of informal talks, or I might call them " confessions," both my own and those of my consultants, than the usual lines that Memoirs as a rule follow.

No statement is made in the following pages that I am not prepared to substantiate, the only reserve being that in the case of some of the " confessions " from my clients, I am entitled to withhold their names or cover their identity, except in cases where I have permission to make them public.

My rôle in writing these " confessions " is simply that of a chronicler —to relate in simple language what happened, to record what I was told. If at times my own thoughts should be heard through my story, it is because a " confession " of any kind must be more or less a personal matter—whether one confesses to a priest, a God, or to the ever sympathetic ear of one's own fellow-man.

" CHEIRO "

INTRODUCTION

By Major W. H. Cross, M.Sc., A.T.S.M., Mining Engineer
of the Tsong Mines of Mongolia

THE publishers of this remarkable book, *Confessions: Memoirs of a Modern Seer*, have asked me to write a few words as a general introduction. My only qualification to be entitled to do so is based on the fact that, although I am purely and simply a business man, I have all my life taken a deep interest in Occultism and the study of persons gifted with occult powers.

Living for the past fifteen years in Mongolia on the borders of that mysterious land known as Tibet, I have come into close contact with many of those Masters who have drunk deep of the eternal springs of Occultism that have flowed and are still flowing since the earliest dawn of civilization.

Away back in those Tibetan monasteries on " the roof of the World " where so few strangers are allowed to enter, as far back as I can remember I have heard the name of " Cheiro " spoken of with respect and admiration.

I had never met this mysterious man who had chosen to conceal his identity under a pseudonym, but I had the pleasure of translating some of his books into Chinese for the benefit of my friends among the Lamas and Abbots of Mongolia. They rewarded me by putting into my possession a set of the famous Chinese tablets made by Confucius.

These wonderful " occult tablets " based on the Law of Vibration, a study more understood and used by these deeply learned people than by any others, have predicted with an accuracy that is astounding the principal events that have taken place in the history of the world to the present day. To my amazement I found that these " tablets " corroborated the statements made in *Cheiro's World Predictions* which he published in 1926, setting out the coming events in history for the next hundred years.

Reading this book decided me to endeavour to seek out and make the acquaintance of the Seer who was gifted with such remarkable prevoyance, especially as many of the predictions in his book have even in the last few years been fulfilled.

But where was this man to be found, that was the question? While turning this point over in my mind, " an incarnate Abbot " in the Monastery of Toussoun Nor, announced to me one day, that one of their monks had been sent to California to find a man whose occult vibrations were of such a high order that perhaps he might be the

Seer I sought and whom they also wanted to find for a purpose of their own. This Abbot told me that I would recognize the man in question, not only by his high vibration but by an extremely old carved image of a Chinese Buddha which would be found where he lived.

As I am allowed a long vacation from my Company every two years, I determined, instead of going to Europe as is my usual custom, that in the autumn of 1930 I would visit California.

On my arrival in California, I found the name of "Cheiro" well known on every side, yet no one appeared to know where he lived, as the rumour was that he had retired from professional work and had recently come from England for the benefit of his health.

For some months I was occupied in searching for Tungsten mines for my Company when one day I ran across the monk from the Monastery of Toussoun Nor, who informed me that he had discovered a man whose vibrations were so in accordance with the indications given by the Chinese tablets, that he believed he must be the Seer that both of us sought.

One day he pointed out to me where the man lived. "In there," he said, "you will find the *incarnate* whom you seek." We were standing before the gates of an old-world-looking house surrounded by over two acres of gardens and half concealed by palms and beautiful trees in one of the principal avenues of Hollywood, California.

As I knew by reports that in various parts of the world many impostors have used or imitated the name of "Cheiro," I determined to make use of the clue the Abbot of Toussoun Nor had given me, namely, the carved image of a Chinese Buddha which I should find in the real man's house.

Walking up the avenue of flowering trees, I entered and was received by a man who closely resembled the photographs of "Cheiro" I had seen in his books. Without any "beating about the bush," I asked: "Have you a Chinese Buddha here?"

"Yes," the man answered; "if you are interested in such things, I hope you will be able to translate the meaning of old Chinese characters engraved on the back of the image."

I entered a room which was evidently used as a study; the carved image, made of some extremely heavy stone, was standing on a shelf before me, its feet surrounded by fresh flowers.

I examined it carefully; it was very old, there could be no question as to its great age. I turned it round; on the back of the image were two rows of Chinese characters belonging to a period so far removed they were extremely difficult to translate.

From what I was able to make out the image had been made sometime about one hundred years B.C. The part I was able to translate ran as follows:

> "He who looks—thinks—and finds good in all men. Blessed thinking attracts success and fortune. Honour cometh to the man in whose keeping this Buddha is found."

The rest being in compound ancient Chinese characters not now in use, in spite of my knowledge of the language I was not able to decipher, but at all events *I knew I had found the real " Cheiro."*

Asking his date of birth I then tested his vibrations by the Chinese tablets I had with me. I found they were higher than those of any man I had ever met, indicating that the man before me must be a reincarnation of some unusual personage of some far-distant past.

"How did you get that carved Buddha into your possession?" I asked.

"It was given to me under strange circumstances shortly before I left London for California," the man I now knew as "Cheiro" replied.

"Why did you come to California?" I blurted out.

"Why? Because I knew it was the one place in the world where the vibrations and climatic conditions would restore my health," he answered.

"These Chinese tablets," I went on, "tell me that you must have been extremely ill in 1925, a year that makes in your case by addition the bad vibration of an 8. In fact it is indicated that you should have died in that year. Is that true?"

"Perfectly true," he replied. "On the 23rd of June in that year, for some reason I never understood, I passed into a sort of comatose state, but not one caused by any form of disease. Doctors pronounced that my heart had ceased beating and that life had become extinct. As the spirit passed out of my body I appeared to see, as in a kind of vision, a man robed like a Lama making passes over me with his hands. His words formed in my mind that my life would be given back to me as it had been once before in a Buddhist temple in India, where after a long ceremony of initiation I had fallen into a state of coma which lasted for fourteen days.

The Lama seemed to say, " For the second time you will be restored to life, when the third time comes—you will *not* come back."

After some considerable period, how long I was not conscious of, the doctor at my bedside thought he detected a slight movement in the heart, then steadily it got stronger and stronger, and to the amazement of those present " I came back to life."

" The ' tablets,' in accordance with your date of birth," I broke in, " indicate that the third test will not come for many years yet. What are your plans now since you came to California ? "

" To get time to write," he answered quickly. " To give back to the world what I have gathered through my own experiences, to travel still more, and finally I hope to get to Mongolia or Tibet, for the ' call ' of those countries I have felt for a very long time."

" I need hardly ask if you believe in reincarnation ? " was my next question. " Do you have at times any recollection of your former lives ? "

" I most decidedly do," he answered, " but that is something I do not wish to talk about. People think it savours too much of the imaginative side of life, so I keep my visions to myself. Perhaps," he added musingly, " I may be the means later on of proving the reality of such things, but the time has not yet come for that."

Quick as a flash my thoughts went back to the words of the Abbot of Toussoun Nor. " In there," he said, pointing to where " Cheiro " lived, " you will find the *incarnate* whom you seek." Perhaps those strange words concealed the secret of " Cheiro's " successful career— an " old soul," one of those whose many reincarnations had taught him the lessons of humanity. How else could he have taken up a study, that for long ages had been downtrodden and despised, and made of it the key to unlock the hearts of Kings, Presidents, Leaders of Commerce, and all classes ?

I was astonished when he told me he was now " in his sixty-fourth year." I had heard many accounts of his radiating life and energy to those who came to consult him. I personally knew of cases where wrecks of humanity left his presence with renewed purpose to begin " the battle of life " over again. Perhaps I had again inadvertently stumbled across another secret of his success. It might perhaps be summed up in those simple words, " to give." While I considered such things, a text passed through my mind, " *It is more blessed to give than to receive.*" It seemed to me this was the basic thought on which this man's whole life was built.

Before I left, I looked through a pile of some thousands of letters from all parts of the world ; one and all they testified to the accuracy of his predictions, to the renewed life and hope he had given by his counsels to his innumerable consultants.

It is not my purpose in writing this introduction to pay this man any fulsome compliments. He does not need them. His work stands above such things : a lesson in itself of those mysterious forces underlying life, which so few of us realize and still fewer—understand.

W. H. Cross,
Mining Engineer of the Tsong Mines of Mongolia.

CONFESSIONS: MEMOIRS OF A MODERN SEER

CHAPTER I

THE MAKING OF A "SEER." SOMETHING ABOUT MY EARLY LIFE AND MY REASON FOR ADOPTING SUCH AN UNUSUAL CAREER

I WILL endeavour to avoid family and personal matters as much as possible, only giving such details as are necessary for readers to understand how and why Destiny found her materials on which to build.

On my father's side I am of Norman descent, and come of a family who can trace their lineage back to Rollo, the first Duke of Normandy.

As he became a Christian in order to marry the daughter of the King of France, I will only mention *en passant* a Pagan ancestor, known as Hamon the Sea-king, who with one blow from his battle-axe struck off the head of St. Hellier to prevent his converting his sailors to Christianity.[1] Historical records show that this incident took place on July 17th, A.D. 526.

I may, however, add that one of his descendants, the uncle of William the First, by joining "The Conqueror" with a fleet of four hundred ships and a large force of men, decided the Invasion of England. He received for his reward six of the largest counties of England and was named Prince of Glamorganshire. Subsequently, this man, Robert de Hamon, became such "a good Christian" that he established the first monastery in Britain, laid the foundation of Tewkesbury Cathedral, and is to-day honoured by a procession of bishops that once every hundred years makes a pilgrimage round his tomb. The last of these ceremonies took place as recently as March 25th, 1925.

Who can tell, if this blend of Christian and Pagan may not in later years have been responsible for my taking up such "heathen studies" as Astrology, Occultism, and "all such works of the Devil," as characterized by Henry VIII when he became "Founder of the Church of England."

My father's principal study was that of higher mathematics; for many years he worked out intricate problems with Gladstone even up to the last years of that great statesman's life.

From my mother's side, who came from Greek and French stock, I inherited poetry, romance, mysticism, and philosophy. The subsequent fusion in the fires of life of these combinations naturally produced a being predestined for a career that *would not run on conventional lines.*

[1] This incident caused the harbour and principal town of Jersey in the Channel Islands to be called St. Helier.

My mother, from her earliest days, was deeply interested in reading works on Astrology, Numerology, and the Study of the Hand. Consequently, almost as soon as I could read, she allowed me to revel in the little library of such books that she had collected. On my tenth birthday my mother passed over to me her little library and jotted down in her notebook the following: "My son has in his left and right hands the sign of the 'Mystic Cross.' For this reason I have given over to him all the books on occultism I possess, and especially those on the Study of the Hand. I believe he will make good use of these books. Even now in his early years I have noticed how he studies such works more than all others. He is certain to become a writer, and will, from what I foresee in his hand, make a name for himself in connection with those subjects."

I was only a little past eleven years of age when I caused a sensation in my family by writing a treatise full of illustrations on the Lines of the Hand, a subject, I must admit, not at all pleasing to my father's way of thinking.

Shortly after, perhaps to combat my "occult tendencies," my father decided to have his only son trained for some religious calling. What that was exactly to be did not trouble him in the slightest; he had some vague idea that I might be useful in converting the "heathen Chinee," the only reason, perhaps, being that his father had lost a considerable sum of money in a speculation in China.

I was accordingly packed off to an extremely strict school where he was assured that all such nonsense as "occultism" would be quickly knocked out of my head.

In his idea of giving me such training, he was, I believe, right, for I am certain that no boy ever began life with a more devotional temperament, or one more fitted, as a missionary, to be boiled alive for the supper of some cannibal race.

Although, at first sight, it may seem a strange anomaly, yet I hold that it was the essentials of that devotional temperament that made me cling to the study of hands with an obstinacy that, in the end, surmounted all opposition.

To my young mind, it was a mystery like religion itself; it contained the language of the Soul in its prison-house, and the lines of the hand seemed many a time to me a more tangible chart of life than the articles of dogma I was forced to commit to memory.

Thus it was that the more I studied creeds, the more the strange threads of Destiny seemed to bind thought, action, and life together, and the more I became convinced that Nature had her secret pages that neither Science nor Religion had as yet unravelled.

I cannot describe with what delight I discovered text after text in that wonderful "Book of Books" that told of the upward progress of peoples and those strange happenings "that the Will of God might be fulfilled."

Can I ever forget that night when, for the first time my mind grasped the idea of the Destiny of races, and the evidence of *Divine Design* in the starry heavens above *and in everything in Nature?*

The next day the " Book of Books " had a greater meaning for me than ever. Predestination became such a force in my thoughts that before I could realize what I was saying, I gave battle to my astonished professor and got punished by the losing of the play-hour for my pains.

Out of every evil comes good—that is, if we can distinguish the good when it does come—so during my punishment, instead of writing exercises, I sketched what I considered ought to have been the hands of some of the great men of Destiny, and became so absorbed in my task that I did not realize the presence of the old professor looking over my shoulder.

Instead of the reproof I expected, the old man sat down by my side and made me explain the drawings to him, line by line.

Then he became still more friendly, and to my utter astonishment he held out his own long, curious-looking hands, and in quite a gentle way asked me what I could make out of them.

To my amazement, I quickly discovered traits that were *even human*. To me, he had ever been something so high and mighty, that the idea of this monument of wisdom having lived as other men had never for a moment entered my mind.

He was a long, lean, anatomical structure, on which I thought someone had hung a professor's coat just to cover the bones ; a grey-eyed, spectacled Sphinx, that history said " had once stroked the Cambridge Eight to victory "—but history tells so many lies that none of us boys believed the story. Yet, as I warmed up to my subject, I forgot that history also said that he had never known emotion of any kind, that he had never loved, had never married, for soon I was telling him of a love in his life such as few men have met, and have cared to live life out afterwards.

I stopped, for something had gone wrong with my subject ; the hands had been pulled aside, and I beheld, for the first time, what tears mean when stern men weep.

After that morning we became friends. Many a difficult exercise he let me off, and many an old Greek and Latin book on Hands he translated for my benefit.

A religious training was, however, not to be my destiny. On the very eve of my entering for an examination which would have decided my career, I received word that my father was ruined by a land speculation that involved hundreds of others ; and so, almost broken-hearted at the sudden ending of my early ambitions, I returned home.

Disappointed and purposeless, I drifted for some time like a helmless ship on an idle sea, until at last, one day, some undercurrent, from where I know not, woke me again. I entered my father's study, and told him that I wanted to steer my own bark and see the world for myself.

My father considered that he had no longer the right to mould my career to his will—he had tried, but Destiny had been too strong—he would let Destiny have its way. So, with a small amount of money and a good, substantial blessing, I spread my own sails, and leaving the quiet harbour of home, I drifted out into the world's wide sea, like so many others have done before me.

It would be out of place to enter into my intervening experiences; the "Call to London" was in my ears, and so, as quickly as possible, I forsook the temptation of quieter routes and steered direct to that great city, where Fate meets Ambition in equal combat.

It is said that "coming events cast their shadows before them." One night, while waiting in Liverpool for the London train, my eyes caught sight of a book with a hand drawn on the cover, which I immediately bought. It was a translation of one of those old books on palmistry that had been printed with the first movable type; it was called in German *Die Kunst Ciromanta*, and as the train started on its journey I became engrossed in its contents.

The only other occupant of the carriage was a gentleman who sat opposite with his back to the engine; he had wrapped round his shoulders a heavy rug that almost concealed his face. When, however, my book was finished, as I laid it down I noticed that his sharp eyes were fixed intently on the drawing of the hand that adorned the cover. As I put it aside, he spoke in a genial, but rather bantering way.

"So you evidently believe in hand-reading. An odd kind of study it must be. But I suppose," he added, "it can find its followers, just as people believe in the shape of the head, and other things of the kind."

"Yes," I answered, "I believe that character makes itself manifest in every portion of the body, but naturally more especially in the hands, which are, after all, the tools that carry out the wishes of the brain. Surely there is nothing far-fetched or illogical in such a belief."

"No," he said laughingly. "Compared with some beliefs, that sounds both moderate and reasonable. But do the hands tell the future? That is the point that would appeal to me, if I could bring myself to believe in such a thing."

"Well," I replied, "as far as our future is made and influenced by our character, and by the tendencies we have inherited, I certainly believe they do, and as success is really the result of the preponderance of our strong points over our weaknesses, I think one might be safe in saying, that, looking at the study from this standpoint alone, the hands may be able to show which of these two forces will gain the mastery."

"Good," he answered, "your theory has really interested me." Stretching out his hands, he added: "Tell me, if you will, which will gain the victory in my case."

I can even now see those slender, intellectual-looking hands that this stranger laid before me; and how they interested me—line after line clearly marked, full of character and of events created by character.

I started with the Line of Mentality. I showed him its superior strength when compared with those of some of the designs in my book, and explained that it denoted his power of will, of organization, and of command over people. Then I called his attention to a well-marked Line of Destiny, deeply traced through his hand until a little past the centre of the palm, and I explained that it indicated strong individuality, a career that must play a marked rôle in life—a destiny, in fact, that would cause him to stand out as a leader above the common herd of humanity.

"But the end," he said, almost nervously. "What does that line show fading out—what does it mean?"

I laughed as I answered, for I could hardly believe, and I felt sure he would not, in spite of his interest.

"Oh," I said, "the stopping of that sign simply means rest for you; another Napoleon sent to St. Helena, I suppose."

"But why?" he demanded, rather excitedly. "What shall be my Waterloo?"

"A woman, without a doubt," I replied. "You can see for yourself how the Line of Heart breaks the Line of Destiny just below that point where it fades out."

Taking his hand away, the stranger laughed—a low quiet laugh—*the laugh of a man who was sure of himself.*

Shortly afterwards the train reached London, and as we got ready our valises and coats, he said:

"It's strange, but that science of yours has been curiously accurate about some things—except about the woman part. There is my card; you will see now how in some things it tallies—but the woman, no—a man with my life has no time for women." With a cheery "Good-bye," he jumped out, hailed a hansom, and was off.

Looking at the card, I read, "Charles Stewart Parnell."[1]

It was some years later, after the O'Shea divorce case and his downfall, that I was able to understand *the meaning of the Heart Line touching the destiny of such a man.*

[1] Charles Stewart Parnell, born June 27th, 1846, Vale of Avoca, Ireland, died October 6th, 1891, it was said of "a broken heart."

CHAPTER II

CURIOUS FACTS ABOUT THE HAND NOT GENERALLY KNOWN. I GET ON BOARD A TRAMP STEAMER IN ORDER TO SEE THE WORLD

THERE are many curious facts concerned with the hand that people have rarely if ever heard of, so I think it will not be out of place if I touch on them here, before I go more deeply into my own reminiscences.

Meissner, the great German scientist, proved that certain tiny molecular substances were distributed in a peculiar manner in the hand. He found that in the tips of the fingers there were 108 to the square inch, with 400 papillæ; that they gave forth certain distinct crepitations, or vibrations, that in the red lines of the hands they were most numerous, and, strange to say, were found *in straight individual rows in the lines of the palm.*

Experiments were made as to these vibrations, and it was proved that, after a little study, one could distinctly detect and recognize the crepitations in relation to each individual, that they increased or decreased in every phase of health, thought, or excitement, and became silent the moment death had mastered its victim.

About twenty years later, experiments were made with a man in Paris, who had an abnormally acute sense of sound—Nature's compensation for want of sight, as he had been born blind. In a very short time, by continual practice, this man could detect the slightest change or irregularity in these crepitations, and through these changes he was able to tell with wonderful accuracy about how old a person was, *how near an illness, or even death he might be.*

The study of these corpuscles was also taken up by Sir Charles Bell, who demonstrated that each corpuscle contained the end of a nerve fibre, and was in immediate contact with the brain.

This great specialist also demonstrated that every portion of the brain was in touch with the nerves of the hand, and that the lines on the palm were more particularly connected with nerves from the brain to the hand than to any other portion of the body.

The detection of criminals by taking impressions of the fingers and by thumb-marks is now used by the police of almost all countries, and thousands of criminals have been tracked down and identified by this means.

To-day at Scotland Yard one may see a library devoted to books on this side of the subject, and to the collections that the police have made; yet in my own short time I remember how this idea was scoffed at when Monsieur Bertillon and the French police first commenced the identification of criminals by this method. If the ignorant prejudice against a complete study of the hand could be overcome, the police would be still more aided by studying the lines of the palm, and by a knowledge of what these lines mean, especially as regards mentality and the inclination of the brain in one direction or another.

It is a well-known fact that, even if the skin is burnt off the hands, or removed by an acid, in a short time the lines will *reappear exactly as they were before,* as do the ridges or " spirals " in the skin of the inside tips of the fingers and thumb.

In connection with the terrible Houndsditch murders in 1911, the Chief Inspector of Police, replying to the magistrate, said that he had taken impressions of the prisoner's finger-prints at the court. The hands were not washed or prepared in any way. The following is a reprint from the *Daily Telegraph*, of February 25th, 1911.

" What is your authority for the proposition that the prints of two different fingers are never alike ? "

" I say that I have never found it so. I am only giving you my own experience."

" I want to know what steps you have taken to come to that conclusion."

" I may be able to help you in this way. We have 170,000 sets of prints recorded in the office. During the last ten years, since the introduction of the system, we have made 62,000 identifications —recognitions—and, so far as is known, without error. I think that will convey to your mind that we deal in pretty large numbers, and I am justified in telling you that *we have never found two impressions taken from different fingers to agree with each other.*"

I will pass over my first experiences in London.

I soon began to feel keenly what it is to be alone in the heart of a great city, without friends and without prospects of making any.

It was in this frame of mind that I found myself, one morning, wandering down by the side of the Thames, until in the end I had almost reached the great docks of Tilbury.

Here, at this gateway to the ocean, ships and boats of every description were loading, unloading, arriving or departing.

A curious longing took possession of my heart, to also pass through this gateway and meet the mysterious " Unknown " that lay beyond.

A battered and shabby-looking tramp steamer, just about to leave, attracted my attention. A hearty-looking man on the bridge was shouting orders—something urged me forward. I went down the gangway and made straight for the man. He was too busy to notice me, another order—the gangway was hauled in, another yell—the dock hawser was thrown off—the engines had already begun to throb. Frightened and desperate, I felt I had to do something. I approached the man again. Instinctively I knew he must be the Captain, no one but a Captain could roar like that, I thought. I got close up to him before he noticed me; I tried to look most respectful and humble and waited for him to speak.

Suddenly he did speak, if I can describe it as speech : " What in the name of Beelzebub d'ye want—who the devil are you ? " he yelled.

" Sir," I very politely said, " I want to go to sea."

"Go to hell!" he said, and turned his back on me.

By this time the boat was already some distance from the wharf, men were hauling in ropes, closing in side rails, pulling cargo under cover, but no one took the slightest notice of me.

I walked down the deck to the stern of the boat and sat down on a big pile of wet rope.

Night was coming rapidly on, the river was widening to the sea, the sigh of the wind against the mast reached me like a cry of pain. Green and red lights flashed from the fast-fading shore, flakes of spray lashed across my face. My wish had indeed been granted—I was at sea—but—alone.

CHAPTER III

I MAKE MYSELF USEFUL ON BOARD SHIP. THE ROUGH SAILORS BECOME MY FRIENDS. MY STUDY OF HANDS IS THE KEY THAT UNLOCKS THEIR HEARTS

HOW long I sat on that coil of rope at the stern of the ship I do not know.

Finally, wet from the spray, cold and very hungry, I determined, come what might, to stretch my limbs and walk up and down the deck.

The hour was late. I had not yet got to know how to tell the time by the ship's bells. I heard eight strokes ring out into the night, a scurrying of feet, a few dark shadows passing rapidly, then all was silence again except for the monotonous throb of the engines and the occasional crash of a wave against the side of the boat.

Light streaming from some portholes in a cabin behind the bridge attracted my notice. It was that same bridge where I had met the man I called the Captain earlier in the evening. Instinctively I felt that that man who had spoken so brutally, was fated to play some important part in my life. A curious idea came into my mind that made me want to peer into the portholes just to have a look at his rugged, weather-beaten face again.

I climbed up a short stairway to the bridge, stole softly round to the back of the cabin, and glued my face to one of the windows. My man was there all right, only looking more angry and brutal, if that could be possible.

His gold-braided cap was pushed to the back of his head, his coat, wide open, showed a striped shirt to the waist. On the table before him stood a pile of papers and some books that looked like ledgers, at his right was a plate heaped up with sandwiches and a large bottle of beer.

From time to time he grabbed a sandwich or gulped down some beer; his whole attention was, however, centred on the mass of papers before him, but his face showed he was working on some task that was not at all to his liking.

" I wonder if I could help him," I thought. Always inclined to act on the impulse of the moment, in another second I was standing in the doorway; the light of a big swinging oil lamp (there was no electric plant on ships in those days) fell full on my face. He did not see me, his head was bent over the papers, and as for me, I was too paralysed with fear to speak.

Suddenly he stood up to reach a book on a shelf. Our eyes met—if he had seen a ghost he could not have given a bigger gasp.

" Great God, he roared, " didn't I tell you to go to hell ? "

" Yes, sir," I answered meekly, " but I couldn't get off the ship

This seemed to strike him as a joke ; a grin passed over his face.

" Well, you're in hell now in any case," he roared ; " before morning you'll be as sick as a poisoned pup. What the devil brought you on the ship, in any case ? "

"I wanted to get away and see the world," I blurted out. Then pointing to the papers on the table, I stammered, "I am good at figures. I am sure I could help you if you would let me try."

I had touched a soft corner in his heart. "Good at figures," he grinned. "Well, let me see if you are. Add up these columns," and he shoved a large sheet before me. "Show me what you can do."

One column he had already done. I ran over it again; he had made a mistake in the pound column.

"How much?" he queried.

"Nearly a hundred pounds," I smiled, as gently as possible.

He pushed the gold-braided cap still further back on his head. "Look here, youngster," he said, "I'm glad you came on board. I'm captain and owner of this tub. I haven't got to report to any Board of Directors as I should have to do if I found a 'stowaway.' I haven't got to put you off at the first port we touch and hand you over to the police as would be my duty to do under other circumstances. You were lucky in choosing this boat, however you did it. Will you stick it out with me to the end of the voyage and take charge of these figures for me? It will be a long run, youngster, we discharge and load at every port. She's a rotten old tub that I mean to sell at the end of the trip, but if you stick to me I will make it worth while. Give me your hand on the bargain."

"Where did you say would be the end of the voyage?" I asked.

"Bombay, that will be the last port."

"India," I said, as I took his hand, "the one place in the world I would rather get to than any other. I will stick it out, Captain, have no fear of that."

"Have a sandwich, youngster," and he pushed the plate before me.

I did not need a second invitation. He rang the bell, another lot made its appearance, and as I would not drink, he ordered coffee.

I felt I was in a dream. Fate had indeed befriended me by leading me to a ship bound for that land of mystery and occultism that I had craved so much to see.

I will not enter into details of the voyage, it was perhaps the happiest one I ever experienced. The man I thought so brutal, whose oaths sometimes seemed to make the very ship tremble, had the kindest heart I think I ever met.

The rough sailors were equally good to me. They had me "read their hands" and tell them of sweethearts and wives they had left behind. At night when work was over we used to lie on the forward deck and look up at the stars together. I told them what I knew of the great Architect of the Universe who had planned all; how not a planet or a sun could vary a fraction of time in its pathway through eternity—and that we are told, "a sparrow could not fall to the ground without He knoweth it."

These rough men, sons of the sea and perpetual danger, seemed never tired of listening to the story. It may not have caused them to cease swearing when the cargo shifted, or the pumps refused to work. Perhaps, however, when Mother Ocean *called for the last time*—some of them may have remembered the story of the " sparrow " and were comforted.

CHAPTER IV

THE MAGIC OF INDIA. AGAIN MY STUDY OF HANDS BRINGS ME FRIENDS

IT would not be suitable in these pages to give more than a brief sketch of my experiences in India. From the letters I have received from all parts of the world, I feel compelled to hurry through these more personal episodes and get as quickly as possible to the "confession" and experiences concerning my professional career.

It may be my privilege some day to be called on to write fully of my life in India, but up to now "the call has not come," and if it does it will easily fill a book by itself.

I just want my readers to visualize, if they will, my feelings as I entered the "gateway of India," as Bombay is so well called—alone—without a friend or a single letter of introduction.

I will not attempt to describe the great city that stretched in the distance before me. Histories of India and guide books have already painted the picture better, perhaps, than I could do.

It was very early morning as I wandered down that great pier—the Apollo Bunder—alone.

Alone—without friends, without money—whatever I had earned on the ship I had spent during the voyage—yet in a way happy. Fate had been so good in bringing me to India, that for the first hour or so that inexpressible feeling of "God is on His Throne—all is right with the world," held my heart high.

And yet, must I confess it?—as I felt the scorching rays of the sun getting hotter and hotter, the strange babel of unknown languages becoming louder and louder, that great enemy of everything good—fear—began to make its appearance.

I began to doubt, I began to wonder at the Destiny that had so mysteriously forced my steps to India.

If you, dear reader, have ever been absolutely alone in a strange country you will realize the feeling of helplessness that was slowly stealing over my senses.

At the end of the pier near the town, I sat down on a stone seat and endeavoured to collect my thoughts. In all the many-hued throng of people that passed and repassed, no one took the slightest notice of me in any way. I was just "another foreigner" who had come to India, and nothing more.

Yet, out of that motley crowd, there was one person who was actually coming to greet me. An old man, garbed as I thought like a Brahmin priest, was even then making his way towards me. I could hardly believe it at first, but our eyes met and that seemed to decide his action.

He held out his hand with a pleasant "good morning," in English, and no music ever sounded sweeter in my ears than those simple words.

We sat down on the seat together ; at first the conversation was the usual commonplace expressions, the splendid view of the Bay, the town, and suchlike. I had just mentioned that I had arrived that morning, when he put the straight question : " Why have you come to India ? "

" Why," I said, " it has always been my most earnest desire. Besides," and I pointed to the Line of Fate on my right hand, " I suppose I am following my Destiny."

Again the study I loved so much had opened another door for me. I shall never forget the expression that passed over the old man's face. He held out his hands for me to read. I told him all I could of the dates of changes in his life, illnesses in the past, and other things.

" Wonderful ! " was all he muttered. After some time he told me of himself, that he was a descendant of the old Joshi caste, who had kept the Study of the Hand, together with that of Astrology, alive since some far-distant date.

He described where he lived and pointed to the Western Glats, or range of low mountains to the north of the city.

He told me of his associates, how simply they lived, the occult studies they believed in and practised.

Of course, I was fascinated. It reminded me so much of a book my mother had let me read, dealing with the Yogis of India.

I expressed a wish to go and live there with him. He held out his hand. Very simply he said, " Come, you will be welcome among us. Whatever our knowledge is shall be yours, provided you pass through certain tests of will-power and faith."

Thus it was that I had the inestimable privilege of living, for upwards of two years, in the society of men who were not only devotees of Indian occultism, but who were masters of whatever branch of it they had especially made their own.

It was here, under circumstances too long to relate in a book of this nature, that I took a vow that if ever I returned to my own civilization I would devote myself for a period of three Sevens, namely, twenty-one years, as a kind of Missionary of Occultism and more especially as an exponent of the Study of the Hand.

After in this way completing my " education," if I may use that term, I was enabled to return to London, by the death of a relation who had left me a considerable amount of money.

Free to carry out any whim I might have, I proceeded at once to make a collection of hands for my favourite study and for some time visited hospitals, asylums, and even prisons, making prints of all kinds and conditions of humanity.

In about a year I found myself the possessor of many thousands of impressions of hands ; still I had no desire to work professionally, for I found the simple life I had led in India had completely unfitted me for the routine and conventionality of life in great cities.

My love of travel also still held me in its grip ; so on the first opportunity that presented itself I turned my steps to another land of mystery, namely, Egypt, and for a certain time became occupied in investigating ruined tombs, temples, and suchlike, in that land where ages past the ancient Masters of Astrology built the Great Pyramid.

On my return from El Karnack to Cairo, I received the disquieting news that the man whom I had left to take care of the property I had inherited had embezzled everything I possessed and I was left without a cent.

It was at this moment, and for the first time in my life, that my study of hands was called into practical purpose; and in my rooms in Cairo I made sufficient money to enable me to return to London to see after my affairs.

Affairs, however, there were none. All my assets were gone; and the unfortunate man who had brought about such a result had disappeared from life's arena by the door of suicide.

Such being the case, I set about facing life from a new standpoint. I developed a literary tendency which I had scarcely dreamed I possessed. At all events, it enabled me to live, and even to enjoy life in a very simple way.

Linked up with my new calling, again there cropped up a practical use of my study of hands. A mysterious murder was committed in the East End of London. A blood-stained hand-mark on the white paint of a door attracted the attention of a detective; he had heard of me and asked me to see if I could make anything out of the impression of the hand.

An examination of the lines in the dead man's hand convinced me that the print could not have been made by his hand, but as there was a similarity in some of the markings, I came to the conclusion that the crime was undoubtedly done by a close relative, most probably a son. This clue led to the arrest and subsequent confession of a son by a former marriage, who up to then had been the least suspected.

Although this again aroused my interest in hands, still nothing was farther from my wishes than to practise such a study from a professional standpoint. Evidently I was not yet ready to preach the truth of what I believed in. (How easily one can see the design of Fate when one looks backward.) I had no self-confidence; the sensitiveness was too extreme, it had yet to be ground down a bit more by the " mills of life "—those mills of bitter experience that crush some to death or grind others to fit the groove in Fortune's Wheel that may one day carry them onward to success.

It was so in any case with me. The gift of writing, or call it what you like, before long began to change or for the time being died out; it had played its part, a step perhaps towards the next, but whatever it was, the faculty that wrote no longer suited the buyers. It may be that it did better work, I am not the judge—those who pay evidently have the right in such matters; but the stern fact remained that the manuscripts came back by every post, and the poems that some religious papers had always accepted before, were returned, sometimes with a pencilled line to say, "Style changed, not suitable for our pages."

A grey October morning found me returning from Fleet Street towards the Strand, utterly dispirited after an interview with an editor of a religious paper, a man who had taken sufficient interest in something I had written to ask me to call.

I had found the Rev. Dr. Richardson, editor of *Great Thoughts*, the most humane editor I had ever met. To my profound astonishment he had pulled up an arm-chair close to mine, and in the kindest manner he had talked to me as a father would to his son. He pointed out the changes that had taken place in my verses and articles in the past few months, and where in place of the devotional tone in which I had at first written, there now appeared ideas and expressions that he said could not possibly be penned by the same person.

This splendid old man, who could so easily recognize evolution in races or in worlds, could not realize the same evolution in the brain; to him I was a young man deliberately choosing "the broad road," and his duty was done when he had told me so, and yet it was almost with tears in his eyes that he added that I was between "the two roadways," in other words: on that narrow strip of thorny ground between the "broad path" that leads to—he graphically implied where, by a significant motion of his hand—and that other path that is evidently so narrow that it accommodates but very few people.

In my own mind, as I returned to Fleet Street, I translated his words to be exactly what I felt, namely, that I was in "the ditch" and had scarcely even the strength left to scramble out.

But life is ever so—the changes in its pathway are often only hidden by the breaks that we think we cannot get over. In a few minutes I was about to scramble out of "my ditch," but on which side I got I will leave my readers to decide in accordance with their own views, for I have long since learned that as the different chords in music make their own harmony—so the different opinions of people also vibrate in accordance with the position in which they have themselves been placed in the harp of Life.

We only make discords when we attempt to force our views of right or wrong upon our fellows.

Better then let each one strike his own chord—leaving to the great Musician of the Universe the finding of the melody.

I had just got beyond Somerset House on my weary tramp towards my rooms when I met a man of decidedly Jewish appearance who looked sharply at me as I passed.

As I had somehow always associated Jews with money, I wondered why this man looked at me so curiously, and I walked on, turning his look over and over in my mind.

Jews had always been a strange puzzle to me. When at school I had made a special study of their history. I had delved deep into their religion on account of its occult significance. I had spent sleepless nights over the wonders of their Kabbala and yet I had always asked, why is this race the most sceptical and materialistic that can be found in the world to-day?

Again these thoughts came to me—this race that God had taught by occultism, whose twelve tribes represented the twelve signs of the Zodiac, whose every action had been predicted in advance, whose prophets were higher than their priests, whose every letter in their Hebrew alphabet was associated with a number and its occult meaning.

Could it be possible, I thought, that by losing the key to the occult mysteries of their own religion, they had paid the penalty by—loss of greatness, loss of country, and the thousand and one privations they had since undergone?

I had often wondered why they were called " God's chosen people," and as there is no statement in Holy Writ that has not its own peculiar message, I had come to the conclusion that they were " chosen " as the race through whom the Creator manifests His design in races as well as in men.

These were the children of Destiny, preaching unconsciously the purpose of God to all people, and the living proof of design in all the happenings of their past—their present—and the—to be.

Such thoughts as these were teeming through my mind, when I felt a touch on my shoulder and saw the Jew I had passed standing at my side.

" What, you don't remember me? " he said.

" I cannot say I do," I replied.

" Well," he answered, " I have reason to remember you. You read my hands in Egypt and the things you told me happened, even down to my divorce case last month."

" Well then, you believe in the study now, I suppose? "

" Oh, no, I don't," he said. " I can't believe in such things; but there's money in it, my friend. You ought to make a fortune. Are you doing it now? I want some friends to see you."

" No," I said, " I am doing nothing; at least, only some writing for papers."

He laughed. " It's only fools who write," he said, and before I could collect my thoughts he already had a glittering proposition placed before me.

We walked round to his office—on the walls were some musty old paintings, on the table bits of china, some Egyptian scarabs and a bust of Grecian marble. He was a Government official, but he made money by anything he could lay his hands on.

Half an hour later I went back into the street, having signed a contract with him to commence at once in London, which contract, by the way, bound me to give him 50 per cent of all the money I made for twelve years from that date.

H.M. THE QUEEN AT THE TIME OF HER MARRIAGE TO H.M. THE KING, THEN THE DUKE OF YORK

Still one must give him credit for his enterprise.

The same day I started out with new-found courage to find suitable rooms to work in, in the West End.

But to find rooms was not an easy matter.

In those days the Study of the Hand was an "unknown and unheard-of quantity" in London.

It was an art relegated to gipsies and associated in the minds of landlords with everything that was evil. It was sufficient to mention the purpose for which I wanted the premises to receive a stern refusal and in some cases a religious lecture on tampering with such works of the devil.

At last I discovered a Scotch landlady (another race whose shrewdness I have since respected nearly as much as I do that of the Jews). She was a good Catholic with a small purse and a consumptive husband, but on my agreeing to pay double the rent, she arranged the affair with her conscience.

But the conscience of a Scotch woman is not a thing so easily lulled to sleep. I soon found she sprinkled holy water night and morning at my door, and on moving to larger premises a month later she charged me heavily for damage done to the carpet.

I was installed, it was true, but another difficulty cropped up; I had no name to work under, for as my father was still living, I would not in fairness take my own.

My Jew friend and myself discussed the question day after day. Biblical names he suggested by the dozen, at one moment he was particularly keen on a *nom de guerre* of "Solomon," but, fortunately for me, he had had that name applied to himself in his recent divorce case on account of his emulation of that monarch's desire to study the book of wisdom called *Woman*, so he finally decided such a distinguished name was too risky for so young a man as myself.

As the days went and no name was found, he began to get impatient at what he called my "capricious fancy."

He quoted Shakespeare's opinion on names every time we met, and wrote long letters on "procrastination the thief of time," the "greatness of opportunity," and so forth, and yet when the right name did come, he was the last man in London to acknowledge it.

One night, more worried than usual by his reproaches, my tired brain dreamt of names by hundreds, till suddenly I seemed to see in Greek and English the name "CHEIRO" standing out before me.

The next morning I announced my discovery. He repeated the name over and over again, and then informed me that I was a fool, that no one could pronounce it, that it had no meaning and was useless.

In vain I explained that Cheir was the Greek word for hand, and that "Cheiro" would thus become identified by intelligent people with the exponent of the hand.

"Fool!" was the only answer he deigned to give, and fearing

"Solomon" might be again revived, I rushed to the nearest printers and so the name "CHEIRO" became launched.

I had a brass plate made with the name "Cheiro" embossed on it in large letters; this was placed on the street door.

It had not been in position an hour before it attracted the attention of a man who was well versed in the Greek language. The word intrigued him; he came upstairs to my rooms. I explained what the plate meant and he insisted on having his hands read on the spot.

He was my first client, so perhaps I did extra well on that occasion. He paid me the great compliment of saying that I had not made a single mistake in anything I had said of his past life or of his very intricate character.

Without any demur he agreed to give me impressions of his hands for my collection. He signed them with his initials, A. J. B., explaining very simply that he was Arthur James Balfour, President of the Society for Psychical Research.

He was, as everyone knows, one of the most distinguished leaders of the Conservative Party in the House of Commons, later still Prime Minister, and farther on in his career as Lord Balfour he visited Washington to make the settlement of the War Debt between Great Britain and the United States.

At a dinner-party that night after he had met me, he related his interview—with the result that the next day my rooms were besieged by clients. From that moment out, I was overwhelmed with work, and by the end of the first month my Hebrew friend had received back whatever money he had advanced, together with the 50 per cent he had bargained for.

He was extremely happy over what he was pleased to call "his occult investment."

His happiness, however, was not fated to last long. One afternoon he rushed up in a very excited state and thrust an evening paper under my eyes. "Look there," he said, pointing to a paragraph; "I shall be ruined."

Looking down the column I found that some reporter in writing about the vogue I had started in London, quoted, to show his extreme learning on the subject (?), an extract from the old Act of Parliament to prove that all such professions were nothing less than illegal.

"My dear boy," my Hebrew friend said, "I shall be ruined. I am a Government official. I should retire with a pension next year. I shall lose all if I am found aiding and abetting a person to break an Act of Parliament. You have paid me back my money with interest; for heaven's sake tear up the contract and burn it, and if you get into trouble never mention my name or that you ever knew me."

Within five minutes the contract was burned, we shook hands, and I was again a free man.

After the contract was broken up, people came more and more to hear what I had to say.

CHAPTER V

INTERVIEWS WITH KING EDWARD VII. I READ HIS HANDS BEHIND CURTAINS. HIS "FADIC NUMBERS" GIVE DATE OF HIS DEATH

I SUPPOSE it is no secret now that King Edward was extremely superstitious in certain matters. Perhaps it would be more correct to write that he had an intense interest in Occultism, believing fervently in fortunate and unfortunate periods, in events foretold by premonitions, and so forth. Even Queen Victoria, strong-minded woman though she was, often incurred the displeasure of her consort by bemoaning a broken mirror or the spilling of salt.

I shall now relate as simply as possible my first meeting with King Edward VII. I need hardly mention that my experiences with him, in the house of a Society hostess and later in his own library, were gossiped about pretty freely, and greatly added to my reputation as a Modern Seer.

The first interview was cradled in secrecy, but Chance—or was it Fate?—upset the carefully laid plans of the lady responsible for my introduction to Queen Victoria's eldest son, then H.R.H. the Prince of Wales.

The scene of my first séance with the late King was not in his own residence, as might be imagined, but at the house of Lady Arthur Paget in Belgrave Square. Lady Paget was a charming American, one of the Stevens' heiresses of Chicago.

Secrecy was the keynote of the meeting, and I was not told the name of the owner of the hands I was to read. My simple instructions at the outset were to come to Lady Paget's house on a certain evening after dinner.

When I arrived, the hostess met me in the hall and conducted me to the smoking-room at the end of the passage. For all her apparent calm, I could see that she was more than a little excited.

"Now," she said, with a charming smile, "I want you to do me a great favour, 'Cheiro.' I would like you to sit behind these curtains I have fixed up, and read, as fully and as convincingly as is in your power, the hands of a gentleman who is coming here expressly for this purpose."

Although, to the reader, this may appear to have been an unusual request, my composure was not affected. Many of my clients adopted all sorts of plans to keep their identity secret from me. The only thing that impressed me was the elaborate nature of the arrangements in this case.

"You will be alone with him," continued Lady Paget, "and you are to say frankly what you see without having any regard for his feelings. Now, you will do your utmost, will you not?"

"Certainly," I answered, "I will do all I can."

Left to myself, I went behind the curtains and arranged the electric light so that I should be able to see the hands of my subject to the best possible advantage. Having done this to my satisfaction, I seated myself and waited.

A few moments later, I heard two people entering the room. Lady Paget directed her companion's hands through the slits which had been cut in the curtain for the purpose, and at once withdrew.

I proceeded to examine the hands before me as calmly as I would have done if the interview had taken place in my own rooms with one of my daily consultants.

The man behind the curtain appeared to be keenly interested. Once or twice he asked questions and occasionally withdrew his hands to note the markings for himself. I, too, was becoming more than usually excited, for the lines on the hands pointed to an unusual career.

Gradually I began to indicate the important years for certain changes and events, which appeared to be beyond his control.

I had reached the point of explaining the days and dates of personal importance, when an unexpected incident occurred that temporarily robbed me of my tranquillity.

Tuesdays, Thursdays, and Fridays, I said were the most important days of each week for him; his important numbers were sixes and nines; while the months representing these numbers, being March 21st to April 20th, April 21st to May 20th, and October 21st to November 20th, had contained, and would contain, the most important events affecting his life.

"Strange," said a deep and somewhat guttural voice, "but that is remarkably true."

At that moment he allowed his hands to rest too heavily on the curtain. The fastening pins came out, the curtain dropped at our feet—and I found myself looking into the well-known face of the British Heir Apparent, as he was then.

My looks betrayed my feelings, for, in the kindest way imaginable, he said: "You have no need to be nervous. You have done splendidly. Proceed with this curious and interesting idea of numbers," he continued, "forget who I am, and be as much at your ease as you were before the curtain so inopportunely fell."

His gracious manner would have restored the composure of the most nervous person.

Drawing over a small table and procuring some paper, I worked out by my system a diagram showing when the most momentous events of his life would happen, and with what exactness they would fall into certain months of the year, and not into others.

Together we figured out the absorbing details, and he himself indicated the year 69, saying, "As this is the only date when these two curious numbers first come together, which you say are the key-notes of my life, I suppose *that must be the end?*"

How far off it seemed; yet he himself, with uncanny precision, had picked out the date. For Fate had ordained that King Edward would be in his 69th year when he died.

By my system of numbers the month of April, the month in which

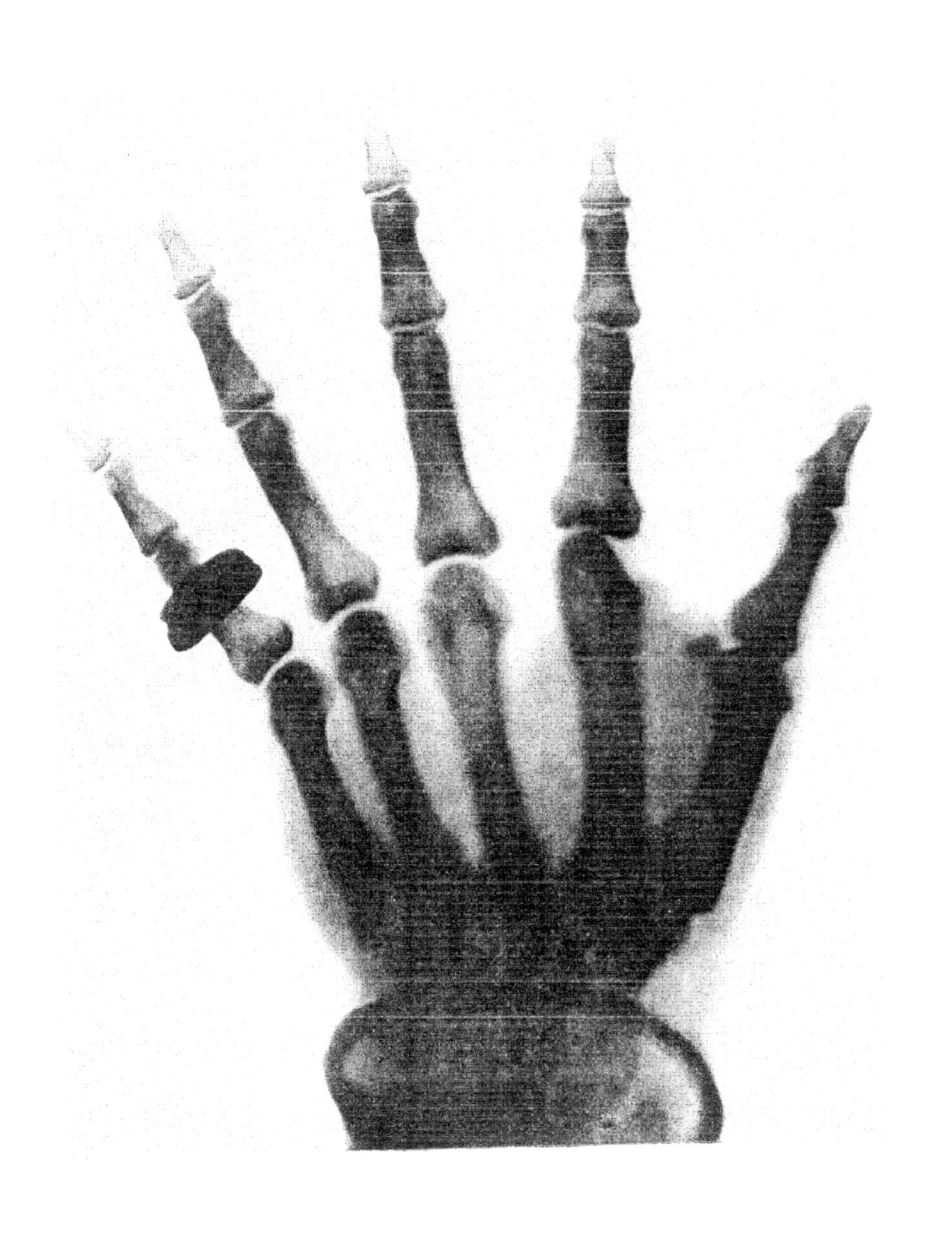

X-RAY PHOTOGRAPH OF THE HAND OF H.R.H. THE PRINCE OF
WALES GIVEN TO "CHEIRO" AT THE INTERVIEW IN
MARLBOROUGH HOUSE

he was afflicted with his fatal illness, has from time immemorial been represented by the number 9. The month of May, in which he died, is similarly represented by a 6.

The addition of the two figures of the age 69, equals 15 ; 1 plus 5 equals 6. He passed away on May 6th, a Friday, which, in the most ancient writings, is also symbolized by the number 6.

At the conclusion, he thanked me most courteously for my delineations, remarking that I had been most accurate in dealing with past events, even if my prognostications had been of a gloomy nature.

"We may meet again," he said, as I took my departure, and he added musingly, "So sixty-nine will mean ' The End.' "

It was some years later when I again had the honour of meeting him and he was still Prince of Wales.

The Boer War had just broken out, and thousands of British soldiers were leaving by every ship for South Africa.

The Princess of Montglyon, who had enjoyed the friendship of the Prince of Wales from her childhood, had come to London with a clever scheme for sending cargoes of biscuits out to the troops.

To further her plans, she had enlisted the interest of the Prince, and, as she had implicit confidence in me, I also had been enrolled to assist her in obtaining options from the big biscuit manufacturers of England.

One afternoon I was in her sitting-room in the Berkeley Hotel, engaged in placing before her the details of the options I had been able to secure, when the door opened and the Prince of Wales entered.

She was about to present me, when the Prince laughed.

"Why this is the man who will not let me live past sixty-nine ! "

"What a pity you are not the Kaiser," she rejoined. "He would already have been executed for *lèse-majesté.*"

Alas for her plans ! The Prince had called to tell her the War Office had just discovered large stores of biscuits that had been overlooked, and already several cargoes of them were on the way to the front.

A few evenings later, I chanced to be passing the Marlborough Club as the Prince was leaving. Coming towards me, he asked me to accompany him.

"I should like to have another chat with you about your theory of numbers," he said. "Come with me to my library, where we shall not be disturbed."

A Royal request is a Royal command, so I obeyed. It gave me great pleasure to do so, and I was flattered by the interest the Prince was showing in my study.

Together we entered Marlborough House and proceeded to the library. First handing me an excellent cigar, and then some paper, he asked me to work out the "numbers" of different people whose birth dates he mentioned.

From six o'clock until nearly eight, I calculated steadily, until a message was brought to him that he had to dress for dinner.

When, finally, he rose to go, he shook hands with me in a gracious manner. Then, making me light another cigar, he walked with me as far as the hall, where he held out his hand again and wished me "good-bye."

During this talk, he got me to work out, without my knowledge, the charts of the Kaiser and the Czar of Russia, as well as those of members of the British Royal Family; he gave me the date of birth, but not the name of any person.

He was extremely interested when I explained the ancient astrological theory that countries are ruled by planets and divisions of the zodiac. I explained that both Germany and England were under the same zodiacal sign—the House of Aries—and that as both were governed by the planet Mars, these nations were bound to fight for supremacy, or be in active competition against one another, but that the better plan would be to form an alliance together. He was so interested in this idea that he had me write it out for all the principal nations of the world.

CHAPTER VI

KING EDWARD'S VISIT TO PARIS. MY SERVICES TOWARDS THE "ENTENTE CORDIALE." I LAUNCH A NEWSPAPER IN THE INTERESTS OF PEACE

FOLLOWING the preceding account of my interview with King Edward VII, it may not be out of place if I relate here how I was later instrumental in helping forward his now famous project of the *Entente Cordiale* between England and France, and, in fact, being, I may safely say, one of the first promoters of the idea, at least in Paris.

I had naturally never forgotten His Majesty's condescension and kind manner towards me, and when living in Paris, shortly after the "Fashoda affair," which excited so much French feeling against England, I did my best in my small way to ensure that at least his name should be respected at the various meetings and gatherings I attended.

During my earlier education one of my tutors—an old man who knew the world well—had once said to me : " My boy, I will give you a golden rule for life's rough journey. It is this : ' Do good to those who do good to you ; and as for those who do you harm—*be sorry for their lack of judgment.*' If you follow this rule, it may not make you a millionaire, but it will at least give you great satisfaction."

I had never forgotten my old tutor's words ; his maxim became one of the fixed principles of my life, and I must admit I have sometimes gone to extremes to carry it into effect.

The feeling in Paris at the time of which I am writing was so bitter against anyone who even happened to " look English " that I often saw Americans when walking through the boulevards hold some American paper prominently in their hands so that the passers-by could see that, though they spoke the language, they yet did not belong to the " hatred race of land-grabbers who had stolen Fashoda."

About this time I had purchased and had become sole proprietor of the *American Register and Anglo-Colonial World*, a newspaper that had been founded during the last years of the Empire and which had the distinction of being the oldest paper published in English on the Continent.

As this newspaper was so well known and so respected by the French people for the impartiality of its politics and its continuous efforts to promote a good understanding between the Latin and Anglo-Saxon races, I conceived the idea that it might be employed in some way to overcome the bad feeling already mentioned.

I had remarked, like so many others, that although King Edward as a man was well liked and his former visits were continually commented on, yet when classed collectively with " perfidious Albion " he bore quite another aspect.

It therefore came into my mind that it might be a good idea to collect together the views of the principal political leaders and public men as to what, in their opinion, would be the reception that King Edward would have if he should visit Paris at that moment.

In pursuit of this plan, I caused a letter to be sent out from the *American Register* which, to put it briefly, asked the following questions:

That, knowing the deep sympathy and profound interest that His Majesty King Edward had always shown towards France, what in their opinion would be the reception accorded to him if he should visit Paris at that period?

And if such a visit would not do much to allay the bad feeling that existed, and be the beginning of an *entente*, both politically and commercially, to the ultimate benefit of both nations?

Some thousands of these letters were sent out, and in a few days, and rather to my own astonishment, replies came pouring in from all parts of France.

And what replies they were, too. Some even went so far as to write no less than eight pages of argument either for or against the idea; some replied very tersely, a mere "yes" or "no"; while others were so abusive as to the very idea of a newspaper asking such questions at such a moment that my very hair at times almost stood on end.

The majority, however, spoke of the King himself in terms of respect and admiration, and many went so far as to say, that, if such a visit were possible, they would do their utmost to make it a personal triumph for His Majesty, even though they might not be able to forget "the last action of *la politique anglaise*."

As Sir Edmund Monson, the then British Ambassador to France, had always been extremely cordial to me, without consulting anyone I made a packet of these letters, showed them to him, and asked if he would send them on to His Majesty.

Sir Edmund, although most considerate to me, told me frankly that, with the tension and bad feeling which existed, he did not believe any good could come from my plan, and so, with my packet of letters, I returned home.

About this time I happened to be introduced to Monsieur Delcassé, who was then Minister for Foreign Affairs. He congratulated me warmly on the attitude taken up by my newspaper, and from what he said, both then and at the second interview, I determined to carry out my plan and forward the letters to His Majesty myself.

I went through them very carefully, but I admit I kept back all those that were too hastily or hotly worded, and which, I am glad to say, I still have in my possession, especially as many of those who wrote them have since altered their opinions, and are to-day staunch upholders of the *entente*.

So that King Edward might, perhaps, remember who his correspondent was, I wrote, in my letter, "Your Majesty may perhaps recall me as the man whom Your Majesty said ' would not let you live past sixty-nine,' " and so the letters were sent off.

Nearly a month passed. I heard nothing; but meanwhile the *American Register and Anglo-Colonial World* continued its articles and published the most important and favourable letters we had received, and special copies of these issues were sent to almost every man of note in the political world in France and England. Many of the leading French newspapers commented on the enterprise of the *American Register*, and quite a large number quoted the published letters and articles in their own columns.

One afternoon I received a message requesting me to call at the British Embassy, and from Sir Edmund's own hands I received the letters returned from the King, "with his thanks for the trouble I had gone to in the matter." Sir Edmund added: "In the next few days you will hear that arrangements are being made for His Majesty's visit to Paris."

It would be superfluous for me to make any comment on "the visit" itself, for almost every writer and newspaper in the world has passed judgment on its far-reaching effect.

I must, however, disagree with the "glowing descriptions" given by so many of the "warm reception" accorded to His Majesty when his carriage first drove through the streets of Paris, on May 1st, 1903.

It was anything, in fact, but a warm, or even a lukewarm, reception. It is true that the Avenue du Bois de Boulogne and the Champs-Elysées were crowded with people, but they were for the most part a very silent crowd; very few even raised their hats.

Everyone knew that President Loubet and the authorities were in the greatest apprehension lest at any moment a counter-demonstration should take place. Every precaution that could be taken for the King's safety was taken, and the police arrangements in the experienced hands of Monsieur Lépine were perfection itself. Still, all this could not arouse the enthusiasm of the people—a people who rather imagined that "the visit" was just "another proof how France had been sold into the mesh of 'perfidious Albion.' "

THE LAUNCHING OF THE "ENTENTE CORDIALE" NEWSPAPER

About a month before "the visit," as it became called in Paris, I thought I would follow up the success of the letters previously mentioned by starting another newspaper whose title would be more in accordance with political interests, and with this view I founded a paper called the *Entente Cordiale*, or, as its sub-heading announced it, "A Journal in the Interest of International Peace."

For this purpose I engaged correspondents in the principal capitals of Europe and several editors capable of carrying out its programme. All went well until the evening before we went to press with the first number, when an episode took place which was perhaps in itself an omen of the difficulties that beset the path of those who, in a world of strife, allow themselves to dream of peace.

This incident, although amusing enough now to look back upon, yet, at the moment it occurred, almost prevented the birth of the journal and nearly altered my own ideas on the feasibility of the enterprise.

On account of the errors made in the English part of the paper by our French compositors, we were compelled at the last moment to make the first issue of the publication through our London offices, and so I rushed over from Paris the night before hoping to find everything in readiness for the press.

My principal editor was an Englishman who had lived the greater part of his life on the Continent, and who was thoroughly conversant with several foreign languages. With his majestic white beard he looked in himself a perfect model for a Statue of Peace, but at heart he was an incarnation of a thorough British bulldog who showed his fighting blood in a second if England's dignity or righteousness was ever called in question.

Another editor was a Frenchman who, although in the end one of the greatest defenders of the *Entente Cordiale*, yet at that time was still " a little sore over Fashoda," and always ready to bring the question up at the most inopportune moment.

The editorial staff in London was completed by an Irishman who had been a war correspondent for the past thirty years.

The Irishman, I need hardly add, was the "powder magazine" of the ship.

His faults may have been many, but he was one of the most brilliant writers it has ever been my lot to meet. No subject was amiss to his rapid pen. International law to the history of an Egyptian mummy —all came the same to him if an article was required at the last moment, provided that one did not question a certain generous allowance of alcohol that " was necessary," he said, " in order that his brain might see things in their proper light."

In such a combination his Irish sense of humour was, however, a somewhat serious drawback. In fact, he thought " International Peace " such a huge joke that he nearly split his sides with laughter the first time he saw our ambitious sub-title.

On the night in question, as I jumped out of my cab, even at the street door the sounds of discord and strife already reached my ears. " What's the matter ? " I said to the porter. With a significant grin he replied : " It's the first night of the Peace journal upstairs, sir ; that's all."

Quite enough for me, I thought, as at the moment there came an appalling crash of glass, and the Frenchman came tearing down the stairs like a madman.

In the editorial room it looked as if a cyclone had paid a surprise

Edward R & I.

*His Most Excellent Majesty
King Edward the Seventh.
by gracious permission of Her Majesty Queen Alexandra.*

visit—proof sheets were flying in every conceivable direction, my venerable editor had a nose so damaged that it spouted blood like a water-cart, while my ex-war correspondent looked as if " he had just returned from the front."

I never knew exactly what happened—for I never asked. " A good beginning," was all the Irishman said as he seized a pen and began to dash off his special article. " England," at the other end of the table, tried to look dignified ; while a diligent office boy gathered up the proofs and solemnly laid them before me.

Not a word was said, but for the few hours that followed I must confess no two men ever worked harder in their lives, with the result that some of the finest articles on the virtues of peace were produced that were perhaps ever written on the subject.

The next day the *Entente Cordiale* appeared on the bookstalls, and I found that we had the honour of giving the King a new title—that of " Edward the Peacemaker." The first time he was ever called by this name was *in the columns of the first issue of this journal.*

In less than two months the *Entente Cordiale* was selling well in all parts of the world, and letters of congratulation poured in from the most unexpected quarters. Nearly every monarch in Europe wrote to acknowledge copies, and from far-distant Japan the Mikado sent the expression of his best wishes for its success.

Financially there was, however, nothing I ever undertook that ended in such a balance on the wrong side. Printed on the best paper, well illustrated, and too well edited, its cost of production every month overwhelmed its income, so that after running this paper for a little over a year I was glad to stop my experiment in " the interests of peace "—and pocket a very heavy loss for my pains.

And the inconsistency of it all ! While all nations praised peace they all actively prepared for war. A certain millionaire, who got the greater part of his fortune from the manufacture of cannon and armour-plate for battleships, gave large donations to build a Palace of " Peace," but no one ever thought of supporting a journal dedicated to its propaganda. Diplomatists were the very last who ever paid their subscriptions, and when they did—it was with a request that their picture might be published in the next issue.

In the end I came to the conclusion my Irish ex-war correspondent's joke had not been far wrong, and that in the great game of politics the superb ideal of International Peace is a dream only to be indulged in—*by the very rich—or the very foolish.*

Before I conclude my humble remarks on this question of International Peace, I feel I must add—even at the risk of displeasing those of my readers who clamour for the curtailing of the Navy of the United States and of Britain—that it is these great navies alone which to-day appear to have the peace of the entire world in their keeping.

It is only those who like myself have lived for many years beneath the flags of other nations, who can realize what such a power for Peace really means. In a menace of war there is only one question asked: " What will England do ? " or, " What will the United States do ? " and it is on the answer to that vital question that so much depends.

Among the many letters I received praising my paper, the *Entente Cordiale*, the one that I prize most was from Buckingham Palace from King Edward VII.

When the Coronation of His Majesty was postponed in June 1902 owing to his serious and severe illness, Queen Alexandra sent an equerry to fetch me to come and see her at Buckingham Palace.

Addressing me in my professional name, she said in the simplest manner possible, " ' Cheiro,' you so impressed His Majesty many years ago that he would not die before his 69th year, in his now serious condition I have sent for you to instil into his mind that his life is good for many years yet. As His Majesty is now only in his 61st year, you must impress on him that his present gloomy fears are not justified and that his Coronation, which you predicted for August 1902, will take place as stated by you."

" Your Majesty, I will do my best," I answered.

Very quietly we entered the invalid's room.

The King, looking very pale and weak, was half sitting up in bed propped up by pillows.

The Queen gave a sign for the nurse to leave and motioned me to a chair by the side of the bed.

King Edward recognized me at once; in fact, the impression I got was that he knew the Queen had sent for me.

On a table by the side of the bed lay a sheet of paper, the same identical paper on which he had jotted down my words at that first interview he had with me at Lady Paget's home; the date 69 was underlined by a heavy pencil-mark.

He nodded and gave me a smile of welcome.

In a very weak voice he said, " I am very, very ill. Do you still believe I will reach my 69th year ? "

Almost impulsively I blurted out, " Your Majesty need have no fear. I know you will live till then. I am *positively* certain of it."

My very assurance seemed to do him good. Quite a bright smile passed over his face as he said :

" Thank you. I hope you are right. I have many things to do before I pass away."

Then it was, I put forth all the will-power I could command. Looking him straight in the eyes, I said, " Your Majesty will remember that I worked out many years ago that your Coronation as King of England would take place in August 1902. We are now only at the end of June; this illness is only temporary, please believe me."

" I am almost forced to do so," he nodded. " Every other date you gave me turned out correctly. I jotted them down on that paper.

Tell me what date, then, in August would be the best one to fix for the Coronation."

"One of your number of nines, sir," I replied. "I would suggest August 9th. The number 9 is your strongest 'fadic' number. You were born on November 9th. From time immemorial in occult studies, November has been considered the House of the Nine, or the House of Mars *negative;* that is why your name will go down to posterity as Edward the Peacemaker. The month of August is called the Royal House of Leo the Lion; therefore August 9th would be the best date that you could decide on."

Fearing of tiring the Royal invalid, I rose to go.

The King smiled and said, "Thank you for your visit. You have made me feel better."

Call it hypnotism or anything one pleases, Queen Alexandra sent me a message the next day that my words had cheered up the King so much that he had slept well that night and showed signs of rapid improvement, and that orders had been given for the Coronation to be fixed for August 9th—the date I had named.

The next occasion on which I met King Edward was at the reception given him at the British Embassy in Paris at the time of "the visit."

I was formally presented to him by the Ambassador, Sir Edmund Monson, among other members of the British Colony. The presentation was naturally made under my own name, but with that wonderful memory for places and names which characterized His late Majesty, he immediately addressed me as "Cheiro," to the great astonishment of Sir Edmund, who it is quite probable did not know me under my *nom de guerre*.

The last occasion on which I met King Edward was just a few months before his death. He was joining the royal train at Victoria Station to make his usual journey to the South of France to escape the winter in London. I happened to be going abroad also and was standing on the platform as he passed. I did not for one moment believe that he would notice me, but he stopped and, smiling broadly, said, "Well, 'Cheiro,' I'm still alive, as you see, but I have not reached that 69 number yet."

A few weeks later he entered that fatal year. By the end of November telegrams were already coming from Biarritz saying that the King's health was causing anxiety, and his own doctor was despatched from London.

In a few months His Majesty returned to Buckingham Palace and the public heard with consternation towards the middle of April of his serious illness that was soon to prove fatal.

On Friday, May 6th, 1910, in his 69th year, the first time that the "fadic" numbers of 6 and 9 came together in his life, King Edward VII was "gathered to his forefathers."

CHAPTER VII

THE REASON "THE LAW" DID NOT INTERFERE WITH ME. HOW I CONVERTED SIR GEORGE LEWIS

DURING my first season in London, some of the newspapers began printing many articles about me; some were extremely flattering, but some were equally hostile and again called attention to the old Act of Parliament, making out that my profession was illegal, and calling on the authorities to have me suppressed.

Questions about me were also asked in the House of Commons, and at last, one Monday morning, I received the visit of a Police Inspector, who politely but firmly told me that no steps would be taken if on the following Saturday I closed my consulting-rooms. He very considerately left with me a copy of the Act of Parliament which read as follows:

> "Any person or persons found guilty of practising Palmistry, Astrology, Witchcraft, or all such works of the devil, is hereby deemed a rogue and vagabond to be sentenced to lose all his goods and possessions, to stand for one year in the Pillory, and to be expelled from the country, or to be imprisoned for life."

The Act in question had been made in the time of Henry VIII, probably because the "much married monarch" did not wish that his many wives should have any chance to find out there unhappy fate by such aids as Astrology or Palmistry.

After the passing of such an Act, it is to be hoped that Henry VIII slept in peace, knowing that Anne Boleyn or Catherine Howard would remain in ignorance that "the axe" was waiting for their heads.

History also states that the King blamed Astrology for the rebellion of the Duke of Buckingham, but whether it was caused by wives or rebellions, in any case this intelligent Act (?) came into being.

Under his daughter Elizabeth it fell into abeyance, due, perhaps, to her belief in the famous old Astrologer and Palmist, Dr. John Dee, and her many visits to consult him at Mortlake. In any case history tells us that her "good Dr. Dee" acted for over twenty years as the Queen's Advisor, Counsellor and Friend, and who knows if the greatness of England to-day does not owe more than anyone may imagine to "Queen Bess" acting on the advice given her from Palmistry and Astrology of which studies old John Dee was a master of at that time?

In the *Life of Dr. John Dee*, published recently by Constable & Co., London, it is disclosed that this famous Palmist and Astrologer was also celebrated for his scientific attainments which were of no mean order. "When Queen Elizabeth desired that a statement of her claims to Greenland and other countries discovered by English explorers should be made, she turned to Dr. Dee, who ably fulfilled the task. He also made a map of the Polar regions for the Queen."

Such was the *savant* under whose tuition Queen Elizabeth studied

Astrology and Palmistry, and " upon whose powers of divination she relied when troubled by Kepler's Comet."

Under George III, whose name is handed down to posterity for the loss of America, the old Act was revived, and as times may change and people may change but Acts of Parliament never, so does this law remain in force in England to the present day.

I had naturally no desire to bring down on my head the threatened consequences involved, so I gave orders to my secretary to book no appointments beyond the end of that week, as on Saturday at six o'clock I intended to see my last client.

I never worked harder or did better than during that week, and at six o'clock on Saturday, as far as my plans were concerned, I had finished my career as "Cheiro."

Fate, however, which had played such an eventful part in bringing into my life actions over which I had no control, had evidently planned otherwise. I heard a lady's voice at the door entreating my secretary to arrange an interview then and there, and so the lady entered.

At the end of the interview, leaning back in her chair, she said: " I have always been a believer in this study of hands. I shall have some very interesting people coming to my house to-night. What will be your fee to come and demonstrate your work ? "

" Nothing, Madam," I said, " absolutely nothing ; since six o'clock to-day, ' Cheiro ' has ceased to exist, but if you will allow me I will give you my services with pleasure, as I only want to convince intelligent people that there are some who carry on this study who are neither charlatans nor impostors."

" Thank you," she said ; " you shall have your opportunity perhaps to-night. Here is my card, ' Mrs. Walter Palmer, Brook Street.' I will expect you at 9.30."

. . . .

The guests tripped up the stairs laughing and talking. The first person they insisted on my seeing was an elderly gentleman whom they addressed as " the doctor." " The doctor," without opening his lips, submitted fairly gracefully to " the operation," and in a few moments I had sketched out the main points of his career, the years in which he had made such and such changes, etc. He became interested, the laughing ceased, and finally when I stopped he said : " Well, I have been your greatest sceptic and have argued all the evening against such a thing being possible, but I don't care whether you have told me these things by my hands or by my boots, you have certainly hit on dates and things that are accurate, but how you have done it I do not know."

" Still," I said, " if you are a doctor this science is all wrong, for you are no more fit to be a doctor than the man in the moon."

" Well, sir," he said, " what profession by ' my lines ' should I then have followed ? "

"Only one," I answered, "that of a barrister, or better still perhaps, a criminal lawyer."

Pulling out his card, my visitor said, "I confess I think you really deserve to know who I am." On the card he handed me I read the well-known name of

Mr. George Lewis[1]

After that, one guest after the other passed through the ordeal, Mr. Herbert Gladstone, Sir Henry Irving, his son Lawrence Irving, and dozens of others, until finally, at nearly three o'clock a.m., Mrs. Palmer said I must be too tired to do more, and she invited me to call the next day and talk over what she said was "her triumph as well as mine."

The next day (Sunday) she said: "You cannot possibly think of giving up this work," and then I told her of the newspaper articles which had been sent to me, of the Act of Parliament prohibiting it, etc.

In her enthusiastic way she said: "You made such a success last night with George Lewis. I will run round and ask him his opinion. Wait here till I come back."

I waited, and when she returned she said: "George Lewis says you are working on such a totally different foundation from what this old Act was intended to apply to, that you do not come under it. You are to send his card to Scotland Yard and tell them to address any further communications to him."

I obeyed these instructions. The next morning I resumed my professional life, and never again at any time did I hear of any interference or talk of this Act of Parliament being applied in my case.

---

[1] Afterwards Sir George Lewis, head of the famous law firm of Lewis and Lewis.

CHAPTER VIII

KING LEOPOLD OF BELGIUM HELPS ME WITH AN "IRISH STEW." THE INFLUENCE OF GABY DESLYS OVER TWO KINGS

HISTORY has by now lined up faithfully the foibles and the follies, the shrewdness and the calculating cleverness in finance and diplomacy of Leopold II, King of the Belgians.

I had the honour of reading his hand and revealing to him his length of years. It was an interesting experience, for King Leopold was a complex man as well as a versatile monarch.

During the run of the Paris Exhibition, I was invited one day to an important lunch given in honour of Senator Thomas Walsh, of Washington, one of the American Commissioners to Paris at that moment.

This luncheon was given in the handsome building called the United States Pavilion, and was attended by the principal Americans in Paris, together with many notable French people, who had contributed towards making the exhibition the success it undoubtedly was.

Mr. Walsh was an enormously wealthy mining man of the State of Montana, whose liberality had done much to make the American section extremely popular with all classes.

After several speeches had been made by the American Ambassador, General Horace Porter, the Commissioner General, the President of the American Chamber of Commerce, and others, the Chairman, for some reason I have never understood, called on me also for a speech.

As I rose to reply, King Leopold, who was a personal friend of Mr. Walsh, entered with his aide-de-camp, Count d'Outremont, and stood at the door. I cannot remember one word of what I said; all I know is, that, at the end I was loudly applauded, and the King sent word that he would like me to be presented to him.

King Leopold congratulated me on making what he was pleased to term " an excellent impromptu speech," and added that " one of the things he most envied was the power of speech." The same week, I again met him at a large reception given by Mr. Walsh; on this occasion, although there were some hundreds of people present, His Majesty with his hawk-like eyes spotted me at the other side of the room, and crossing over, held out his hand, at the same time saying : " I have been told that you follow a very strange and interesting profession. I would like to have your address and perhaps in one of my leisure moments I may want to avail myself of it."

I heard later that many people were amazed at his condescension in talking to me, and I know I suffered in consequence from the jealousy it aroused.

Two days later, I was sitting down to an early lunch, when my servant announced that an elderly gentleman who had great resemblance to the King of Belgium, was in the *salon*, waiting to see me.

Through the dining-room door, to my amazement, I saw that my visitor was indeed none other than King Leopold, and hastily entering, I apologized for the smell of lunch that pervaded the apartment.

He stood up, his great height towering over me. Very gravely he said: " Monsieur ' Cheiro,' I want you to do me a favour. I am sure I smell Irish stew; it is a dish I always relish, so do me the favour of asking me to help you with it."

" But—Your Majesty——" I stammered.

" There are no ' buts ' when I want anything," he laughed, " so don't let us allow the dish to get cold—believe me, there is nothing I would like better."

Fortunately, the stew was really a good one, for my " French cook " happened to be an Irish woman, united in marriage to a chef at the Café de Paris, and Irish stew was to her a kind of sacred memory of all that was best in her Motherland.

In a few minutes, we sat down to the table and my illustrious visitor did full justice to my Irish dish.

I found His Majesty of Belgium was enormously interested in the United States, and as I had travelled all over it, many were the questions he asked me about its marvellous development and also about the different Americans I had had the good fortune to meet while there.

After a cup of coffee and some cigarettes, we adjourned to my consulting room, and I explained " the lines " in his long and highly intelligent-looking hands.

He became apparently interested in what I told him; a good hour had already passed, the clock on my table struck four o'clock. He started up abruptly, " I cannot stay longer," he said, " but I want to hear more. When can you come to me at Laeken Palace ? To-day is Thursday—I leave to-morrow for Brussels; can you come on Saturday at six in the evening ? "

With kings, to hear is to obey. Full up though I was with engagements, I decided to cancel them at once. The magnetic personality of this monarch, at the time the most-talked-of King in Europe, gripped me with intense fascination.

" Good," he said, after I had mapped out my movements, " I shall expect you at six. Take this "—he placed a card in my hand—" present this to the officer of the guard at the Palace and you will be admitted without question."

With this he strode out of the room.

I made a fast journey from Paris, and arrived in the Belgian capital in ample time to keep my appointment. I found Laeken a fine-looking palace, originally an old château very much modernized, and surrounded by beautiful woods. I made my way to the main entrance, was stopped by the guard, handed over to an officer, and quickly found that the card given me by the King was an *Open Sesame*. On the stroke of six, I was seated in a small room, plainly furnished, and not unlike an ordinary hotel sitting-room.

Suddenly one of the inner doors opened and His Majesty appeared. He was dressed very simply, in a morning suit and smoking his eternal cigar. He bade me come into his study and quickly made me feel quite at home. For some minutes the conversation turned upon the British Royal Family. One remark I can repeat, as it was so shrewd: "When King Edward gets his 'head' in foreign affairs, he will be a big surprise. He is a born diplomat." He also made some penetrating remarks upon the character of the Duke of York, now King George V. I was amazed to see how closely the Belgian King had studied various Royalties.

I had expected to be called upon to give His Majesty another demonstration of my art of reading hands, but to my surprise, he suddenly said:

"You are hungry; you must have something to eat."

I protested that I required nothing.

"Nonsense," he replied, getting up and touching a bell. "You gave me an excellent 'Irish stew' in your house, you shall now have one in mine." As he said this—and I must confess I thought my ears deceived me—he laughed his peculiar sardonic croak, and repeated again in commanding tones that had a touch of foreign intonation: "I will show you how to make one, it is my favourite dish."

I certainly was not prepared for the gastronomic exhibition that followed, and incidentally I may reveal that I stumbled upon one of the most curious Royal hobbies. For in response to the ring, a servant appeared.

"Kitchen!" was the curt word, and the servant vanished. This servant, by the way, was an ex-guardsman, a Scotsman, who had been for some years in the service of King Leopold.

"Come with me," said the King, rubbing his hands.

I followed him into a small kitchen, wonderfully fitted up with every device for cookery, and entirely dominated by electricity.

On the side of the electric range a copper pot was gently simmering; going up to it His Majesty took off the lid and sniffed the savoury smell with evident satisfaction.

It was while he was earnestly engrossed with the task of watching the stew, that I was amused—I hope the expression is not disrespectful—to learn that the King of the Belgians often cooked his own supper.

"I'm so tired of the elaborate dishes cooked by the chef," he told me, "and have no intention of digging my grave with my teeth. To this end, some time ago, I thought out the idea of doing some cooking myself. I have found it real fun, and I am going to say that nobody can cook better Irish stew than I can."

I remained silent, when suddenly he added:

"Is it true, 'Cheiro,' that King Edward is a great gourmet? It is so gossiped in European courts, and when he came to Brussels as Prince of Wales, my chefs vied with each other in preparing wonderful dishes. But most of them were passed by."

I was able to assure His Majesty that so far as I had heard, King Edward was extremely simple in his taste, and I repeated the anecdote concerning the occasion when, as Prince of Wales, he was asked to dinner by Lord Randolph Churchill and consented on conditions: "Churchill, you must give me liver and bacon." The King of the Belgians laughed heartily at this.

With such light conversation, the time went on until the stew was ready. His Majesty poured it out into two dishes and there and then sat down, His Majesty opposite to me at a small table *in the kitchen*. I can honestly say that it was the most perfect Irish stew I have ever tasted. It was a curious introduction to a séance with Royalty.

Afterwards we returned to the smoking-room again—for such I found it was—and after he had pressed me to have something to drink, he began:

"Now, 'Cheiro,' I want you to continue the examination of my hands from where you left off the other day. I have heard from several sources of your remarkable skill in predictions of death-days, and important dates in life. I want you to tell me of any striking events that you see, and anything that portends in the near future."

As he uttered these words, the King's manner became very serious; I felt that he realized that the shadow of "The End" was creeping over his long reign, and that he half dreaded, yet longed, to peer into the "Future."

With this he laid his strong, masterful hands upon a small cushion, and remained absolutely silent while I again made a careful examination of the clearly marked lines in his hand. Sixty-two years of crowded life seemed indexed on the right palm; while on the left I saw graved the hereditary pointers that told their own tale of the inherited nature, the weak and strong points that are just as visible on the palm of Royalty as on any other hand.

Born son of a king known as the "beloved Uncle of Queen Victoria" (Leopold I), he inherited to the full the peculiarities of the Saxe-Coburg-Seafeld dynasty; proud, obstinate, strong in love and in hate. I must confess that as I studied the maze of lines that confronted me, I became fascinated with my subject, until at last I involuntarily exclaimed:

"A wonderful hand! It holds what it grasps!"

"No flattery," replied the King sternly.

"Sir," I said, "if your hand was that of a peasant I should say the same."

I explained to him the peculiar significance of the Line of Head so clearly marked across the centre of the palm. It showed not only remarkable intelligence, but, above all, the power *of acquisition*. It need hardly be explained that the King's conduct of the Belgian Congo exploitation has been acknowledged to be a masterpiece of high finance.

"But tell me," he said, "my physical condition."

As briefly as I was able, I explained that the indications pointed to remarkable lung development, a sound nervous system, while the heart and circulation were excellent. I may state that it is beyond dispute that upon the palm of the hand is graved a chart of health, which is closely described in the many books I have written on this study.

" Quite sound then, ' Cheiro ' ? " he questioned, fixing his imperious eyes upon my face. I paused, for I saw written there one fatal defect which I knew must soon bring the Royal frame down to the dust of dissolution.

" Not quite," I said diplomatically ; " you will, I fear, before long develop some serious trouble in connection with the digestive system and internal organs."

" That is your revenge for being made to eat Irish stew in a Royal palace," he laughed. " You are wrong, ' Cheiro,' I can eat anything."

I let it pass and went on to other matters. When, two years later, on December 17th, 1909, death called for the King at his palace, the official bulletin gave the cause of dissolution as *a complete breakdown of the digestive organs, and intestinal obstruction.*

I passed over the matter of his various love affairs, and the dark cloud that had settled over his domestic affairs. Few monarchs have been more cursed in their matrimonial life than Leopold II. His Austrian wife was estranged from him ; his heir, the Duke of Hainaut, died of consumption ; his daughter Stephanie was involved in the tragedy of Meyerling whereby her husband committed suicide ; whilst in his later days, only one of his children, the Princess Clementina, would come near him.

" What are my years ? "

This was the next question shot out in his commanding voice. I knew that the birth date of His Majesty was April 9th, 1835, and I had already made the calculations necessary for divining the predominating position of the planets when he came into the world. The prevailing influences were favourable for success in business undertakings, but decidedly unfavourable for matters of affections. According to my computation, the figure 9 was the key numeral in the life of His Majesty of Belgium. It would take up too much space to show how astoundingly this figure dominated his whole existence, just as 6 and 9 were the overruling figures of King Edward.

I was certain that 1909 was King Leopold's " fatal year," and probably at the end of the year, as the planetary conditions would then be unfavourable to him. I asked him point-blank if he wished me to give an opinion.

" Yes," he said, " why not ? "

I then said :

" I should predict 1909 as being a year of greatest import to your physical health, and the utmost care should be taken all through that particular year."

I may here observe that while I believe a man's Fate is, as the Eastern saying puts it, "bound invisibly about his forehead when he enters this Vale of Tears," yet it is possible by knowledge to avoid the ill-effects of unfavourable aspects of the planets. Thus I warned W. T. Stead years before his death by drowning, that a certain month in a certain year was highly dangerous to him should he be travelling by water. He laughed and said: "Don't you know, 'Cheiro,' that I am to die at the hands of a London mob?" This was a fixed idea of his, and I have often wondered whether he remembered my prediction, in that solemn moment when he saw Death approach him on the sinking *Titanic*.

Leopold brushed aside my prediction concerning 1909; for he was nervously sensitive upon the subject of his health.

In December 1909, on the 10th of the month, I happened to be turning up my notes on this interview at Laeken, and observed to a friend in London: "I should not be surprised if there is news of the death of a Continental monarch before long, and I believe it will be the King of the Belgians." At the time there was no hint that Leopold was failing; in fact, the official newspaper reports gave his health as excellent. But on the 15th came the news that he was ailing; on the 17th he died suddenly. The post-mortem revealed the cause of death to be intestinal trouble.

I cannot reveal all the conversation that followed. It has been said that Leopold was a harsh father and a hard taskmaster to his Congo workers. But I may chronicle that he found abiding happiness in his companionship with the Baroness Vaughan—some recompense after the extraordinarily unhappy scenes that made up his married life, and culminated in his quarrels with most of his family.

After an interview lasting nearly two hours, we were interrupted by the appearance of a short, stout, remarkably handsome lady, to whom I was introduced. This was Baroness Vaughan. Leopold was said to have gone through a marriage ceremony with this lady some time before; but as the ceremony was not recognized by the Belgian Parliament, she was not regarded as Queen; it is not correct, however, to call the match a morganatic marriage. She was a very great comfort to the monarch in his declining days, and was with him to the last.

As the King evidently did not wish the Baroness to remain, she very tactfully left the room, and His Majesty went on to discuss with me my system of numbers and lucky and unlucky days.[1]

He disclosed that he was a shrewd speculator on the Stock Exchange, and wanted to know what his "lucky days" were. I explained to him exactly which would be the most favourable times for matters connected with money, and he carefully noted down all I told him.

I left His Majesty of the Belgians feeling that I had been in the presence of a very remarkable man, one who possessed qualifications that would have made him successful in many walks of life, if he had

[1] This system is described fully in "Cheiro's" *Book of Numbers*.

THE LATE KING LEOPOLD OF BELGIUM AT WIESBADEN

not been born beneath the purple. He had a clear brain, great power of concentration, inflexible will amounting to hardness, and real gifts of diplomacy. Against this must be set his predilection for the fair sex, which caused his frequent visits to Paris in his later days to amount to a scandal. In this connection I cannot forbear touching upon a rather interesting visit I had from a lady whose name is still remembered with affection.

I was in my apartment at Paris one morning when I received a visit from a heavily veiled woman. On examining her hands, I saw certain lines that are unusual in denoting influence of remarkable men of the highest rank.

As I have explained before, a kind of clairvoyant picture often appeared in my brain during my consultations.

"Madame, there must be considerable perplexity in your mind at the present time, for you have excited interest in the hearts of two men, both much older than yourself, and who have the means to gratify their wishes." I hesitated, and she said in a singularly sweet voice:

"Do not shirk, 'Cheiro,' from telling me everything."

"These two men both wear a crown, but up to now, you have repelled them both."

She removed her hands from the cushion and put them up to her veiled face, as though to control her thoughts. Then she said in a low voice:

"My name is Gaby Deslys. You know all about me by repute"—at this time she was making a triumphant success at the Folies Bergères in Paris—"I have had invitations to supper from both King Carlos of Portugal and King Leopold of Belgium. I do not wish to seem discourteous, or refuse what is practically a command, but I do not know what to do; up to now, as you say, I have kept free from both."

The more I studied the palms of this talented dancer, the greater was the sense of bewilderment I experienced. For here was one of those radiant creatures of sunlight, born to delight thousands, yet as surely doomed to sadness and premature death. All those who knew this enchanting woman intimately, know that she was singularly unselfish and anxious to help everyone who was in trouble. But death beckoned her away at the zenith of her career.

I saw, too, that here was one of those women destined to cause the formation of events of far-reaching importance. It is no secret that the open rivalry between Carlos of Portugal and Leopold of Belgium, as to which could shower the greatest attention upon Gaby Deslys when she rose to triumphant fame, was most unfavourably commented upon in the Press of both countries. The assassination of Carlos and his heir marked the culmination of this revulsion of respect for the House of Braganza. Gaby Deslys was one of those lovely but "fatal" women, born to set in motion many currents leading to trouble.

The extraordinary mystery concerning her birth and who she really was, has never been cleared up.

Hundreds of thousands of people the world over have seen her on the stage. Her photograph has been published in every continent, yet no one has come forward with any definite proof of *where she was born*.

After her death persons rose up like mushrooms from almost every country claiming that they were relatives of the celebrated beauty, but as she had left a fortune of some hundreds of thousands, it may have been the cause of such universal interest. These claims, however, were never proved and have only increased the mystery.

Gaby herself always avoided the subject by merely saying there was a mystery about her birth and that when the right moment came she would herself disclose who she was—*but that moment never came*.

During the last War when she was playing in London and when everyone was more or less " suspect," a woman in very bad circumstances turned up claiming to be her mother, but instead of being welcomed as under the circumstances one might expect, she was denounced by Gaby as an impostor and ordered to leave her hotel.

This woman retaliated by saying she was a native of Hungary and that Gaby had been born in that country. If this had been true, the famous beauty would have been ruined and probably interned as an enemy alien. Scotland Yard investigated the story, but decided there was nothing in it, and Gaby's public career went on as before.

On her return to Paris, in view of the persistent rumours set afloat by many war-maddened persons, Gaby suddenly produced what she called " her real mother." This woman, who called herself Madame Caire, actually produced a birth certificate to prove that she had a girl born in Marseilles at almost a date that might have fitted in with Gaby's age. She told a story of how out of her small savings made from selling papers and magazines, she had educated and trained her brilliant child.

With the advance of the German Army on Paris, no one had time to investigate the story and Gaby was accepted as French.

This woman remained in Gaby's sumptuous apartment for some time, but when the War ended, a clerk of the Bureau of Records at Marseilles declared that the certificate of birth belonged to another mother and child. From this out it is said that the certificate had become mislaid and nothing more was heard about it.

A third equally unknown woman put in an appearance one evening in the star's dressing-room in one of the Paris theatres and claimed her as her daughter. Gaby fainted when she saw her; whatever happened no one knows; the woman disappeared and was never heard of again.

One of the mothers turned up just after the War and told newspaper interviewers that Gaby's rael name was Fraulein Navratel, the end of it. You, yourself, will lose everything by this coming war and will die in poverty in a strange land."

A week later, I was taken out by this Minister to see the Czar's Summer Palace at Peterhof. He first drove me through the wonderful gardens surrounding it. Below us lay the private yacht with steam up and ready at a moment's notice if the Czar had reason to escape from the country.

"What a terrible way for the Czar to live," I exclaimed.

"Yes," His Excellency replied, "but this is Russia. You did not notice perhaps that this car we have driven in has not an atom of wood in its structure, *it is all steel and bomb-proof.*"

Just then we passed the famous waterfall of the golden steps, sheets of crystal water flowing over wide steps of beaten gold. What a land of contrasts, I thought.

As we drove near the Palace, my friend the Minister said: "I will now tell you that I have brought you out to dine with the Czar to-night. I do not know if the Czarina will be present, but if she is, I want you to avoid all subjects touching on occultism. She may very likely recognize you, as she has all your books sent her from London; but remember, I shall depend on you to change the subject as quickly as possible should she talk about predictions, or her dread of the future, or anything of that kind. With the Czar, however, it is quite another matter; I have told him of your gloomy predictions for me, he has asked me to bring you, and after dinner he will probably take you with him into his private study."

"But, Your Excellency," I said, "how can I possibly dine with the Imperial Family like this—a blue serge suit will be impossible."

"On the contrary," he laughed, "it will be quite all right. We will dine in a private apartment with probably one servant to serve us. I am in a blue serge suit myself, and it would not surprise me if His Imperial Majesty, the Czar of All the Russias, will not be in blue serge also, as it is by his own request we are coming in this informal manner."

At this moment the motor stopped at the door of the Palace, and an officer of the Imperial Guard met us. After passing through one long corridor after another, we were shown into a beautiful room that looked like a library. At first I thought we were alone, but no. There, seated in an easy chair by the window, was the Czar of All the Russias, looking for all the world like an ordinary English gentleman—and reading *The Times*, too, from London.

I stood still as if riveted to the floor. I could not make a mistake— before me was decidedly the same man who had visited me in my consulting-rooms in London many years before. He came forward with his hand out. I bowed, but he took my hand all the same. We walked over to the window and looked out over the gardens and down to the beautiful yacht moored underneath. There was nothing worth recording in the conversation that followed; the three of us smoked

Russian cigarettes, one after the other, and as the clock struck eight, a door opened and dinner was announced. At that moment the Czarina entered. She simply bowed to the Minister who was with me, then to me, and we went in to dinner.

His Excellency had been right. It was indeed a private dinner and without any ceremony whatever. Her Majesty wore a kind of semi-evening dress, but with no jewels, except one magnificent diamond at her throat. There was nothing extraordinary about the dinner; the zadcouskies were numberless, the sturgeon was excellent, but the rest was like what one would expect at any gentleman's house.

I had no difficulty in avoiding questions on occultism from Her Majesty—she hardly spoke, in fact she did not seem to notice me. She appeared very distraught, spoke of Alexis a few times to the Czar, and the moment dinner was finished she bowed to us in a very stately way and left the room.

When we had finished our coffee and cigarettes, His Majesty said some words in Russian to the Minister—it was the only time I had heard Russian spoken all the evening, for the conversation had been entirely in English and French, and mostly in English.

As we left the dining-room His Excellency whispered, "Go with His Majesty, I will come back for you later."

I did what I was told and soon found myself in a rather odd-shaped room alone with the Czar. This room was, I expect, his own private study, as it led into a very handsome bedroom which I could see through the door, and from it the Czar later came out with a large leather case in his hands. Taking a small key from the end of his chain, he opened the case, and to my amazement laid on the table by my side the identical sheet of paper with my own writing and numbers on it which I had jotted down in King Edward's library, and had seen once again in my consulting-rooms in the hands of the man now sitting opposite to me.

The Czar saw my look of surprise. Pushing across the table at which we were seated a very large box of cigarettes—the box looked made of solid gold with the Imperial Arms of Russia set in jewels—he said slowly and impressively: "I showed you this paper once before. Do you remember?"

I gasped with astonishment. Yes, I did indeed remember. And I knew the words on the paper were the terrible words of impending fate.

"Do you recognize your writing?" he asked.

"Yes, Your Majesty," I answered, "but may I ask how that paper came into your possession?"

"King Edward gave it to me, and you confirmed what it contained when I called on you in London some years ago, although you certainly did not know who your visitor was. Your written predictions to Isvolsky again bears out what is given on this sheet of paper. To-night there are two other lives I want you to work out."

I gave the Czar my word of honour that I would not reveal what passed between us that evening in his study in the Summer Palace of Peterhof. Sufficient to say that he knew—that he was a fated monarch. At his request, I worked out before his eyes the charts of two other lives he asked about; both showed the same thing, that 1917 was "overwhelmed by dark and sinister influences that pointed to 'The End.'"[1] I was amazed at the calm way in which he heard my conclusions; in the simplest way he said:

"'Cheiro,' it has given me the deepest pleasure to have this conversation with you. I admire the way you stand by the conclusions you have arrived at."

He rose, we went out and joined Isvolsky on the terrace. Beneath us on the summer sea, the Imperial yacht lay like a painted toy, by my side stood His Imperial Majesty, the Czar of All the Russias, the Anointed Head of the Church and the "Little Father" of his people, and yet even then there were outward and visible signs that all was not right with the heart of Russia.

A short time later I was awakened one morning in my hotel to be told by a police officer that on that day from nine o'clock until midday, no one would be allowed to look out of any windows having a view on the Nevsky Prospect. His Majesty the Czar was about to pass to dedicate the church built over the spot where his predecessor had been assassinated.

Every window was closed and the slatted wooden shutters bolted.

I could not resist the temptation when in the distance I heard the procession coming nearer and nearer. I crept across the floor on my hands and knees, to where one of the slats did not fit closely. What a sight it was—from that third-floor window. The Czar's carriage surrounded by the Imperial Guard swept past rapidly, the long Nevsky was lined by troops so close together that they were shoulder to shoulder like two walls of armed men; but, was it possible to believe one's eyes—each soldier had his rifle pointed at the windows of the houses along the route, with orders to fire if any person disobeyed the order and looked out—and yet we hear that "the Little Father was loved by his people."

On another occasion, a few months later, when the first snow of winter made the streets almost impassable, I met a procession of some fifty men with a few women handcuffed together being driven to a station to be entrained for Siberia. They had been arrested at their work, some were in shirt-sleeves, some in their overalls, but just as they were, they were being marched through the streets *with the thermometer at 18 degrees below zero.*

As if it were a funeral that was passing, my droshky driver held his

---

[1] March 12th, 1917, the Russian Revolution.
March 15th, 1917, Abdication of the Czar.
July 16th, 1918, the Czar and Imperial Family massacred.

66 CONFESSIONS: MEMOIRS OF A MODERN SEER

fur cap in his hand and made the Sign of the Cross—involuntarily I did the same.

Nevertheless, the gay and gorgeous life of the Court of Petersburg pulsed merrily on. There were balls, dances, dinner parties, and assemblies; there was hardly an evening but I was whisked off to some lordly mansion to meet beautiful Russian women, highly placed soldiers and naval officers, diplomatic figures, and those who then emphatically made up the ruling class.

One day there came to my hotel one of those travelling monks so often met with in Russia; this man was a close friend of the Monk Heliodor, who with Hermogen, Bishop of Saratov, had great power in all ecclesiastical matters.

Heliodor himself was a cultured, gentle mystic, who was deeply learned in occult matters. The Monk, who called on me, said that Heliodor had exercised considerable influence over the Czar, and was profoundly interested in the study of the Kabalistic System of Numbers, together with Astrology. Several times he came in to have a talk with me, and on one occasion he brought the ill-fated Stolypin to see me.

The black-bearded burly statesman, who tried to rule Russia with a rod of iron, at first pretended to be indifferent when I suggested I would examine his hands. He became interested when I showed him the " broken Line of Life " that was marked clear and distinct on his right hand. I foresaw a violent death. He laughed at my fears, he told me he was guarded night and day by the agents of the *Ochrana*, or secret police, yet it is a matter of history that he was shot down through the treachery of one of the secret police whom he employed.[1]

One day the Monk came to me.

" ' Cheiro,' " he said, " I want to bring to you a colleague of mine who seems to have extraordinary occult powers. For reasons of my own, I want you to read his hands, even if he should appear to pose as a sceptic."

Later on that afternoon in January 1905, the Monk opened my sitting-room door, and behind him strode a figure that could not fail to make a powerful impression upon me. Habited as a kind of peasant monk, corresponding to the old-time wandering friars in England, he walked with long strides across the carpeted floor, halted in front of me, and speaking a few words in very bad French, then rapidly in Russian, which Helidor translated, scornfully said something to the effect that he did not believe in hand-reading—*but he believed in Fate*.

This was my first view of the now notorious Gregory Rasputin, who at the time was at the head of an extraordinary sect known as

[1] In August 1906, a bomb was exploded at his villa, which was practically destroyed, seriously injuring one of his daughters. But all attempts to kill him proved futile until 1911 when he was shot in a theatre in Kieff on September 14th, before the eyes of the Imperial Family, by a Jew named Mordka Bogrov. Stolypin died of his wounds September 18th, 1911.

the Khaysty, at first composed of poor people, but now spreading its influence into Court circles. This sect held the strange doctrine that in order to obtain perfect forgiveness they must commit sin. Rasputin had not long come back from Jerusalem where he had made a pilgrimage ; he had struck up a friendship with Heliodor, and through his Court influence had already begun that amazing course which culminated in his violent death, and contributed so largely to the downfall of the House of Romanoff.

There was no mistaking the fact that my visitor was an unusual man. His height was not noticeable owing to his broad-shouldered, powerfully built figure, clad in a heavy brown cassock ; round his waist was a girdle which the Monk told me he said he had brought from holy Mount Athos.

His features were large and coarse, his eyes brilliant, his mouth mobile and the lips full and red. He wore an overgrown light brown beard, partly reddish, and his head was covered with a tangled mass of unkempt hair. On his forehead was a dark patch-like scar of an old wound. His voice was deep, authoritative, and sonorous.

He allowed me, after some demur, to examine his hands. They were thick and coarse and very dirty ; the lines were strongly marked. The Fate Line showed unusual vicissitudes, the Line of Life appeared cut through ominously, half-way down the hand.

While I was looking at his left and right hands, he suddenly roared :

" I know the Future—you do not ; my Future is to redeem the People, and save the Emperor from himself."

I hardly knew what to reply to this arrogant statement, but at length I said quietly :

" Would you care for me to tell you anything about the Future ? "

He smiled scornfully.

" I shall laugh at whatever it is. I am called to be the Saviour of Russia. Fate is in my keeping. I am the maker of Destiny."

I wondered for the moment whether the man was mad. My profession had brought me in contact with not a few crazy individuals, yet his eyes were clear enough. Besides, I was in " Holy Russia," where all sorts of mystical creatures were then at large. But I must confess that what I saw in the hand before me was baffling in its extraordinary message.

" You have before you," I began, " a future that is filled with wonders ! You have been raised from the lowest to associate with the highest, from the utmost poverty you will command wealth, you are destined to wield enormous power over others—*but it will be a power for evil*—do you want to hear more ? "

While I had been speaking, he had listened attentively.

" Yes, yes ! " he said impatiently ; then correcting himself, he added grandly :

" But, of course, I knew all this before ; I am a prophet, and a greater one than you. I know all things."

"But what of the Future?" asked the Monk, who was listening with rapt attention.

I remained silent. Dare I reveal the terrible vision of blood that seemed to have formed before my mind. As I studied the hands of the boastful man seated before me, I seemed to see him gliding from the Cabinet of the Emperor, with an evil smile upon his dark face, insinuating himself into the deepest confidences of the Empress who knelt reverently before him, and hailed him as "Holy Father," and at last yielding up his life mid a scene of terrible ferocity.

"Well, what is it, Seer?" asked Rasputin, in a taunting voice.

"I foresee for you a violent end within a palace. You will be menaced by poison, by knife, and by bullet. Finally I see the icy waters of the Neva closing above you."

There was silence for a few seconds. My words had evidently made an impression upon the Monk, because before this I had sketched out his early home life—how he had married a woman much better off than himself.[1]

I told him that he had two daughters and one son, and that the latter would turn against him—which came true shortly after I made the prediction.

Moreover, I told him that he had turned against his wife, and had allied himself with a woman who was destined to work great harm. At this he had smiled cunningly, and uttered his famous formula that afterwards became the watchword of his sect:

"A particle of the divine is incarnated in me! Only through me can they hope to find salvation. The manner of their salvation is this: They must be united with me, *body and soul!* The virtue that goes out from me is the destruction of sin."

As he uttered these astounding words, he drew himself up to the full height of his powerful figure, folded his arms upon his massive chest, and his great haunting eyes seemed to fill with almost supernatural fire.

When I had finished speaking of the terrible picture that had formed in my mind, our eyes met across the table at which we sat. Those piercing eyes wanted to strike terror into my soul. For some reason which I cannot explain, I felt no fear whatever. I returned his gaze without flinching. The Monk passing behind me, slipped the large silver Cross he always carried, between us; he expected some tragedy to happen and wanted to protect me.

The sight of the Cross broke the spell. Rasputin sprang to his feet, giving vent to a torrent of words I could not understand; his companion rapidly translating them, he roared:

"Who are you who can predict the end of Rasputin! Rasputin can never die. Knife, nor bullet, nor poison can harm him."

Then drawing himself to his full height, he said slowly and impressively:

[1] Olga Chaningoff.

"I am the Saviour of my people. I am the Protector of the Czar. *I am greater than the Czar.*"

With that he left the room, while the Monk making the Sign of the Cross slipped out after him.

Whether I made an enemy of this extraordinary man or not, I cannot say.

I do not know whether he saw in me a rival to his occult powers or not, but later on I underwent an experience that showed that he would have caused me injury if he could.

The following year I was back in St. Petersburg in connection with a very large financial operation. Returning one day to my hotel, I found that some of my most important papers had been stolen.

I went at once to my friend, Monsieur Isvolsky, at the Foreign Office and protested. He listened, smiled his enigmatical smile, and said:

"Take my card to the Chief of Police and explain the loss of your papers to him."

I must confess I was astounded at the deadly swiftness of the movements of the Russian police when animated by the highest powers. Within twenty minutes I was shown into the presence of the Chief. By the time I returned to my hotel, the police were already at each entrance to prevent anyone leaving. Within an hour my papers were restored; a secret agent of Rasputin joined a Siberian chain-gang that night, and never again was I subjected to any molestation.

When I first met Rasputin, I could not help but realize—although I had no idea who my visitor was—that I was in the presence of one of those extraordinary men who are born into the world as instruments of Fate. There was no question about his overpowering will-power and magnetism, but it was what I might call "animal magnetism." By his luminous compelling eyes he attempted from the first moment to hypnotize me as he had done so many hundreds of others. It was only my long experience of such things that saved me. Instead of looking into his eyes, I concentrated my attention on a point between his eyebrows, with the result that he could have no power over me.

But what defence could the gentle Czar or the religious emotional Czarina have against such a man? Absolutely none.

They were as helpless as a bird fascinated by a snake into whose jaws it was about to fall.

About this time I was introduced to one of the mystery women of the Imperial Court, one who was largely responsible for the introduction of Rasputin to the notice of the Czar.

Many rumours have been afloat in Europe as to the identity of the woman often spoken of as "Madame X," who was for some years famous as a medium in St. Petersburg. Her real name was Madame Gutjen Sund, a Swedish woman who married a German officer, who afterwards was a prominent assistant under Herr Stanmers, the chief of the great Spy Bureau in the Wilhelmstrasse, Berlin.

This woman had undoubtedly remarkable occult gifts. When King Edward visited the Czar at Reval, Madame Sund was brought into the circle of notables after dinner and was invited to read the future of those present. The Czar himself told me on that evening when I dined with him at Peterhof how impressed he had been by what she had said. One statement that filled him with especial sorrow; it was she who told him that "the little Czarevich would not live to reign."

Madame Sund, for some time before the coming of Rasputin, occupied a very extraordinary position in the Court, and was daily consulted by the Emperor and Empress. Most of the Grand Dukes hated her, for she worked against their influence; twice she narrowly escaped death by poison.

By some means she became acquainted with Rasputin, who immediately exercised over her a fatal influence that set in motion a whole train of significant events. Knowing how the mind of the Imperial pair had been influenced by her prediction, Rasputin prevailed upon Madame Sund to go to the Empress and to tell her that she was mistaken; that she had been converted by a wonderful saintly Father who could work miracles, and who had the power to save the life of the Czarevich.

The Empress sent for Rasputin. He came, arrogant, dirty and impressive, striding into the presence and crying in his bell-like voice: " Repent, ye who wear purple; repent, ye who are clothed in garments of gold and silver."

The Empress was so impressed that she fell upon her knees, and the Court entourage witnessed the amazing spectacle of the Consort of the Emperor of Russia kneeling before a dirty peasant.

Rasputin told her positively that he alone could restore her son to health. After that, the Imperial pair were as clay in the hands of the so-called Monk, and when the Imperial child fell ill shortly afterwards, and was apparently at the point of death, Rasputin dismissed lal the physicians and announced that " faith alone would prevail."

It was one of the doctors who described the scene to me: " I was in attendance with other Court physicians grouped around the bed of the heir to the throne, who was gasping for breath. Suddenly Rasputin strode in, made no sign that he saw the Czarina, but shouted:

" ' Away, unbelievers! Away! This is the work of faith! '

" The startled physicians drew back as the Empress came forward, and kneeling before Rasputin cried: ' My Father—save my child! ' —' Turn out these dogs,' cried the Monk, sweeping his fiery glances round their outraged faces. At a look from the Empress nearly all the doctors left the apartment, even Imperial etiquette hardly restraining them from shrugging their shoulders with disgust.

" Then, like Elisha the Prophet who raised the widow's son, Rasputin bowed his great form over the fevered little Czarevich. He stretched himself in the form of a cross upon the Hope of Imperial Russia. Those present stood petrified with amazement. The Empress, her hair falling about her shoulders, knelt at the foot of the bed, her breast heaving, her maternal tears falling like rain.

" Then the miracle happened.

" The physicians had said that natural sleep alone would save the child. Rasputin rose and stood before the Empress.

" ' Behold thy son ! ' he cried, his voice booming through the great apartment. The Czarevich was sleeping peacefully, his little hands relaxed upon the gorgeous coverlet, the fiery flush of fever dying to a rose-pink upon his cheeks.

" That night the news flew through the capital, and spread through Russia that Rasputin was responsible for a miracle—that the heir had been dead, and that he had raised him up.

" In a burst of gratitude, the Czar presented Rasputin with a million roubles ; the Czarina loaded him with gifts, but even more, his influence was fixed ; nothing could shake it. Once in power, he threw off Madame Sund. She died after a short mysterious illness, and Rasputin pronounced her epitaph. ' She had finished, my work has commenced.' "

CHAPTER X

THE REAL STORY OF RASPUTIN. HIS INFLUENCE OVER THE CZARINA. THE TRUE CAUSE OF RUSSIA'S DOWNFALL

IT will not be out of place, I think, if I relate in as brief a way as possible, the real story of Rasputin. I have gathered my facts from reliable sources. As this man was decidedly one of the most extraordinary personalities and one who was instrumental in bringing about the fall of the great Romanoff dynasty, the world is entitled to know as much about him as possible.

Rasputin, or to give him his real name, Gregory Effimovitch, was born in the little village of Petrovskoie in Siberia, on July 7th, 1872.

His father was a notorious horse thief and the worst drunkard in the place. He was nicknamed " Rasputin," which means, in Russian, " corrupt." His son inherited this nickname, and according to the police records, well merited this distinctive title. Dr. Litchernoff, who was called in to treat him for smallpox, gave the following account of his patient:

" He was," he said, " a fine, dark child, with such an ardent expression in the eyes that even I felt strangely affected by it. He was thickset and strongly built and soon became the terror of the district. I remember how Father Alexis, the priest of Petrovskoie, used to give him ten kopecks every week *to keep him away from church on Sundays.*"

At fourteen years of age he robbed an old man of his savings after nearly murdering him. For this he received twenty strokes of a whip in the presence of all the inhabitants in the village in the market-place. The extraordinary thing was that this public flogging roused in him one of those fits of religious fervour so associated with him in later years, and was the commencement of his fanaticism.

From this out he began to visit churches and monasteries in the neighbourhood, and was often to be seen on his knees on the roadside lashing his body with thistles and reciting long incomprehensible prayers.

This religious fervour was as suddenly brought to an end as it had begun by an assault he made on an old beggar woman. After the police enquiry that was held over this affair, he abandoned religion and threw himself whole-heartedly into thieving and drink. According to the official register of Petrovskoie, he was about this time arrested for horse-stealing.

In spite of his reputation, he had the good fortune to marry in 1895, when he was twenty-three years old, a charming innocent girl named Olga Chaningoff, who brought him as a dowry " a pair of horses, a cart, three thousand roubles, and a few acres of land."

Three children were the result of this strange union, two daughters, Mariska and Zenia, and in 1899 a son whom he called Michel Gregorovitch.

One night in the middle of the winter, February 5th, 1903, he was forced as a carrier to drive a priest to the seminary of Teoumene, which event completely changed his career and led to the remarkable adventures that followed.

En route the priest, who was named Zaborovsky, persuaded him to abandon his drunken habits and go and make a penitence at the monastery of Verkhotourie. He remained here for some weeks; on his return to his home, he declared that St. Michael had appeared to him and had commanded him to build a great church to the name of the Archangel.

From this moment he was a changed man. He went from village to village, and from monastery to monastery, collecting money for the future church and so earned the name of a " Staretz," or holy man.

On his return to the little village of Petrovskoie, he refused to live with his wife and children, but lived by himself in a small cottage surrounded by sacred icons he had collected in his travels and numberless wax candles that had come into his possession.

From all sides people came to hear his words, the words of a prophet, they said, who had once been a demon.

Men, as well as women, begged to be allowed to kiss the hem of his raiment, and in return for gifts of money they were allowed such a privilege.

It was during this stage of his career that he conceived his extraordinary doctrine of " Sin for Salvation," which of all religious revivals that perhaps the world has ever seen, had in the end the most far-reaching results.

Across the dreary wastes of Siberia the slogan, " Sin for Salvation," spread like a battle-cry, and the name of " the holy Rasputin " echoed far and wide.

While on a pilgrimage to Kazan, in April 1904, Rasputin met for the first time a wealthy widow named Lydia Bachmakow, who became another rung in his ladder of ambition.

This lady had just passed the dangerous age of forty, when her husband was considerate enough to die and leave her his fortune. She thanked God for the end of what she called " her conjugal martyrdom " and threw herself into every form of religious fanaticism.

With the most passionate devotion, she journeyed from monastery to monastery, squandering her money wherever she went, and submitting herself to the severest penance that could be imposed.

In spite of all her piety, charity, and devotion, she had not found the satisfaction she sought and was about to abandon all religious persuasion, when at this psychological crisis Rasputin entered her life.

" Sin for Salvation," he whispered, " and the Gates of Heaven are yours to enter."

Lydia Bachmakow had never dreamt of such a wonderful creed; she had tried every other—she would now try it. She declared this doctrine must have been made expressly for her benefit, so without reserve, she placed herself and her money in the hands of " the holy Rasputin."

Like the usual run of converts, she commenced to have "visions," the most important being that the days of pilgrimage by foot were ended, so she carried Rasputin off in one of the most magnificent motor-cars that money could buy in Russia.

The new pilgrimage started at Kazan; helped by the splendour of the millionaire widow, every door was thrown open for "the chosen of the Lord." Even Rasputin's bad manners were turned into a blessing; it showed, his followers said, that a "holy man" was above the petty details of convention and because he disdained forks and ate with his fingers, he was declared to be "the apostle of simplicity."

It was here at Kazan that Rasputin came in contact with Sturmer, who was at that moment Inspector General at the Ministry of the Interior, and in a position to be of great use to Rasputin.

Rasputin arrived at St. Petersburg, as it was then called, on the evening of December 5th, 1904. (I was then living at the Hôtel de l'Europe, and within about a month of Rasputin's arrival I met him, as I have related in the previous chapter.)

Madame Bachmakow rented a magnificent apartment in the best part of the Nevsky Prospect and when it was suitably furnished with every luxury, she installed "the holy father," as she now began to call him.

As an advance agent the millionaire widow was without an equal; she had already sent reports on miracles worked by Rasputin to Bishop Hermogene, John of Cronstadt, the monk Heliodor, and the principal newspapers.

In less than a few weeks, his apartment in the Nevsky Prospect was besieged by members of the highest aristocracy of St. Petersburg. In a police report dated April 12th, 1905, it is noted:

"Crowds assemble at Rasputin's place, people have to wait two or three days before being able to approach the 'Monk' (he never was a monk or had holy orders of any kind). He works miracles when it pleases him to do so. He has been seen to take a handful of earth and by simply breathing upon it, to turn it into a magnificent rose tree covered with flowers."

The writer of this report counted more than four hundred women before Rasputin's house in a single afternoon. As a rule, the report proceeded, "he receives only the young and pretty ones, because, he says, the others have fewer sins to be forgiven."

"Rasputin makes considerable sums of money. He has no fixed price for his consultations, but his secretary, a man called Striapcheff, never introduces anyone to him without first receiving at least one hundred roubles.[1]

"Those who give more get special attention. A certain Madame Narukkine offered a thousand roubles to be received. These amounts are said to be put on one side for the church in honour of St. Michael that Rasputin has promised at Petrovskoie."

[1] About £10 in English money.

If a police report could say so much one may easily imagine the reports that were circulated in ordinary society.

There are two versions of the way in which Rasputin reached the Palace. One gives the credit to Madame Sund, as I have already related—the other relates that the Czarina sent her confidential companion, Anna Vyronbova, to consult him. Which account is the true one does not greatly matter.

Rasputin, there is no doubt, converted this rather ordinary woman. His wonderful doctrine of "Sin for Salvation" made an instant appeal to her senses.

He very quickly made an *entente* with her. He threw over the millionaire widow, Madame Bachmakow, and gave Anna Vyronbova the title of "Sister-in-Chief" as a reward for her promise to open the gates of the Czar's Palace and establish him in the favour of the Czarina.

It was Anna who taught him to give up the name Rasputin and take the name "Novy," meaning innovator—as she explained the name Rasputin was not pleasing to the Imperial ears.

Shortly after her first visit Anna made the arrangement that he could come to the Palace whenever he pleased.

About this time the widow, Madame Bachmakow, received an order from the police to leave St. Petersburg at once.

From this moment Rasputin's influence over the Czarina and the Court was established.

In 1908, for some unexplained reason, except that of vanity, he spent the summer months at his old village of Petrovskoie.

He was at first received by the simple peasants as a god who had returned to save them, but the twelve young and beautiful "sisters" who accompanied him caused a scandal that reached the ears of the Czarina, who recalled him to St. Petersburg.

Many stories at this time became circulated about his drunken orgies, so much so that the Archbishop commanded him to present himself before an ecclesiastical tribunal composed of a bishop, two canons, and three important officials of the Civil Courts.

Near the conclusion of this investigation, at the moment when a unanimous verdict was about to be pronounced against him, Anna Vyronbova called on the judges and informed them that it was the express wish and command of the Czarina that "the holy man" should be found "Not Guilty."

Rasputin was acquitted on the spot, the Tribunal saying that they accepted his own statement that the charges brought against him were false.

The day after the mock verdict the Czarina sent for him to come to the palace of Tsarskoie-Selo. As he entered her presence, she bowed to kiss his hands and begged forgiveness for the annoyance his enemies had caused.

The Czar asked if he could show him some special favour.

Rasputin thought for a moment and gravely requested that the friend of his youth, Barnaby, the gardener, might be made Bishop of Tobolsk—and within two days this was done.

Rasputin's next step was to be appointed "Spiritual Adviser" to the young Princesses and the Czarevich, but after the bishop incident anything equally grotesque could only be expected.

The day after the attempt on his life by the young girl, Kheone Gousseva, who on June 28th, 1914, shot him in the stomach, the Czar sent a special telegram to the Governor of Tobolsk commanding him to see that nothing should be left undone " to save the life of one of the best friends of the Crown ! "

A month later the Great War broke out. Rasputin was absent recovering from his wound. The Czarina wrote to the Innovator, as she always called him, as follows :

> "I am happy, my beloved master, to be able to inform you that 'Niky' has realized the importance of your dear presence at Tsarskoie-Selo. Come back quickly, as my poor heart suffers to know you are so far away and I feel lost if I cannot hold your hands in mine and find, in your eyes, the light of my soul.
>
> "I hope this time our troubles are at an end and that we shall never be separated again. As for me, I shall thank God if He allows me to die with you and gain—in your company—the heavenly paradise for which you have so prepared me.
>
> "I am not the only one wishing for your return. Anna is also dying of impatience.
>
> "Take pity on two women who adore you and can no longer live without you.
>
> "Give me, in your thoughts, your most ardent blessing, in anticipation of being able to give it to me in person, my whole being in touch with yours.
>
> "Your daughter who cherishes you.
>
> A."

Rasputin returned and his influence at the Palace was greater than ever. He now determined to turn it to good account. Although he had received rich presents from both the Czar and Czarina—on one occasion His Imperial Majesty gave him a diamond valued at thirty thousand roubles that had been given to him at his coronation—he determined to take advantage of the War to increase his wealth. Large orders for munitions by his influence were passed to those who paid him for his trouble, one order alone bringing him 360,000 roubles.

Judging by extracts from the diary of Anna Vyronbova which came into the hands of officials after the revolution, there is no doubt that from April 1915 Rasputin used his influence over the Czarina to make peace with Germany at any price. What his reward was to be has never been disclosed, but had he lived, no doubt it would have been very considerable.

About this time, Count Tolstoi, the Grand Master of Ceremonies in charge of the crown jewels at the Hermitage, made the amazing discovery that the real stones had been abstracted and paste put in their place. The blue diamonds that edged the saddle of Alexander II, the priceless garnets of Catherine the Great, the matchless pearls of the Crown of Ivan the Terrible, all these and others equally valuable had been stolen and replaced by worthless imitations.

The Czar was furious with rage when this news was first broken to him, yet the next day he wrote in his own handwriting to Count Tolstoi: " Do not continue the inquiry about the Hermitage. Let it remain a profound secret."

The only comment I make about this is that a woman named Cecilia Werner, an Austrian and intimate friend of Rasputin, was furnished with a diplomatic passport which enabled her to travel every few months to Stockholm without having the inconvenience of *having her trunks opened*.

As I am not writing a life of Rasputin, I must pass over many episodes of his career and come to the dramatic end that I had so clearly indicated when I first made his acquaintance at the Hôtel de l'Europe in the Nevsky Prospect.

I heard the details of his horrible death from one of those who assisted at it, and as many versions have been made public, it may interest my readers to have, what I have every reason to believe is, the true one.

I have dealt with Rasputin's career at some length, on account of the remarkable role he played on Russia's lurid stage, leading up to the fall of the curtain on the great and all-powerful Romanoff dynasty.

It is my firm belief that if this man had not come into the Czarina's life, the revolution would never have occurred, and the lives of many millions of people would have escaped the horror and destruction that fell on them like an avalanche of disaster.

That strange word " if " is, however, the pivot on which so many lives turn, that it becomes the Key of Destiny in all languages, to unlock the future for good or evil.

If—Judas Iscariot had not been born, the tragedy of Calvary would not have happened.

If—Rasputin had not crossed the Russian stage, how different things might have been.

Speculation is useless—nations rise and fall—men and women are but threads on the loom of Fate—the weaving of the pattern lies in the hands of Design, before which one can only bow the head and murmur: " Thy Will be done on earth *as it is in Heaven*."

Like Napoleon, the ex-Kaiser, or the late Nicholas of Russia, Rasputin was but a servant of Destiny; as such, he obeyed those unknown forces of Life that make themselves manifest in all, whether born in poverty or under the greatness of a throne.

Rasputin was born a peasant, the very lowest kind at that, so ignorant that he could scarcely read or write—yet this man became a power that destroyed a dynasty, wrecked a civilization, and caused more ruin and upheaval than any other man of the age.

In the short period of twelve years from that night of February 5th, 1903, when the words of a young priest changed the current of his life, Rasputin strode boldly across the Russian stage, until he reached the climax of his career in 1915. In that brief period, he had turned a gardener into a bishop, amassed wealth, built a church to the honour of St. Michael, and brought an Emperor and Empress to his feet.

In 1915, he brought about the dismissal of the Grand Duke Nicholas, as Commander-in-Chief of the Army. By his influence a man named Khvostov succeeded Prince Tcherbatoff as Minister of the Interior, and Sturmer became Prime Minister.

By 1915, Rasputin, masquerading under a monk's robe, was the undisputed Master of Russia.

If he had been a clever man, he might have kept his position, but that " if " I have already spoken about, was switching over the points of doom on the railroad of Fate.

Vanity, his besetting sin, blinded his eyes, drink and boastfulness did the rest.

One night in a restaurant in Petrograd, surrounded by some of the pawns he had placed in power, exhilarated by champagne and flattery, his sonorous voice rang out in criticism of everything Russian.

People sitting at nearby tables were horrified, others laughed, some encouraged the wild-eyed man to go still further.

Looking round like a mad bull, he may have noticed at a table not far away, the Grand Duke Dimitri, first cousin to the Czar, the Prince Youssoupoff, and three other guests.

" I don't care a damn for all the Grand Dukes in Russia," Rasputin roared, " nor for the Holy Synod, or all the Generals of the Army."

The Grand Duke Dimitri rose to his feet—he was about to accept the challenge, there and then—when a member of the Duma entered the restaurant and passed between the two tables.

Turning towards Rasputin this man, the well-known Pourichkievitch, sneered : " Care for nothing, vile impostor. Your reign of terror is nearing its end. Blind yourself with drink and orgies, before long some man will rise to rid Russia of your presence."

To the amazement of the other diners, Rasputin made no answer—turning deadly pale, he got up and left the restaurant with the members of his party.

Prince Youssoupoff crossed to the table of the new arrival and held out his hand.

" Thank you, Pourichkievitch," he said, " you have expressed the wish that a man may be found to rid our country of this infamous impostor. I offer myself as that man."

The Grand Duke Dimitri joined the party. " Count on me also," he said. " We have all put up with this moujik to the breaking-point.

Let us pledge ourselves here to-night, to redeem Russia by ridding her of the presence of this monster."

In the corner of this restaurant, in the heart of Petrograd, a solemn oath was taken. Fate had forsaken her favourite—the doom of Rasputin was sealed.

It took some months to prepare the stage for the last act.

On December 15th, 1916, by the Russian calendar, all was ready. The principal actors had already arrived, the Gand Duke Dimitri, Prince Youssoupoff, Pourichkievitch, another man, and the beautiful Karali, the dancer whom Rasputin had for a long time pestered with his attentions. The scene was set in Prince Youssoupoff's palace in the Moskaia.

Karali was to be the inducement for Rasputin to come to supper. The other conspirators were to keep in the background until their presence became necessary.

The bells of St. Izaac's Cathedral struck eleven.

An automobile stopped at the private entrance to the house in the Offizerskaia.

Rasputin got out, he dismissed his motor, he looked up and down the deserted street, he hesitated some time before he rang the bell.

A presentiment of danger, perhaps, passed through his mind—the thought of the beautiful Karali overcame all prudence—he pressed the bell.

The door was opened by the Prince himself.

"I have allowed the servants to be away to-night," he said. "I promised you to take every precaution that your romance would never be known. Come in and wait for her, I am sure she will not be late."

Together they entered the dining-room; an appetizing supper was set out on the table.

Two exquisitely carved decanters held the famous red Crimean wine from the Youssoupoff estate; one placed at Rasputin's chair contained enough cyanide of potassium to kill any six men, while on a solid gold plate on his right, were some zakouskies, also treated with the same poison.

Rasputin would neither eat nor drink.

"Time enough," he said, "when Karali comes. My brain must be kept cool if I am to taste the most exquisite morsel of womanhood that I have ever seen. What can I do for you, Prince, in return? Name any honour you wish to have and I promise you the Czar will sign the decree before to-morrow night."

"Let us drink to to-morrow then," the Prince laughed, "it would take more wine than is in that bottle for such a man as you to fail to do justice to a pretty woman."

The flattery did its work; Rasputin filled his glass and finished it in one gulp. He then took another; turning his attention to the zakouskies he cleared the plate in a few minutes.

And yet nothing happened.

The Prince got nervous, beads of perspiration glistened across his forehead.

"Have a cigarette," he said, as he pushed his jewelled case across the table.

"No," the monk said, "some women object to the smell of tobacco; I cleaned my teeth for the first time in my life to-day."

"Karali would be flattered if she knew that," the Prince smiled.

If at that moment Rasputin had looked round he would have seen in the shadow of the staircase going to the next floor, the gleaming eyes of Karali and her clenched hands.

Behind her a little higher up, stood the other men, one of them with a revolver in his hand.

"Don't care much for your famous Crimean wine," Rasputin sneered, "it seems to me to have a bitter taste."

"You are not accustomed to its flavour," the Prince answered, "it is famed as a tonic and gives strength; finish the decanter and let us have some more."

Rasputin emptied the bottle—*and yet nothing happened!*

The Prince could hardly hide his nervousness; in order to regain his self-possession, he made an excuse and went up the staircase to where the others were waiting.

He really went up to get his revolver—on his return he found Rasputin pacing up and down the floor.

"I don't feel well," he said, "those zakouskies have upset me. I won't wait for Karali, when she comes tell her she can go to the devil, she is the first woman that Rasputin has ever waited for," and he reached for his fur coat.

"Don't be impatient," the Prince said, "she will arrive any moment now, but while waiting come and see this wonderful bit of carving and which, if you like, you can take away with you to-night."

Rasputin was never known to refuse a present.

He took it in his hands, it was an exquisite ivory crucifix, he bent over a light to examine it closely.

At that moment Prince Youssoupoff passed his revolver from his left to his right hand and fired straight at the monk's heart.

Rasputin, with a groan, fell in a huddled mass on the floor.

The Grand Duke Dimitri went to get his automobile—it was decided they would take Rasputin's body and throw it into the Neva.

They went as far as the street door, they were overjoyed at the success of their plan.

"Russia, Holy Russia is at last free," they said.

"Listen," someone said—a noise came from the dining-room.

No! it could not be possible.

Rasputin, with his monk's robe open—with blood streaming from him, was clutching at the back of a chair in the centre of the room.

Before they could recover their senses he had already walked out into the garden in an effort to gain the private entrance.

Blood marked every step he took in the snow.

He reached the door, his hand was already on the catch.

Pourichkievitch and Youssoupoff fired together.

Rasputin fell without a word.

The body was taken in the motor to the Petrovsky Bridge.

With a great effort they raised it to the top of the balustrade.

Horror of horrors—the monk was still alive—with his right hand he clutched the epaulette on the shoulder of one of the officers and tore it from the uniform.

Fate could not, however, be cheated at such a moment. Four strong men with grim faces pushed him over, the body rebounded on the stone buttress below, crashed on a block of ice and rolled over into the swirling icy waters of the Neva.

CHAPTER XI

STRANGE EXPERIENCES IN RUSSIA. "THE ANGEL OF THE REVOLUTION." THE CZAR'S EFFORTS FOR A WORLD-WIDE PEACE. I AM FORCED TO WITNESS AN EXECUTION IN THE FORTRESS OF ST. PETER AND ST. PAUL

I COULD tell of many wonderful experiences I had in "Holy Russia," and they would fill a volume. I have been whirled off in a *droshky* drawn by six fiery horses, driven by a demon driver wrapped in furs, through the moonlit night, travelling through a seemingly endless forest, the black trees standing up in sharp contrast to the snowy track. The ching! ching! ling! of the bells upon the horses mingled with the distant woof! woof! of the wolf pack, borne to my ears by the melancholy winter wind. But suddenly, when I felt that the journey would never end, the white road ran sharply in a dizzy curve through giant sentinel trees—a noble avenue, two miles long. At the end, lights twinkled from myriads of windows; great doors rolled back; a gorgeous majordomo received me with six footmen at rigid attention behind him. Thus in state, I came out of the cold winter night into the blazing splendour of the *salon* of the Princess Kienia Yvesky.

Her party included the cream of Russian society; some had come in their *droshkies* and sleighs for many miles through the vast forests that stretch for leagues round this château. It was hard to believe, looking round at the luxury, the toilettes of the ladies, the perfect organization of the house, that it was miles from everywhere, and that wolves bayed almost up to the château gates. But—it was Russia.

Alas! I revealed the fate of the Princess that night. A shout of incredulity greeted my predictions:

"Widowhood—Poverty—Death." They laughed—"How ridiculous." Among the victims of Bolshevik terrorism was the accomplished Prince Yvesky, while his beautiful wife died of privation, after escaping to Finland with a few jewels sewn up in her petticoat.

I will include in this part of my revelations a strange tale that sheds a light on Russia, when she was staggering downwards into the abyss of revolution.

I was visited in my hotel by an aristocratic Russian gentleman, who spoke frankly.

"'Cheiro,' I have heard of you from my chief, M. Isvolsky. Do me the honour to be frank with me."

I examined his shapely hand with attention. I saw there a wonderful capacity for organization and business ability, courage and faithfulness in friendship. But the indications pointed to some menacing sorrow, and a violent death for himself and two other persons closely connected.

I spoke first of his past life, and sketched out the circumstances of the present.

When I had finished, he said:

"'Cheiro,' you have been wonderfully accurate. So much so that

I dread to have the veil lifted from the Future. But I must. It hangs over me with a menacing aspect that fills me with a sense of depression. I am determined to know all."

I looked at his hands—they quickly told me what was the matter.

" You have a loved one who is in trouble," I began.

He started violently and his face became deadly pale.

I went on : " She has come into this trouble through helping someone else. This other person is a near relative—I should suppose her brother. He has been indiscreet and has been arrested. His sister—if it is his sister—has now fallen under the suspicion of the Government."

" 'Cheiro,' " he whispered, and seemed to gaze fearfully round the apartment, " you—you are marvellous. My fiancée has been arrested by the secret police, simply because she expressed the hope that her brother would be treated fairly and allowed a trial. He was a student at Tobolsk, a hot-headed boy, and he spoke injudiciously about ' Liberty and Equality '—he is in a dungeon in the fortress of the capital of the province, I know—for I am in the department of Justice —that there will be no trial, but an expulsion to Siberia. Now his sister is being drawn in. Good God ! Is my beloved to be sacrificed as well ? "

I comforted him as best I could. The working out of Fate bore hardly upon these three people. The woman, maddened by the fate of her brother, who was slashed to death by the *nagaika*, or *knout*, wielded by a Cossack guard, threw herself heart and soul into the revolutionary movement. She was liberated at first owing to the strenuous efforts of her lover, who risked his reputation with his superiors in order to do so. Known as " The Angel of the Revolution," she planned the assassination of the Czarevich, and was implicated in the mysterious attempt that partially succeeded when the Heir to the Throne was upon the Imperial yacht, cruising in the Baltic.

Frantic with fear that even there the child was not safe—for although official reports were suppressed, it is known that a woman gained access to the yacht in the guise of a trusted nurse—the Empress demanded that the full force of the fury of the Government should be let loose against all suspects.

" The Angel " was arrested, exiled to Siberia, and died in those frozen solitudes. Her lover blew out his brains in an elegant flat in St. Petersburg.

One fragmentary tragedy of mighty Russia, when she was tottering dizzily to the brink !

In view of the Czar's effort for a world peace in the years gone by, it may be interesting for my readers to glance over the following particulars of the famous Hague Conference of 1899.

It may be that the Czar was impressed with my prediction when he visited me in London in 1894, and endeavoured to alter his destiny by making the effort for peace which he did a few years later ; it is often that the smallest things give rise to the greatest results.

On January 11th, 1899, the Czar sent round letters to the leading Powers, inviting them to meet at a Peace Conference at the Hague. Twenty-six of them agreed to meet.

The Conference resolved itself into three committees. The first one dealt with the method of limiting armaments and the use of needlessly destructive engines in warfare; the second with the extension of the principles agreed to at Geneva in 1864, and at Brussels ten years later; while the third handled the question of international diplomacy and arbitration.

The First Committee's object was achieved, Russia gaining her point that explosive bullets and asphyxiating shells should be prohibited, an interdict being laid for five years on the employment of balloons to discharge explosives.

The Second Committee proclaimed neutral all vessels equipped solely to save human life.

The Third Committee discussed the Russian proposal to establish a permanent Court of Arbitration for the settling of international disputes.

In spite of severe opposition from Germany, the following principles were approved by the Conference:

That one or several Powers should have the right of offering mediation in impending conflicts; its exercises should not be regarded as an " unfriendly act."

A permanent Court of Arbitration was established at the Hague, composed of judges, selected from a list on which every state was represented, and this body formed an International Council.

A protocol embodying the decisions was signed by the representatives of sixteen states, and subsequently executed by sixteen more, including Great Britain, Germany, Austria-Hungary, China, Japan, and Italy.

As though by the irony of Fate, some of the most terrible wars broke out shortly after this Conference. I could not help remarking, when talking to a very distinguished pacifist one day, that when the foundations of the Hague Palace of Peace were laid, we had the Boer War; when the building was erected, the Russo-Japanese War; and when it was ready for its furniture, the Great War.

Yet what can one expect when one remembers that the £300,000 that Mr. Carnegie gave to lay the foundations of this Palace of Peace came chiefly from the manufacture of cannon and implements of war!

Russia recalls many memories to my mind, some pathetic, others humorous, and not a few on the verge of the sensational. It is of one in the last-named category that I have most vivid recollection.

Several times after my interview with the Czar in the Peterhof Palace I paid visits to Russia.

On my arrival in Petrograd for the third time, I was invited to dinner at the house of a lady who had great influence in Court circles.[1] It was a lovely night in August, and when I took leave of my hostess, I determined to walk to my hotel for the sake of getting some exercise.

[1] Princess Golitizen, Lady-in-waiting to the Czarina.

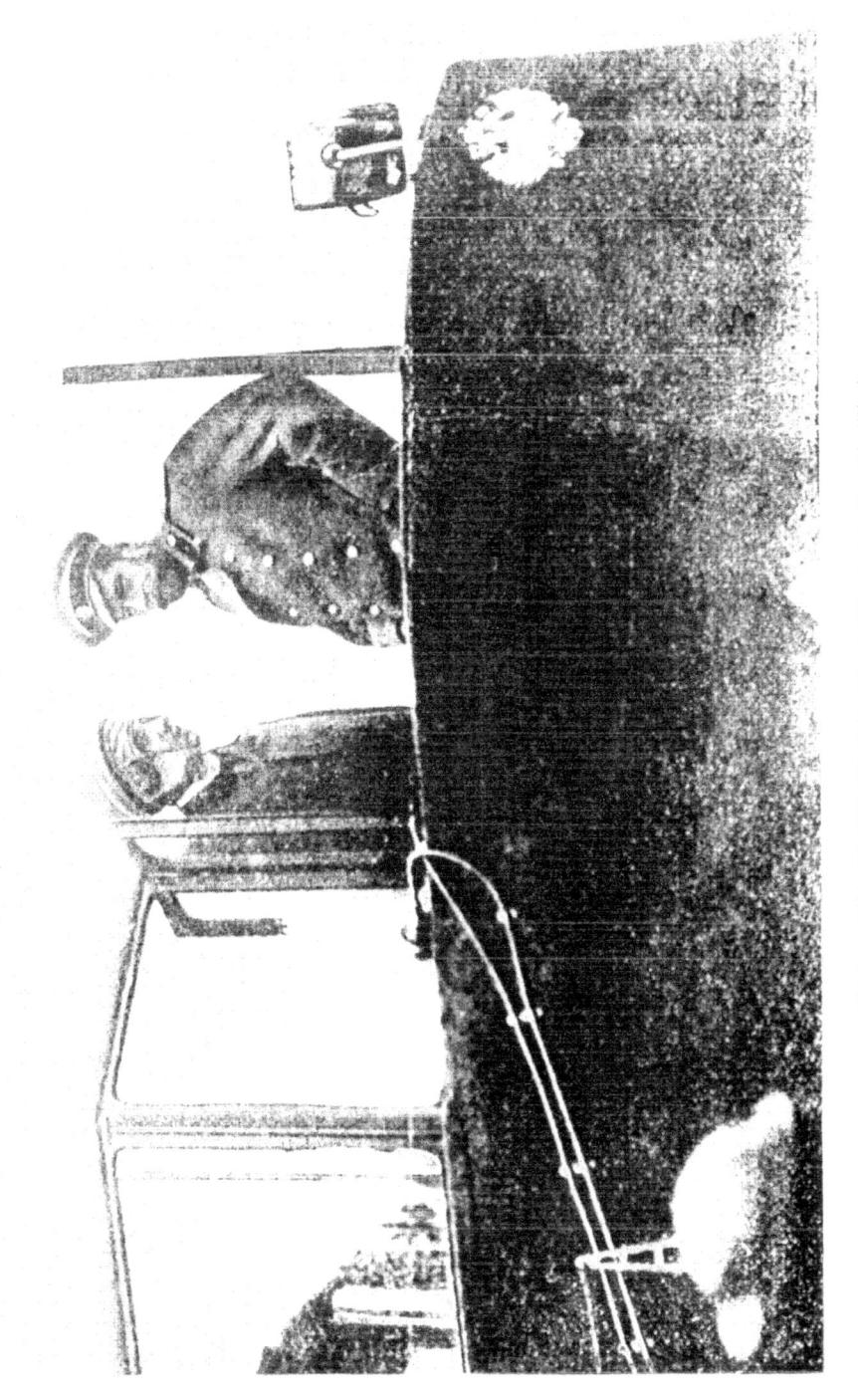

THE LAST PHOTOGRAPH OF NICHOLAS II AS CZAR

It shows him in his private aeroplane and was taken very shortly before his abdication.

The driver of a solitary *droshky* standing near the house importuned me as I passed, but I shook my head negatively and set off at a brisk pace towards the Nevsky.

Quite casually, I observed that the man was following me at some yards distance; I thought nothing of this, as I knew how persistent these drivers were in their endeavours to secure a fare.

Abruptly the weather changed. Spots of rain fell and I realized that unless I availed myself of the shelter the *droshky* offered I should receive a drenching.

Accordingly, I signalled to the driver, announced my hotel, and jumped in. Almost at the same instant a man stepped from the shadow of a house, and in perfect French said: " Pardon me, Monsieur, but may I share your *droshky*? I am also making for your hotel, and it is going to be very wet."

I consented, of course, and the stranger seated himself beside me. We set off at a furious pace towards the Nevsky, and I was observing what wonderful horses the Russians had, when I noticed that we turned down a side-street towards one of those long bridges that span the Neva.

" The fellow is going wrong," I laughed. " Tell him in Russian the address of our hotel."

" No, Monsieur," my companion replied, " the fellow is not wrong! You will not see your hotel to-night."

Despite the menacing nature of the words, his tone was polite, almost casual.

" What do you mean? " I demanded.

" Only this," he replied, still in that pleasant but significant tone. Gripping my arm with his left hand, he showed me a glimpse of the revolver held in his right.

After a long drive, we turned into the courtyard of a house standing alone on the very outskirts of the city.

We descended from the *droshky*, and, still holding my arm in a firm grip, my companion entered the house and conducted me into a heavily shuttered room in which four men of the artisan class were filling small brass cases that looked ominously like bombs, or hand-grenades. Through a door at the end of this room, we gained access to another and smaller apartment. There seated at a table, head in hands and the very picture of abject despair, was a woman.

" Ah, Monsieur, she is broken-hearted," said my companion.

" But what has happened? " I asked in wonderment.

This atmosphere of mystery was stifling me. " Can I do anything to help her? "

As though galvanized to life by an electric current, the woman started up at my words. The next moment she was on her knees at my feet, her tangled black hair thrown back, revealing a face beautiful yet drawn with an agony that was painful to witness.

" Indeed you can! " she moaned in French. " That is why I made them bring you."

In calmer tones the woman told me of her life. She was a revolutionary. Her people had always been rebels and had suffered for their beliefs. She had seen, first her grandfather, then her brothers, knouted to death, while her husband had been executed soon after their marriage.

"But it is of my son I wish to speak," she cried. "It is for him I beseech your help!"

"Is he a revolutionary, too?" I asked, bewildered at the turn the night's adventure had taken.

"No, Monsieur," she sobbed. "On the contrary, he was, alas! *born without the spirit of revenge*."

I could not fathom this strange statement. But all was revealed to me as she proceeded to tell me how this son she adored had pleaded with her to give up the revolutionary cause; how, instead, she had gone on blindly, year after year. Men and women had looked to her as their leader; they had suffered exile or died for the cause, yet she had gone on, determined to give up her life if that were necessary. After "Bloody Sunday," when the police could not find her, they had taken her son; his family record was against him, and he was at that moment in the fortress of St. Peter and St. Paul under sentence of death.

"But what can I do in all this tragedy?" I asked. "I, a stranger here—what good can I do?"

Again the woman lifted her head.

"Yes, you can indeed help, that is why I made them bring you to me. The lady you dined with to-night could plead with the Czarina that my only boy may be spared. She, too, has an only son; she knows what it is to love."

I had grasped by now the terrible difficulties of the situation. They told me that the sentence of death would be carried out in two days—surely not much time in which to work, and even then, could there be any hope of success?

I was in despair. I attempted to reason with the grief-bowed mother, but at the first words the tears stopped, the sobs ceased—a terrible light came into her eyes, and, ordering the man to open the door, she pointed to where the four figures were silently filling the bombs in the outer room.

"If my son dies," she hissed, "the Czarina and her son will die too!"

Full of emotion, I could only repeat my promise to try to help. "I will try to-night," I added.

With a sob that wrung my heart, the half-mad mother knelt down and kissed my feet. Without a word, the man and I went to the door, and in another moment the *droshky* was tearing back towards the city.

Although it was extremely late, my friend the Princess received me at once. I told her exactly what I had heard and seen, and she promised me she would go to the Empress at the earliest hour in the morning.

At four the following morning, the Princess sent for me.

"I have not been successful," she said, "but I have at least obtained one slight concession. The boy is to be shot at six o'clock to-morrow morning, but I have been promised that his body will be placed in a coffin and given over to his relatives. Further, you and that man who brought you will be allowed to witness the execution and can take the coffin away with you at once afterwards."

"There may be some hope," she added, "that I shall be able to arrange something between this and six o'clock to-morrow morning, but don't ask me any questions now."

With a heart like lead, I returned to my hotel and found my companion of the previous night waiting for me. He knew from my face that my news was not reassuring, but he did not say much and quietly agreed that he would meet me at the gates of the fortress of St. Peter and St. Paul at 5.30 in the morning, and that he would have a hearse there waiting to carry away the body.

I do not think I ever passed a more wretched night. The dawn at last came, heavy, foreboding, and as the clock struck 5.30, I kept my appointment at the gates of the prison fortress.

We found the lad wonderfully calm and resigned to his doom. He gave me a gold cross which he had always worn, to hand to his mother, and, saying good-bye, we left him to the care of a priest who had just arrived.

The firing-squad were already in position as we returned to the yard, and while the men waited for their officer, they leaned nonchalantly on their rifles as if the terrible scene were but part of the ordinary routine of their daily life.

The officer came, the men stood to attention, and at the word of command loaded their rifles. A bell was rung, the condemned man marched into the yard, escorted by two jailers and preceded by the priest, mumbling words that no one seemed to hear.

When all was ready, the officer walked up to the boy and said something. The condemned lad seemed to bow his head. A moment later three sharp commands rang out; the rifles answered with a volley, and the boy's body fell forward in a huddled heap into the coffin at his feet.

I was spellbound with horror. Mechanically I saw the warders straighten out the body, screw down the lid of the coffin, and throw, rather than lift it into the hearse.

Then I felt myself being helped into a *droshky* at the prison gates, the other man with me, and without speaking a word, we followed the hearse to that same lonely house where we had been so shortly before.

Men carried in the coffin and placed it on the bench in the centre of the room—the same bench where I had seen the bombs being filled.

A wild, haggard-looking woman staggered out from the inner room and ordered the men to unscrew the lid.

The lid was lifted; respectfully the men stood back. The woman, with a tenderness almost divine, bent down and lifted the head gently against her breast. There were no sobs from her heart, yet silent tears rolled down the cheeks of the men present.

I felt I could not stand there a moment longer. I turned towards the door, but as I did so, I heard a scream that seemed to freeze the blood in my veins.

I rushed forward. The mother was clasping her boy in her arms, as if waking out of a dream, his eyes opened and were looking straight into hers.

"Maya, Maya," he said in Russian. "Don't be frightened! I am not dead."

In a few minutes the seeming miracle was explained.

The Princess had kept her word. She had influenced the officer in charge of the firing-party to have the soldiers served with blank cartridges. He had, in his turn, told the boy to fall forward as though dead when the shots rang out, and the youth had involuntarily added realism to the deception by fainting at the fateful moment.

I need not dwell on the joyous scene that took place in that sombre house. It affected me deeply, and I was glad when I was able to make my departure—not, however, before I had been overwhelmed with sincere expressions of a mother's gratitude.

It was that very boy who three years later saved my own life in an experience which I will relate later.

CHAPTER XII

THE GREAT CATHEDRAL OF KIEFF. THE HOLY PICTURE ON HUMAN SKIN IS LOWERED FOR ME TO KISS

IT was about three years later when I again visited Russia, this time chiefly directing my attention towards the south.

I got off the train at Kieff and stopped for a week to thoroughly enjoy this remarkable city—the one-time capital of what was known as " Little Russia."

Situated as it is on the crest of a hill overlooking the Steppes and the Dnieper, which sweeps in almost a circle round its feet, there are not many cities which occupy a more commanding position. I know few sights more impressive than when looking down from the public gardens on the crest of the hill, one looks across those endless plains below, where they seem in the far distance to join the sky. In the rays of the setting sun, one sees the great river like a path of gold flowing from the horizon where sky and earth have met and sweeping onward in majestic curves past this fairy city of the heights.

Set like great jewels in emerald foliage, the churches rise with their glittering domes; higher still and dominating all, stands the Grand Llarva, or Great Cathedral, holding as it were the last gleams of light in its golden dome and shedding them back to the city at its feet like some glittering blessing from the Giver of Good.

And what a cathedral that Grand Llarva is—what a monument on the pathway of Religion ; can one wonder that pilgrims wend their way to see it once before they die, from the farthest stretches of the great Russian Empire ?

Esquimaux from the White Sea, a thousand miles to the north, have taken years to tramp that distance, just to live a few days in the shadow of its arms, to die perhaps with hunger on their homeward march.

From the borders of China in the east ; from the hot plains of Turkestan in the south, they come year after year.

All bring presents to the great shrine, jewels that have no price, gold the purest that can be found, carpets of silk that lifetimes were spent in weaving, everything that one can imagine or that homage can give.

And some again come with nothing, only rags that cover skin and bone—weary and worn out they creep into the great courtyard, glad to get a crust of bread from the black-robed monks and happy to even see the incense that every few hours rises upwards towards the dome.

I had come with a letter of introduction to the Grand Patriarch from my friend, the Minister of Foreign Affairs, Monsieur Isvolsky, and counter-signed by the Czar himself. The Grand Patriarch was a marvellous-looking old man in his robes of black and gold, and a beard white as snow that almost reached his feet.

He gave me a monk as a guide to show me the wonders of the place and his patriarchal blessing which I often felt I needed when gazing at the treasures in the vaults below. Through catacombs cut out of the solid rock by human hands we wandered, past the mummified heads of the hundred monks who had in far-off ages built the cathedral and who when their work was finished carved out their own tombs one by one in the heart of the solid rock below.

Wonderful, wonderful, is all one feels able to say as finally the tour is ended and one comes upward into the light and into the heart of the great cathedral itself.

I was indeed a favoured person. What did it matter what my own religion might be, or for the matter of that, what could any other religion matter in such a place.

I was indeed a favoured person and yet I was going to be favoured still further.

As we stood in the centre of the chancel, opposite the gates of solid gold that separate the public from the high altar, my guide, the monk, drew my attention to a small painting of the head of the Mother of Christ that hung suspended on two chains of gold directly above the altar. Looking upwards I saw the painting which was not more perhaps than twenty-four inches square, but set in an enormous frame of gold in which thousands of diamonds seemed to sparkle. While looking at it, he told me the following curious story :

" That picture," he said, " was painted by a monk about the year A.D. 400 ; it is made on human skin taken from the breasts of those monks who started the foundations of the cathedral.

" When the Saracens overran Asia, they invaded Russia and conquered it as far north as Kieff. They sacked the then cathedral, and, finding this painting hanging over the altar, they took it and threw it into the Dnieper ; they ravaged the entire country, but later were beaten back again towards the south.

" When the monks returned to their cathedral they commenced to rebuild it, but their greatest sorrow was the loss of this picture that they prized more than all the jewels and precious things that had been stolen. The day, however, when the cathedral was restored and the first Mass held—on that same day, the picture was discovered floating on the surface of the Dnieper exactly opposite the church as if the current of the river had never in all that time been able to carry it away. It was found to be undamaged in the slightest degree and was brought back and hung by chains of gold over the altar in the same position where it is to-day.

" From then on, it became the custom in Kieff and for a hundred miles round, that every rich person who died within that circumference had to leave to the picture one solitary diamond, *but the best and whitest that money could buy.* The frame has had to be enlarged many times and it now contains so many thousands of diamonds that to-day it has perhaps a depth of several feet. It is only lowered to be kissed by exceptionally favoured persons ; the last person it was lowered for was the German Kaiser when he visited Kieff as Crown Prince.

"It will be lowered again to-day," the monk added, "for I have instructions that you are to be the favoured person to be allowed to press your lips to what is considered here as the most venerated object of all our treasures."

It was useless my expostulating that I was far too humble an individual for such an honour. I was led up to the altar, the gold chains were loosened, and the picture slowly descended to where I knelt. When the ceremony was over I looked outwards to the chancel. To my amazement I saw the monk and I were not the only participants in such a strange ceremony—the entire cathedral was filled, and the courtyard beyond, with pilgrims lying flat on their faces in mute devotion and awe.

CHAPTER XIII

TIFLIS AND THE WONDERFUL KASPECK MOUNTAIN. I AM GIVEN A CONCESSION WORTH A FORTUNE, BUT AM MADE PRISONER BY BANDITS ON THE ROUTE OF GEORGIA

LEAVING Kieff, I went by automobile by the once great national road to Jitomir. This wide, magnificent route was made for military purposes and is almost a straight line across the country for a distance of about forty-five miles between the two towns. As this part of the country is very badly served by the railway, the traffic is carried on by the most old-fashioned diligences that one could possibly imagine. To see these odd-shaped vehicles drawn by six or seven horses lumbering along would make one believe one was suddenly transported back to the heart of the Middle Ages.

The Zemstvo of Kieff had offered me a concession to replace these diligences by a service of auto-omnibuses, but as I found a German firm had already been in negotiation for the same service, and as their tender was a ridiculously low one, I did not entertain the business. The German motors proved to be too light for that terrible road, and within two years travellers were glad to go back to their old-fashioned conveyances and the German company came to grief.

This is just another of the many instances of German enterprise in Russia. A few years before the War one could find them in almost all Russian factories, and if the War had not come on, in a short time Russia would, at least commercially, have become not much more than a kind of German province.

From Jitomir I went on to Baku, the city of petrol on the Caspian Sea. A city of oil wells and huge refineries, where even the very water one drank seemed to taste of petroleum.

After crossing the Caspian and getting a glimpse of the old-world Oriental civilization in Turkestan, then on to Mount Ararat where I was shown a supposed piece of Noah's Ark, I was glad to retrace my footsteps and make my way to Tiflis, the capital of the Caucasus and the principal town in Southern Russia.[1] Here I presented a letter of introduction from His Excellency Monsieur Isvolsky in Petrograd to Count Vorontzoff-Daskoff, the Viceroy, who received me in a most courteous and charming manner. I carried with me from the Minister of Ways and Communications, a signed Government concession to place motor omnibuses for both the post and passengers on the famous military route of Georgia to serve the towns of Vadikaffquas and Tiflis. This concession had been represented to me to be worth a fortune.

I wanted, however, to see one of the greatest sights of Nature that perhaps the eyes of man can behold. I wanted to cross the Alps of Russia to see the famous Kaspeck with its peaks of perpetual snow, many thousands of feet higher than Mont Blanc, and at the same time inspect the famous route of Georgia for myself.

[1] The City of Tiflis was founded by Vakhtang, King of Georgia, in the fifth century.

It was a strange sensation to swelter in the streets of Tiflis and look upwards to those glistening heights of the Kaspeck that rose like white steps into the very heart of Heaven.

One day I told the Viceroy, whose guest I was, that I was planning to see for myself the route of Georgia across the Caucasus from Tiflis to Vadikaffquas. He laughed and said, " If I gave you an escort of my best Cossacks, I doubt if you would ever get half-way."

Perhaps seeing my look of incredulity, he added, " It is true it is our great military road from north to south constructed by Peter the Great, but since the past few years it is so infested with bandits that it would take as long as the late Japanese War to clear them out, and it might cost us as much in lives and money."

In spite of all warnings, the love of adventure called me on, and seeing occasionally a peasant caravan that made the journey, apparently without mishap, I finally made up my mind to try.

I had made the acquaintance of a Georgian prince, who in a wonderful uniform of a Cossack officer, with revolvers in his belt and a row of cartridges all round his body, looked so fierce that I confided in him my plan. Of course, he laughed at danger, he was a Georgian, he said, and Georgians had no fear. His race had fought for centuries the troops of every Czar who had reigned since Peter the Great ; besides, he added, his own brother was Chief of the Bandits, so we need have no fear.

For a paltry present of a few hundred roubles he would be glad to accompany me, and so one morning as the sun rose we started.

We took a carriage with four splendid Cossack horses, a lot of provisions, together with winter clothing and furs which would be necessary when we reached the snow.

I bought the latest pattern Browning revolver, and feeling very brave away we started.

Far out on the famous route of Georgia, our carriage wound in and out among the mountains, climbing higher and still higher till the town of Tiflis beneath looked like a pack of cards that some pigmy had played with at making houses.

No painter's brush, no poet's pen could depict such savage and grandiose scenery. At one moment we swung round at the edge of a precipice, at another we passed through walls of giant rocks that guarded the road with the shadows of night ; on past firs and pines and forests of oak that had reared their heads for ages ; on again till the peaks of the Kaspeck seemed toppling over upon us.

At last we stopped, we had reached the edge of the ice, a place where the forest had ceased to grow, where the birds had ceased to sing, where silence reigned upon her throne, where edicts of Czars or men had never reached.

I still tried to look brave, but I did not feel it. My companion no longer looked the fierce Cossack of the town, but rather like some toy I had bought in a child's bazaar.

Our horses were dead beat and they had to rest, our men too were hungry and they had to eat. We opened our provisions, we spread them on the upturned face of a massive granite rock. We filled our glasses—we had brought with us a bottle of French champagne, it sparkled in the sun, but, like ourselves, it looked out of place in such surroundings.

For hours we had not seen a human being, not a single bandit—as if such worms could live in such a scene!

We clinked our glasses, we had raised them to our lips, when from behind our shoulders two huge hands appeared, took them out of our fingers and with a laugh emptied them into two big fierce-looking mouths.

There was no dream about it, we were surrounded by bandits, there was not even a shot fired, not a word had been said.

My Georgian prince expostulated, argued, raved in Georgian, Russian, and every other language he knew, in vain he cited his bandit brother. They first ate our provisions, drank our champagne, and with charming consideration gave us two chunks of dry bread for ourselves. Then our horses were led away, we were pushed into the centre of the group and marched for about an hour across the side of the mountain. At last we reached what they called their fortress— a natural stronghold where Nature had piled up enormous masses of rock on the edge of a precipice, while on the other sides it was surrounded with an equally inaccessible and impassable sea of ice.

In the centre of this rock-bound enclosure was a large hut made of logs, in which a good wood fire blazed brightly and around the chimney were some rough benches which my companion and myself were very glad to appropriate to our own immediate use.

Cups of very good chi (tea) were handed round by a deaf and dumb youth who appeared to be a kind of general servant, and then most of our captors picked up their rifles and went out, leaving us to ourselves.

My companion, who of course understood everything that was said, told me in French that from their conversation he had learned that they were planning to hold me for ransom, but the amount would not be decided on until their principal Chief would come back the following day.

He had also gathered that this Chief was from the north of Russia and although very young and only with them for a little over two years, had in that time become the leader of nearly all bandits in that part of the Caucasus, and, further, had enormous influence with the revolutionaries in St. Petersburg.

" We are in a bad fix indeed," he added, " and if a ransom for you is not easily arranged, God only knows what may happen."

" But surely if I can send word to the Viceroy," I suggested, " he will send and obtain our freedom."

My friend smiled. " You don't realize where you are," he said.

"In the first place no message could ever reach him, and if it did, it might take years to find us here."

"But they don't seem to watch us closely," I replied, "there does not appear to be a soul about, let us go out and have a look round."

Outside the hut there was no one to be seen, we could wander where we liked. We climbed the edge of the rocks; on two sides there was a precipice with a wall of unbroken rock that looked straight down as far as our eyes could see, and on the other side there was a wide plain of unbroken ice and snow whose edge seemed to lose itself in great glaciers that appeared to rise without end up to the highest peaks of the Kaspeck itself.

We next worked our way round to the entrance by which we had been brought in. It was very simple—a wide cleft in a sheer wall of black rock and one man with a rifle that commanded the winding path by which we had entered.

"But our drivers," I said, "they were allowed to escape. By to-morrow, they will have reached Tiflis and will have given the alarm."

"They may reach Tiflis," my companion answered, "but even if they do, they will not dare say one word. You forget you had to pay them in advance before they would start, as likely as not they are friends of the bandits; besides, in the Caucasus people do not go about helping the police or Government with information, and even if they did, it would not be of much use."

We returned to the hut; a savoury smell of cooking made us feel desperately hungry. Over the fire was swinging a huge pot that the deaf and dumb youth occasionally stirred; with greedy eyes we both watched it and began to long for our bandit hosts to return.

At last they came. They were in excellent spirits. A foolish merchant from Moscow had attempted to reach Tiflis by "their" road, with the result that several thousand pieces of gold, a handsome watch and one of Faberger's jewelled cigarette cases had become their property. Like children they played with the gold, they handed me cigarettes from the merchant's case, and finally they invited us to their wooden table and we all sat round for dinner.

The stew was excellent, it was a close cousin to "Irish stew," only of venison instead of meat, but I never ate anything in my life that tasted better, especially washed down as it was by a couple of glasses of old vodka which they poured out like water from a curious-shaped stone jar. In the end they drank so much that one by one they rolled off to sleep upon the floor, and if we had not known of a man and a rifle posted at the entrance to the stronghold, I feel sure we would have been tempted to make an effort to escape.

Morning came at last; one by one they woke up. The youth brought in several jugs of hot coffee and chi (tea), vodka was also served round, the gold which was still lying about the table was picked up and put in a chest, and I was actually offered the rest of the cigarettes out of the robbed merchant's case.

To my amazement nearly every member of the band washed and tidied himself up. One man struck a magnificent osprey into the front of his turban and filling their belts with cartridges they picked up their rifles and went out.

"They have gone to meet the Chief," my companion said. We went and sat down by the fire and with mixed feelings of dread and anxiety, waited for the arrival of the man who was to decide our fate.

In about an hour we heard their footsteps returning. They entered the hut—one man a little in advance of the rest.

My companion rose, gave a military salute, and stood at attention. I heard a lot of voices, but as they spoke in Georgian I could not understand a word that was said, but as the Chief walked to the middle of the room I also turned round, stood up, and faced him.

I had barely noticed his tall, slight form, the contrast he made to the men around him, his steel grey-blue eyes that in a flash of memory I felt I had seen somewhere before—when in one bound he had clasped me in both arms, and I heard him say in French, "My God, to imagine we should meet like this!"

For a second I did not recognize who he was, but the wonderful had happened; those same eyes I had seen facing rifles in a prison in Petrograd; he was the man whose life I had saved three years before.

In a few words he told me what had taken place. His mother had been killed in the end by the police. The spirit of revenge which she thought he had not inherited *had come to life in his veins at her death*, he had become an outlaw against all society, and the money he gained as a bandit was to help the revolutionaries in the north. "All men are bandits," he said bitterly, "until they become successful; if they have luck enough to rob countries, they become kings."

A few hours later we were on our way back to Tiflis. My bandit friend accompanied us to the very outskirts of the town.

"Good-bye," he said, and kissed me on both cheeks.

CHAPTER XIV

HOW I MET LORD KITCHENER. THE ONLY IMPRESSION OF HIS HAND THAT WAS EVER OBTAINED. HOW I PREDICTED HIS EXACT DATE OF DEATH

ON July 21st, 1894, I had the honour of meeting Lord Kitchener and obtaining the autographed impression of his right hand, which accompanies this chapter.

The day I had this interview, the late Lord Kitchener, or, as he was then, Major-General Kitchener, was at the War Office. To take this impression I had to employ the paper lying on his table, and, strange as it may appear to those who read symbols, the imprint of the War Office may be seen at the top of the second finger—the finger known for ages as that of Fate—in itself perhaps a premonition that he would one day be the guiding hand in that great department in the most terrible war that up to now has threatened the Destiny of Britain.

As I related in one of my recent books,[1] Lord Kitchener was at the moment of my interview (1894) Sirdar of the Egyptian Army and had returned to England to tender his resignation on account of some hostile criticism over "The Abbas affair." His strong-willed action was a few weeks later completely vindicated. He was made a K.C.M.G. and returned to Egypt with more power than before and not long afterwards brought the Egyptian Campaign to a successful close.

It seems only yesterday to me, that most memorable morning at the War Office, when after sending in my card I was in a few minutes ushered into his room.

He received me most cordially. "Well," he said, "so you want to have a look at my hand again?"

"Again?" I said in astonishment.

"Yes," he replied. "Years ago I went to see you like so many others and I can only say you were most singularly accurate in everything you told me."

"I am so glad," I stammered, "for I hardly dared come and ask you to let me have an impression of your hand as I had no idea you believed in such studies."

"Look here"—he turned and pointed to a small blue vase about three inches high that was standing on his table—"can you tell me anything about that?"

Utterly taken aback, I took the vase in my hands, looked it all over, and then put it down, saying, "I am sorry, but I don't know one vase from another. I have never had the inclination to study such things."

"Just so," he laughed. "You have answered yourself. I have never studied hands and you have. If a man makes a lifelong study of a thing, I expect him to know more about it than anyone else—so now you know why I went to see you many years ago."

This little incident had put me completely at my ease and in a few moments this great man, before whom so many trembled, was quietly

[1] *Palmistry for All.* Putnam and Son.

leaning back in his chair asking me the meaning of the lines in his own clearly marked palms, also those of some famous men, such as Gladstone, Stanley, and others, the impressions of whose hands I had brought with me.

He was then forty-four years of age, and I remember well how I explained the still higher positions and responsibilities that his path of Destiny mapped out before him.

The heaviest and greatest of all would, I told him, be undertaken in his sixty-fourth year (1914), but how little either of us thought that in that year the most terrible war that England has ever engaged in would have broken out.

Believing as I do in the Law of Periodicity playing as great a role in the lives of individuals as it does in nations, it is significant for those who make a study of such things to notice, that the same "fadic" numbers—or, as they are also called, "Numbers of Fate"—that governed Lord Kitchener's career when he was planning out the Egyptian Campaign, by which he made his greatest name, and which resulted in the victories of Atbara and Omdurman in 1896, 1897, and 1898—produce the same final digit number for 1914, 1915, and 1916.

These years added together from left to right give the following numbers :

1896—24—6. Opening of Egyptian campaign.
1897—25—7. Atbara and Omdurman.
1898—26—8. Rest from Labour—Honoured by Nation.
1914—15—6. Opening of the Great War.
1915—16—7. Creation of Britain's Army of 4,000,000.
1916—17—8. Rest from Labour and death—Honoured by Nation.

"Tell me what you like," he said, that morning of July 21st, 1894, " as long as the end is some distance off." And yet, when I pointed out to him that the 6 and 7 and the 8 were the most important numbers of his life, as quickly as the late King Edward worked out from my figures that 69 was likely to be the end of his life, and joked with me and others about it afterwards—so Kitchener, with perhaps the same mysterious flash of intuition, ran his pencil down the figures I had just worked out to the date of 1916 which was indicated as " Rest from Labour." " That then is perhaps ' The End,' " he said.

" Strange, isn't it ? " he laughed. " But is there any indication of the kind of death it is likely to be ? "

" Yes," I said. " There are certainly indications, but not at all perhaps the kind of ' end ' that one would be likely to imagine would happen to you."

I then showed him in as few words as possible, that having been born on June 16th, 1850, he was in the First House of Air, in the Sign of Gemini, entering into the First House of Water, the Sign of Cancer, also House of the Moon and detriment of Saturn. Taking these indications, together with the kabalistic interpretation of the numbers governing his life, the fatal year would be his 66th year,

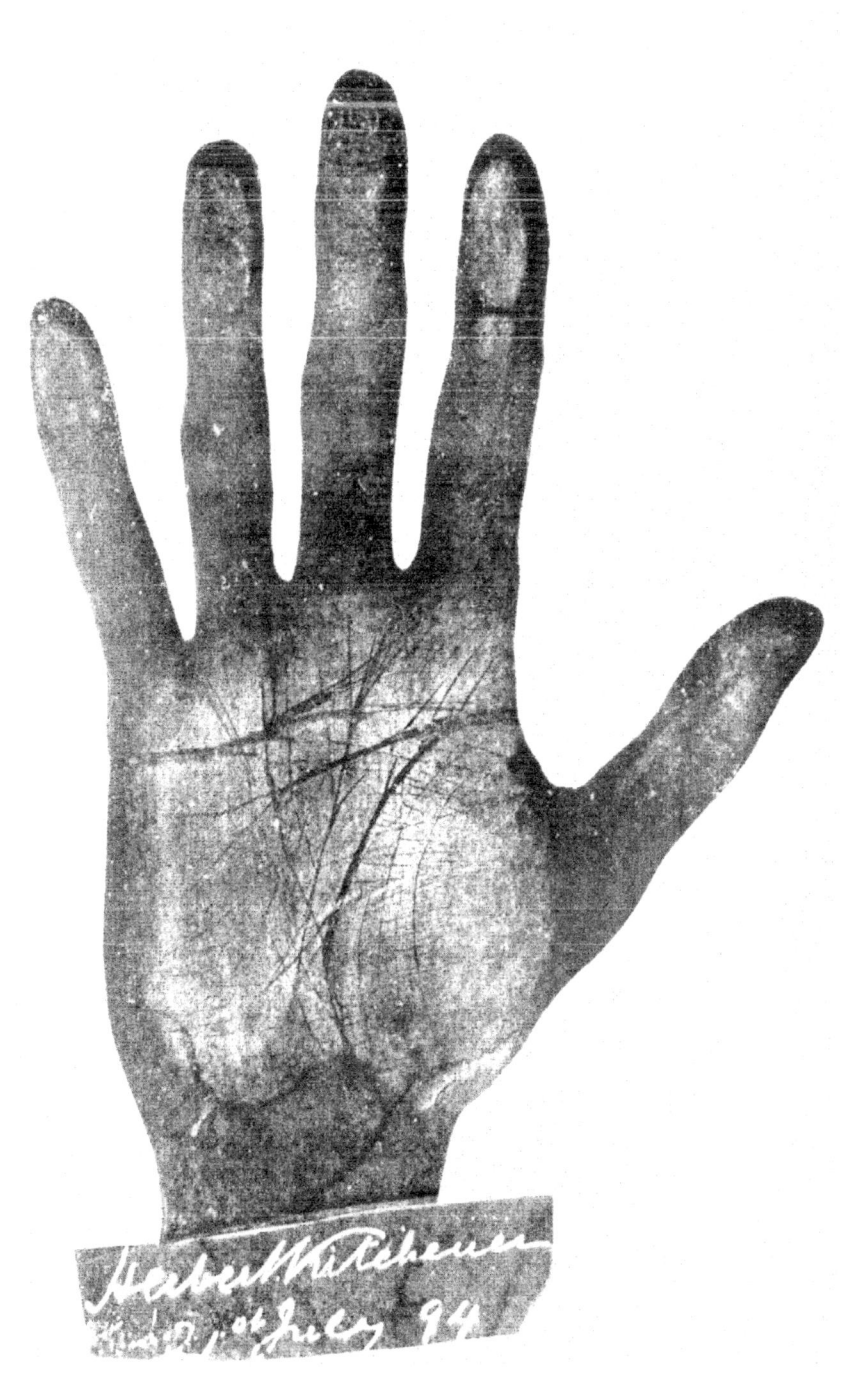

AUTOGRAPHED IMPRESSION OF THE HAND OF LORD KITCHENER
OF KHARTOUM
The only one that was ever made.

about June, and the death would be by water, probably caused by storm (Air) or disaster at sea (Water), with the attendant chance of some form of capture by an enemy and an exile from which he would never recover.

"Thanks," he laughed. "I prefer the first proposition."

"Yet," he added, "I must admit that what you tell me about danger at sea makes a serious impression on my mind and I want you to note down among your queer theories, but do not say anything about it unless if some day you hear of my being drowned—that I made myself a good swimmer and I believe I am a fairly good one— for no other reason but that when I first visited you as quite an unknown man many years ago, you told me that water would be my greatest danger. You have now confirmed what you told me then and have even given me the likely date of the danger.

"Good-bye," he said, "I won't forget, and as of course you believe in thought transference and that sort of thing, who knows if I won't send you some sign, if it should happen that water claims me at the last."

That he did remember is, I think, established by an Exchange Telegraph Company's message on June 19th, 1915, mentioning that " when Lord Kitchener came to the British Front, he met at Dunkirk Commandant de Balancourt, to whom he mentioned that a ' Jack Johnson ' had dropped not far from him. ' That did not alarm me,' said the Field-Marshal, ' *because I know I shall die at sea.*' "

I must now allude to a strange occurrence on the night of the disaster and yet one that, had it not happened, I doubt very much if I would ever have felt the desire to write this chapter.

Many persons will, of course, call what I am about to relate " a strange coincidence," but to others it may be just another illustration of one of the many mysteries that make up the sum-total of what one calls " the unexplored side of life."

The occurrence I am about to relate does not rely on myself for its testimony, for I wrote an article on this subject for the *Strand Magazine* and showed the editor the written testimony and confirmation of the persons who were present with me when it occurred.

Almost at eight o'clock on Monday evening, June 5th, 1916, the hour when the disaster to the *Hampshire* happened, I was sitting in a long music-room in my house in the country with some friends, when during a pause in general conversation about the War, we were startled by a *crash of something falling in the north end of the room.* Going to the place where the noise was heard, we saw a large oak shield on which the arms of Britain were painted lying on the floor— *broken into halves.*

Picking it up, I noticed that the shield had been broken through that part representative of England and Ireland, and showing it to my friends I could not help saying, " This is evidently an omen that some terrible blow has at this moment been dealt to England. I feel that some naval disaster has taken place in which Ireland or at least the name of Ireland is in some way concerned."

But how little did we think that at that very minute the illustrious Irishman, Lord Kitchener, was perhaps standing on the quarter-deck of the *Hampshire* facing his death at sea.

A few seconds later the clock struck eight.

I have often asked myself since—did Lord Kitchener remember and keep his promise?

Returning to the accompanying illustration of Lord Kitchener's hand, low down in the palm one can hardly help but notice that the Line of Life (encircling the ball of the thumb) has a line shooting out through it crossing the two main lines of the hand—(the Line of Fate going up to the first and second fingers and the Line of Success going up to the third)—the line shooting across from the Life Line is called the Line of Voyage or Travel, and it is a strange fact that it is on this hand seen *breaking* the Line of Fate and Line of Success at the very period where all my books on this subject show to be about the 66th year of age.

We have been told by Him, whose words all Christendom venerates and believes, that "not even a sparrow can fall to the ground, but that the Father knoweth it." Considering all these things, perhaps then it is not too much to believe that in the case of Lord Kitchener "the appointed time" had come. The work of the life had been accomplished, and the year of 1916 was even at his birth written in the Book of Destiny as the year of the final "rest from labour."

The following appeared in a London paper a few weeks after the publication of the account of my experience with Lord Kitchener in some of the English periodicals.

KITCHENER A VICTIM OF A WOMAN'S REVENGE?

Strange Question to "Cheiro" in Mystery Letter

BOMB IN WARSHIP STORY

"I wonder if by chance you told him (Kitchener) he would be the victim of revenge?"

This strange question was put to "Cheiro" in the course of a letter he received from a Boer woman who shrouds her identity under the signature "Johanna."

The writer of this remarkable letter states:

"I was fascinated at your foretelling his fate by drowning. I wonder what else you said—if by chance you told him he would be the victim of revenge?

"As you are perhaps the only man who may have guessed the truth, or part of the truth, from what you saw in Kitchener's hand, I am going to give you the real facts."

Then, in strange foreign handwriting, and using the German script lettering, the writer proceeds dramatically:

LORD KITCHENER OF KHARTOUM

"Twenty-five years ago I was a happy woman, married, and my son was ten years of age. We lived with my parents and my three brothers in a fine homestead farm in the Transvaal.

"We were Boers and loved our home and worked hard. I will be brief as to what happened. War came to our unhappy people. Our homestead became our fortress.

"Kitchener gave the order to burn us out. Our brave men were shot before our eyes as rebels. My mother, my little son and myself were imprisoned in a dreadful concentration camp where the horrors drove my poor old mother insane and my little boy wasted nearly to a skeleton.

"In that plague and disease-stricken camp hell, I swore to revenge my beloved ones; and so it was that when I found myself free I devoted all my mind, body and soul to be revenged on the man who gave the order to kill *all that I held dear in this world*.

"I planted the flame of hate in my son's soul and fanned that flame till his hatred of the man who had killed his father was as fierce as mine.

"Alas! my son had developed consumption, caught in that horrible camp, the like of which cannot be described.

"Enough to say that I and my son in the end got our chance of revenge. When the last war came on we were living in Scotland where my son had employment in loading ships at Scapa Flow. An infernal machine was taken on board the *Hampshire* in the disguise of stores. All the world knows the rest.

"A few months ago my dear son coughed himself to death and I am alone, an old woman. I am going back to my country to end my days and am glad to have confessed this to you.

"'An eye for an eye!' I have done no murder. *I have had my revenge.*—Johanna."

The letter is dated October 19th, and, as the postage stamp shows, was posted at 7.45 p.m. on that date at Tilbury.[1]

---

[1] Tilbury contains the great docks on the Thames from which so many South African liners leave.

CHAPTER XV

I AM RECEIVED BY HIS HOLINESS POPE LEO XIII. CONVERSATION ON THE SUBJECT OF "FADIC NUMBERS." HIS HOLINESS PRESENTS ME TO CARDINAL SARTO, FATED TO FOLLOW HIM ON "THE THRONE OF ST. PETER"

OF all the remarkable experiences in my professional career, perhaps the most remarkable was my interview with His Holiness Pope Leo XIII. It remains in my memory an unforgettable experience; many people have pressed me to tell the full story of that visit to the Vatican, and the hour's conversation I had with His Holiness.

Even the circumstances that led to the interview being granted were quite out of the ordinary; although to penetrate into the Vatican's mysterious interior had long been the dream of my life, I could see no prospect of the wish being granted. Still, I clung to the impression that it would some day be accomplished; until at last, in an unlooked-for fashion, events so shaped themselves that the dream became reality.

It came about in this way. I had the honour of knowing Prince Marco Colonna from almost the commencement of my career as "Cheiro," and I had had the good fortune of being extremely accurate in predictions concerning him and the many persons he sent to me.

Here I may mention that the Colonna family is one of the most ancient and honoured in Italy. While associated with the Court, they have for generations been more particularly identified with the service of the Popes. No history of the Popes of the Vatican could be complete without telling the story of the Colonna family—who devoted their fortunes and swords to supporting the occupant of the Papal Throne.

During my season in Paris, one afternoon the Prince dropped in to see me, and we fell to discussing occult matters in general. He told me of the marvellous library of the Vatican—the world's greatest collection of books, some of which, so to speak, it was almost unlawful for a man to peer into, so great was the mysterious knowledge contained in them. He spoke with reverence of the sainted life led by Pope Leo XIII in the Papal Palace, surrounded by his cardinals and attendants, while the precincts are guarded night and day by the famous Papal Guard.

As I listened, I felt a renewed desire that I might be admitted to this Palace of the Popes, guarded so jealously. On the spur of the moment, as people say—although I would prefer to record that these "spurs" are impulses governed by Fate—I said to the Prince:

"For years I have longed to have the privilege of seeing the Vatican!"

He looked thoughtful for a moment, and then said quietly:

"'Cheiro,' why not?"

Emboldened by this, I proceeded:

"Yes, but that is not all. I have for long cherished an audacious desire to see and converse with the Pope himself. It may be but a mad dream, but now that you have come to see me, and I have heard your conversation, it makes me wonder whether it would be possible."

It was then that the Prince Colonna told me that he was going back to Rome, and urged that I should not fail to call upon him if I visited the Italian capital.

"Then," he added, "I have no doubt your wish could be granted."

At the time I was so busy that I saw no prospect of getting away even for the briefest holiday. But a few days later a doctor friend called to see me.

"You must forgive me," he said, "for seeming officious, but you are seriously overworking; your nervous system cannot stand the strain without some rest, if you do not take even a few weeks off, there will be a collapse."

It is, of course, obvious that the work of concentrating upon clients day after day must be extraordinarily exacting. Many an evening I found myself too worn out to seek amusement beyond music. Like a flash it came to me that the doctor was right, and that I ought to ease up, whatever the difficulty of putting off pressing clients might be. Just then I received a letter from an old friend who was living in Rome, asking me if I could come over and be his guest for a few weeks.

In a moment, the sequence of events shaped themselves before my mind. My longing for years to visit the Vatican—Prince Colonna's kind invitation to see him in Rome—the doctor's orders—and now this cordial request that I should come to the Italian capital. *I saw in it Fate.* I determined to go and wired that night that I would come.

On arriving in Rome, I sent a message to the palace residence of Prince Colonna, mentioning that I had arrived. He immediately sent a message by a servant that he would like to see me the following day.

When I met him, he said:

"My dear 'Cheiro,' to-morrow eight hundred pilgrims are to be received by His Holiness, and he will be tired out. But leave it to me, and I will do the best I can. In the meantime enjoy yourself by seeing the sights of our ancient city."

Later, he told me that he had arranged for the interview to take place in two days' time.

On the appointed day he called at my hotel and drove me to the vast Palace prison, as it used to be, of the Popes of Rome, and what a wonderful place it is. Housed within its precincts is the world's largest collection of Greek and Roman sculptures; there is an Egyptian museum; a marvellous picture gallery, with a collection of great masterpieces without an equal in the world, while in the Lateran Palace are indescribable treasures of gold and silver objects, jewels, and vestments encrusted with precious stones. Much of this was related to me by the Prince as we drove along, and naturally heightened my anticipation.

My interview was to be strictly "informal"—which meant that I was to be presented specially to His Holiness. The Prince told me that the Pope desired to hear something from me on the question of numbers dominating human life.

The only ceremonial part of the visit was our reception by the splendidly attired officers of the Papal Guard, while we waited for the arrival of a Cardinal to conduct us to the inner apartments.

We passed through what seemed endless corridors, each dim with mystery and antiquity, wrapped in a brooding silence that impressed me with a sense of awe. At length we traversed a suite of rooms overlooking the noble gardens of the Vatican.

There, seated in a massive chair drawn up in one of the window-spaces, sat His Holiness Pope Leo XIII. We halted some paces away, while the Cardinal who was with us went forward and announced our arrival.

Leo XIII, the two hundred and fifty-seventh successor of St. Peter, was admittedly one of the most remarkable occupants of the Vatican. At this time (1900), he was very aged, but his long life had been packed with exciting events before he came, in 1878, to succeed Pius IX.

As Cardinal Pecci, Leo XIII was for some time Roman Catholic Archbishop of Belgium, and was presented by King Leopold I to Queen Victoria and the Prince Consort. This, it may be remembered, gave great offence to the extreme Protestant party in England.

The day after his election as Pope, Leo XIII crossed the Tiber in disguise to his former residence in the Falconieri Palace, to collect his papers, and then returned to the Vatican, to commence what was a virtual imprisonment in the vast Palace of the Popes. He died in 1903 shortly after he had celebrated his jubilee. Such was the venerable personage to whom I was about to be presented.

He looked exquisitely frail and spiritual. He first spoke rapidly in Italian to Prince Colonna, and I was then bidden to approach. He made a sign to one of the cardinals and to my surprise a low chair was pushed towards me, and the cardinal said it was the wish of His Holiness that I should use it. I felt nervous at first, yet there was no reason to be so. The Pope spoke very softly in French, but soon his voice became quite animated.

" Prince Colonna has told me about you," he said. " I am interested in meeting a man who has met the remarkable people you have. But more particularly I should like to hear something from your lips about your strange theory of the coincidence of numbers in human life. Now please proceed, but speak slowly, and as distinctly as possible."

I then proceeded to show how certain numbers dominated the lives of individuals, explaining that the occult symbolism associated with them had come down to us from the most ancient times.

I gave an example in the chief events in the life of St. Louis of France and that of King Louis XVI, showing that whenever the interval number of 539—which *was the number of years between the birth of one and the other*—was added to the known events in the life of St. Louis, an exactly similar occurrence took place in the career of King Louis XVI. This extraordinary series of dates was as follows:—

St. Louis.		Louis XVI.	
Birth of St. Louis, April 23rd	1215		
Add interval	539	Birth of Louis XVI, August 23rd	
	1754		*1754*
Birth of Isabel, sister of St. Louis	1225		
Add interval	539	Birth of Elizabeth, sister of Louis XVI	
	1764		*1764*
Death of Louis VIII, father of St. Louis	1226		
Add interval	539	Death of the father of Louis XVI	
	1765		*1765*
Minority of St. Louis commences	1226		
Add interval	539	Minority of Louis XVI commences	
	1765		*1765*
Marriage of St. Louis	1231		
Add interval	539	Marriage of Louis XVI	
	1770		*1770*
Majority of St. Louis (King)	1235		
Add interval	539	Accession of Louis XVI (King)	
	1774		*1774*
St. Louis concludes a peace with Henry III	1243		
Add interval	539	Louis XVI concludes a peace with George III	
	1782		*1782*
An Eastern Prince sends an Ambassador to St. Louis desiring to become a Christian	1249	An Eastern Prince sends an Ambassador to Louis XVI for the same purpose	
Add interval	539		
	1788		*1788*

Captivity of St. Louis	1250		
Add interval	539		
	——	Captivity of Louis XVI	
	1789		*1789*
St. Louis abandoned	1250		
Add interval	539		
	——	Louis XVI abandoned	
	1789		*1789*
Beginning of Pastoral under Jacob	1250		
Add interval	539		
	——	Beginning of the Jacobins in France	
	1789		*1789*
Death of Isabel d'Angoulême	1250		
Add interval	539		
	——	Birth of Isabel d'Angoulême in France	
	1789		*1789*
Death of Queen Blanche, mother of St. Louis	1253		
Add interval	539		
	——	End of the "White Lily of France"	
	1792		*1792*
St. Louis desires to retire and become a Jacobin	1254		
Add interval	539		
	——	Louis XVI quits life at the hands of the Jacobins	
	1793		*1793*
St. Louis returns to Madeleine en Provence	1254	Louis XVI interred in the cemetery of the Madeleine in Paris	
Add interval	539		
	——		
	1793		*1793*

This, I believe, is one of the most curious examples of history repeating itself at a fixed interval; further, the addition of the interval number 539 reducing it to the single digit gives the number 8, and the addition of the number of letters in the name L.O.U.I.S XVI gives also an 8.

This number in Kabalistic Symbolism is called Justice.

His Holiness followed my exposition with the closest attention, nodding his head slowly and occasionally asking a question. When I finally paused, he said:

"You must meet Cardinal Sarto.

"Cardinal Sarto has also made a deep study of such things. He believes there is a curious coincidence in numbers in the events of his own life."

At the conclusion of this deeply interesting and wonderful interview, I was taken to Cardinal Guiseppe Sarto, who held the position of Patriarch of Venice. He was at the moment in Rome. One afternoon he sent for me and in the kindest possible way showed me over some of the treasures of the famous library of the Vatican.

There, in one of the recesses of the windows, we fell into an animated discourse on numbers and their significance, and I soon found that this was an absorbing subject with Cardinal Sarto.

The Cardinal, without mentioning what he considered was his dominating number, asked me if I would work it out, to see if it coincided with his own method. I willingly assented. He gave me particulars of his birth, June 2nd, 1835, at St. Riese, Italy, and he said that if I wished during my stay in Rome, he would arrange for me to look through the books and manuscripts on occultism and numbers in the Vatican library. That is how I was able to avail myself of the inestimable privilege of wandering at will amid this storehouse of human wisdom.

In due course I presented the Cardinal with the result of my labour. He was pleased to find that my number system agreed with his and that the number 9 was the dominant one in his career.

Readers may be interested to know that " nine " ruled his life in a very remarkable fashion :

For nine years he was at school at Riese.
For nine years a student at Padua.
For nine years a curate at Tombolo.
For nine years a priest at Salzano.
For nine years a canon at Treviso.
For nine years a bishop at Mantua.
For nine years a cardinal-patriarch of Venice.

I knew from my study of his numbers, that an even more wonderful life was shortly opening out before him. In due course he was elected Pope Pius X, in succession to Leo XIII. He died in his 80th year on August 21st, 1914.

CHAPTER XVI

AN EXTRAORDINARY INTERVIEW WITH KING HUMBERT OF ITALY. HIS ONLY QUESTION, "WHEN SHALL I DIE?"

I HAD met many times in Paris, Prince Borghase. One evening he gave a dinner in my honour and invited the Princess Demidoff and her two daughters, Vera and Olga, beautiful and talented girls, who with their mother, the Princess, were murdered in their château in the middle of Russia during the Revolution.

Shortly after my interview with Pope Leo XIII, I was dining with him in Rome when he startled me with the following proposition:

"'Cheiro,' I have been commanded to bring you to meet King Humbert in the Quirinal Palace." He hesitated and then added: "I happened to mention to His Majesty your uncanny gift for predicting the future, and he was very interested. He is sensitive, almost morbidly so, as to his length of days—I will leave it at that."

A few days later he called for me at my hotel and drove me to the Quirinal—a vast but by no means imposing palace. King Humbert received me very simply, in a small room that he used for the homely purpose of a smoking lounge. Throwing himself into a big easy chair and lighting a cigarette, he quickly put me at my ease.

While I was telling him some events of the Past, he interrupted and asked bluntly:

"But tell me, 'Cheiro,' when shall I die?"

Having read before I went to Italy of the activities of the anarchists in the chief Italian cities, I had for my own curiosity worked out the significance of the Fadic Numbers and astrologically the events in relation to King Humbert's life.

Keeping these things in my mind, I asked the King to let me examine his right hand. The narrow escape he had from assassination in 1897, when the miscreant Passavante attempted to kill him, was clearly indicated.

I was conscious that King Humbert was a brave man—that he wanted to know *the truth*, because of his responsible position, and therefore I would be right in telling him all I could.

As I stood examining his hands with their characteristic marks, I saw as in a tableau the sword of Fate suspended over his head. The few months that lay between him and the fatal day stood out clearly before my occult consciousness. I dared to tell him all.

"Your Majesty," I said slowly, "you have already escaped the attack of the assassin, and you may escape again. But I must tell you that three months from now all the signs point to the end of your life."

He turned pale, withdrew his hand, leaned back in the chair for a few seconds, and then shrugged his shoulders.

" Well, then, if it is Fate—*che sarà sarà!*"

Then he relapsed into silence. There was no sound but the ticking of a great clock. It seemed almost as if the moments of Time were running swiftly away for His Majesty of Italy.

I must mention here that three months later His Majesty was assassinated by the anarchist Bresci, at Monza, on July 29th, 1900. I was in Paris at the time, and the striking confirmation of my prediction, which got into the Continental Press, led to my momentous interview with the late Shah of Persia, which I will relate in a coming chapter.

On the evening of the day that I visited King Humbert, I dined again with Prince Borghase; he was very eager to know the result of my meeting with his King. I told him of my prediction of danger, if not death, through the machination of anarchists. He was much moved, and revealed how for years King Humbert had been dogged every day of his life by the haunting fear of assassination, that on one occasion a sudden movement on the part of a man in a crowd had brought on those nervous twitchings of the King's face that disfigured him to the end of his days.

We discussed the fascinating question: Can Fate be averted? Later, with the encouragement of the Prince, I worked out a horoscopic chart of all the crowned heads of Europe, and this, together with my system of Fadic Numbers, proved of extreme interest. In the case of King Edward, the attempt upon his life by Sipido at Brussels, when he was Heir Apparent, was most clearly indicated. The unhappy Czar of Russia might be said to be the sport of malignant Fate. As all the world knows, he had the inspiration that led to the Hague Conference and certainly dreamt of world-wide Peace. Yet his country fell a prey to anarchy, while he himself was foredoomed to a violent end.

One may certainly say that Nicholas of Russia could have averted Fate. There was a time when he might have escaped from Russia; indeed the Empress implored him to get away to England, and a scheme was formed, but like a man in a dream, he could come to no decision until his abdication was followed by arrest and the final blood-red tragedy of Ekatrinberg.

Among others, I worked out the life-chart of that fated Prince Rudolph of Austria, whose tragic end in the château of Meyerling remains a Mystery of the Purple.

Rudolph was fatally unlucky in love, for his marriage with the Princess Stephanie, daughter of Leopold of Belgium, was a ghastly failure; while his passionate love romance with Mary Vetsera ended in death for both of them.

The Great Napoleon originally wrote his name as Napoleon Buonaparte. Later on in his life he changed it to Napoleon Bonaparte. This change had a curious significance, when worked out by the

Hebrew, or Chaldean alphabet which is clearly explained in my *Book of Numbers*.[1]

    Napoleon equals in Fadic Numbers a 5
    Buonaparte also equals   5

The number of 5 is considered a magical number, and was carried by the ancient Greeks as a mascot when they went into battle. The two numbers of 5, which if added produce 10, are equally important and strangely significant in this case.

When Napoleon altered the spelling of his name to Bonaparte, it altered the vibration of this word to an 8, which represents revolution, anarchy, waywardness, conflict with human justice, and on the lower plane, a tragic ending to the life.

Although a great man, Napoleon was on the lower plane of existence —as can be seen if one looks up how the number 8 (Saturn) and the 9 (Mars) dominated the chief events of his career. As Napoleon Bonaparte, the two names total the number 13, which number, in occult symbolism which accompanies the Fadic system of letters and numbers, bears the curious picture of a skeleton with a scythe, mowing down men; it is also a symbol of " power, which, if wrongly used, will bring destruction upon itself."

This was so borne out by Napoleon's career that further comment is needless.

In the case of Napoleon III, the compound number became 44, which, in my Fadic system, " is a number of the gravest warning for the future; it foreshadows disasters brought about by association with others, and bad advice "—exactly what happened to Napoleon III who went down to prosperity as the " man who lost France."

The addition of the separate figures of important dates often appears to bring out subsequent dates of equal importance.

The following is a striking illustration from French history :

Revolution in France and fall of Robespierre took place in	1794
The numbers of this date if added together give	21
	1815
The fall of Napoleon	1815
1815 added, gives	15
Fall of Charles X and revolution in France	1830
1830 added, gives	12

---

[1] Cheiro's *Book of Numbers*, Herbert Jenkins, Ltd., London.

THE LATE KING HUMBERT OF ITALY

Death of King Louis Philippe	1842
1842 added, gives	15

End of Crimean War	1857
1857 added, gives	21

The famous Treaty of Berlin	1878
1878 added, gives	24

Danger of war with England over Fashoda	1902
1902 added, gives	12

The Great War	1914
1914 added, gives	15
	1929

A date which was evidently of considerable importance in French history.

It is a somewhat remarkable coincidence that a similar series of fateful dates governs the present history of Great Britain. The details are as follows:

Battle of Waterloo	1815
1815 added, gives	15

Ascension of William IV	1830
1830 added, gives	12

Scinde War	1842
1842 added, gives	15

Indian Mutiny	1857
1857 added, gives	21

Afghan War	1878
1878 added, gives	24

End of Boer War	1902
1902 added, gives	12
European War	1914
1914 added, gives	15
	1929

The fall of the Conservative Government and the overwhelming triumph of the Labour Party, one of the most drastic changes in the history of the British Empire, took place in 1929.

CHAPTER XVII

HOW I MET MUZAFFER-ED-DIN, THE SHAH OF PERSIA, AND WHY HE GAVE ME THE DECORATION OF "THE LION AND THE SUN"

ONE of my most disconcerting encounters with crowned heads was my first command appearance to come before the Shah of Persia, Muzaffer-ed-Din.

How I came to meet the Persian ruler makes an interesting story. While working out the "fatal years" of various crowned heads, I noted that the danger period for King Humbert of Italy coincided with one for Muzaffer-ed-Din, the Shah of Persia.

I had openly made the statement that if my system of prediction proved correct in the case of King Humbert, that one might expect about the same date an attempt on the life of the Shah.

At this time the Shah was a guest of the French Republic during the famous Exhibition of 1900. By some means my prediction reached the ears of his Grand Vizier.

In due time came the tragic announcement of the assassination of King Humbert, by Bresci, the anarchist, on July 29th. Hardly had the Paris papers printed the news before I received a visitor to my apartment in the rue Clément Marot, a street just off the Avenue des Champs-Elysées.

Without stating who he was, he introduced himself as a Persian who was greatly interested in predictions and occult subjects in general.

"I have heard," he said, "of your remarkable foretelling of the death of King Humbert, and it is also said that you have predicted danger to the Shah of Persia. Is this true?"

I replied that, so far as my work revealed, danger, and very grave danger, threatened the Shah. I said further that if he knew any of the suite surrounding the Shah, I hoped he would warn them, so that every precaution could be taken, or there might be a repetition of the Italian tragedy in Paris.

I did not know until afterwards that, upon leaving, my visitor went straight to Monsieur Lépine, the Chief of the Paris police, and asked for a double guard of police to watch the residence of the Shah, and to "shadow" him whenever he went out. It was, in fact, this extra guard that saved the Shah's life when it was attempted a few days later by Salson the anarchist.

The day after the attempt, the Persian stranger called upon me again, and this time he revealed himself as the Grand Vizier. He had his hands examined and prints taken, giving me an autographed impression that I have before me as I write. He told me that his Imperial Master had been profoundly impressed by my prediction, and was most grateful for my timely warning. Further, he had commanded that I should be brought before him the following evening at five o'clock.

It was arranged that I should call at the Palais des Souverains, where the Shah had been installed by the French Government, and at the appointed hour I presented myself before the lordly mansion where the Ruler of Persia was in residence. I will confess that I felt a little trepidation at having to face such an ordeal. However, I determined to keep myself well in hand and to endeavour to treat him exactly as though he were an ordinary consultant.

I was struck forcibly by the silence—the almost unearthly silence—of the vast mansion when I was admitted, and while waiting in a small antechamber for the momentous interview. The servants, in Persian national costume, moved upon velvet felt; great rugs and carpets deadened all sound. Then suddenly the silence was ended by the most exquisite bird-like song I have ever heard, like a singer in the Paradise of the Blest. It was entrancing! When it finished, I realized that I had been holding my breath with sheer delight the whole time.

I learned afterwards that the singer was one of the Persian wives of the Shah, who had accompanied him on his European tour. It was her custom to sing to him every evening in order to ward off the attacks of melancholy that seized him.

Soon afterwards I was received by Amin-es-Sultan, the Grand Vizier, the man whom I have already mentioned—a very remarkable personality who was mainly responsible for the reorganization of Persia in 1900, when a British loan was floated in London. The Grand Vizier gave me a few hints as to my deportment upon being ushered into " the Presence," and added in excellent French:

" His Imperial Majesty is somewhat difficult to-day! On no account contradict anything he may say."

We ascended the splendid staircase, and came out upon a wide landing. Standing before a closed door were two Persian officers with drawn swords.

I found the Shah seated on a small gilt Louis XVI settee, on a kind of raised dais. He was dressed in national costume, and was wearing a black fez, ornamented with an enormous white diamond. He was at this time about forty-seven years of age, rather small in stature, with sharp features, long black moustache, and keen dark eyes. His expression was remarkably dignified.

For some minutes after I entered, he took no notice of my presence. I remained standing rather awkwardly, wondering what I ought to do. After speaking for a few moments with the Grand Vizier, he suddenly abruptly addressed me in French:

The Shah: " Well, Magician, I have heard of you. My people tell me it was owing to your words that the fool the other day failed in his purpose. They say that you are a wizard and can read the Future."

" Cheiro ": " I have had some success, Your Majesty."

The Shah: " In some ways, doubtless. But I have travelled and learned a great deal. I have my own Wise Men in Teheran and one of them travels with me."

Upon this he indicated a very old Persian who stood at some distance. After some further conversation, the Shah stretched out his

MUZAFFER ED-DIN, THE SHAH OF PERSIA

hands and laid them upon a cushion placed upon a small table; while I was studying them I could feel his quizzical eyes boring into my soul.

They were remarkable hands, and the lines were distinctive of a man who was at once weak and strong in will; swayed by self, yet easily led; crafty yet simple—in short, a bundle of temperamental contradictions. I told him this as carefully as I could, and he listened with the keenest attention. I also explained the meaning of the remarkably strong Line of Destiny running up from the wrist to the base of the second finger.

I felt I was making good progress, when suddenly my Imperial client pulled me up short.

Tugging his long moustache, as if to conceal a smile, he turned to his Grand Vizier, and said something in Persian. Speaking in French, the Grand Vizier said:

"'Cheiro,' His Imperial Majesty says that all you have told him might have been read in a book dealing with his life, to which you might have had access. But to make a final test of your powers, he propounds this question: Tell him exactly what is happening in Teheran, his capital, at this moment. Your statement will be tested by a cable sent off at once. Speak, 'Cheiro,' for the Shah commands."

Bowing dutifully, I desired from the Shah some personal object that I might hold in my hand. He immediately gave me a silk handkerchief plucked from his breast. Crushing this in my palm, I closed my eyes and concentrated with all my force of will.

For a few seconds—it seemed like an age—I found my mental canvas a hopeless blank. It seemed to me that a dry chuckling laugh issued from the sarcastic lips of the Ruler of Persia. Then suddenly—how, I cannot explain—a picture formed with startling distinctness before my inward sight. I did not hesitate any longer. Opening my eyes and looking the Shah full in the face, I said in French:

"Your Majesty, grave events are happening in Teheran, your capital, at this very hour! The Governor of the city has been thrown into gaol by the mob, on account of serious food riots that have raged for several days. He is in danger of being a victim of the rage of the people against the price of bread and wheat."

The Shah gave a gasp of astonishment and then his face grew a shade darker.

Half rising from his settee, he said loudly:

"You know nothing. You are an impostor. What you say is impossible in my kingdom. Go!"

I found myself being ushered out of the room by a rather scared-looking Grand Vizier.

I returned home to my consulting-rooms with mixed emotions. I felt convinced that my clairvoyant picture had mirrored the truth, yet—supposing that it did not! I had done my best and I certainly did not relish being called an impostor when the charge was unjust.

A few days later, a Persian aide-de-camp rushed into my rooms. He seemed labouring under an unusual degree of excitement.

"Come at once," he shouted, and began to drag me towards my coat and hat. "His Majesty the Shah wants you immediately." I must confess that my heart sank, but not a word further could I get out of the officer.

I was ushered into "the Presence." As soon as I entered, the Shah inclined his head to me gravely, while at the same time I noticed that he held something that looked like a telegram in his hand.

"'Cheiro,'" he said, with infinite courtesy, "I have done you an injustice. You *are*—wonderful!"

He handed the telegram to the Grand Vizier. He explained to me that it was in response to one sent the day of my interview, announcing that serious riots had been quelled with difficulty, that the Governor whom the Shah had appointed in his absence had overtaxed the people on their wheat and bread, that revolution had broken out, that the Governor was in prison, and imploring the help of the Shah in the difficult situation.

Congratulations showered about my ears.

I treasure among my possessions a decoration bestowed upon me on this occasion by the grateful Shah, Muzaffer-ed-Din, the Order of the Lion and Sun of Persia.

At this second interview, the Shah desired that I should work out my system of numbers as relating to his life. He gave me his birth date, March 25th, 1853, and in due course I worked out a chart of his years. According to this he ran at times grave danger of assassination. He had succeeded his father when the latter had fallen a victim to a fanatic who had imbibed anarchistic ideas. It was remarkable how fatal was the figure 2 in the life of the Shah. An attempt to assassinate him in Paris on the second day of August 1900 might have succeeded if my warning to the Grand Vizier had been ignored; while on the second day of the second month (February of 1906), *two* bombs exploded under his motor-car while in Teheran. Two persons were killed. On September 2nd, 1907, the Shah abdicated under pressure, and retired to Russia, where he died the same year.

SIR H. M. STANLEY, THE AFRICAN EXPLORER

CHAPTER XVIII

H. M. STANLEY, THE FAMOUS EXPLORER, INTRODUCES ME TO GLADSTONE

I WAS introduced to Mrs. H. M. Stanley (later Lady Stanley), the wife of the famous explorer, and I was invited to meet Stanley himself at luncheon at their house in Richmond Terrace, London.

I must say that I rather dreaded this interview, for I had heard a good deal of Stanley's brusque manner with people in whom he took no interest, and I rather imagined that he should have no interest in common with me.

I was, however, completely mistaken. It is true that all the way through the luncheon he never opened his lips; but when the ladies had retired and we were left alone, to my astonishment he put out his hands for me to read, and in a few moments we were talking as if we had been old friends.

He went back over the past, reviewed it step by step, explained to me how he had been misjudged by those who had not heard from his own lips of that memorable tramp across "Darkest Africa." He seemed to live every moment again as he spoke of the anxieties and responsibilities he had to meet, but not one word did he say of his own personal dangers.

It was a memorable afternoon for me, but I am glad to say it was not the only time I had the honour of meeting the man I must always remember as "the great Stanley."

At a subsequent visit to Richmond Terrace, to my astonishment he suggested that I should meet Gladstone.

"Mrs. Stanley will arrange it for you, if you like," he said. Mrs. Stanley agreed, and sat down at once and wrote the letter.

By return of post came one of Gladstone's famous postcards, offering me an appointment for the following day at Hawarden Castle.

It was a hot day in August. Mr. Gladstone had, on the day before, made, what was, I believe, his last public speech, when he addressed the Horticultural Society of Chester.

Mrs. Gladstone met me in the hall, and my heart sank as she said that Mr. Gladstone was so fatigued that she must refuse to have him disturbed on any pretext.

I told her how sorry I was to hear of Mr. Gladstone's indisposition, but that I should be only too happy to come again from London at any time he wished, and I turned to go.

At this moment the "Grand Old Man" opened the door of his study. "My dear, is that the gentleman who has an appointment with me at three o'clock?"

"Yes, but you must not see anyone to-day," Mrs. Gladstone replied.

"But, my dear," he pointed out, "this man has come all the way from London at my invitation. He is a friend of the Stanleys, and it will interest me to see him."

"Sir," I said, "please do not consider me. I will come up another day from London when you are feeling better."

"I will see you now," he answered, and then, with a sad tone in his voice, he added, "I may never be better than I am to-day."

We walked into his well-known study, and he motioned me to a seat by the window. One of my own books lay on a table at his side, and I saw to my surprise that he had evidently determined to know something about my work before he met me. This, I have since heard, was his invariable custom—the reading up beforehand of any subject on which he was about to be interviewed.

But there was a still greater surprise in store, and also an example of his wonderful memory.

"I have been told that you are the son of Count de Hamon," he said. "Your father had the same love of higher mathematics that I have. We have corresponded many times on difficult problems—here is one which he worked out a few years ago, and which has interested me many times since."

As he spoke, he unrolled several sheets of paper, covered with calculations and algebraical figures in my father's handwriting.

"Is your father still living?" he asked.

"No, sir," I answered; "he passed away only a short time ago."

"And you," he said, "have you inherited the same love of figures and mathematics?"

"Alas, no," I replied, "my calculations only relate to occult things, and they probably will not interest you."

"We shall see later," he said. "Now please let me hear your theories about this Study of the Hand of which the Stanleys tell me you are a master. Speak slowly and clearly, so that I may follow you if I can."

The gentleness and kindness of this wonderful man—this man who had so often swayed the destinies of nations—whose intelligence was acknowledged even by his enemies—completely conquered my nervousness, and, astonished at my own confidence, I plunged at once into my subject.

At first I rapidly explained the theories associated with the study, and backed them up with the impressions of hands, showing heredity and other signs, and then attempted to show that man, like everything else in life, has his number as well as his place in this universe, and that if this number could be determined, so could the years that correspond to this number be equally determined, either for his good or evil as the case might be.

Taking as an illustration the different vibrations in each tone of music, with a very simple instrument I had with me, I showed him how each vibration produced different forms in matter, and that the same vibration repeated dozens or hundreds of times, always created *a distinct figure of its own* that never varied in its basic principles, that these tones or vibrations had their distinct number—and so on through the scale of creation up to man, who, as the image of the universe, vibrated in exact accordance with the vibrations of those

GLADSTONE.
A photograph he autographed for "Cheiro."

planets which, as the instruments of God, called the universe into being.

I had brought with me my friend, Savary d'Odiardi's "Thought Machine," and placing it on the study table, I asked Mr. Gladstone to test for himself if every person brought before it did not affect it in a distinctly different manner, according to their will-power, radiating outward through the atmosphere.

Standing near the instrument, I showed him how far I was able to will the needle to turn; he then tried it himself, and calling some of the servants into the room, he quietly tested it with one after another.

When we were again alone, I asked him to allow me to take a chart of the movements of the needle when operated upon by his will, and may I add that of the thousands of examples I have made with this instrument, Mr. Gladstone's stands out as the most remarkable for will-force and concentration, as shown by the length of time he was able to make the needle remain at certain points.

Before the end of the interview, he allowed me to take impressions of his hands for my collection, and further to show his appreciation of what I had explained to him, he autographed and gave me the photograph which I reproduce here.

The date on it is August 3rd, 1897. Mrs. Gladstone finally broke the interview by coming in and announcing that it was half-past six. I felt rather guilty, but as if to save me from her anger, he said: "My dear, this has been one of the most interesting afternoons I think I have ever spent. I am not fatigued, I am now going to show this young man the gardens, for it is he who must be tired."

Together we walked out over that lawn, so beautifully kept that it looked like a piece of green velvet set with those gorgeous crimson geraniums which he loved so much.

He made me talk of Canada and the United States, and said how much he regretted that he had never visited those countries, and he went on to speak of the deep interest he took in the rapid progress the United States had made during those long years over which his remarkable memory could go back.

Finally, he said good-bye, and as I reached the gate, I stood for a moment and watched his retreating figure pass on through the gardens, and disappear among the growing shadows of evening and the dying glory of the sun.

CHAPTER XIX

A STRANGE STORY OF PRE-NATAL INFLUENCE

THE following story may be considered gruesome by those who would, if they could, drift down Life's tide to the sound of perpetual laughter; or who would treat existence as the joke of some idle god, who will not hold them responsible for their actions towards their fellows.

The study of humanity proves, on the contrary, that we are as often held responsible unto others for even the most thoughtless action, as we are for what we may consider the most deliberate and well-thought-out plan that we could have conceived.

That " pre-natal influence " may toss the rules of society to the winds is now accepted by many students, as the story I am about to relate is in itself a striking example.

One morning, the post brought me the following letter:

THE VICARAGE,
——, ENGLAND.

" DEAR SIR,

Having read your work in analysing character and disposition from the study of the hand, I take the liberty of enclosing you the impression of a boy's hand, aged eighteen last June, and I shall be indebted to you if you will take the trouble of giving me as exact a description of his character and tendencies as you can, for I confess that this boy is a puzzle to me as to the career (if any) that he should be trained for.

As I feel I cannot offer any fee that would repay you for your trouble, perhaps you will be good enough to regard this case in the light of a study and let me have whatever advice you can.

Thanking you in advance,

Faithfully yours,
——."

Although I was literally " worked to death " at that moment of my career, I gave my time for nothing in many cases—in fact, more than people could possibly imagine. In this case, the impression of the boy's hand interested me so much that I could not refuse, and so one night after the world had gone to sleep, I went to work, and endeavoured to unravel as curious a bit of tangled humanity as had ever been brought to my notice.

The impression of the left hand showed all the indications that this boy, whoever he was, had inherited unusual brain-power and character from good ancestors, highly intelligent, refined and cultivated in every way; yet one glance at the right hand showed me in an instant that every good quality given by heredity had already, even at the age of eighteen, been twisted and warped in the most inconceivable manner.

The superior brain-power indicated on the left hand was only employed by the right in planning and working out any form of crime

"CHEIRO," IN 1897, BEFORE THE "THOUGHT MACHINE" WHICH HE DEMONSTRATED TO GLADSTONE

or vice that would interest him. The refinement given by heredity had already become the refinement of cruelty ; affection and the nobler instincts of nature had been strangled at the very beginning. In fact, I saw before me nothing but a distorted brain that could not help but choose a life of crime, and that such a life had already commenced, I was absolutely certain.

As for any sign of a legitimate career, there was none—such a boy could only be from his earliest age but a clever thief. Even at eighteen, he would not hesitate to murder, if it suited his plans, and the only hope I could hold out was, that at that early age some of his crimes might already be discovered and that for his own good he would be locked up.

But what could have caused such a change ? That was the question that puzzled me. With all the signs of heredity so good, what could have launched such a twisted, distorted brain into the world ?

As I studied the hand, I became convinced that some pre-natal influence alone could cause such an abnormal creature.

I finished my study and enclosed it to the Vicar the same night. I had not long to wait for an answer At five o'clock the following day, the most enraged man I ever saw in my life stood before me

Stamping his feet with passion, he demanded how I dared write such a thing to him ; that the boy was his own son—his only son—that he had the most wonderful brain it was possible to imagine—that his queer ways were only a sign of genius ; and, lastly, that my absurd theory of some pre-natal influence was a proof of my own madness, for his wife was a saint, or as near one as a clergyman's wife could ever expect to be.

He swore he would denounce me as the greatest impostor that ever lived ; he would move heaven and earth to drive me out of the country ; and so on he raged, for over half an hour.

There was nothing he said, however, that could make me angry ; there was something that told me that I had been right in my conclusions, and, further, that before long that unfortunate man would be broken down by the trouble that very son would cause him.

I kept silent, as he described how piously this boy had joined him in prayer the night before, when the Vicar was asking God's help to find his daughter's wedding presents, which had disappeared.

At last, he left me to go to the police and denounce me as an impostor—but this very act of his was the means of bringing about the dénouement, and saving the whole family from a still worse disaster. The police took up the case about the missing presents, but after a month, they acknowledged they had not the slightest clue to work on, and to all intents and purposes gave up the search.

Then it was that the Vicar's anger against me appeared to grow worse than ever. He pestered the police with letters until, one day, an inspector called and questioned me as to the reason for the unfortunate man's vindictiveness.

I explained what had happened, and why I had stated in my letter that my conclusions were that the boy's hand I had examined was that of a thief, if not already something worse. Well, to put it as briefly as possible, within a short time the police discovered that, for at least two years previously in the village near the boy's home there had been many clever robberies. These robberies were, however, so skilfully planned out and executed that the police had believed none but a master mind could have done them.

But there was still worse to follow. For some weeks past, the Vicar, his wife and daughter had got into extremely bad health. Doctors had put it down to the worry about the missing presents, and one can hardly tell what might have happened if the new man-servant, who was in reality a detective, had not one night discovered the boy mixing powder into the flour from which the bread was made.

In the end, the boy was sent to a reformatory for a very long term. When the father was able to leave his bed, the first thing he did was to call and see me, and we remained very good friends up to his death, which took place only a short time ago.

One evening, he told me the following story:

"I never thought much about such things as pre-natal influence until that remark in your letter made me think it out as a possible cause for my poor son's extraordinary mental distortion. After a good deal of questioning and reasoning, my dear wife told me recently something that I had not the faintest suspicion of before, namely, that for more than seven months before the birth of our boy, she had the most unaccountable craving to read the history of criminals and murderers of every description.

"One book she had read no less than three times and, strange to say, in it there was the account of a boy of a most respectable family who was an expert thief before he was fifteen, and who, later, *was executed for poisoning every member of his own family*."

When he had finished speaking he took my hand in his and made me promise that I would one day make this story public. "Who knows," he said, "the good it may do by warning mothers of their enormous responsibility during the pre-natal period?"

CHAPTER XX

MORE INTERVIEWS WITH FAMOUS PERSONALITIES. LORD RANDOLPH CHURCHILL. CECIL RHODES. JOSEPH CHAMBERLAIN—MY PREDICTIONS FOR HIS SON, NOW SIR AUSTEN CHAMBERLAIN. LORD BALFOUR. SIR LIONEL PHILLIPS. THE BISHOP OF BIRMINGHAM. THE REV. FATHER BERNARD VAUGHAN. THE DUKE OF NEWCASTLE. LORD PIRIE AND " BOSS " CROKER OF TAMMANY HALL

LORD RANDOLPH CHURCHILL was extremely superstitious on the matter of the number 13, and attributed many adverse events to the fact that he was born on the 13th of a month, namely February 13th, 1849. He was interested in my explanation that the idea that 13th was an unfortunate number was nonsense, and that it was simply regarded as ill-omened because in Occultism in ancient times it had been regarded with veneration. The early Christian fathers had in fact spread the impression that it was evil, and was connected with thirteen sitting round the table at the Last Supper.

Just before his lamented death in London on January 24th, 1895, I had another brief interview with the then enfeebled statesman, and he reminded me that my theory of numbers had interested him very much. From King Edward he had gathered that I said 4 and 8 were his Fadic numbers, and that his lowest point of vitality would occur in the part of the year considered most influenced by the planet Saturn, namely, the month of January.

Cecil Rhodes was another remarkable personality whom I met during one of my many seasons in London. He was brought to me one afternoon by his great friend Dr. ——, who took every possible occasion to state that I had been extraordinarily accurate in my predictions for himself.

Cecil Rhodes was really interested in the subject of numbers. Until he met me he had an idea that the number 6 had followed him through life. I worked out his birth date and found that, in fact, 5 was his ruling number. He was born on the 5th day of July, the fifth son of his father, and he went to South Africa on the 5th of the fifth month of 1879. I recommended him to carry out important events on dates producing this number. It is significant that Rhodes severed his connection with South Africa by resigning on January 5th, 1896, and he told me, that after he met me he carried out all important speculations on dates in any month that made a 5, such as the 5th, 14th, and 23rd, the single digit of which produces a 5.

Another interesting interview which I had was with Mr. Joseph Chamberlain, and also with his son, now Sir Austen Chamberlain.

On the morning of June 23rd, 1894, I had called at the House of Commons to keep an appointment made for me with Mr. Chamberlain.

My theory of heredity, as shown by the lines of the hands, interested him deeply. I showed him an impression which I had just taken of the right hand of his son, Austen Chamberlain, and together we compared the " markings " with those on his own hand.

The two impressions bore out what I had said so often in my books about heredity.

On nearly every hand there can be found a line going from the wrist towards the second finger. This line is called the Line of Individuality or Destiny, and when turning towards the first finger, it indicates that the individuality will point, lead, or dictate to others —the first finger is also called the Law-giver or Dictator. This strong line seemed strangely appropriate to the career of Mr. Joseph Chamberlain, and also to the future indicated for the son, who has followed in the political career of his distinguished father.

The lines of the hands of Mr. Chamberlain showed very clearly, when compared with my system of dates, the exact years when he occupied positions of great responsibility. At the very zenith of his career, Joseph Chamberlain was stricken down with paralysis, and as a complete invalid was compelled to live a life of inactivity until death finally released him on July 2nd, 1914.

On that morning of June 23rd, 1894, as we sat in his private room in the House of Commons, Mr. Joseph Chamberlain did not talk to me about Tariff Reform. All thoughts of politics seemed very far from the mind of the great statesman, as he looked over the many impressions of hands of celebrated people I had brought with me. It was that strange question of heredity that appeared to occupy his attention the most, and especially that remarkable illustration of it shown so clearly in the shape of his own right hand and the right hand of his eldest son. Again and again he remarked how the lines in the two hands resembled one another.

" So you say," he added reflectively, " that means that my son Austen will have a career in every way similar to my own. He has entered Parliament only two years ago, having been returned for East Worcestershire in 1892."

" Yes," I answered, " he will also, like you, reach some of the very highest positions in parliamentary life, and will reach the zenith of his career in 1925. In that year he will secure a great international triumph and will undoubtedly one day be the Leader of the House of Commons, but as the lines and markings in his hand, although lying in the same position as those in yours, are not so clearly marked, he may not perhaps have as strong a personality as you have, but in every way he will be your double."

" Perhaps the difficulties of political life may be greater when he comes to play his role, and, if I am any judge, I think they will," the great statesman added very gravely.

Since then I have often thought of this remark, as I watched Mr. Austen Chamberlain, now Sir Austen, filling such high positions as Postmaster-General, Chancellor of the Exchequer, Secretary of State for India, and Leader of the House of Commons.

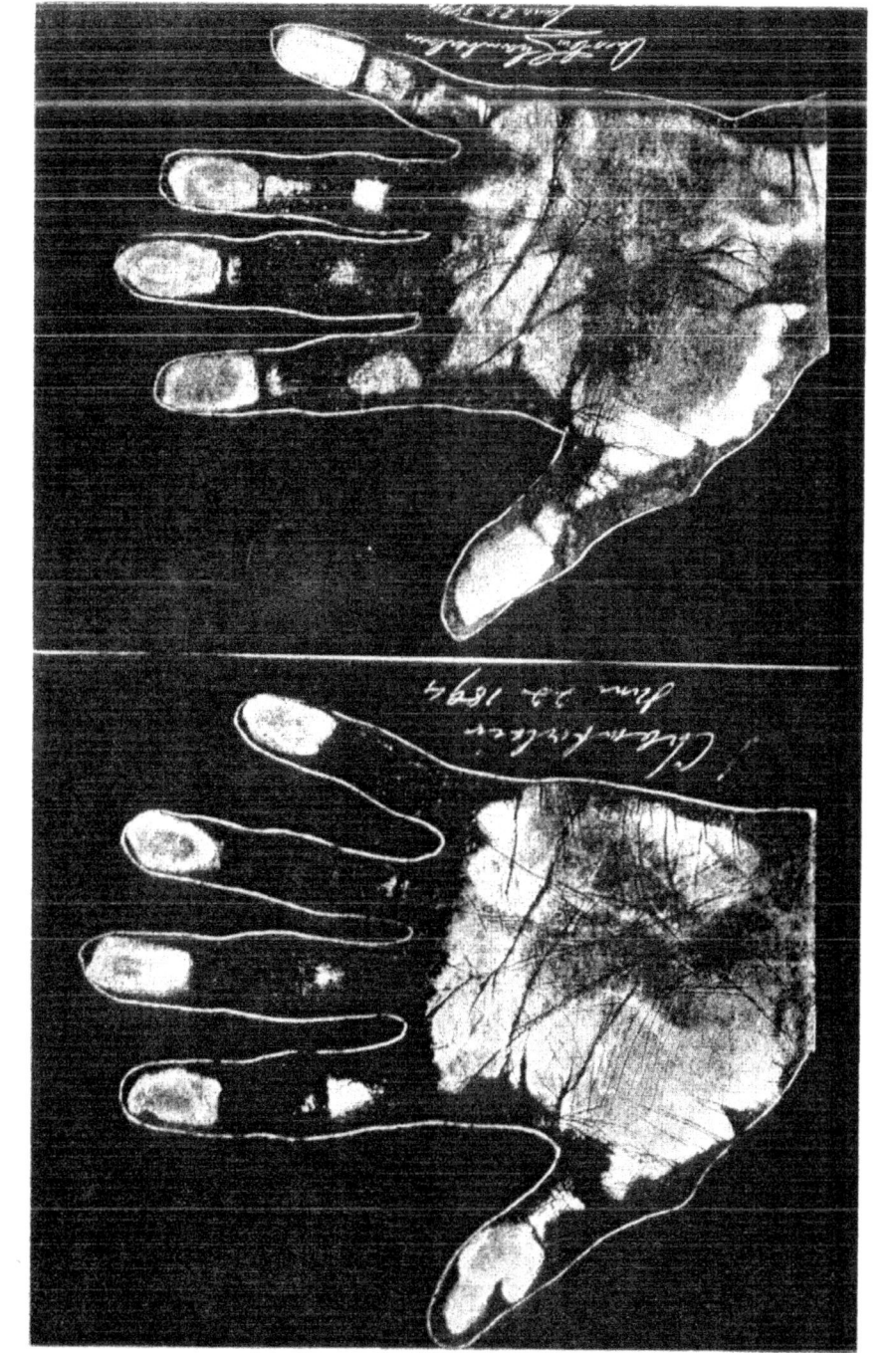

JOSEPH CHAMBERLAIN   SIR AUSTEN CHAMBERLAIN
Example of heredity shown in the lines of the hand.

My predictions were carefully written down by Mr. Chamberlain, and I have reason to know that they were found among his papers at the time of his death.

But it is somewhat ominous to see that in the hand of Sir Austen there is the same tendency in the Line of Health as I found upon the Health Line of his father. It most certainly indicates a tendency towards overtaxing the mental and physical strength, with a possibility of nervous collapse. Sir Austen should be careful to avoid overstrain and undue fatigue, threatening forced retirement at the very climax of his career, and likelihood of a nervous breakdown.[1]

The position of the Life and Head Lines is somewhat unusual, and is almost alike in the hands of both father and son.

The late Lord Balfour gave me an impression of his hand which he signed A. J. B., and which lies before me as I write. In his hand the important line is that of Destiny, turning towards the base of the first finger, indicating great success and prominence in public life. Yet the hand itself is full of complexities, being that of a philosopher accustomed to weigh judgment, while also having that agile type of mentality that could see both sides of a subject at once. The Line of Mentality on his palm is so well marked that, like Gladstone's, it traverses the entire palm.

It was interesting to notice in his hand the entire absence of indications relating to marriage. I mentioned this to him, and he laughed heartily.

"Quite right, 'Cheiro,'" he said. "I am determined to remain a bachelor to the end of the chapter, and I am glad that Fate reveals nothing to the contrary."

Sir Lionel Phillips, the famous South African millionaire, and one of the four uitlanders condemned to death for participation in the Jameson Raid in South Africa, visited me and wrote in my autograph book:

> "Until I visited 'Cheiro,' I had no conception that the secrets of one's life were imprinted upon the hands. To those who would conceal their history from the gaze of a fellow-creature, I would say —avoid an interview with 'Cheiro'!"

I met Sir Lionel recently, and he told me that my previsions in his case had been remarkably fulfilled, and especially in one particular.

I had said that he would have a hairbreadth escape from death in the spring of the year 1914. He told me, in that year, in April, he was walking in the street in Johannesburg, and was suddenly attacked by a man who fired at him three times with a revolver. He was badly wounded, and for weeks hovered between life and death, but eventually recovered.

I will now give my readers some details concerning quite another type among the numerous people who consulted me. I have sometimes

[1] This, unfortunately, took place shortly after his knighthood in 1925.

been asked whether I have ever been consulted by members of " the cloth."

Let me say that the number of clergymen who have come to me at one time or another is extraordinarily large. Some came openly, others with their coats turned up to hide their tell-tale clerical collars.

Yet I cannot recall a single instance in which they disputed the exactness of my descriptions of their lives and character. I have many testimonials to this in my autograph book, in which many famous clergymen, among other people, have written their appreciation of my work. One I prize very highly reads:

> "To 'Cheiro': The past quite accurate. May you prove right as to the future. Many thanks for your clear statements and charming way of telling the tale of life."

The signature is "*H. Russell Wakefield*," later in life the distinguished Bishop of Birmingham.

Father Bernard Vaughan, of Farm Street, London, also consulted me, and, upon leaving, wrote in my book. "God bless you; be a reaper as well as a sower."

Among my clerical friends was a very charming man whom I only knew as the "Padre." He came to visit me several times.

One day he turned up accompanied by a gentleman whose hand he wished me to read. I did so, and after they took their leave, I noticed my client wrote in my autograph book:

> "'Cheiro' has told my past and future with wonderful accuracy, especially with regard to the immediate future, which he could not possibly have known.
>
> NEWCASTLE."

It was only when my visitors had gone that I realized that the "Padre's" friend was none other than the gentleman who was the late Duke of Newcastle.

Lord Pirie was also one of my consultants. What a wonderful career, people exclaim when his name is mentioned.

There is probably no equal to such a successful battle with fortune to be found, even among the merchant princes of the United States, if indeed in any other country of the world.

He was simply the Honourable W. J. Pirie when I first met him. He walked into my reception room on one of my busiest days and asked my secretary how long he would require to wait for an interview.

My secretary replied that as there were three people ahead of him, it might be as well if he were to return some other day. Through the half-open door of my consulting-room, I heard the reply that was so characteristic of him.

"When I have set my mind on something, I can afford to *wait* for it," he said. "So, if you do not mind, I *will* wait."

Until I visited Cheiro I had no conception that the secrets of one's life were imprinted on one's hand. To those who would conceal their history from the gaze of any fellow creature, I would say, avoid an interview with Cheiro

Lionel Phillips

A CANDID EXPRESSION FROM SIR LIONEL PHILLIPS, THE SOUTH AFRICAN MILLIONAIRE

More than an hour had passed before I was free to see him. When he did enter my consulting-room, it was with a bright, cheery smile on his face, which showed that he harboured no resentment at having been obliged to wait.

He put his hands out on my table and said encouragingly: "Well, I wonder what you will be able to make out of me?"

I sketched out the hard commencement Destiny forced him to pass through in his early years, then the success that came to him and the still greater positions that lay before him, and gave him dates when important happenings had occurred, and when others would occur.

After the consultation, he checked the dates I had given of the past events, and spoke of the various stages in his life to show how accurate my statements had been.

On returning to Ireland, he wrote me the following letter:

QUEEN'S ISLAND,
BELFAST.
August 14th, 1899.

"DEAR 'CHEIRO,'

I really feel constrained to tell you how much I enjoyed my interview with you on Friday last, and to hear so many facts respecting my past career from the lips of a perfect stranger was perfectly amazing.

I was sceptical on the subject of the Study of the Hand when I went to you, but your little sketch of my life from childhood until now was so wonderfully accurate, that I am bound to say I was thoroughly convinced I was wrong in my estimation of this Science.

In view of your having so distinctly stated on Friday that I was about to receive a great honour, it is remarkable that I should have received a private intimation this morning that I am to have the honorary degree of LL.D. conferred on me by the Royal University of Ireland, Dublin—a distinction that I shall regard as the greatest that has been bestowed upon me.

If you are passing through Belfast, I hope you will give me the pleasure of showing you round our works.

Yours very truly,
(Signed) W. J. PIRIE."

A year later I accepted his invitation. The Boer War was in progress and I wanted a ship to carry out the plans of Princess de Montglyon, to transport large quantities of biscuits and provisions to the soldiers in South Africa. I went straight over to Harland and Wolff's, sent in my card to Mr. Pirie, and explained the plan to him and what I wanted. He did not hesitate one moment.

"I will have a boat at your disposal whenever you are ready to load it at Liverpool," he said. "Now that we have settled that matter, come with me and let me fulfil the promise I made you in London."

For over an hour he personally conducted me to every point of interest in those great shipyards—shipyards with which he had grown up and which are now famous the world over.

Not many years later he was created Lord Pirie, and during his wonderful career he has received some of the highest honours that the King or nation can bestow. In spite of it all, however, he always remained the same genial, kind-hearted, but exceptionally practical, man he was when I first met him.

Although he became possessor of one of the handsomest mansions in Belgrave Square, I believe he preferred his long, splendidly equipped office in the front of Oceanic House, with its walls covered with models of those great ships built by his firm, and where I often had the honour of seeing him in later years.

When I met Richard (" Boss ") Croker, he was the active head of Tammany Hall, New York, a political organization that for power is without its equal in the world.

Croker confessed to having a curiosity as to what I could tell him of the future, as he had " heard his friend, Mr. W. T. Stead, speak of me."

Strange to say, what I told him was the very thing which at that time seemed to be most unlikely.

I said he was " at the parting of the ways," and was about to relinquish his command to another and to exchange his political life for one of quietness and peace.

He had evidently no intention of doing so, and told me so very bluntly when I made my prophecy.

Not more than a year later, however, he surprised everyone, with the exception of myself, by retiring and buying an estate in Ireland, where he bred a winner of the Derby and won the blue riband of the English Turf with Orby.

> Cheiro has exposed my character to me with humiliating accuracy. I ought not to confess this accuracy, still I am moved to do it.
>
> Mark Twain

> To Cheiro—
>
> The past quite accurate—May you prove right as to the future—Many thanks for your clear statements, and charming way of telling the tale of life
>
> H. Russell Wakefield

A PAGE FROM "CHEIRO'S" VISITORS' BOOK: "MARK TWAIN" AND THE REV. H. RUSSELL WAKEFIELD (LATER BISHOP OF BIRMINGHAM)

CHAPTER XXI

A DINNER WITH LOUIS PHILIPPE, DUKE OF ORLEANS AND PRETENDER TO THE THRONE OF FRANCE. I MEET BARON VON BISSING, THE INFANTA EULALIE OF SPAIN, AND PRINCE ALEXIS KARAGEORGE-VITCH OF SERVIA

I HAVE a vivid recollection of a very interesting dinner that I had with the ill-fated Louis Philippe, Duke of Orleans and Pretender to the Throne of France, on board his yacht, when he discussed with me the subject of Occultism and displayed a remarkable knowledge of the Chaldean system of predicting future events by numbers.

The dinner was perfect. I found the Duke a charming and unaffected companion. For some hours we discussed the interesting question of Kabalistic Numbers, and I showed the Duke how remarkably they ruled in certain lives. I ventured to say that I feared his years would not pass 57, and his death has confirmed this.

He was born in 1869, the 6th of February, the year adding to 24, 2 and 4 equalling 6. In 1887 he was finally exiled from his beloved France, the addition of 1887 again giving 6. On taking up a military career in England, he was appointed to the 60th Rifles, again a number 6, with a zero added. He married the Archduchess Maria of Austria in 1896, and the addition gives 24, again the predominating 6. His last period of ill-health, ending in death, commenced in June, the sixth month.

Concerning the misfortunes of his life, he was keenly sensible, and he spoke of himself as " fated." He had in his possession a remarkable chart of the lives of his ancestors, drawn up by the Abbé Thurvillier, the Astrologer of Paris, in 1656. It held out no hope of a restoration, although it clearly showed gleams of hope that were destined to be quenched in disappointment.

The late Duke cherished many curious superstitions.

He was very much afraid of cats, and shared with Lord Roberts an almost painful aversion to them. He had also a hatred of green as a colour, and this fact was so well known to his miniature court that any ladies wearing that obnoxious colour were severely barred.

About this time I met the lovely Princess Lavalia, one of the most bewitching women in Paris in the nineties, who was introduced to me by Lady Arthur Paget.

The Princess was somewhat of a mystery, a woman at home in every capital. She was a born gambler and would spend whole nights in some of the chic gambling saloons in the neighbourhood of the Champs Elysées.

She had had a long spell of ill-luck and had lost very heavily. When I saw her in my consulting-room, the conversation turned upon lucky and unlucky days, and I found that unquestionably a 6 in any combination would be her fortunate number.

Acting on my advice, she altered her style of roulette play from a random staking upon any number that caught her fancy, to stakes upon numbers that gave her a 6 in combination. The result was gratifying and she won back her losses many times over. As a souvenir, I possess a valuable gift from the Princess.

It has been rumoured that the ex-Kaiser had long made a study of numbers in relation to Occultism, and has toyed with the idea that the "6–6–6" mentioned in the Book of Revelation referred to himself. If this number is added together, it produces 18, which, if added, gives the final digit of 9, the same as the ex-Kaiser's birth number, the 27th of January. When the number 9 is the important cypher, the series number of 3, 6, and 9 governs the events of the life. These numbers work out very clearly in connection with the Hohenzollern dynasty. Add together the figures of the fateful year, 1914, it gives 15, the final digit of which is a 6.

It was in 1904, a lovely spring afternoon, that a tall and smart-looking gentleman, with a decided military appearance, stepped into my consulting-room in Paris. He had a letter of introduction from a German friend of mine, Prince von Putbus, a cousin of the ex-Kaiser. Speaking in excellent English, considering his Teutonic origin, he said he desired to know something about the future.

Baron von Bissing, for this was my visitor, had rather an engaging personality, although ruthlessness and force were strongly in evidence.

I could not help seeing, however, that a dark curtain would be drawn over his latter days. I indicated this as frankly as I could. I found, to my surprise, that he had also studied the science of numbers, and added that he believed his days would not be long.

Our conversation drifted to the Kaiser, at that time enthroned as the Great War Lord. He mentioned that the Emperor was very interested in Occultism, and that in the library of Potsdam were several of my books.

Finally, he spoke of the theory of survival after death.

"No, 'Cheiro,'" he said emphatically, "when one is dead, it's the end—the finish. Nothing will ever convince me differently." He added with a laugh, "If I change my mind, after I am gone, I will let you know." The strange thing is he did let me hear from him *about two years after he died*.

One of my great friends in Paris was Madame Lambert de St. Croix, a lady of Spanish and English descent, who was an exceedingly clever and remarkable woman.

She was Lady-in-Waiting to the Infanta Eulalie of Spain, aunt of Alfonso XIII, and used to attend her on her frequent visits to Paris. One day she gave a lunch in order that I might meet the Princess.

The Infanta was a delightful person, sparkling like champagne, and full of witty sayings. She insisted that I should read her hands, which I did. In return she gave me a signed impression of a print of her beautifully formed hands.

She told me many interesting things about the Court in Spain—how extremely superstitious King Alfonso was, and what dread he

God bless you

Be a reaper as well as sower

Yours truly

Bernard Vaughan

WHAT THE REV. BERNARD VAUGHAN, S.J., WROTE IN THE VISITORS' BOOK

had of unlucky days. It will be remembered that a dastardly attempt was made upon his wedding day to explode a bomb beneath his carriage. He had said before the wedding that the day was ill-omened, a fact he learned from the extraordinary Spanish friar, Philipo Stelato, a mysterious professor of the occult.

The Infanta asked me if I would work out a chart of the life of the Spanish monarch, and I gladly complied with her request. I was struck by the constant hoverings of disaster, and yet the succeeding almost miraculous escapes. It is common knowledge that again and again the throne of Spain has been said to be tottering; again and again, too, assassins have menaced the King. But the danger passed, notably when he faced the peril of a horrible death at Barcelona, going smilingly to his hotbed of anarchy, although his Prime Minister threw up his hands in despair and said: "You will never come back alive." My prediction to the Infanta was that the King would hold his throne until the year 1931, in that year he would fly from Spain and by doing so save his life.

Incidently it may be mentioned that the father of Alfonso was shot on his honeymoon, while driving with his bride, who, as Princess Maria de las Mercedes, created a furore by her wonderful beauty when she came to London just before the marriage.

Prince Alexis Karageorgevitch consulted me after he had made his plans to go to America to be married there, to the wealthy heiress of the Swift millions, whom he had met some months previously in Paris.

I did not know to whom I was talking, but after an examination of his hands, I told him very decidedly that the journey he was about to take could only end in disappointment, and that he would not marry for many years, and then only after a great tragedy had altered the position and fortunes of his family.

Notwithstanding my warning, he went to America, and met with disappointment in his marriage plans, exactly as I had predicted.

Years passed, and the family tragedy I had foretold took place in the horrible murder of the Serbian monarch and Queen Draga, his consort. Following upon this double assassination, Prince Alexis' cousin became King Peter of Serbia.

Prince Alexis was thus lifted into the position of being cousin to a ruling monarch, and shortly afterwards he married a very charming and wealthy American lady.

Again he came to me in Paris, and I predicted that his country would soon be drawn into war and would be practically swept away in the upheaval.

That prediction was fulfilled by the world-shaking tragedy of the War. To-day the Serbian Royal Family is impoverished.

The last time I saw him he was with his charming wife on a visit to London, and as he said good-bye, he added:

"Every prediction you have made has been fulfilled to the letter. I wonder——" then he smiled and left me.

CHAPTER XXII

AN AMUSING EXPERIENCE WITH SIR ERNEST SHACKLETON, THE EXPLORER. A NIGHT WITH FLAMMARION, THE CELEBRATED ASTRONOMER, IN THE OBSERVATORY AT JUVISY

I HAD a very amusing experience with Sir Ernest Shackleton, the famous Antarctic explorer, and one so unlike what my readers could imagine that bluff and hearty sailor going in for, that I am sure they will enjoy it as much as I did at the end. Before he came to see me, Sir Ernest had, I believe, the fixed idea in his mind that I told my visitors as much from their appearance as from their hands.

In order to baffle me, he got a lady to ring up my secretary and fix an appointment for a certain afternoon (February 10th, 1912). According to her account, a famous tenor would come to consult me, and to throw me still more off my guard, she requested that I would have no windows open, so as to endanger his sitting in a current of air.

When the appointed hour arrived, a very peculiarly dressed man made his appearance. He had a curious kind of black coat with a cape thrown across his shoulders such as one associates with artistes and singers in the Latin Quarter of Paris; the lower part of his face was covered by a well-cut beard and moustache of the vandyke style which matched a handsome head of blond hair.

To make the disguise all the more complete, my strange visitor spoke with a foreign accent and had a large roll of music that he laid very carefully on the table by his side.

When at last he spread out his hands before me, I quickly forgot my visitor's artistic appearance and plunged ahead into a description of the characteristics as shown by his very clearly marked hands, the leading points being, that in the first place he was a born "leader of men," a man as brave as a lion, one who courted and loved danger as few men would dare, and one who at that moment of his life should be, from all the indications of his hands, planning one of the most hazardous enterprises of his career.

He could not restrain himself from asking a question. "Will it be successful, Monsieur?" he said.

"Only in the way that you will escape losing your life while engaged in it," was my reply.

"And after?" he asked.

"After, you will carry out another enterprise exactly similar, and it is while engaged in this second one, that then, I fear you will lose your life, in or about your forty-eighth year."

"Interesting, eventful, hazardous life, I suppose you would sum it up," he laughed.

"Yes," I said. "Just such a one as would suit Shackleton, the explorer."

To my astonishment, my visitor removed his false beard and wig. "Well," he said, "as you evidently don't tell these things by the face you may as well know now that I am Shackleton."

> I have been much struck by Cheiro's
> extraordinary power of analysis
>
> June 9, 1893. H. Drummond Wolff

> Cheiro has inspired me with
> with veneration for Palmistry
> to an appalling extent.
>
> Melton-Prior.

IN "CHEIRO'S" VISITORS' BOOK: SIR H. DRUMMOND WOLFF (AMBASSADOR TO PERSIA) AND MELTON PRIOR (LATE WAR CORRESPONDENT, *DAILY TELEGRAPH*, LONDON)

We met many times after that interesting afternoon, and I have his letter before me as I write now, wishing me the following Christmas the best of good luck and at the same time telling me that he had arranged for his expedition to try and discover the South Pole to sail the following July, 1914.

Everyone knows the results of this great effort; from his second expedition he never returned, but lies buried at the gateway of the Antarctic.[1]

I was indebted to my old friend, the Marquis d'Oyley, for an introduction to the famous French Astronomer, M. Camille Flammarion, and a little later I received an invitation to go and dine with him and Madame Flammarion *en famille* in their apartment near the celebrated Observatory in Juvisy on the outskirts of Paris.

It was an interesting evening for me; I not only met the most famous Astronomer of the age, but I persuaded him to talk on his favourite study of Stars and Planets for the best part of two hours.

He then questioned me as to my own study and also on the system of Astrology I used in connection with my work. Finally, I read his own wonderful hands, and as a souvenir of our meeting, he gave me a signed copy of his book called *Uranie* which had just been published. On the front page of it he wrote: " Au savant Chiromancien ' Cheiro ' sympathique homage, Flammarion."

Shortly afterwards he invited me to go with him to the Observatory and see, through one of the largest telescopes then in the world, those planets we had been talking so much about. So, one magnificent night in June, a night I shall never forget, high up in the Observatory, we watched the stars rising and setting for hours, until the dawn came.

It was a memorable evening for me. Our conversation had turned from the wonders of Nature to the probabilities of Life after Death, and my host listened with rapt attention to some of my experiences in research work in Spiritualism, and I believe I was the means of stimulating his interest in such things. His investigations in Telepathy, Spiritualism, and such subjects had already dated back many years. He lately gave the world several remarkable books on the subject, such as those recently published in London by Fisher Unwin & Co., *Death and its Mystery*, and another volume called *At the Moment of Death*.

Camille Flammarion does not hesitate to state boldly and clearly in these works, not only that " communication with those who have passed to the Great Beyond " is a proved fact, but also that the future can be seen and foretold by those who have a special gift in that direction. On page 318 of his book *Death and its Mystery*, after giving many examples of proved cases in which future events were

[1] Sir Ernest Shackleton was born February 15th, 1874, died 5th January, 1922, within a month of his 48th year.

foreseen and predicted in advance, this great scientist and thinker writes, " conclusion—*the future can be seen.*"

Again on page 221 of the same book, he writes, " future events can undoubtedly be seen in advance," and he gives examples he had collected from priests, lawyers, doctors, and eminent people to prove his statement.

He has himself recently passed to " the Great Beyond " where I feel sure he is continuing his investigations.

CHAPTER XXIII

HOW I MET THE LATE SIR EDWARD MARSHALL HALL, Q.C. I AM NEARLY MADE A CO-RESPONDENT IN THE DIVORCE COURT. A CURIOUS EXAMPLE OF CLAIRVOYANCE

I FIRST met Sir Edward Hall (at that time Mr. Marshall Hall, Q.C.) under rather unusual circumstances. I had been subpœnaed as a witness in Keighley versus *Modern Society*. The famous Queen's Counsel was the leading counsel for the defendants and my evidence was called on the side of the plaintiff.

Briefly the case was as follows :

About this time a Palmist had started with a great flourish of trumpets in Bond Street and had announced himself as the " greatest Palmist in the World," etc. He had as a secretary a woman who called herself Mrs. Cornwallis, whose name had unfortunately a few years before been mixed up with a man called Callan, implicated in the alleged attempted murder mystery of one Hubert Birkin at Tangiers.

Modern Society, in a burst of religious zeal for the exposure of Palmists in general, had in an article mixed this woman up with the man's rightful wife, Mrs. Keighley, and the much abused wife had defended her honour by bringing an action for libel and suing *Modern Society* for £1000 damages.

As I was in the position of being able to identify Mrs. Keighley as the man's real wife and of testifying as to her honourable reputation and that she could not possibly be mistaken for Mrs. Cornwallis, when the case came on I was called as a witness.

I had never, even out of curiosity, seen the inside of a Court of Justice before, and I felt extremely nervous when from my seat at the back of the court, I heard the name "Cheiro" called, and I found the plaintiff's solicitor ushering me into the witness-box.

" You will have the redoubtable Marshall Hall to cross-examine you," he whispered, " for God's sake keep your head."

Such a warning was enough to have made me " lose my head " twice over, and youth as I was, only a little over twenty, I only wonder I did not drop dead with fright.

I remember well how very earnestly I took the oath, " to tell the truth and nothing but the truth," kissed " the Book," then turned and faced the dreaded Q.C.

Marshall Hall was already standing up, looking at me with a curious, sarcastic, ironical expression on his face that pulled me together as nothing else could. He was the handsomest Q.C. I believe at the Bar, and to my mind as I stood there he seemed a kind of intellectual god calling me before the judgment seat of Truth.

What passed between us was so clearly set out in the leading papers of that date, that I cannot do better than quote a notice of that part of the case as it appeared.

"CHEIRO" HITS BACK.
SOME AMUSING PASSAGES WITH
MR. MARSHALL HALL.

" The well-known ' Cheiro ' was the next witness. All he could add to the evidence was, that when he saw the article in *Modern Society* he took it as referring to the plaintiff.

" There were several passages of arms between this witness and Mr. Marshall Hall, counsel for the defendants, in which ' Cheiro ' did not by any means get the worst of it."

Mrs. Keighley won her case, the jury gave judgment in her favour with £1000 damages and costs.

And now comes the sequel to my first appearance in court, a sequel that in itself throws more light on the magnanimous side of Marshall Hall's character and his sportsmanlike nature than anything else that I might write.

That same evening I happened to be dining at the Carlton with Major Alexander Davis and his daughter, who later became Lady Fletcher Moulton. After dinner we were sipping our coffee on the terrace of the Palm Garden next the restaurant entrance, when my opponent of the morning, Marshall Hall, with two gentlemen passed out.

Again his eyes met mine, but this time there was a friendly smile in them. Apologizing for intruding, he asked if he could have a moment with me. I stood up, he held out his hand.

" ' Cheiro,' " he said, " after our battle this morning let us be good friends and shake hands, and let me also congratulate you as being the only witness I can remember who up to now got the better of me."

Very warmly we shook hands, then to my amazement he added :

" I want to come and consult you myself, when can you give me an appointment ? "

We fixed it up for the following day at five o'clock. Punctually to the moment he arrived, I read his hands, he took notes of every word I said.

Our next meeting was in his chambers in the Temple. I was worried and in great anxiety ; a terrible blow had as suddenly as a " bolt from the blue " fallen on me and completely upset my plans.

I had signed an agreement with the famous Major Pond of New York to sail to America in the coming September and deliver a series of lectures in the principal cities of the States.

I had inserted notices in *The Times* and *Morning Post* of my approaching departure, when I was served with that horrible-looking paper that all men dread the most, namely, *a citation as co-respondent*.

Where could I go to ask advice ? Marshall Hall, Q.C., came into my mind, and without hesitation I drove to his chambers and sent in my name.

I was not kept waiting a moment. I was ushered into his private room with its magnificent view of the Temple Gardens and the Thames Embankment.

Marshall Hall sat at a long table in the centre of the room, with a pile of papers in his hands that he was rapidly going through.

I looked at him, and hesitated. "How could I possibly take up the time of such a busy man with my wretched troubles," I thought.

I had not, however, much time to think. He threw down the papers and with a hearty hand-shake, he exclaimed :

"Great heavens, 'Cheiro,' what's the matter, you look as if you had seen a ghost ?"

"I wish it were only that," I answered, "but it is ten times worse. I have come to ask if you will help me out of this awful thing," and laid the citation on the table before him.

Very gravely he read it through, then with a kindly human expression in his eyes, he said :

"I am very sorry"—and then under his breath, he added, "Guilty, of course."

I hardly knew what to answer for a moment. I was still very young, very inexperienced in the world, and most terribly frightened of the Law in every shape and form. I am sure I looked "guilty," for he very gently pushed me into a chair and with a quiet laugh said :

"Well, don't be frightened, better men than you have been in the same position, but let us hope the woman was at least pretty."

"But there was no woman," I blurted out.

"Nonsense," he laughed, "how can you be a co-respondent without a woman. Come on now, tell me all about it."

As quickly as possible, I told him all I knew. I admitted the lady had called to see me about once a week ; I also admitted that seeing my approaching departure announced in the papers, that she had called to say good-bye, but at the same time I assured him on my word of honour that she had been nothing more to me than one of my ordinary clients.

"It will upset all your plans of going to the States in September," Marshall Hall said. "My advice to you is—wait about till the case comes on ; if you go to America they will plead you ran away. When the case comes on you can depend on my acting as your counsel. If you don't know any solicitor I will give you my card to a reliable man, who will immediately get in contact with the petitioner's lawyers. Then take my advice, go and have a good holiday and wait for developments."

I could hardly thank him enough for his kindness. I took his card and with a lighter heart than I had entered I went round at once to see the solicitor he had recommended.

I found Mr. Fairbrother, of Messrs. Fairbrother, Ellis & Co., Craigs' Court, most sympathetic and kind. Marshall Hall had added to his goodness by telephoning that I was coming. Mr. Fairbrother read the citation through and although most sympathetic, appeared very sceptical of my denial of the charges brought against me. It was in vain I pleaded that I only regarded the lady in question as one of my ordinary clients.

"Nonsense," he said. "An ordinary client would not have come on an average of say once every fortnight for the past six months."

"I could not prevent her," I pleaded, "and on one of those special dates they mention, when she must have been followed by detectives, she only came to say good-bye, and did not remain longer than ten minutes with me; surely that disproves the charge."

"Not one bit," he laughed. "With the epidemic of divorce at the present moment a good old-fashioned British jury might take it into their heads that ten minutes was quite long enough for you to have been guilty ten times over.

"Was the door of your consulting-room open?"

"No, of course, it was shut," I answered.

"Did you receive any letters from the lady?"

"Yes, I had piles of them."

"Never kept letters from ladies, I suppose you will say next."

I know I flushed scarlet. "Yes," I admitted, "I did keep them, but they were beautiful letters."

"Of course they were. Ladies' letters under such circumstances always are. You had better bring the pile down here and let me see them."

"I am sorry I won't be able," I answered, "the whole packet was stolen from my desk in the last few days."

"Indeed," was all he said, but at the same time he looked as if he did not believe me. Then he added, "It's quite a pity about those beautiful letters, they might have been interesting if read out in court."

After a few more questions, he pushed the citation into his desk. "I will get in touch with the petitioner's solicitors and will send for you in a few days. Good-bye, don't worry too much about it."

In about a week, Mr. Fairbrother sent for me. "This case is not as simple as it looks," were the first words I was greeted with; "it appears this lady kept a diary—a most indiscreet thing for any woman to do—and in this diary she recorded very freely her emotions whenever she saw you. All very flattering for you, my young friend—but rather compromising, and may require a good deal of explanation. Do you remember a fancy-dress ball at Covent Garden on the night of June 3rd?"

"Yes, indeed, I do."

"Do you remember anything rather romantic that happened, such as dancing with a veiled lady or anything like that?"

"Yes," I said, "but what can that have to do with the case? There was a lady in an Eastern costume so veiled I could not see her face; she was an excellent dancer and I had several waltzes with her."

"Was there anything else that impressed the charming dancer on your memory?"

"Yes, she never spoke a word the whole time, no matter what I said she never answered. She attracted me all the more for that reason."

"On your word of honour, you never knew who she was?"

"On my word of honour, I have no idea who she was. I even went to the following fancy ball hoping to meet her again."

Mr. Fairbrother pushed back his glasses. He was the true type of lawyer that I don't believe anything could surprise. Very quietly, he said:

"Would you be interested to learn, that it appears the veiled lady you danced so much with was none other than the respondent in the present case? Now, tell me exactly what you remember as to the finish of the evening, did you drive the lady home or anything like that?"

"No, not exactly that, I lost the lady that I had danced with about three o'clock in the morning. I searched the place hoping to find her. At last I thought I saw her having a glass of champagne at the refreshment counter, her back was towards me, and as I imagined her veil would be up, I thought it would be a chance to see her face. I stole up beside her, but just as I was about to speak, a man dressed as Mephisto struck me across the face. I lost my head and hit him back as hard as I could, he dropped to the floor, and two men in fancy dress carried him away."

"Well, what happened then?"

"I turned to apologize to the lady. I found to my horror I had made a mistake, that though dressed in a very similar costume and the same type of figure, she was not the lady I had been dancing with. I hardly knew what to do, she said she was leaving the ball and that the least amends I could make would be to drive her home. I was glad to get away myself—so I did so."

"Where did you drive her to?"

"To the Savoy Hotel."

"And?"

"There was no 'and,' Mr. Fairbrother. I had reached a full stop, that was all. The lady went up to her room, I went out by the Embankment entrance on the other side of the hotel, took a cab and got home as soon as I could."

"Have you any idea of the lady's name whom you so gallantly drove to the Savoy?"

"No, not the faintest, I did not dream of asking her."

"Rather a pity, my friend; if you had, it might save you a lot of trouble."

"What on earth do you mean?" I asked.

"Simply this: the man you struck was the co-respondent's husband, the two men in costume who carried him away were his own private detectives; they had watched you dancing nearly all the evening with the veiled lady, who was his wife. The husband followed you to the refreshment room, and believing you were going to speak to his wife, struck you in the face. A few minutes later you were seen driving off with a lady in Eastern costume, the detectives followed; in their report they state that you were seen to enter the Savoy with the lady, and though they watched till morning, *you were not seen to leave the hotel;* of course they did not think of the other exit. Worse still, the man's wife was actually stopping that night in the same hotel and was registered there, openly under her own name. If you could find who the other lady was, it would certainly clear you, but without her evidence, considering the diary, the packet of letters which I believe they have got, and all the circumstances—the case is beginning to look very serious for you, I am afraid."

"But I am perfectly innocent, I swear I am, Mr. Fairbrother."

"You may be, but you will have to persuade a British jury that you are, and that may not be so easy. In any case, the petitioner is so furious that he is absolutely determined to bring you in as co-respondent."

"Well, what do you advise me to do?"

"Do! You can do nothing, but wait. Give up your tour in the States, have a good rest at some seaside place for the rest of the summer, get yourself in good form, and make the best fight you can when the case is called after the courts open next October, that's all the advice I can give you at present."

"But when the case does come on," I begged, "suppose the co-respondent swears it is all a mistake, that I had nothing to do with her, never stopped in the Savoy and so on, won't that end it?"

Mr. Fairbrother laughed, "Suppose," he said, "she gives her evidence badly—suppose you are not believed, suppose she is divorced, what then? A man of honour is expected to marry the woman he has compromised. I may be drawing up your marriage settlement next."

"I hope not," I said, "I don't want to marry."

"Well, what do the lines of your hand say about it?" he chaffed.

"They say I won't be married till late in life," I answered quickly.

"Well, then, my friend, as you have so little belief in the Law—you had better trust to Fate to get you out of the mess you are in."

I thanked the old gentleman for his advice, but I walked away with a very heavy heart, wondering if Fate would indeed help me out.

I did go to the seaside, for I wanted to get out of London, away from anyone I knew—so I went across the Channel to Boulogne-sur-Mer for the rest of the summer. August came to a close and I was preparing to return to London with no happy anticipations of going back. To me, those great buildings of the Law Courts that I had so often stopped to admire, now cast a shadow over London that I could not get away from. Of course, it is only those who have experienced what " waiting for the case to come on " means, who may realize what my feelings were. I was too sensitive, I knew, yet it was that very sensitiveness by which I had lived and made whatever success I had. I realized the absolute torture I would undergo in the witness-box, but the one thing I clung to was, that Marshall Hall had agreed to be on my side.

As the season at Boulogne drew to its close, the sands became more crowded than ever, and like many others, I was in the sea nearly all day.

One very hot afternoon, the boat from England landed an unusually large number of visitors ; many of them came to the bathing-place to have a dip before returning by the evening boat.

I was in the water as usual, swimming about, when I noticed a woman not very far off getting into difficulties—she must be from England, I thought, from the unbecoming costume she wore. I had judged rightly, in another moment she was floundering about out of her depth and the good old English word " help, help " came from her lips between each gulp of salt water.

In a few strokes I reached her ; seizing her by the neck of her very solid-looking bathing dress, I kept her head out of water and got her in towards the sands.

She was fainting with fright, so I half carried her close in to the shore.

Standing before us, and not ten yards away, stood two men both actively engaged in taking snapshots—not of the beach with its array of beautiful bathers, but of myself and the half-fainting woman by my side. One glance told me they were detectives, but the woman, who could she be ? Not the fair respondent surely ; no, but someone so like her that a few yards away one might easily be deceived. I looked down, I thought I had seen her face before. I looked again. Yes, the other woman in the Eastern costume at the Covent Garden ball—the lady I had driven back to the Savoy.

Fate had indeed been good to me. The detectives returned to London to develop their snapshots, believing they had snapped the respondent and myself together.

Result, in a few days, a letter from Mr. Fairbrother giving me the good news that the petitioner had withdrawn his charges, apologized, and agreed to pay all my costs and expenses up to date.

I sailed to the States in September after all, took over my discarded lecture tour that had been cancelled, and have had no more " citations " to enliven my memoirs and for which I trust Fate will accept my humble, *but very grateful thanks*.

Very recently, Sir Edward Marshall Hall, hearing I was about to publish my reminiscences, sent me over the following notes which he had jotted down after his interview with me in 1899.

He headed them " The Prevision " and " The Fulfilment," and I publish these notes exactly as he sent them to me.

THE PREVISION

"Notes jotted down after my interview with 'Cheiro' in 1899. Cheiro' then said : ' I see something so vividly that I feel bound to tell you of it, though at the same time it seems to me of such small importance, and in fact so impossible that I hesitate.' I asked him to tell me what he saw, he replied : ' The whole thing is so anomalous that I cannot make it out. I see you standing on the balcony of what looks like a large country house with a big garden below and big trees all in front. But the strange thing is, that the grounds seem lit up with very vivid electric lights and even the trees are lit up with coloured lamps—what makes it still stranger is that there are thousands of people trampling down the flower-beds and looking up at the balcony, and you are apparently trying to speak or actually speaking. There are several people on the balcony, men and women, and the faces of the crowd are very white in the strong light. Beside you *on your left is a woman, much shorter than you are, waving a white pocket-handkerchief in her left hand* and the people below are shouting. That is what I see, but what it means is more than I can tell you.'

"After this he told me much more about various matters and then the impressions of my hand came back and we compared them with those in his book, *Cheiro's Language of the Hand*, which he afterwards gave me."

THE FULFILMENT

" In August 1900 I had declined to stand as a candidate for Parliament, and this although I had received three invitations to do so. I had gone down to Ellen Terry's cottage at Winchelsea with my wife and daughter to play golf at Rye.

" One day as I was playing golf, I saw my groom coming towards me with a telegram which he had brought from Winchelsea. It was from Sir Edward Carson asking me to come to London at once to meet Lord Derby.

" Knowing he would not send such a wire unless it was important I replied that I would come and I went the next day, and thereupon was asked to fight the Southport seat at the next election.

" I was shooting with Hudson Kearley (Lord Devonport) at Marlow and had to leave early to catch a train at Liverpool Street for the North where I was going to shoot the next day. My intention was to send a wire from Liverpool Street announcing my refusal to stand for Southport, but my train on the G.W.R. had been late and I all but missed the train. In fact, my guns and luggage were handed in to me as the train was moving off.

" Then a strange thing happened—I fell asleep in my corner back to the engine and after a time woke up to find what seemed an endless line of trucks running on a parallel line in the same direction as we were going. I watched and watched, and fast as we were going it

SIR EDWARD MARSHALL HALL AT SIXTY-NINE
The last photograph taken shortly before his death on February 23rd, 1927.

took a long time to overtake them. What they were I know not, but eventually we ran abreast of the engine that was drawing them, and there in big gold letters on the engine was this name SOUTHPORT. This struck me as very curious that this name should be on what I thought was a G.W.R. engine, and being a little superstitious I began to think. It seemed to me a direct omen and when I got to Chester I stopped at the Telegraph Office and sent a wire to say *I would stand for the constituency.*

" As time pressed I had to go up almost at once, and it was a very strenuous campaign in which I had no doubt a very uphill task. The polling took place on October 11th, 1900, a day I had chosen as it is always a number that enters into my life—on the polling day my wife and I had been for a tour of the constituency from 8 a.m. to 7 p.m. in a coach and four, lent to us by Mr. Formby. We came back dead tired, and at dinner my wife asked if she might come to the counting which was to take place that night at the Town Hall.

" I said NO and I particularly asked that she might not come as I knew she was very interested and I was afraid if I lost, she would be bitterly disappointed, and as the betting was then 10-1 against me, I had ground for my anxiety, especially as she was not at all well. I went to the counting and all people present had to sign papers promising not to divulge what took place. When the counting was half-way through I suddenly saw my wife standing at one of the tables with my old friend Sam Bigas, and I do not conceal the fact that I was very much annoyed. I went up to them and he said, ' Don't be angry, I brought Mrs. Marshall Hall with me.' Well, I had no choice and presently one of our people told me that I was beaten by about 300 votes. I had already been down the tables counting the clips and I did not think the margin was so big. We had another count and found that four clips of my votes had been accidentally put into red clips, my opponent's colours, and counted for him. This, of course, made a big difference, and the result was that I was elected by 209 votes, which if added together make the number 1192.

" At this moment the Returning Officer said that the formal announcement of the result would be made in two minutes' time to enable the Press representatives to get away first, and then he added : ' May I ask that no one present will signal the result to the crowd outside by waving red or blue handkerchiefs as has been done on a former occasion.'

" We waited two minutes and then some twelve or more of us went out of the big windows on to a balcony where I had never been before and the very existence of which was unknown to me.

" When I got outside I very nearly fell over the low parapet in front, for there before me and below me, *was the exact reproduction of* ' *Cheiro's* ' *prevision.*

" There was what looked like a big country house, there were the big trees all lit up, there were the thousands of people with their upturned faces showing white in the brilliant electric light of the arc-lamps, and there were the flower-beds being trampled down by their feet.

"And then a most weird thing happened. I recognized the scene in a moment, and equally instantaneously I remembered the other detail, and almost chuckled when I thought that that *at any rate could not be reproduced*, but turning around I saw standing beside me *my wife, who was waving a white pocket-handkerchief in her left hand*.

"She had anticipated the instruction of the Returning Officer literally and did not think that a white handkerchief came within the prohibition of red and blue.

"I believe Southport is the only place in England where this scene could have been reproduced as it was. You can make what you like of it, but what I have written actually happened some 16 or 17 months after 'Cheiro' *had seen it* during my interview with him."

When sending me these notes, Sir Edward enclosed the following letter :

November 1924.

"Dear 'Cheiro,'

It may interest you to know that I have just been reading the deductions you drew from the lines on my hand in August 1899, and I find throughout *they have proved to be wonderfully true*.

Yours very truly,
(Signed) E. Marshall Hall."

CHAPTER XXIV

WHY THE LORD CHIEF JUSTICE OF ENGLAND, LORD RUSSELL OF KILLOWEN, GAVE ME SIGNED IMPRESSIONS OF HIS HANDS

IN preceding chapters I have explained that by finding the key to the number which seems to govern a person's life, I was able with considerable accuracy to foresee what year, and, in some cases, in what month, the climax of the life's career would be attained. The following is a remarkable instance of this.

One day in the middle of one of my seasons in London a very exacting and apparently severe elderly gentleman came to see me; he was dressed in tweeds like some country squire. There was certainly nothing in his appearance or dress to lead me for a moment to imagine that he was even then a very big man in the legal profession.

Dates, however, seemed to interest him, and when I told him certain years in his past life which had caused important changes in his career, he did me the honour to delve back into his memory of the past and give me the satisfaction of knowing that the years I gave him were correct. I then told him that in a certain year, and further in a certain month in that year, he would reach the summit of whatever his ambition was, and that he would at that moment hold the highest position that his career could confer on him.

He carefully took a note of what I told him, and then in a rather mocking way he said: "And now, sir, as you have gone so far, you may as well make a guess at the exact date of this wonderful event."

"Call it a guess if you wish," I replied, "but by my calculations the day should be any one of those days which make by addition the figure of 1 in the month of July, 1894, such as the 1st, 10th, 19th, or 28th, but I will decide for the 19th of that month."

This he carefully noted, and then when I asked him to give me an impression of his hand for my collection, he turned and said: "You shall have it on one of the days you have mentioned, provided your prediction should become verified," and so my strange visitor left.

Some three years passed. I had completely forgotten the incident, when one morning a messenger called and without any explanation, informed me that my attendance was required at twelve o'clock that day at the High Courts of Justice.

I will not enter into my feelings or tell you my fears, but in a very nervous state of mind I went with the man and finally found myself waiting in a plainly furnished room at the back of one of the principal courts.

Minute after minute passed until nearly an hour had gone. I had imagined myself tried and executed in a hundred different ways, when suddenly a side door opened and the Lord Chief Justice appeared before me in all the majesty of his robes of office.

I admit I did not recognize my client of some years before, but, without waiting a moment, rolling up his ermine sleeves, he said:

"I am willing to keep my promise; you can have impressions of my hands now."

I had no apparatus for doing such work with me, but there was not a moment to be lost. I lit a legal-looking candle standing on the table, blackened some sheets of papers which the Lord Chief Justice himself found in a drawer, and in a few minutes I had obtained an excellent impression of his hands.

Taking a pen, he wrote: "Russell of Killowen," with the date, July 19th, 1894, and simply said: "You see, I have kept my promise; this is the first day I have put on these robes as Lord Chief Justice of England—*your date was exact*, though how you did it I cannot imagine."

As it may interest my readers the impression is here reproduced, and the curious thing is that the imprint of the High Courts of Justice which was on the paper he gave me can also be clearly seen in the impression at the ball of the thumb.

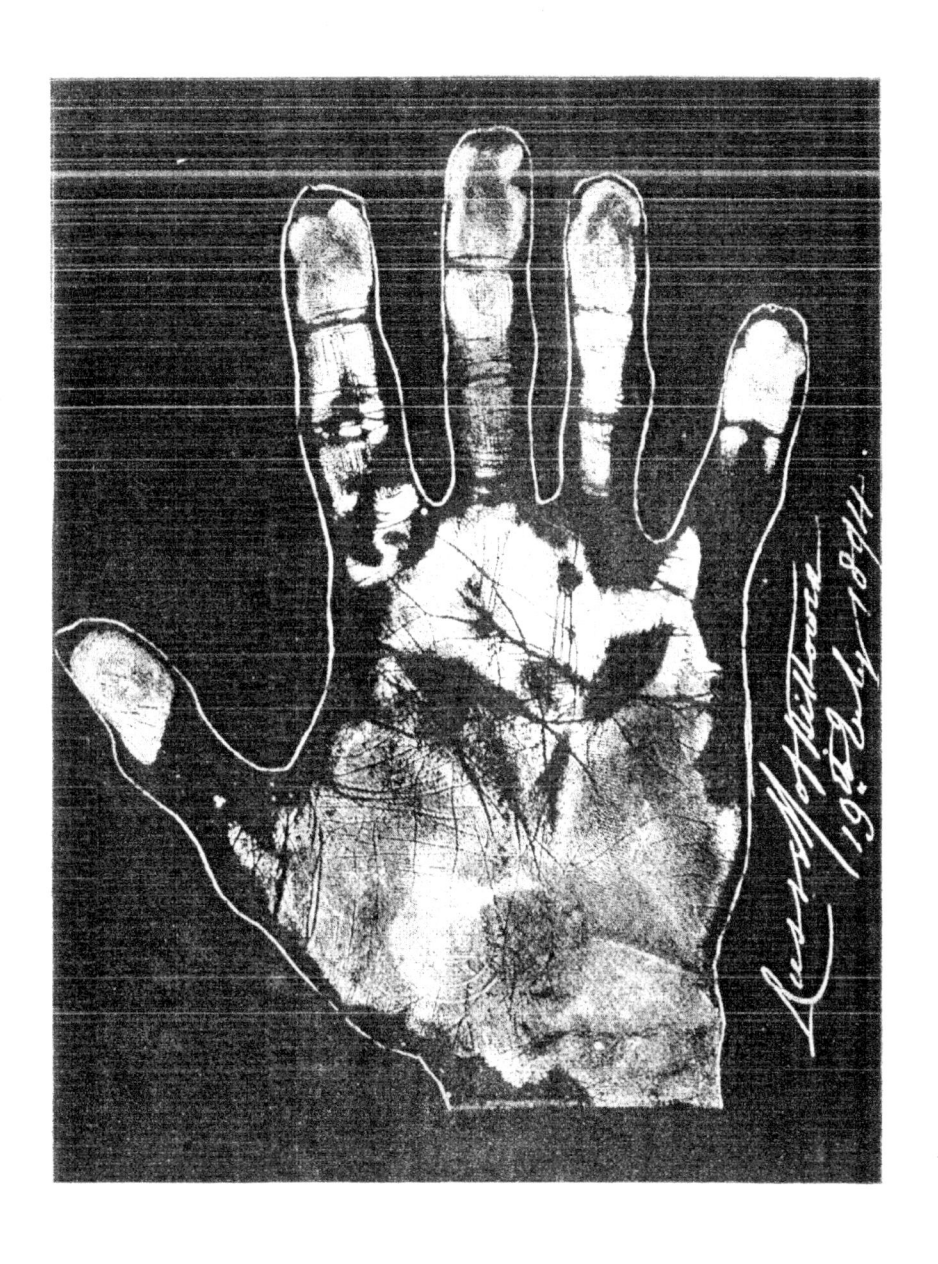

AUTOGRAPHED IMPRESSION OF THE RIGHT HAND OF LORD RUSSELL
OF KILLOWEN, THE FAMOUS LORD CHIEF JUSTICE

CHAPTER XXV

SARAH BERNHARDT—AN INTERVIEW UNDER STRANGE CONDITIONS

ONE evening, a gentleman came to my rooms and asked if I would drive out with him and meet a lady whose hands he thought would be of great interest to me. I agreed, and together we went to a house standing in a large garden near St. John's Wood.

I had been made to promise to ask no questions, but I must confess that I was somewhat anxious when, after what appeared to me a considerable time, the door at the end of a corridor opened, and a lady, with a heavy black lace mantilla covering her head and face, came towards me and held her hands out under a shaded electric light.

What hands they were! From my point of view, of lines and marks, they completely fascinated me.

I scarcely knew what I said, for I was keyed up to a pitch of nervousness and intensity, especially as my subject broke in every now and then with the exclamation, "Mon Dieu, comme c'est bien vrai." Then, after my description of the pathway of brilliancy and success—the glory of the conquest—the triumphs, and also the trials of the successful, I painted the ending of the day—the burning out one by one of the lamps of life, the slow, levelling process of the hills of hope and ambition, and something else, that seemed like a long-drawn-out tragedy—and the end.

The white hands were drawn away, sobs came from under the veil, until suddenly it was thrown back, and the eyes of the great Sarah Bernhardt, those wonderful eyes, looked straight into mine.

It is not my part in these rough sketches of the past to tell of my own feelings or of my emotions, but I must admit that at this stage of my unusual career, I felt a flush of pride, and gratitude, to the study that had brought me so close to the one and only Bernhardt, especially as, in the sweetest of voices my young ears had ever heard, she murmured over and over again in French: "It is the most wonderful thing I have ever known, wonderful, wonderful, wonderful."

But quickly I thought that the sceptical public would never believe that I had seen "the divine Sarah," so I handed her my autograph book, and asked her to write something in it as a souvenir. Without hesitating for a moment, she wrote the following words and signed it with her own characteristic signature:

(TRANSLATION)

"Since God has placed in our hands lines and marks which tell our past and future, I only regret that from these lines we cannot know the future of those dearest to us, so that we might warn them of coming troubles or sorrows. But God doeth all things well—so be it then. Amen.

SARAH BERNHARDT."

Before I left, I took the impression of her hand, which I published years ago in my well-known book, *Cheiro's Language of the Hand*.

Even the shape of Sarah Bernhardt's hand was in accordance with her well-known artistic temperament. As regards the shape of hands, a short explanation may, I think, be of interest to my readers.

In the first place, the formation of a hand to the student of such things should surely tell as much as the shape of the limbs of a horse to a judge of horse-flesh.

To the latter every movement, every line is an indication of breeding, " form," and the like, while an experienced eye is able in a moment to " place " the horse, as suitable for one class of work or the other, to tell its weak points, its strong ones, and if success or failure is likely to attend its career.

In the same way, the shape of the hand to the person experienced in such matters, shows the characteristics of the person, the heredity, breeding, peculiarities of temperament, and so on, upon which the mentality will play as upon an instrument.

Surely there is nothing illogical in such reasoning. People with square-shaped, heavy hands, with square-looking, blunt fingers, are found to be methodical, solid, materialistic in their thoughts and actions; whereas those with plump, rounded hands and pointed fingers are found to be impulsive, excitable, artistic, and so forth.

The same study which has demonstrated that the shape of the hands has its meaning, has also proved that the lines on the palm are the indication of the mentality; it has been found that all persons who have straight, decided-looking lines have strong, decided personalities, which stamp all they undertake with their will-power, their precision and purpose. Some may have only the one line straight and clearly indicated, and all the others slightly marked or wavering; then they will be found to be decided in purpose *in whatever that line represents*.

In Madame Bernhardt's case, all the principal lines were strangely clear and straight, indicating that she marked all she undertook with an unmistakable personality of her own. Madame Bernhardt's career is too well known for me to draw examples of this from the various things she has undertaken, but it is admitted that even her sculpture has always been as decided in its character as her dramatic power has been in another branch of art.

In every way I found that the hands of the great Sarah were in exact accordance with a career which dazzled the world even in her earliest years, and which has continued all through the brilliant pathway of her life.

Many times in the years that followed my first interview with " the divine Sarah," we met again, both in London and Paris.

Towards the closing years of her life, in spite of the accident which

WHAT SARAH BERNHARDT WROTE AFTER HER INTERVIEW
WITH "CHEIRO"

caused her to have her leg amputated, her will and courage never gave in. During the Great War when she gave her last performance at the Coliseum in London, she remained seated while delivering her speech as the " Spirit of Lorraine." When the curtain fell, she sent for me to come to her dressing-room. " ' Cheiro,' " she said, as she took my hands in hers, " the tragedy you foretold for the end of my life has come, my voice is all that is left to me now."

Shortly afterwards she went to New York, and on her return to Paris the end came as everyone knows.[1]

In my many works published on the Study of the Hand I have spoken of the natural dramatic quality indicated when the Line of Head is separated from the Line of Life, as the reader will easily notice on the hand of the greatest actress that has been seen in modern times.

In Sarah Bernhardt's case, in preceding pages I have called attention to the remarkable Head Line, as if drawn by a ruler across the centre of her palm. I would also like to mention here the two lines that rise above the wrist and proceed upward to the base of the second and third fingers.

The one to the second is called the Line of Fate or Destiny, and that to the base of the third the Line of the Sun or Brilliancy. They are very fully explained in my works on the Hand.[2] In a book of this kind it would take too much space to set out in detail the extraordinary manner by which these lines tally with Sarah Bernhardt's well-known career. I will only say, *en passant*, that such lines are extremely unusual, they promised brilliancy and success in all she undertook from her very earliest years. She made her debut at the age of fifteen when she entered the Paris Conservatoire.

Unfortunately, as will be noticed, both these strong lines appear to break up in the latter years, namely, before they reach their termination at the base of the fingers.

When this wonderful woman returned to Paris from New York on her last visit she was on the verge of bankruptcy. All her property had already been sold or seized to pay her debts. It is well known that in order to raise immediate money she had agreed to pose for a Cinema Company, even although she knew she was dying.

In the morning of her last day on earth, she sent for the Film operators to be shown up to her bedroom. In a voice very weak and shaky, she said to the doctor who was present, " Please, my dear man, do not object, they pay me Ten Thousand Francs every time I pose."

Using her strength of will to the last, she had herself propped up in bed, the Cinema men took the picture ; as they left the room the great Sarah sank into a coma from which she never awakened.

[1] Sarah Bernhardt, born Paris, October 22nd, 1845, died March 26th, 1923, in Paris.
[2] *Cheiro's Language of the Hand ; You and Your Hand ; Cheiro's Guide to the Hand ; Palmistry for All*, by " Cheiro."

And the irony of it all; the Film Company failed, the money that might have paid for her funeral never materialized, yet nearly a million francs worth of flowers followed her hearse to the grave. She was buried in the rosewood coffin she had herself designed and with which she had travelled all over the world for more than thirty years.

CHAPTER XXVI

BLANCHE ROOSEVELT'S PARTY AND OSCAR WILDE. A STARTLING PREDICTION AND ITS FULFILMENT

ONE afternoon an unusually handsome woman called. She was my last client that day; after she had left I mentally reviewed all I had told her. I had been unusually accurate with her, she had told me, and I passed over and over again in my mind the things I had mentioned, and the dates I had worked out for events that I thought must happen. From a peculiar system of my own, in which dates, numbers, and time can be worked out to a remarkable extent, it seemed to me that my late visitor would be threatened with a serious danger from fire *on that very evening*. Some people might probably call this a species of clairvoyance, but to my way of thinking, with certain calculations as a base, the trained and intuitive mind is enabled to interpret the "shadows of coming events" and feel them, as even animals sometimes feel the approach of danger hours in advance.

Be this as it may. I became so convinced of this danger of fire threatening my late visitor that, in spite of a hundred reasons against my doing such a thing, I determined to see her at once, and give her the warning. I had no idea of her name, for my visitors never gave them, but when leaving she had told my servant to tell the cabman the name of a certain well-known hotel, and so I at once proceeded there.

My description at the hotel office was sufficient; my card was sent up and she received me. At first she thought I was mad and frankly told me so, but finally she became impressed with my earnestness and agreed to leave the hotel and stop the night at the house of a friend, Mrs. Charles Hawtrey of Wilton Crescent.

And now came the strange part of the story. No real fire took place. But her pet dog which she left behind in her bedroom was during the night asphyxiated *by an escape of gas* which occurred under the floor *in this very room*.

It was in this way I became acquainted with the famous and beautiful Blanche Roosevelt (Comtesse Machetta d'Algri). Blanche Roosevelt was one of those creatures that, like Halley's comet, only pass over life's horizon once in so many hundred years.

Blanche was an American, everyone loved her, from the beggar in the street to the prince in the palace, and everyone called her Blanche, for no title seemed to adorn her more than her own simple Christian name.

This strange being, a veritable spoiled child of the gods, was gifted as few women have ever been. She was an authoress and poetess of no small merit; her *Copper Queen*, with its vivid picture of the Chicago fire, was considered one of the best novels of the day. She could paint as few artists could, and sing as few prima donnas.

Liszt worshipped her and encouraged her in music, while the great

Sardou and Bulwer Lytton tried to draw her into the world of letters.

Apart from her talents, she had a charm of beauty and the apparent guilelessness of not knowing it that drew women to her as much as men. Even Queen Victoria after her presentation at Court had requested to see her again.

If I could only sketch her you would perhaps understand it—the whitest teeth, the fairest skin, the bluest eyes and hair like beaten gold that any artist has ever imagined, a figure divinely tall with the bearing of a queen, the grace of a thoroughbred, and with it all the simplicity of a child. Such in a few words was Blanche.

Shortly after the "fire" incident I mentioned, she gave a dinner where it was arranged that I was to read hands through a curtain so that I might not know who my consultants were. When my work was finished, I was presented to the Prince Colonna of Rome, the Duke of Newcastle, Madame Melba, Lord Leighton, Henry Abbey of New York, and many others.

The greatest hit I made that evening was in the case of Oscar Wilde, who was then at the height of his fame. He had produced that very night *A Woman of No Importance*, but I little thought when his rather fat hands were passed through the holes in the curtain that such hands could belong to the most-talked-of man in London at that moment.

I was, however, so struck with the difference in the markings of the left and right hands, that from behind my curtain I explained that the left denoted the hereditary tendencies, while the right showed the developed or attained characteristics, that as we use the left side of the brain the nerves cross and go to the right hand, so the right hand consequently shows the true nature and development of the individual.

I pointed this case out as an example where the left had promised the most unusual destiny of brilliancy and uninterrupted success, which was completely broken and ruined at a certain date in the right. Almost forgetting myself for a moment, I summed up all by saying : "The left hand is the hand of a king, but the right that of a king who will send himself into exile."

The owner of the hands did not laugh. "At what date ?" he asked rather quietly.

"A few years from now," I answered, "at about your fortieth year."

Of course, everyone laughed. "What a joke !" they said, but in the most dramatic manner, Wilde turned towards them and repeated gravely, "The left is the hand of a king, but the right is that of a king who will send himself into exile," and without another word he left.

That was the end of the evening. Blanche was rather annoyed (at least as much so as she could ever be at anything) that I had sent her lion of her party away. She told me I was too realistic for drawing-room entertainments, so my curtains were taken down and supper

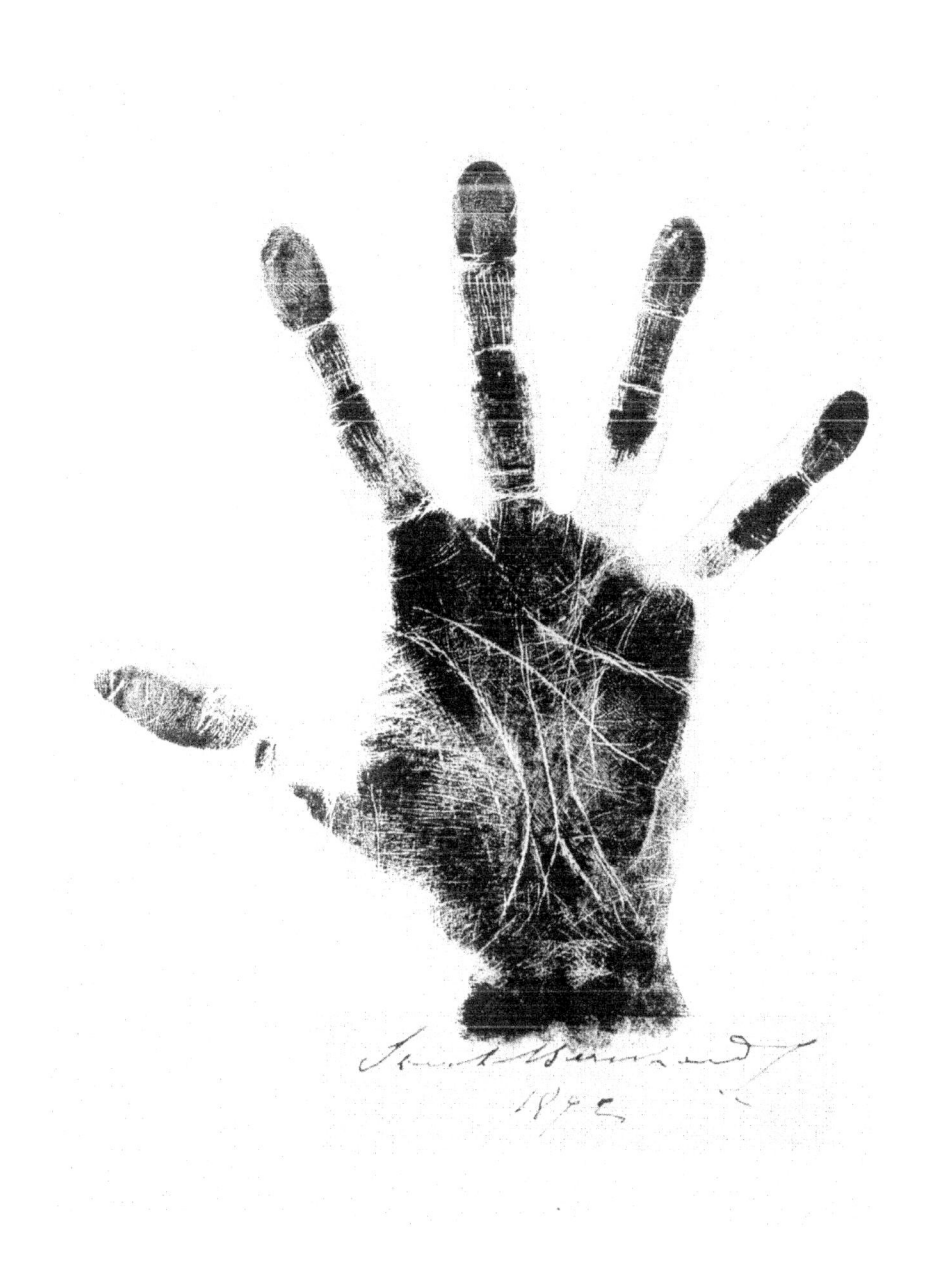

THE RIGHT HAND OF SARAH BERNHARDT

was served instead of science. The next day I received from her the following letter:

SAVOY HOTEL,
October 24, '92.

" DEAR ' CHEIRO,'

I am afraid we were all too inconsiderate last night and yourself too yielding. Pray take some rest to-day and treat your marvellous gift with proper respect and delicatesse.

You amazed and terrified us all last night—I am sure some are still wondering whether you are a human being or a creature of another world—I know what I think—I told you last night—I repeat it this morning and wish you every good luck, and success triumphant.

Always faithfully yours,
BLANCHE ROOSEVELT."

The end of her remarkable life was of the nature of a tragedy which I had predicted many years in advance; it would be too long a story I fear to include in these memoirs.

I did not meet Oscar Wilde again until shortly before he commenced the case that was to end so fatally for him. He came then to see " if the break was still there." I told him it was, but that surely his Destiny could not be broken. He was very, very quiet, but in a far-off way he said: " My good friend, you know well Fate does not keep road-menders on her highways."

I never met him again until I had wandered half round the world and had reached Paris in 1900.

It was a lovely summer evening in the Exhibition. I had been dining there with friends, and as we sat on the terrace of one of the principal restaurants, a strange, gaunt, broken figure passed and took a seat far away from the crowd.

I should not have recognized him if some of our party had not exclaimed, " Why, that's Oscar Wilde ! " Instinctively I rose. " I must go and speak to him," I said.

" If you do," my host replied, " you need not return."

I accepted the challenge and went to Wilde and held out my hand.

In his terrible loneliness he held it for a moment and then burst into tears.

" My dear friend," he said, " how good of you ! Everyone cuts me now. How good of you to come to me ! "

And then we talked—talked till the music ceased, till the sound of voices and passing feet grew silent and the great Exhibition wrapped itself in gloom.

He went through the trial again—the mistakes he had made, the life in the prison, the joy of liberty—all. And then he told me the bitterest part of all, the hopelessness of despair, of the slights and cuts by old friends and the impossibility of getting back into his place in the world again. He passed all in review like the reading of a human document written in blood.

It was no use offering him comfort or hope—his brain was too great to feed on dreams—it was awake to the terrible reality of life, to the cruel truth *that Fate for him was broken.*

Suddenly after an outburst of words where foam and froth and depth like a mighty torrent of language tore down the banks of conventionality, the river seemed to give him an idea, and in a second he was at its side. As he stood on the parapet the moon shone out and outlined every curve of the massive, broken figure that seemed about to plunge into the quiet river at his feet.

I reached his side, and clutched his arm, but he as suddenly turned, and with the most satirical laugh I have ever heard, said: " No, my boy, they shall not say that Oscar took his own life. How the dogs would yelp and the Press would ring with their graphic descriptions! They have hounded me enough, God knows, but to-night has given me the courage to face them, and the pain—and the death—that is every day coming nearer. If you never did a kind action in your life, you did one to-night by coming to me with your sympathy and your friendship. You have walked in the Valley of the Shadow with me—the Gethsemane of life that some pass through sooner or later.

" Your presence brought the dead past out of its grave. You remember that night at Blanche's—the very night on which I had made one of my great triumphs, and you remember what you told me. How often I have thought of it since, and while I picked oakum I used to look at my hands and wonder at that break so clearly shown in the Line of Fate, and also wondered why I was unable to take your warning.

" You have done me good to-night. You have brought me back to myself. Now let me walk home alone through the quiet streets. We shall surely meet again in this great village of Paris."

We never met again, but I was one of the few who followed his coffin to the grave in the little cemetery of Bagneux a few months later. When the lease of that grave was up, his body was put into a new coffin and transferred to Père la Chaise, where it now rests.[1]

I regret I cannot publish the signed impressions of Oscar Wilde's hands which I have in my collection, as I promised him I would not do so.

[1] Oscar Wilde, born in Dublin, October 16th, 1854. Died in Paris, November 30th, 1900, in his 46th year. He was sentenced at the Old Bailey, London, on May 25th, 1895, to two years' hard labour. He was then 41 years of age.

He died, practically speaking, in poverty, in a small room in a hotel at 13 rue des Beaux Arts. A few weeks before his death, the Curé of St. Germain des Pres converted him to Roman Catholicism and from that time on two nuns attended him to the end.

*It is only shallow people
who do not judge by
appearances.
   The mystery of the
world is the visible, not
the invisible.*

    Oscar Wilde

For my friend
   Cheiro
      from.
         S.2.

OSCAR WILDE IN THE VISITORS' BOOK

CHAPTER XXVII

A CURIOUS INSTANCE OF PREVISION

THE name and fame of James K. Hackett, the distinguished American actor, are well known in London, where he has made several brilliantly successful appearances.

He was one of my earliest consultants in New York, and, as the following letters show, all that I predicted for him came true.

These two letters have a peculiar interest in themselves, apart from the fact that they stand out as a testimony to the accuracy of the study I have so often defended.

I received Mr. Hackett's permission to publish the two letters in question, and I am happy to add that the honours I also foretold would be showered on him, have been accorded.

I have before me as I write the programme of his famous performance of *Macbeth*, in Paris, on June 6th, 1921, and the subsequent announcement of June 9th, that " Mr. Hackett was awarded the Cross of the Legion of Honour " ; also that the miniature Cross of the Legion of Honour, set in diamonds, was presented to him by the Society of Dramatic Authors and Writers, " As a mark of their admiration for his art."

I believe this is the highest honour that France has ever given to a foreign actor.

En Tour,
London, *April Eleventh,*
Nineteen Fourteen.

" My dear ' Cheiro,'

It gave me a great deal of pleasure to meet you again after twenty years, and to tell you that everything I remember of your predictions as you read my hand, when I was twenty-three years old, in the Grand Central Station in New York, through the good offices of a friend, who treated you as the average Catholic treats his priest—as an adviser and counsellor—has come true.

You told me as you sat in the railroad car in the Grand Central Station that I was then engaged to be married, which I was, and that that engagement would be broken, and for the lady's sake, I congratulate her that she had the good taste to break it.

You told me that when I was twenty-six I would make a very great success. You could not state what it was, but that it would be very great. When I was twenty-six, I played the ' Prisoner of Zenda ' in the Lyceum Theatre, New York City, and the very importance of that success has artistically strangled me ever since.

You told me that when I was twenty-seven I would meet a very charming and beautiful woman, with whom I would fall in love and afterwards marry. You also told me that shortly thereafter I would have a very serious illness, during which I would be very near Death's door, but would finally recover. All of these predictions came true *absolutely to the year*. You told me that I would eventually go into management, which I did.

You further told me that ultimately I would receive every honour that my profession could bestow upon me. That has not yet come, but let us hope that this prediction may also come true.

I have not mentioned names, because they are unnecessary. The names are a matter of public record, and this letter is written to you to confirm the accuracy of your judgment as expressed to me at that time.

I am leaving London for Paris on Tuesday. On my return to England, which will probably be in about six weeks, I hope I may get in touch with you and that we may have a smoke together.

With kindest regards and every assurance of esteem,

I remain,
Most sincerely,
JAMES K. HACKETT."

The second letter bears the same date, and is as follows:

"MY DEAR 'CHEIRO,'

Since dictating my other letter to you, a very curious incident has just been recalled to my mind, which, in my hurried interview, I forgot to tell you.

A very estimable lady, who had refused some of the biggest nobles in Europe, partially because of her great wealth, and with whom I had an intimate and most charming friendly acquaintance, returned to New York. She had been abroad for about two years.

I had just been jilted by my fiancée, whom I mentioned in my other letter, and my visits to the lady, who had just returned from Europe, and with whom I had a most sincere and warm friendship, and for whom I held and still hold the greatest respect, were very welcome to me.

On a certain day I proposed to her and she accepted me. Suddenly an impulse seized her. She went upstairs and brought down a book, and read me a date you had given her, saying, that though she would hesitate about accepting either of two European gentlemen, she would ultimately accept, *on the date set down*, a man born in the United States, whom she had known for some time, and the description you gave of the man exactly fitted me.

The date and the other details were in ink and in her own hand, and it was *on that exact date I proposed to her*. I merely recite this for your information and because I think it is extremely interesting.

Most sincerely,
JAMES K. HACKETT."

Mr. Hackett's father, who was born in 1800, was one of the greatest comedians on the American stage. After gaining enormous success in the States, he made his début in London in 1827, exactly ninety-three years before his son made his triumph in *Macbeth*, on November 2nd, 1920, when the English Press pronounced him to be "the greatest ' Macbeth ' within living memory."

The elder Hackett gained the friendship of the most famous men, and every leading English actor of his day, just as the younger Hackett made lifelong friends of Irving, Tree, Wyndham, etc., and counted among his friends the most notable families in England ; while at a recent Royal garden party at Buckingham Palace, the King had him specially presented to him.

In America, the elder Hackett was considered the greatest " Falstaff " of the age. He was a lifelong friend of President Lincoln, and it is a matter of history that Lincoln sent an order to the famous General Grant, in the middle of the Civil War, to leave the front for two days' vacation, to come to Washington and witness Hackett's performance of " Falstaff."

In the same way, the younger Hackett was one of President Roosevelt's most intimate friends, and, as he was as good a sportsman as he was an actor, he accompanied Roosevelt on many of his shooting expeditions.

James K. Hackett was born *when his father was sixty-nine years of age*, and it is a curious coincidence that when his mother was being congratulated on the birth of such an extremely vigorous and healthy-looking boy, she made the remarkable prediction that, as his father had been the greatest " Falstaff " of the age, the baby in her arms " would one day be the greatest ' Macbeth ' that would ever be seen on the stage."

Whether this may have had some influence on the boy's later destiny is, of course, mere conjecture, but from his boyhood days he made a special study of the character of " Macbeth," and his only real regret in life was that his mother never lived to see or hear of his tremendous success as " Macbeth," in both London and Paris.

It is an interesting story of heredity, and helps to illustrate how ignorant we are of such laws of nature. Perhaps when I met young Hackett—then an unknown actor—in the railway car in New York my subconscious brain got in tune with his, and his mother's message in the long-dead past came again to life and re-echoed itself through my lips.

CHAPTER XXVIII

LILLIE LANGTRY'S ACKNOWLEDGMENT. MELBA, NORDICA, PERUGINI, LILLIAN RUSSELL, CALVÉ, THE GREAT DUSE, AND JANOTHA, COURT PIANIST TO THE EX-KAISER

THE famous Mrs. Langtry, who later became Lady de Bathe, wrote in my Visitors' Book as far back as 1899:

"'Cheiro's' predictions of my future will influence me in all my dealings—because I am so impressed by the extraordinary precision with which he read my past.

November 11th, 1899. LILLIE LANGTRY."

Many years later she invited me to tea with her in her suite of rooms in the Carlton Hotel.

How well I remember that afternoon, with her charming sitting-room filled with beautiful La France roses. She was looking so radiant, so happy.

While we were talking, a large box containing a handsome silver inkstand, and a friendly letter of good wishes for her birthday arrived from King Edward. She had quite forgotten what day it was,[1] but with the King's usual thoughtfulness he had remembered it, and I feel sure no present he ever gave brought more pleasure than this one.

Before I left, she presented me with the excellent photograph which I reproduce here, but those who have had the privilege of meeting Mrs. Langtry will agree with me that no picture ever did full justice, or gave the faintest idea of her wonderful charm of manner, or that kindliness of heart that made those who really knew her so devoted to her.

I afterwards received the following letter from Lady de Bathe, and as it is an instance of that kindliness of nature which I have mentioned, I believe it will be of interest to include it in these records:

28 REGENT'S COURT,
HANOVER GATE,
April 15th, 1911.

"MY DEAR 'CHEIRO,'

I have heard that you have returned to London, and I think it is only fair to tell you how very accurate your remarks were in my case, and the strange fulfilment of what you said would happen during the past ten years.

You told me that I should not be accompanied by my husband to America, although I had planned my tour there expressly for that purpose. I could not see how your words could come true, but the Boer War broke out, and events happened exactly as you said they would.

You foretold a scandal and trouble for me in the States during

[1] October 13th.

the tour I was then contemplating. In this I again doubted your accuracy, as I was taking an excellent company, and a play that had been a great London success; but you were again right, for I reached America during a political campaign, and the play in question, *The Degenerates*, by Sydney Grundy, was dubbed immoral, on account of the title, by those who, in such a moment, were glad to seize on anything to further their party interests. I had all the trouble and scandal which you had indicated, being in some cases hounded from town to town.

But perhaps the most curious incident was the following. You told me that in the following month of July, I would have an accident in connection with a horse, which would cause a shock to my nervous system which would take me some time to get over. This happened when my favourite racing mare, Maluma, ridden by Tod Sloan, broke her shoulder in the race for the Liverpool Cup and had to be killed. I must confess, whether people believe it or not, that this affected me so much that it was a long time before I could again get up my enthusiasm for racing.

These are only the things that stand out more clearly than others in the years that have passed since I last saw you, but in minor details even, *you were equally true in all you said*.

I think it is only fair to write and tell you how accurate you have been. Encouragement does us all so much good in our work! If people could only realize this, the world would be filled with much better efforts.

Believe me,
Very truly yours,
LILLIE DE BATHE."[1]

MELBA

Madame Melba was one of my earliest consultants when I first came to London; she had no appointment, but just came in one afternoon as she was walking up Bond Street. This was about November 1888; she was not known then, she had not made her début in London; so much so, that two ladies who had booked their appointments and were waiting in my reception room, resented her intrusion and though she asked them to oblige her and let her have the first interview, they would not give up a moment, so the unknown intruder had to wait—it was nearly an hour later when she finally was ushered in. She took the waiting very good-humouredly and chaffed me for being such a public favourite.

She had such a sweet smile and was such a change from the two

---

[1] Lillie Langtry was born on October 13th, 1854, her father was the Dean of Jersey. She was painted by Sir John Millais as "The Jersey Lily." Her entrance to London society and presentation to Queen Victoria made a "furore" on account of her beauty.

About this time (1878) she met the Prince of Wales (later Edward VII), also Beaconsfield, Gladstone, and all the celebrities of that time.

She died in her villa at Monte Carlo on February 12th, 1929.

"cats" that had preceded her, that I threw myself heart and soul into reading the very expressive hands that she put on the table before me. She did not interrupt or say a word until I had finished—then she gave me the great satisfaction of telling me that I had told her every important detail of her past life and that every date I had given her had been exact. "But there is one thing," she said, "that I cannot understand. You predict, 'Cheiro,' that I am on the verge of some great triumph or success and you have gone so far as to say that my career should be that of a singer, and at the same moment of success, I am to have a loss and bitter disappointment—how can you reconcile the two things?"

I was puzzled. "I can't answer," I said, "I can't explain, but I am certain if the one happens, the other will also."

She opened her card-case, took my pencil and wrote something on a card. "There," she said, "I hope you will come and witness my success to-morrow night, and we won't bother about the other thing."

I looked at the card, it was an order on Covent Garden for a box for me, and signed Nellie Melba.

Of course, I went. I had never been to an opera in my life before. I brought with me a huge bouquet of roses which I was told was the correct thing to do—and I am glad I did so.

Melba made her début that night in *Lucia de Lammermoor* and had indeed a triumph. The packed audience rose to its feet and cheered her; flowers, bouquets, and baskets of roses were thrown on the stage from every side—it was indeed a triumph such as few great singers have ever had.

Just before the Opera was over an attendant handed me a card. It was nothing less than an invitation to join her party at supper at the Savoy.

An hour later she sat at the head of a table covered with flowers in the private dining-room of the Louis XV suite; flowers were everywhere and still they kept on bringing in more bouquets. I can't remember who half the guests were, but I know Augustus Harris, the chief man of London Opera, was there, also Henry Abbey of the New York Metropolitan Opera House, Lady de Grey, Blanche Roosevelt, Prince Colonna, Jean and Edouard de Reszke, Madame Nordica, and many others.

Melba told them the story of her visit to me the previous day and I was placed next to her at the table.

There was still a vacant chair—no one seemed to notice it but Melba. Just then her maid came in and whispered something; for a moment her face clouded, the bright smile had gone, she turned to me and said in a low tone: "You were right, 'Cheiro,' the triumph and the loss did come together."

It was only the next day that some of her most intimate friends learned, that while she was having her great success at the Opera a Russian protégé, a young fellow whom out of the goodness of her

LILLIE LANGTRY (LADY DE BATHE)

heart she was helping to start in a musical career, had slipped back into her hotel and, making off with at least five thousand pounds worth of her jewels, had caught the night train to the Continent.

Some years later Melba and I again met in New York; she came again for a consultation and on leaving wrote in my autograph book:

" You are wonderful. What more can I say ?

NEW YORK, 1894. NELLIE MELBA."

On her return to her hotel she sent me the signed photo that accompanies this chapter.

The great Melba was born in Melbourne, Australia, on May 19th, 1859; she took her stage name from the city in which she was born. She died on February 22nd, 1931, in Melbourne. In recognition of her work on behalf of British soldiers during the Great War, she was created a Dame of the British Empire.

Madame Nordica

On my first voyage to America, Madame Nordica sent me a charming little note inviting me to come that evening to tea in her state room.

I found Signor Perugini, the well-known tenor, had also been invited; after tea the conversation turned to my work, and Nordica asked me to see if Perugini was really going to retire into a religious life, as he had for months before been planning to do.

You can imagine their incredulity when I announced that Perugini would instead, in less than a year, marry a woman in his own profession, be congratulated by all, and yet the marriage would be over before six months and in a little over a year would end by—hopeless separation and divorce.

" A little rapid even for the States," they laughed—and yet it was what actually did take place. As everyone knows, he was on landing engaged to sing in Lillian Russell's Company at the Casino; in a few months he married this beautiful prima donna, at that time the goddess of the American stage; in less than six months the marriage was over, and in little over a year a divorce was agreed on by this curiously ill-mated pair.

This prediction and its fulfilment did much to make my name known in New York.

Madame Nordica was one of the most famous singers of her day in London and Paris, but she had been so many years absent from her own country that her fame was almost unknown in New York.

She was to make her reappearance at the Metropolitan Opera House on the gala night when each of the other great prima donnas, Melba, Calvé, and Eames, were to sing an act from their repertoire. As the others were certainly sure of meeting with a great reception and receiving a large quantity of bouquets, it came to my mind that it would be a nice action on my part if I had a basket of flowers sent up to Nordica on her reappearance in her own country.

I had only been six weeks in New York, and in the innocence of my heart, I entered one of those flower-shops in Fifth Avenue that in " the city of skyscrapers " are more like golden palaces than shops.

Very quietly, I said to a statuesque-looking person, who looked like the " Queen of Flowers " herself, " I want a handsome basket of roses sent to Madame Nordica at the Opera House to-night."

" What kind of roses ? " she smiled.

" Oh, the very best of course," I answered, forgetting in my excitement that it was in the month of December and that I was in New York with two feet of snow on the ground.

Again the " Queen of Flowers " smiled. " What size of basket and about what price do you want to pay ? "

Once more forgetting I was in the Land of Large Ideas, I very loftily waved my hand, " I will leave it all to you," I said. " I give you carte blanche to send something I shall be proud of. Madame Nordica's act comes on about 9.30, please see that it is there in good time. Send the bill in to-morrow at my address."

" Yes, sir, it shall be done," and the " Queen of Flowers " smiled me out as if I were one of New York's millionaires.

That evening at nine o'clock I was in a box at the Opera when Henry Abbey, the manager, sent for me.

" You have sent a basket of roses to Madame Nordica," he laughed, " that is so large it would be impossible to get it through the doors of the front of the house. What shall we do about it ? "

Looking through the glass doors, on a lorry in the street we could see a crowd of people gazing at what looked at first sight to be a small mountain of roses, but it was in fact a basket about sixteen feet high by perhaps four feet across, made entirely of those famous " American Beauty " roses costing many dollars apiece at that time of the year.

Mr. Abbey saw my look of dismay.

" All right," he laughed. " I'll have the scenic doors on the stage opened—it will be there when Nordica comes on."

The curtain went up on the temple scene of *Aïda*—as the light gradually increased all eyes were attracted to the basket of flowers standing at the corner of the stage.

My " Queen of Flowers " in the shop had indeed excelled herself— she had also known what giving her " carte blanche " meant, and, further, she had not forgotten to gracefully festoon a small silk flag of Stars and Stripes to the handle of the basket.

For a moment a hush of astonishment crept over the crowded house, then realizing the compliment to an American singer, the basket received an unstinted round of applause, to be repeated still louder as in a few moments Nordica made her appearance.

The bill for the basket duly reached me the next morning. I will

MADAME MELBA

not go into details—it is sufficient to say that it taught me not to give " carte blanche " to anyone in America again.

CALVÉ
I had an unforgettable experience with that gifted child of song, Madame Calvé. She came so disguised and covered up in a black Spanish mantilla, that no one could even see her face. When the interview was over my strange visitor wrote in French, which I translate for the benefit of my readers :

> " ' Cheiro ' (she spelt the name as it is pronounced—Cairo) has to-day from the lines of my hand told me things that are terribly true. By his advice I will hope to escape many sorrows and evils.
> EMMA CALVÉ."

Years later I was in Paris and she showed her good-heartedness in a way which few great prima donnas would have done. I was giving a reception at the close of my season, and had invited quite a number of friends to bid them good-bye. Calvé heard of it and insisted on coming with her friend, Madame Guy d'Hardelot, whose beautiful songs are so well known in England. Her presence had, however, made all my other singers so nervous that they declined to sing. Calvé took in the situation at a glance and beckoning me to where she was sitting, said : " ' Cheiro,' do ask me to do something. Nothing would give me greater pleasure." A night of song followed such as my friends and myself have never forgotten.

CHARLES W. CLARKE
One of the many letters sent me recording the accuracy of predictions made by the study of the hand, is one I received by post from Paris after I had retired from professional work.

A man had called to see me one afternoon during my season in Chicago. He told me he had been a failure in everything he had attempted and he just asked me if I could make a suggestion of some career for him to go in for. He had a few thousand dollars left, he said, and wanted to know what he should invest them in.

After examining his hands, I surprised him by saying he should invest the money in himself. " You have the hands of a musician," I said ; " have you ever had your voice tested ? "

" A few years ago I thought I had a voice," he answered, " but I was told it was only fit for singing in the streets, so I did not continue. Do you really think I could ever do something with it ? "

" You have not only got a voice," I laughed, " but you have an intensely dramatic nature ; besides, you have the Lines of Success and Fame marked to commence in about five years from now—I would strongly advise you to give it a good trial."

He took my words seriously and for the next few years studied under some of the best voice-producers on the Continent. The result was that Charles W. Clarke, before the five years had run their course, was considered without an equal as a basso and became in constant demand for all the great oratorios and received enormous fees wherever he sang.

The following is a copy of the letter I received:

12 Rue Leonard de Vinci, XVIᵉ,
August 29th, 1912.

"My dear Friend 'Cheiro,'

To me it is most remarkable that all the important events of my life should have been predicted by you fifteen years ago, the *events and time have been as you predicted.*

I am truly grateful *for the help derived* from the many things you told me of myself.

Sincerely yours,
Charles W. Clarke."

The "Great Duse"

While in London for my third season, I was visited by a lady who studiously concealed her identity. I saw that she had unusual hands; in fact they reminded me remarkably of Madame Sarah Bernhardt's that I had studied in the earliest days of my career, when called upon to meet the famous actress.

My visitor certainly had wonderful triumphs imprinted upon her hands. But in the story of Love, there was nothing but disaster; moreover, I could see that before the end, clouds of darkness and depression would have settled down, and that poverty and death would take place in a foreign land.

"You have a wonderful career of success—much glory and prosperity has already been yours—more is still before you. But in Love you will be wounded to the heart."

Before my visitor left, I learnt that she was the incomparable Duse, the great tragic artiste of the Italian stage. In the time of her joy, she was inclined to laugh at my predictions of sorrow; for she said boldly that the most wonderful lover in the world was at her feet— Gabriele d'Annunzio, poet and novelist, destined later to have a spectacular reign in his ivory and gold palace, as the Dictator of Fiume. For her, he had written a tragedy, while his love-letters transcended all beauty and adoration.

Before a year had run its length, Duse called upon me again. I was struck painfully by the change in her. Her wonderful lover had tired of romance; he had shown the world his soul, with a cynical disregard for Duse's feelings. Sick to the heart, she went off on a foreign tour, although her health was breaking up. It was not long

Cheiro's remarkable predictions when crossing the Atlantic in September 93 on the S.S. Paris were not alone curious but have been verified — Truly "there is more 'twixt heaven and earth than are dreamt of in our philosophy."

New York. U.S.A.

Gio. Perugini

25.1.94

My compliments to Cheiro.

Lillian Russell Perugini

Jan 25th 94. New York.

LILLIAN RUSSELL AND SIGNOR PERUGINI

after she left me that she died in a hotel in America—far from home, a wreck of her former genius and actually suffering from poverty.

JANOTHA

Another interesting personality, of a totally different type, whom I met about this time, was Mademoiselle Janotha, the famous Court pianist to the Emperor of Germany, a lady who has received, perhaps, as many decorations and honours from Royalties as any other woman in the world of music.

This weird lady (for if one has ever heard her wonderful playing, one is inclined to believe that the spirits of the great dead play through her subtle fingers) came accompanied by her famous black cat, " Prince White Heather," rolled up in her muff.

En passant, I must remark that " Prince White Heather " had been Mademoiselle's mascot for many years, and was always seen with his mistress at those numerous bazaars where this generous-hearted little lady was found working in the cause of charity.

Her great talent was so distinctly marked in the lines of her hand that I could make no mistake about it, and the following week I had the pleasure (at the old St. James's Hall) of being one of a large audience, who were carried away by enthusiasm at her rendering of some difficult pieces from the great works of Chopin and Liszt. It may interest my readers to hear that this great artiste played over three hundred times at this famous house of music, and as a special mark of appreciation, she was asked to play at the last concert before the old St. James's was demolished. The handsome iron crown which had capped the summit of the structure for forty-seven years was presented to Mademoiselle Janotha as a souvenir.

CHAPTER XXIX

INTERVIEWS WITH W. T. STEAD—HIS TRAGIC END ON THE ILL-FATED "TITANIC" FORETOLD. MARK TWAIN, ELLA WHEELER WILCOX, THE FAMOUS AMERICAN POETESS; MARY LEITER, WHO BECAME VICEREINE OF INDIA

ANOTHER of the remarkable personalities I met about this time was W. T. Stead, the celebrated editor of the *Review of Reviews*. He asked me to come and see him in his well-known offices at Mowbray House.

I must here explain that in all cases when I knew who my subject was I considered myself at a great disadvantage, and for this reason I had made a rule with my secretary at my rooms that should he know the name of any intended visitor he was on no account to tell me.

My idea was (and I believe my readers will agree with me) that the brain in an ordinary way is carried away with the thought that such and such a person will lead such and such a life or do such and such a thing. The exact reverse is, on the contrary, more often the case, because men and women on life's stage play more or less of a role, while their real character is often extremely different from what it appears to the general public.

For this reason I have never cared to interpret the lives of those I knew intimately, and I often disappointed my friends by refusing even to look at their hands.

It was thus I felt on going to see Mr. Stead. He was one of those big personalities with the limelight of public opinion playing so strongly on every action that even the "man in the street" had heard of his character in a dozen different ways through the columns of every newspaper in England.

I explained my difficulty to him; he thought it was logical and reasonable, and so I contented myself with taking an impression of his remarkable hand for my collection and explaining to him the meaning of the difference of the lines as shown in his hand and those of other well-known personalities.

Years later, however, we met in Paris, and as I was wearing the decoration which had been given me by the Shah of Persia on account of my having predicted the date of his attempted assassination, and thus caused his Grand Vizier to ask for a stronger guard of police, which as may be remembered, saved the Shah's life, Mr. Stead made me explain how I worked out by my theory of numbers what might be called "Fadic" dates.

We were sitting at a table in a well-known restaurant, in the Boulevard de Capucines, Mr. Stead, the famous Miss Maud Gonne, and myself. Mr. Stead had returned from his visit to the Czar over his great Peace Movement, and Miss Gonne, who was called by Parisians, "the Irish Jeanne d'Arc," had just come back from one of her brilliant "peace-breaking" tours in Ireland.

When I had finished explaining my reasons for picking out the date

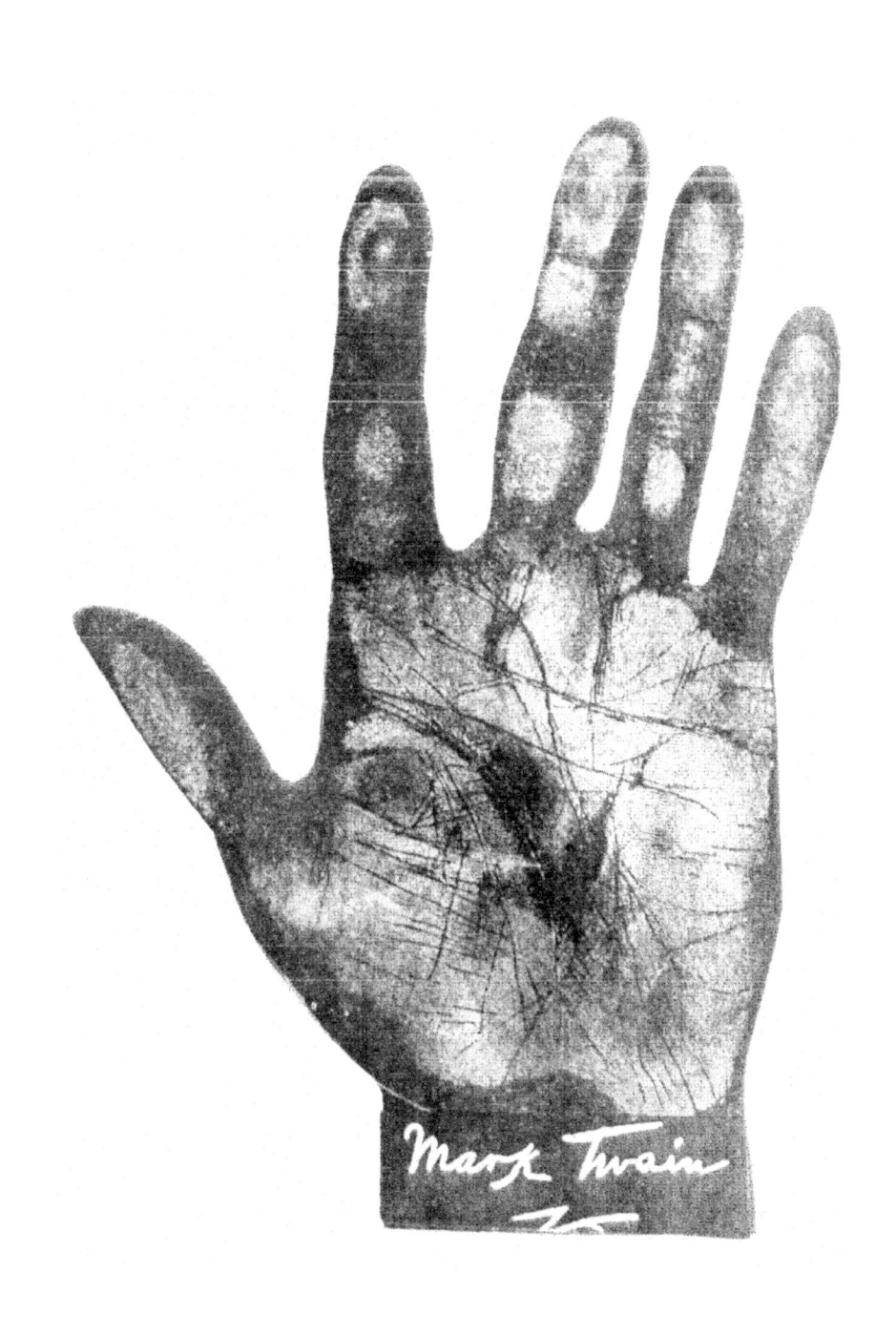

THE RIGHT HAND OF "MARK TWAIN"

of the attempt on the Shah's life, Mr. Stead made me tell him some things about the characters of people whose numbers, according to my system, were "keys" to their characters and the chief events of their lives.

When I had finished he told me that the numbers he had given me were those of his own sons, and as far as he could judge, the picture I had made was exact to even the smallest details of character, and some ten years later I had the satisfaction of hearing from him that even the events which I had indicated at that *déjeuner* in Paris had also been fulfilled.

Mr. Stead had, as doubtless many will remember, the firm conviction that his death would be one of violence at the hands of a London mob.

I believe he had this idea from the time a mob attacked his offices and smashed the windows, apparently as an indication of the feeling engendered by his opposition to the Boer War.

Mr. Stead on more than one occasion referred to this extraordinary belief of his. The last time he brought the matter up was in the middle of June 1911, when he had lunch with me at my house.

I argued against his view, as I always did, but again on that occasion I failed to make him change his mind. My words, however, had made some impression on him, for a few days later he telephoned me and asked me to consider the matter again, letting him know the result.

The following is a copy of the letter I sent him:

June 21st, 1911.

"MY DEAR MR. STEAD,

Yes, I remember very clearly our discussion at lunch here the other day, but I see no reason to go back on what I said then, namely that as far as I can judge, you need have no reason to believe that your life will end by violence from a London mob.

I have gone over very carefully the impression of your hand that you gave me many years ago, also the more recent notes I made on it, and judging from it and from your date of birth in the Sign of Cancer, otherwise known as the First House of Water,[1] in my humble opinion, any danger of violent death to you *must be from water and nothing else*. The most important months for you to avoid travelling in are December and next April of 1912.

Very critical and dangerous for you should be April 1912, especially about the middle of that month. So don't travel by water then if you can help it. If you do, you will be liable to meet with such danger to your life that the very worst may happen. I know I am not wrong about this "water" danger; I only hope I am, or at least that you won't be travelling somewhere about that period.
Always sincerely yours,
'CHEIRO.'"

---

[1] W. T. Stead was born July 5th, 1849. He was drowned in the disaster to the *Titanic* on her first voyage to New York on April 15th, 1912.

The following month I went to Spain, and nine months later, in April, I was on board an Italian liner in the Mediterranean when the captain announced to the passengers that he had received a message that the *Titanic* had sunk, and among other names of those lost he read out that of W. T. Stead.

" Mark Twain "

" Mark Twain " came to see me one afternoon, and the famous humorist was never more serious, I think, in his life, and I was sorely at a loss " how to place " the curious rugged piece of humanity that had called to consult me.

As I fell back on my system of working out the dates at which the important happenings took place in the life, my consultant began to check off the years I mentioned, and then asked me to explain to him by what method or system I was able to arrive at such conclusions.

" The past may leave its mark, I admit," he said, " and character may be told, even down to its finest shades of expression ; all that I might believe—but how the future may be even foreshadowed, is what I cannot understand."

I reasoned with him that the subconscious brain may know in advance what we shall attempt and where we shall fail, that nothing in the world was left to blind chance, and that our very failures were as necessary to our development as were our successes. Seeing that I was making no headway towards convincing him, I took up the question of heredity, as shown by the markings of the hand.

I showed him the impression of a mother's left and right hands, with the impression of five of her children's hands, until we came to one where the right hand of the child almost exactly tallied with the markings of the mother's right hand.

" In this case," I said, " which you can follow up and prove for yourself, every section of this girl's life repeated, even to dates, the actions of the mother's life, although twenty years separated them in time."

The girl had passed through similar illnesses at the same ages at which they had occurred to the mother ; she had married at the same age, also had five children, and was a widow at the same age.

" Now," I concluded, " if one had known the events of the mother's life and seen that the same markings appeared in the hands of the child—then, even say at six years of age, one could have predicted the events which would take place in the fate of the daughter."

This interested my visitor so deeply that he took notes of the various hands I showed him, and we examined with a microscope the lines in the tips of the fingers of the mother and this one daughter, whose dates had been so nearly the same, and we found that even the circles in the finger-tips and thumbs also agreed.

As he was going, he said, " The one humorous point in the situation is, that I came here expecting to lose money by my foolishness, but

"MARK TWAIN"

I have gained a plot for a story, which I certainly think should be 'a winner.'"

A short time later, he published *Pudd'n-head Wilson*, dealing with thumb-marks, which had an enormous success.

Before he left my rooms he wrote in my Visitors' Book the following:

> "'Cheiro' has exposed my character to me with humiliating accuracy. I ought not to confess this accuracy, still I am moved to do it.
> MARK TWAIN."[1]

ELLA WHEELER WILCOX

The world knows Ella Wheeler Wilcox through her vivid human poems. It has formed all kinds of opinions of her, according to the personal views of her critics. Her famous *Poems of Passion* brought her a torrent of abuse, and a whole army of friends. I know of some who would not give this unpretentious little volume room in their houses. I know of others who read and devour each line—as they did Bunyan's *Pilgrim's Progress* in their early days.

It may, therefore, interest both sides if I recount my own experience with this very strongly marked personality. She came, as so many did, without giving any inkling of her name or position; I quickly picked out her wonderful poetic gift, but classed it as of the most dramatic character; at the same time telling her that her versatility of mentality could make of her a brilliant success in any line of literature she would be pleased to make her own.

My description of her home life, so sweet and simple, so entirely opposite to what the world might suppose would be the home of the authoress of *Poems of Passion*, so impressed her that in her quick, impulsive way, she said, "You must know my husband, for my life is just as you describe."

Then, at the end of the interview, she told me her name, and I confess I was astonished, for I had heard of her fame long before I had left England, and I also had probably formed a wrong conclusion from what I imagined such an authoress would be like.

I have since learned how much public persons are judged wrongly, and as I have, later still, followed her career, I have become more and more impressed by the fact that the soul in its prison-house writes its biography in the lines of the hand, with a faithfulness of description that is nowhere else to be found.

Before she left she wrote in my Visitors' Book:

> "The study of people gifted with occult powers has interested me for several years. I have met and consulted scores during these studies. In every respect I consider 'Cheiro' the most highly gifted of all. He *helps* as well as astonishes.
> NEW YORK.
> ELLA WHEELER WILCOX."

[1] "Mark Twain" (Samuel L. Clemens) was born in Florida, 1835, and died at Redding, Connecticut, April 21st, 1910.

A Vicereine of India

Now that the grave has unhappily closed over the head of the great Lord Curzon, I should like to relate the story of his first romance, and how I foreshadowed it.

It was while I was fulfilling a season in Washington that I was informed that two ladies desired to see me. I was exhausted after a heavy day—physically and mentally unstrung—and had given my secretary peremptory orders that I would see no more clients. However, though " Man proposes, Woman disposes," and eventually there entered two ladies—an elder and a younger. In an imperious tone I was bidden unravel Fate for the latter, but with this somewhat uncompromising prelude :

" ' Cheiro,' I believe you to be an impostor. However—do your best—or worst ! "

" A short and brilliant life," were the first words I uttered, and the hand upon the cushion seemed to vibrate with inward feeling. " In a few years you will marry a man of different country from your own, and by him you will be raised to a position in an Eastern land equal to that of a queen."

" Nonsense ! " snorted the elderly lady, and then gave a thin, cynical laugh.

" Equal to a queen—really, quite a fairy story ! "

I continued to the end, and when I had finished, the elder lady gave me her hands to read, with the remark :

" Tell me about my myself, and I shall soon catch you out."

I commenced, and her anger melted away and a look of real wonder was seen on her face. When I had finished she said, " ' Cheiro,' you have truly amazed me, although I cannot see how your prevision with regard to my daughter can be fulfilled."

She took out her card and laid it upon my table. Upon it was engraved : " Mrs. Levi Z. Leiter."

The years passed on, and there came a day when I received a letter from the Vicereine of India, the wife of George Nathaniel Curzon, once Mary Leiter. She wrote :

> " Is it not wonderful, ' Cheiro,' that I am now occupying exactly the position you foretold—equal to that of a ' Queen in an Eastern land ' ? All that you foretold in Washington has come to pass."

All, indeed ! For it proved a " short and brilliant life." Death quenched the love romance of Mary Leiter and Lord Curzon in a premature grave.

Lady Arthur Paget

One of my warmest friends in London was Lady Arthur Paget, by birth an American lady, and the great friend and confidante of King

LADY ARTHUR PAGET

Edward. She was the acknowledged leader of British society during the great Edwardian days, she ruled the best social life, and her will was law.

On one occasion when she consulted me, I observed that I feared she was in great danger of a terrible accident caused by a fall, and I advised her to take the greatest care during the coming month of August.

She told me afterwards that my warning had so much effect upon her that she used the greatest caution whenever she went out. But, alas, in an unguarded moment she fell down the lift shaft in her well-known home in Belgrave Square, London, on August 4th following, and shattered her limbs from the hips to the ankles. When she was able to receive callers she sent for me and gave me details of how the accident had happened, adding that when she recovered consciousness she thought, " So ' Cheiro ' was right after all."

She suffered intensely for over a year, but bore all with wonderful resignation and fortitude. King Edward frequently called upon her, and during one of his visits, Lady Paget mentioned how I had predicted the sad accident. The monarch then retold the story of how I had given him " sixty-nine as his age limit."

Lady Paget was a Spartan where Court duty was concerned. She attended a reception at Buckingham Palace when barely convalescent, even though she was hardly able to stand. King Edward ordered a chair to be brought for her, but she refused such consideration and stood during the entire ceremony.

CHAPTER XXX

SOME NOTABLE EXPERIENCES IN THE UNITED STATES. MY FIRST LECTURE IN BOSTON. I MEET JULIA WARD HOWE, THE AUTHORESS OF THE " BATTLE HYMN," AND OTHER INTERESTING PEOPLE

AT the conclusion of my first season in New York, I made up my mind to start off on a lecture tour and see as much as I could of the great continent of America. I had never lectured before in my life, nor addressed a public audience of any kind, and I was consequently rather nervous of the issue. Knowing nothing of the routine of engaging halls, advertising, etc., I put myself into the hands of an enterprising American, who assured me that the correct thing to do was to make my début before the public in that centre of culture and home of learning, otherwise known on the map of America as the City of Boston.

It is hardly necessary to explain that this famous city is not far from the two celebrated universities of the States, namely, Yale and Harvard.

It may be on account of the close proximity of such seats of wisdom that Bostonians give themselves such a superior air of learning, or at all events—look wise. I have heard it said that more men and women wear glasses in Boston than in any other city of the same size in the world!

As a matter of fact, I was on one occasion served by an Irish waiter with a mutton chop, who was so affected by the atmosphere of the place, that he wrote out my " check " on the back of a Greek grammar, which he carried with him on all occasions.

Bostonians are, however, considered to be the finest lecture-goers in the world; and it was perhaps for that reason that my " advance agent " determined that my lecture tour should be started from such a seat of culture.

I, quite naturally, I think, left all the arrangements to him; just giving him a synopsis of what the lecture was to be about; and suggested that the leading line of the advertisement should be " ' Cheiro's ' Lecture Tour "—" The Study of the Hand, and What it Means."

On the eve of the fateful day on which I was to make my appearance, I took the night train from New York, and in fear and trembling arrived at the " City of Learning " whose verdict was to decide my destiny, as far as lectures were concerned.

Imagine my amazement, as in the early morning I drove to my hotel, to see the following bills on the hoardings:

" CHEIRO'S " TOUR OF THE WORLD

CHICKERING HALL,

To-day, 2.30

Not a word about Hands, or anything else ! My " advance agent " met me at the door of the hotel ; he had a smile on his face, from ear to ear. " I thought I knew Boston," he said ; " every seat is taken in the entire hall."

" But, my good man," I said, " there's not a word about Hands, or the subject of the lecture."

" Don't teach me my business," he grinned. " The less Bostonians know of the subject of a lecture, the more reason for them turning up to find out."

Events proved he was right, in this case at least. I had a splendid audience, the hall packed to the doors, and excellent notices in the newspaper the next day.

Of course, I told them the trick my " advance man " had played on them, and the compliment he had paid them. They roared with laughter, and Bostonians and I have been the best of friends ever since.

I finally stopped almost a year in this city. My rooms at the Hotel Brunswick were always crowded with visitors. I met charming and delightfully cultured people. I made some lifelong friends, and will carry with me to the end of my life the happiest souvenirs of " the Hub of the Universe."

It was in Boston I met Mrs. Ole Bull, the widow of the famous musician. I spent a delightful day in her curiously picturesque home in Cambridge. It was she who took me over to Longfellow's home, and Miss Longfellow showed me many of the original manuscripts of her father's poems—and how wonderfully cleanly written those manuscripts were ! That beautiful *Psalm of Life* had, I think, only two corrections.

It was also in Boston I met that now celebrated writer, Miss Lilian Whiting. In a letter which she sent to *Light*, and which appeared on January 18th, 1913, she refers to me and my visit to Boston in the following generous terms :

" SIR,

I have read with much interest the various references in *Light* to ' Cheiro,' and should like to add a word of my own experience. It is not too much to say that I owe to his remarkable power as a seer and diviner of conditions *an immeasurable debt of gratitude.*

Many years ago, I found myself at one of those ' parting of the ways ' which recur in our human experiences, when the resource on which I had been relying vanished, and no other appeared.

To put the matter plainly, the journal of which for some years I had been the literary editor was sold and changed in character, and I was intent on finding another similar place in journalism, as my only means of earning a living.

At this time, I accidentally met ' Cheiro.' He was just then the 'storm centre' of Boston Society—who crowded his rooms, waited in throngs on his secretary for appointments, and eagerly secured his 'readings' to a degree that taxed his time to the utmost. At that moment he was the idol, so to speak, and there was not wanting those who would gladly have paid one hundred dollars or more for a half-hour's interview. As I have said, I chanced only to meet him (not having gone for a professional séance), and this is the sequence.

'There is a line in your hand that is lived out,' he said, 'and you are trying to live it over again. This is impossible. As well try to put a chicken back in the shell and make an egg of it again. There is much that is awaiting you, but you are keeping it all away by not letting go of the past and turning towards *another side of literary work*, such as writing books.'

'I understand exactly what you mean, "Cheiro,"' I replied; 'from this minute I will let it go.' Within that year (1894) my first book, *The World Beautiful* (first series), was published, followed within the seventeen ensuing years (1911 inclusive) by the other twenty-one works that I have published; and for all the possibilities involved in these, and my fourteen visits to Europe within these years, I feel that I am indebted to this remarkable psychic and seer *to an incalculable degree*.

Yours, etc.,

LILIAN WHITING."

"The Grand Old Woman of America," as she was called, Mrs. Julia Ward Howe, was also one of my dear friends. She gave me an autographed copy of her famous "Battle Hymn," which was known by every soldier during the Civil War, and many a delightful evening I spent in her home.

And Dr. J. Heber Smith! I cannot conclude this chapter on Boston without speaking of him. He was a famous physician, who performed all his cures by the aid of Astrology; and a wonderful astrologer he was, too! This remarkable man worked out a chart of the heavens for every patient; he prescribed for them according to the indications of disease, as shown by their planets; and he had more grateful patients than any doctor it has ever been my lot to meet.

He, finally, two years in advance, predicted his own death from the effects of an accident. When the appointed time came, he "put his house in order"; every paper and document was in its place; and so he met his death as calmly for himself as he had often studied it for others.

It was while I was in Boston, and perhaps owing to the literary atmosphere of this city, that I published my first volume of poems. These were unique, in one way at least, namely, that I had to correct

"A little knowledge is a dangerous thing," then the power which Cheiro possesses of seeing into hidden secrets might undermine the social system.

Minnie Paget. — Nov. 1899

LADY ARTHUR PAGET'S OPINION

the proofs by telegraph, my publisher in New York having wired me that he had to catch the Christmas trade, and had to go to press immediately or delay them for another year.

These poems were extremely well received by the Press, and Boston alone sold over a thousand copies a week for the following few months; but as an illustration of the prejudice a man following such an unorthodox profession as mine had to bear, I may mention that one poem —*If We Only Knew*—was quoted far and wide through the world but in almost all religious papers it was printed *without my name to it;* when I protested at such injustice, I was told that " they could not advertise in their columns the name of a man associated with such an illegal profession," yet these same people did not see the inconsistency of making use of the work of my brains.

The only claim for this poem was, perhaps, its simplicity and human pathos; in answer to numerous requests for copies of it, and to set all doubts as to the authorship once and for all at rest, I hope it will not be considered out of place if I reprint it here:

IF WE ONLY KNEW

If we only knew, if we only knew,
But a little part of things we see,
Methinks the false would be oft more true
Than what is truth—or what *seems to be.*
If we only knew—if we only knew !

If we only knew the pain we cause,
By the slighting look or the word of shame,
By the seeking out of those old, old flaws
That one scarce could help, in the race for fame.
If we only knew that the deeds we scorn
Might some day fall to ourselves to do,
Or if not to us, to our babes unborn:
If we only knew—if we only knew !

If we only knew how the man we spurn,
Had fought temptation—aye, day and night.
If we only knew, would we so turn
And cast him off as a loathsome sight ?
Ah me ! instead of the sinner's brand,
We'd gladly help him the right to do ;
We'd lift him up with each honest hand,
If we only knew—if we only knew.

If we only knew how the woman fell,
Would we shun her as now, whene'er we meet ?
Would we leave her then to that bitter hell
Of self and sin and the homeless street ?
Would we shrug our shoulders and shake our head
For trusting too much, or being too true,
Or sinning, perhaps, as some do, for bread ?
If we only knew—if we only knew !

If we only knew—*that the hearts we miss*
Would have stayed so short in this vale of woe,
How much more sweet would have been each kiss,
But we did not know—we did not know.
Regrets are useless, and tears but blind,
And empty words can no past undo;
It's no good sighing—" *I'd been more kind
If I only knew—if I only knew!* "

CHAPTER XXXI

A LECTURE AT SYRACUSE THAT NEARLY SPELT—FAILURE

I AGAIN started on my lecture tour and reached the enterprising town of Syracuse, in the middle of New York State. My " advance manager had preceded me, and he met me as I arrived, with an air of self-satisfaction that it was impossible not to notice.

In answer to my questioning look, he said : " I have made a wonderful business deal here ; I have engaged the largest hall in the town for a mere bagatelle, provided I took it for three nights running ; so, of course, I took it," he added.

" How did you get it so cheap ? " I asked.

" I don't know," he replied, " except that the owner must be a fool or a disciple of your study, or something of that sort. I have advertised you extensively and I expect you will have crowded houses for your three nights' stay."

At the appointed hour, I arrived at the hall, and immediately went on the stage behind the curtain to see that nothing had been forgotten, such as the large lecture sheet, lantern-slides, etc.

It was a few minutes before the advertised time, and feeling a strange emptiness about the place, I peered through a hole in the stage curtain, and, to my dismay, discovered that the hall was, practically speaking, empty ; not more than perhaps forty persons sitting in the reserved seats.

Before I could recover from my surprise, the curtain was rung up, and I was left nothing to do but to make my bow and commence.

In that first moment, I thought I had better retreat, but fortunately a sense of humour came to my rescue, and, instead, I announced to my limited audience that I would try to reward them for their bravery in coming by endeavouring to give them the best lecture I ever gave in my life. At the same time, a happy thought struck me, and I announced that instead of giving my usual lecture—" The Hands of Celebrities I have Met "—I would devote the evening to a kind of lesson on the Lines of the Hand ; and that if they would give me their attention for a couple of hours—or longer, if they chose—by the close of the evening, every member of my audience would know sufficiently of the subject to be actually able to read the hands of their friends the following morning.

Americans, I believe, admire resourcefulness more than any other race on earth. My poor little audience of two score murmured their approval ; slide after slide was switched on by the lantern, and I threw myself heart and soul into my subject as perhaps I never had done before.

Two hours passed quickly away. I asked if they wished for more ; they replied with one voice : " Yes," and off we went again. Finally twelve o'clock struck and, thoroughly exhausted, for I had been speaking from eight, I came to a stop. It was fortunate I did, for the hydrogen of the lantern had also given out and its light had become suddenly yellow. I then announced that as I had the hall engaged for another two evenings, and as there was no way to get out of my contract, that on the following nights, whether there would be one person or one hundred in my audience, I would again give these lectures as lessons, so that if I ever returned to Syracuse, I would find the Syracusians more educated and appreciative of the subject.

When the audience filed out, I learned the hall was let cheap because the Grand Opera Company of New York was also in Syracuse for the same three nights; and the proprietor, in consequence, believed there could be no chance for any other attraction.

However, my happy inspiration of giving the lecture as a lesson had saved me. During all next day, my little audience, proud of their possession of the knowledge they had gained, "read," I believe, everybody's hands in Syracuse. There had also been two of the leading newspapers of the town represented in my audience. The next day, to my surprise, each paper spoke of the lecture in a most flattering manner, and when night came, the hall was packed to such an extent that the door had to be closed half an hour before the advertised time; and the same was repeated the following night.

It is so easy to be successful—if one can *only get the right inspiration.*

CHAPTER XXXII

HOW THE VANITY OF ONE MAN NEARLY BROKE MY CAREER

BUFFALO, one of the leading and most prosperous cities in New York State, was my next place to visit after Syracuse, but my advance manager had lost his nerve over his last experience in taking halls, so instead, he had simply arranged that at least my first lecture should be very unostentatiously given in the handsome ball-room of my hotel, the Iroquois.

Contrary to all expectations, people came in such crowds that every inch of available room was in demand, so much so that I had barely space on the platform to stand on; the result was, that the following week I engaged one of the largest halls in the city, and every lecture I gave was to a crowded audience.

In all my experience in America, I do not think I met with greater hospitality than I did in Buffalo; the newspapers as well as private persons seemed to vie with one another in showing me every possible kindness; and yet in the middle of it all, I had one of the saddest experiences of my career, and I realized to what an extent jealousy and vanity could go, and what harm a few slanderous words could do at any time—to one dependent on the public for his career.

I was nearly a fortnight in Buffalo when I began to notice that some of those who had been extremely lavish in their hospitality at the commencement, suddenly became quite distant and reserved. One man in particular, who had asked me to accept the privilege of his club, during my stay in the city, acted so strangely that I could stand it no longer and asked him for an explanation.

At first he said " he did not wish to hurt my feelings," and it was only after the greatest persuasion that he finally agreed to tell me, but only under the provision that I would not ask him to give the name of the person who had spread the cruel slander about me.

Anxious to get even some information that might be of assistance, I gave the promise he asked, and then in a quiet corner of his club, he told me the following:

" There is a certain Mr. X in this city," he began, " who knows everyone and goes everywhere; whose word has the greatest weight, both on account of his wealth and the position he occupies socially. On the night of your big lecture, when your name was on everyone's lips, this man stated at a supper party that not only did he know you from your very boyhood, but that it was due to his generosity that you were educated and launched into the world. This man knows something about the study you have, he admits, become a master of, but he states you are only proficient because *he first taught you the rudiments of the Art;* and, later, *because you robbed him of all his valuable books on the subject.*

" Recently, to cap all, he has gone further, and at a dinner a few evenings ago, he stated that he had proofs that you had married a young and beautiful girl in England in order to possess her money—

that she was now dying broken-hearted and in poverty, in a London garret, and that you had left England in order to avoid the vengeance of her relations."

As I listened in silence to this terrible accusation, I realized that the man who told me, believed every detail of it in all sincerity, and that no words of mine could possibly alter his opinion.

It was in vain I begged him to give me the man's name, or to bring me face to face with my hidden accuser—it was all to no purpose. He did not wish to be brought into a scandal, he said; and realizing that I could get no farther with him I took up my hat and walked out into the street.

I cannot describe how I felt, or, in a way, *how helpless I felt*. I had up to then no real personal experience with the world at large, for I had lived in a little world of my own. My books, and the study of the one subject I almost reverenced, had, in a sense, cut me off from the rest of humanity. My very success had blinded me; it seemed impossible to believe that the arrows of jealousy or envy, which might strike others, could have been hurled against me.

Besides, I could not see what motive any person could have for inventing such a story, especially as my friend had told me that my accuser was "a wealthy man with good social position." If it had been from a rival in my work, I could have understood perhaps, but not someone whose interest could never clash with mine.

I thought of all kinds of things; I made all kinds of plans; but in spite of all, I felt such a feeling of helplessness and utter loneliness that my very blood seemed to have turned into water.

If I could only find who my accuser was, I thought, I would force my way into his presence and demand the most absolute denial of the infamous story; but how and where could I find him, what length of time would I have to wait? were the questions that racked my brain with such veritable pain that, when finally I reached my hotel, I was as worn out as if I had passed through a long illness.

A pile of letters were lying on my table. I had not the courage nor the desire to open them, and I would not have noticed them a second time if the handwriting of one of the envelopes had not caught my eye.

It was from a man who had always been a staunch supporter of mine, a well-known lawyer, whose daughter, some time before, I had been the means of saving from a most unhappy marriage.

Mechanically, I opened the envelope. Would he, I wondered, also turn against me? Perhaps this very letter would be a notification of it, but to my relief I read:

Wednesday.

"My dear 'Cheiro,'

You said you would be free to-morrow night, so I want you to come to dinner—only a few people, but I will have the best in the city to meet you. You won't be bothered to look at any hands, for I shall not introduce you as 'Cheiro' (they can know afterwards, if necessary), but I want them to know you as you are—your own self, without any halo of fame round your head; so come and don't disappoint me.

Yours always sincerely,

————————."

I gave a sigh of relief, but the next second I threw the letter aside, for I felt I could not go under the circumstances. It was only when morning came I changed my mind, but in my letter I said: "I shall want you after dinner to give me a quiet half-hour, as I need your advice, and I know you won't refuse to give it to me."

I will not waste words describing how I got through the long day before me; every moment of my time had been booked in advance; and perhaps it was as well it was, for like an artist, I was so devoted to my work that I forgot my own trouble in the troubles of those who came to consult me.

I had so many appointments that I was late getting dressed for dinner, and when I arrived at my friend's house, I had already kept the company waiting, and we were ushered immediately into the dining-room.

During dinner, the conversation ran on every possible subject except that of Occultism in any form. I was evidently regarded as a young Englishman travelling through America for pleasure, and so I was entertained with all kinds of ideas on sport, what to see and such-like.

When the ladies retired, and we "mere men" were left to our cigarettes, cigars, and coffee, I took the opportunity to draw my host into a corner of the large room and had just commenced to tell him how much I wanted his advice, when a remark from an elderly man, whom I had not particularly noticed during the dinner, struck my ears and seemed for a moment to turn me into stone.

"Oh, yes," he was saying, "I know the man who calls himself 'Cheiro' well—too well in fact. No, I have not been to see him and don't intend to either, for I have seen him a good many times too often. When I lived in London years ago, in one of my philanthropic quests to aid what I considered talent in any form, I had him educated as a youngster. I taught him all I knew about hands, which was a special hobby of mine, and the young scoundrel rewarded me by robbing me of all my most valuable works on the subject."

I could not wait to hear more—in a second I was before him, but controlling myself with all the will I could master, I said very calmly: "You would recognize him again if you saw him, would you not?"—"Oh, yes," he laughed, "indeed I would; but he will take care not to meet me, as he knows I would take him at once to the nearest police station."

It is under the stress of moments such as these that one acts so totally different from what one expects one would do, that our actions and force of will become a mystery; if someone had told me an hour before that I could appear so calm while I heard my character and name dragged so low, I would have considered him mad. But, quietly looking the man straight in the eyes, I took my cigarette from my lips and said slowly and deliberately:

"Sir, you are either an escaped lunatic or an infernal liar; the man who stands before you is the ' Cheiro ' that you say you could recognize. I demand a full explanation of your words, or else it will be this very ' Cheiro ' that will take you to the nearest police station, if he has not in the meantime strangled you."

I cannot describe the short scene that followed. In a death-like silence, we heard some sounds choking in his throat, but the next second he had fallen a helpless mass at my feet.

Fortunately, there was a doctor among the guests, but even he had hard work to save him. An hour, perhaps, later, my friend and I leaned over the couch on which he had been placed, and an utterly broken, shattered piece of what I suppose was humanity blurted and gasped out the following sentences:

"For God's sake forgive me. I can't think why I did it—vanity, perhaps, for I could not bear to think that anyone could have made a success of what was my hobby for so long. Give me a pen, I will sign any declaration you like that every word I said about you was false."

He did sign a statement, for my friend thought it was right that he should do so. I had, however, never occasion to use it—and I never shall now, for it was not so very long afterwards that Mother Earth swallowed up even his memory.

.   .   .   .

It was years later that I learned the lesson that those who follow *unusual* lives *must have unusual experiences*, and must meet more calumny than those enviable ones who follow life's beaten track.

I confess I have had to pay the price of whatever little fame I earned, and especially in later years. As my name became more and more known, so did the penalty at times become all the greater. I made legions of friends, but that very fact made me also legions of enemies, and the wildest and, at times, the cruellist stories were circulated about me.

Some put my success down to " black magic," others to " spirits," others, again, to the agency of the Devil. Few, if indeed, any, put my success down to something so very simple, so very commonplace, that they would never perhaps have thought of it—*simply hard, earnest work* and nothing *but work;* and coupled with it, the real desire to help those tangled or tinselled lives that for a few moments came into contact with my own. How few out of those hundreds of society butterflies, who came to jest or pass an idle hour, ever thought that many a time I silently asked for help to read their lives from that one great Source that never fails to help; and when the jest passed from their lips and the tears started to their eyes, I did not take the credit for unlocking the secrets of their hearts.

I was only thankful that I was the instrument that had, perhaps, awakened them to the knowledge that our thoughts leave their traces, and that there are records of the things that one often would fain conceal.

I did not pretend to be a saint, for had I been one, they would not have come. I did not preach, for they would not have listened; but by the lifting of even a corner of the veil of the Mysterious, I led on those whom the churches would never have reached, to penetrate still farther—and some of them, I know, went onward—until they finally found the Mystery of Life from the lips of things that spoke to them of the Creator of all.

CHAPTER XXXIII

I VISIT DETROIT AND CHICAGO. I MEET MR. ARMOUR, MARSHALL FIELD, H. GORDON SELFRIDGE, AND JOE LEITER, MAJOR LOGAN, AND A PREDICTION FULFILLED TO THE EXACT DATE

DURING my visit to Buffalo, I was invited to run over to Detroit, a few hundred miles away, and give a lecture in aid of a charity kindergarten that was being established there. One thinks nothing of distance in the land of comfortable trains, so the following night saw me before a packed audience of Detroit's Four Hundred.

In a few eloquent and flattering words, I was introduced to my audience by Mr. Don M. Dickinson, an ex-Postmaster-General of the United States Government. I hardly think I ever had a more interested or appreciative public in any city in America, and a large amount of money was turned over to the charity for which I had given my services.

The next morning, a very remarkable man, the Mayor of the town, called on me without announcing who he was. He was a man famous in Michigan for his love of argument, but before he left, he wrote something in my Visitors' Book which, considering his nature, was the highest compliment he could have paid me. It read: "'Cheiro' is so accurate, there is no chance for 'argument.'" This remarkable testimony is signed J. S. PINGREE, Mayor of Detroit.

Before I pass on from this city, I must say that from a picturesque standpoint alone, Detroit should not be ignored by visitors to the States. Magnificently situated as it is, on the junction of the great lakes, it is one of the most attractive cities I know of. The streets are wide and well laid out; the buildings are handsome and imposing; it is to-day the principal centre of the automobile industry.

From Detroit, I reached Chicago, the great central metropolis of the States—the Clearing House of the West and the East, I think one might fitly describe it. For some reason that I never could understand, Chicago is one of the most abused of all the American cities; its streets are criticized, its buildings held up to ridicule, its men and women stuck into every melodrama that requires money or a villain, and its climate held up to scorn as the worst in the States.

Three times I visited this great city, and I must say that each time I left it, I took away with me only renewed feelings of admiration for the enterprise that seemed to flow like a tide through its streets, and the hospitality and splendid good fellowship of its inhabitants.

In Chicago, men and women don't think that " it is a crime to work "; on the contrary, they think it is a crime to be too lazy to toil. These people make a sport of life's hardships. They laugh at her blows, they gamble with her coin, if they lose, or if they win, they laugh all the same—or at least they are too plucky to show their tears.

But do not think for a moment that these people have not " the milk of human kindness in their breasts "; on the contrary, let the

Flood come, or the Cyclone strike, be it north, south, east, or west, and Chicago responds quick as a wounded heart to the touch of sorrow.

Some people think that humanity is the same the world over, but in my way of thinking, I believe that climate and even the soil have as much effect on races as they have on flowers and vegetables. Plant the champagne grape in another district and it will no longer give the " wine that cheers " ; in fact, in many cases it will cease to yield grapes at all. Geologists explain this by the statement that the champagne district is one with chalk and gravel for its subsoil, but if such things affect as they do, a hardy plant, such as the vine, how much more so may not the magnetic influence of subsoil affect the most sensitive organism of all, namely, the human being !

Is there no reason for the difference that exists in the character of the French and the Germans, or the English and the Irish ? Why should there not be equal divergencies between the people of Chicago and, say, New York, with their eight hundred miles of separation !

In any case, I do not think the soil of Chicago, whatever else it may breed, gives birth to snobs, for in my opinion this city is particularly free from this species of objectionable parasites.

In the great world's workshop I allude to, men worth millions are as humble and unassuming as if they were worth so many pence. They are happy to work, happy to play the game, and, as long as they are not playing against loaded dice, such men are bound to win in the long run.

As a passing example of what I am citing, I wish to mention the following incident that happened to myself :

I had a letter of introduction to Mr. Phillip Armour, the head of the great establishment that bears his name. One morning, I found myself in that quarter of the city and so thought I would present my letter. Entering one of the big stock-yards, I saw an elderly man, very plainly dressed, who appeared to be occupied making some notes on a slip of paper ; going up to him, I asked where I could find Mr. Armour, as I had a letter of introduction to him. " What do you want him for ? " he asked. " Oh, only," I replied, " that he may, perhaps, send some clerk with me to show me over the factories."

" Don't bother about your letter," the man said, " I'll show you all you want to see."

I thanked him and away we started ; we passed from one building to another in this most wonderful business organization that perhaps the world has ever seen. The workmen, packers, and others took no notice of us as we went from place to place, until at the end of perhaps an hour I again reached the street. I thanked the man who had been my guide, and taking a dollar from my pocket, I was handing it to him, when, to my astonishment, he said : " There is no need to do that, I am Mr. Armour. Now give me your letter."

The millionaire, Marshall Field, was just as unassuming, so also was his partner, Harlow N. Higinbotham, even while he was President of the World's Fair. H. Gordon Selfridge, also a millionaire partner in the same gigantic establishment, was one of the quietest and most unassuming men I have ever met, and he remains the same to-day, even though he is in London and " Selfridge's " the talk of the town. In fact, if one wanted to select an example of the best kind of business men that America can produce, I do not think we could do better than to take H. Gordon Selfridge as that sample.

A " self-made man " and one proud to have such a title ; a man who rose from the ranks, but who, in the stern battle of life, won his commission by hard, honest, upward fighting. A man who at thirty was one of the principal directors of Marshall Field & Co., and who at a little over forty, sold out his interest in the great Chicago firm, and taking himself and his money to London, created in less than two years one of the largest, and certainly one of the most successful, establishments that the great heart of England's commerce has ever seen.

How well I remember the first evening that I had the pleasure of dining at his home in Chicago. He had come to me as one of my many unknown clients a few days before ; he had admitted he was amazed at the accurate delineation I had given him of his character, and perhaps also of the picture I had drawn of the still more successful future that lay before him. He was surprised that an examination of his hands could give such a record of his past career, and such indications of half-dreams and desires that like meteors from time to time had lit up the long nights of his early life. He felt, however, that I had told him the truth ; so before leaving, he handed me his card and invited me to his house to meet his wife and his aged mother who so recently passed over to the " Great Beyond."

Fifteen years later, I met him again in his London offices, with the plans spread out before him of the magnificent business building he was about to create. Pointing across to the other side of Oxford Street, he said :

" All those ramshackle shops and buildings you see there are coming down ; in their place, in a few months, I hope will rise a veritable Temple of Commerce, worthy of this great city."

H. Gordon Selfridge kept his word, and London owes to him to-day not only a magnificent building, but a House of Business that for organization and efficiency has, I believe, no equal in the world.

But to return to Chicago. At the Hotel Auditorium, I had a very fine suite of rooms on the first floor, and from these windows I enjoyed every day the view of Lake Michigan—an inland sea—that stretched away to the far-distant horizon. It was hard at times to realize that this great lake at my door was larger in extent than England and Wales, or, in fact, the British Isles with poor old Ireland thrown into the bargain.

My rooms became so crowded by applicants for interviews that it was finally found necessary for them to book appointments for as much as three or four weeks ahead ; and one point I specially admired about Americans was, that not only did they keep their appointments, but invariably *they were punctuality itself ;* also, when their allotted time—half an hour—was up, they willingly gave their place to the next visitor, so as not to keep others waiting.

I worked regularly, from nine o'clock to five, with just an hour off for lunch. As well as the appointments, I had classes every second evening, from eight o'clock to ten, and public lectures as well.

At my first lecture in Chicago at Steinway Hall, I was introduced to the audience by Judge William A. Vincent, and nearly always some public man acted as my chairman. These lectures, at which I showed, by a large stereopticon lantern, the autographed impressions of the hands of the most famous men and women of the day, were from a financial standpoint most successful, often in fact bringing in between one and two thousand dollars a lecture.

By a strange occurrence, the Chicago people themselves instituted a custom that brought me in more money for the last hour each afternoon than I often made during the entire run of my business day.

One evening, at five o'clock, just as I had finished with my last client, a lady and gentleman, strangers to one another, arrived in my outer reception room at the same moment, and the lady tried to persuade my secretary to arrange an appointment with me at once, when the gentleman said : " You are taking an unfair advantage both of ' Cheiro ' and of your sex, madam. We have arrived here at the same moment, if anything I was in advance."

" Very well," the lady replied, " if you think so, let the secretary auction off this extra appointment, and let it go to the highest bidder."

No sooner said than done. They began to bid against one another, the lady only stopping when the figure reached one thousand dollars (£200). Very politely the gentleman paid his money, took his appointment slip, and with a courteous bow, presented his ticket to the lady and walked out.

I never knew who one or the other was, but that was certainly the highest fee I ever received for a half-hour consultation.

In some way, however, the incident got known, and from that time it became quite a customary thing for two men or ladies to arrive about five o'clock and auction off that extra appointment, at prices ranging from five hundred dollars to one thousand.

It was in this way I made the acquaintance of Mr. Arthur Caton. Mr. Arthur Caton was one of the best-known men in Chicago. He strolled in one afternoon and bid up to five hundred dollars for his interview against another man. When his interview was over, he insisted on my coming out to dinner with him, at the Calmette Club, and from that day on to the time of his death, he always remained one of my best friends.

As a curious example of a prediction being verified almost literally and to an exact date, I cannot pass my experiences in Chicago without mentioning the case of Major John A. Logan. This man had bought one of my appointment cards from one of his friends, and as no names were ever asked by my secretary, and only numbered cards given, I had not the slightest idea who my visitor was.

His strong personality, however, attracted my attention, and I put my heart very much into my work. I fathomed out very quickly his tendencies and peculiarities, and then I proceeded, step by step, to unravel his future; but I had not gone very far before I came to a standstill, perhaps rather abruptly. "You have not so very long to live," I said; "I would strongly advise you to get out of business as soon as possible, straighten out all your affairs, as with your disposition, you would regret leaving things in a chaotic state."

He was a man of such a determined, strong will that I knew I could give it "straight from the shoulder," and that he would prefer me to do this.

"What do you imagine is likely to happen?" he said; "but weigh well your words before you answer, for I frankly admit," he added, "you have told me my past career so accurately that your words now may have great weight on what I may decide."

"Well, as you really want to know," I said, "I am sorry to say everything points to death for you just as you reach the age of thirty-five—and, further, the cause will not be from illness or disease of any kind, but instead, from a blow or injury to the head—instant death from this cause will be what I see will happen."

"I cannot imagine what it may come from," he said, very seriously, "unless it may be from the intense love of horses and riding which you have so well described as one of my chief enjoyments; but if it is possible to avoid the danger, well, when I come near the age you mention, I promise you I will not cross a horse's back. But let us leave this gloomy subject and tell me if you can about my business outlook at the present moment."

Giving me his date of birth, I worked out the immediate conditions for him, and the following was what the figures clearly indicated: "You must be risking everything at this moment in an enormous gamble; at the present time you may be able to get out of it, and perhaps make a considerable profit, but if you wait for even another few days, instead of gaining, you will, on the contrary, be a ruined man."

The prospect of death a few years off had not unnerved this well-dressed, handsome-looking young man, but my last words had such an effect that for a moment I thought he would faint.

"'Cheiro,'" he said, "I must tell you how close you have hit it. I will put the facts before you and then see if you still stick to what you say. I admit I am engaged in the biggest gamble of my life. You perhaps have seen in the papers that Joe Leiter has cornered the wheat market? Well, I am one of Joe's greatest friends, and I am in it with him for all I can carry. Now let me show you why I am going to argue the point that I am not running any danger of loss." So saying, he pulled back the curtains of the window and pointed out to Lake Michigan, which was covered with ice as far out as one's eyes could reach, and lay glistening like a sheet of silver under a brilliant moonlight sky.

"There," he said, "as long as this frost continues, not a wheat boat can leave Duluth, and enter Chicago. The price must go up by leaps and bounds.

I admit I was puzzled to answer him. I worked my figures out again and I tried to force my brain to find the solution. There was only one that would come. "I can't tell you where the danger lies," I replied, "I can only repeat, sell out as soon as possible every dollar you have in this gamble, and, believe me, you won't regret it."

He left me in a very undecided state of mind, but to the surprise of everyone, the following day he sold out every cent he had in that famous wheat corner.

All day long prices rose—the papers said a wheat famine was threatened, and that this was the greatest wheat corner ever known.

Towards six o'clock, Joe Leiter himself came in to see me and laughed good-humouredly at my forebodings. He was wearing a very handsome memento of his triumphs in the shape of a diamond bull scarf-pin that a lady had just given him, emblematic of his being at that moment the "bull" of the wheat market. He insisted on my coming out to dinner with some friends, and, of course, chaffed me several times during the evening.

It was, however, like the Feast of Belshazzar before the fall of Babylon.

At that very moment, a master mind was issuing his orders by wire and telephone, to thousands of men and boats at the icebound shore of Duluth, and wherever his enormous reserves of wheat were stored.

The famous Armour, whom Leiter had believed he had caught napping, roused himself as a general might have done on the eve of battle. All night long, his fleet of ice-breakers and boats with huge chains broke the passage clear at Duluth and across the lake into Chicago. When morning came, billions of tons of wheat were already *en route* and the great wheat corner was broken.

As everyone knows, Leiter lost millions of dollars and his father had to come to his rescue to preserve the name of the family that was later to give a Vicereine to India.

Major Logan not only saved himself, but had made a considerable profit, and a few days later he gave me a very handsome present as a souvenir.

I met him again during my last visit to Chicago. A Mr. Allen had given a dinner to me as a farewell, for I had announced that I was returning to London for several years. As I bade good-bye, Major Logan stood at the door and said : "Well, 'Cheiro,' this time I suppose it may be good-bye for ever, as in a few months I will have reached my fatal year of thirty-five "—(I had quite forgotten my prediction) —" Still, I may prove you wrong," he added; " I have sold every horse I possess and no one will catch me risking my head till I get my thirty-fifth year well over."

But how little we know whether it is given to us to avert our destiny or not! In less than three months, the Spanish-American War broke out and Major Logan was shot through the head when leading his men in a volunteer regiment, in one of the very first engagements.[1]

---

[1] " Of course you read of the death of Major John A. Logan. Was it not terrible? One of the last things he said to me before going to the war in the Philippines was that he was going to take good care of his head and not get killed as Cheiro had predicted. But alas! Cheiro's prediction was only too true. He was killed by a bullet wound in his head and was exactly thirty-five years old when it happened."

HARRIET HUBBARD AYER."

New York World, December 31st, 1899.

CHAPTER XXXIV

VISIT TO SALEM WHERE THE LAST WITCH IN THE UNITED STATES WAS BURNED AT THE STAKE. A BEAUTIFUL WOMAN SENT TO TRAP ME

BEFORE I left the Eastern States, I was invited to visit Salem and give a lecture in that historic town, where more Palmists and Astrologers had been tortured than any other place in the world, and where the last witch was burned at the stake in America.

I confess I thoroughly enjoyed the idea of giving a lecture on Hands, and proving the truth of the old study in such gruesomely historic surroundings.

Salem is not very far from Boston, and as the papers had made my name well known there, I found an extremely large audience assembled for the lecture. I had brought with me a large steriopticon lantern and slides to throw on the screen the impression of famous hands, such as Gladstone's, H. M. Stanley's, Joseph Chamberlain's, Bernhardt's, and dozens of others. I was just about to ring for the curtain to go up, when, to my amazement, a police inspector walked across the stage from the back, and holding up his hand, forbade the curtain to rise.

He was extremely polite but told me very firmly that by one of the old laws of that State which had never been altered since the last poor witch was burned, it was absolutely forbidden to allow any person to expound in any form whatever such a subject as Palmistry, or any other such "works of the Devil," and that any person found doing so for payment of any kind would be arrested and subjected to the direst penalties.

After reading the enactment, he requested me to step before the curtain and announce that the lecture could not take place.

I think it must have been the spirit of that last poor witch that was burned at Salem that prompted me to do what I did, for I am sure my poor brain would never have thought of a way out of such a position.

I stepped before the curtain and informed the audience that by an old law of their State no lecture on such a subject as Palmistry could take place in Salem. The most absolute silence followed my statement.

"Now, ladies and gentlemen," I proceeded, "as law-abiding citizens, you cannot be expected to break the laws of your own State, no matter how obsolete or absurd some of them may be; but as intelligent men and women you may be expected to adapt yourselves to the altered conditions under which you now live; and, further, to derive benefit from having used your intelligence to circumvent the stupidity that called this law into existence, I will now proceed to suggest to you how this may be done, and at the same time, with your help, let us try to bring good out of evil.

"The Act says that no exposition of Palmistry or any such studies

191

of the Devil can be given *for payment of any kind whatever*. I therefore propose that you will accept my services to-night as a gift to you, and that all moneys you have paid for your seats be given to whatever charities you may wish to benefit by this lecture."

As unanimous applause greeted this proposition, I returned behind the curtain and asked the inspector if he were satisfied now that the lecture under these conditions could proceed.

"Yes," he said, laughing, " you can go on—the only pity is that you were not born an American."

I did not wait for the subsequent division of the profits, so I can only hope that *the police charities* of Salem were included in the benefits derived from that evening's lecture on one of the principal studies of the Devil.

A Beautiful Woman sent to Trap me

In reading these confessions of a strange career, people must not be carried away by the idea that a man so favoured by making hosts of good friends may not also have had some dangerous traps laid for him, either by enemies or by those envious of his success.

In a later chapter I will give an account of the attempt made on my life while practising in New York. Now I will give the following account of a trap laid for my honour in Chicago.

One afternoon as I was finishing my work for the day, my secretary informed me that there was a lady waiting who had specially insisted on having the last appointment. She had explained her insistence by saying that she had a great deal to ask me, and that an ordinary half-hour would not be sufficient for her purpose.

As I knew well that when Americans insist on a thing it is only waste of time to argue the point; although very tired after a long day, I agreed and my secretary ushered the lady into my consulting-room.

A tall and extremely well-dressed woman entered; she threw back her veil and disclosed as beautiful a face as I think I have ever seen. I would not have been human if I had not admired her. She was dressed in black—a curious mixture of silk and jet, that showed every line of her slight, graceful figure to perfection. As she drew off her gloves her delicately shaped hands were a positive delight; they were so exquisitely formed and so artistic that an artist would have been enchanted by them.

To my amazement, instead of placing them on my cushion before me, she drew out a finely carved cigarette-case and offered me a very tempting Turkish cigarette.

I was, however, thinking of my work; and in spite of my long experience, wondering—even half fearfully—whether I would be successful with my client or not. Seeing my hesitation, she laughed sweetly, and said: " My dear man, don't bother trying to convert me.

Cheiro's predictions of my future will influence me in all my dealings, because I am so impressed by the extraordinary precision with which he read my past.

Lillie Langtry.

Nov. 11th/99.

A STRIKING TESTIMONY FROM LILLIE LANGTRY
(LADY DE BATHE)

Life is like the cigarette I offer you—very quickly consumed and but a little dust and ashes at the end."

She had forgotten, however, that I was nothing more nor less than a sensitive instrument, and that although I looked young, I had the experience of many lives crowded into my own; and that in spite of her laughing mask, I had already come into contact with her crushed and wounded soul, *and pity was the only feeling* she had aroused within me.

"We can smoke a cigarette afterwards," I said, "but meanwhile let me see your hands."

"Oh, my hands have nothing in them," she said, "at twenty-four a woman has neither lines in her face nor in her hands."

"And yet a baby an hour old," I replied, "has lines that tell its future—lines that could they speak would even tell its burden of heredity—*the fate that perhaps its mother made for it*, and that later she would give her life *to unmake*, if it were possible."

I had unknowingly touched the tender spot in the nature of that mysterious piece of humanity before me; her hands opened, and very quietly she laid them before me.

The chart of her own life appeared so clear that I could hardly have made a mistake in it had I tried. The early surroundings, the strict home life, the beautiful voice that had promised to make her a great singer, the love affair at eighteen—her desertion at twenty—the birth of her child. Then the struggle for existence, the flight from one city to another, her desire for money that her little one might be fed, the strangling of everything that was refined, so that *it might live*. The tiger-like fierceness of that mother nature that was willing to cover itself with blood or crime, *if only she could protect her child from the same fate*—such had been the making of the woman before me.

She drew her hands away; taking a letter from a satchel, she handed it to me without speaking. The heading of it was a Chicago newspaper, and the letter ran as follows:

"Dear Miss So-and-so,

Almost every paper in the City has had laudatory articles about this man 'Cheiro' at the Auditorium Hotel. I want to take the opposite track to get up some sensation about him—*some scandal*, if possible. You are the woman to do it; the price will be good. Let me have the story as quickly as possible.

Yours, etc."

The woman rose and went across to the writing table and wrote the following:

"Dear Mr. Editor,

I tried this evening to obey your instructions—but I have failed. Further, let me tell you if you attempt to get up 'some scandal' about this man I will immediately publish your letter and show up your game.

Yours, etc."

I tried to thank her, but with a sob in her voice she said:

"It was my child that saved you. You can thank her 'Cheiro.' I can only ask you to forgive me."

CHAPTER XXXV

AN EXTRAORDINARY GAMBLE. THE SHARES OF A METALLURGICAL COMPANY THAT ACTUALLY MADE GOLD

DURING my last winter in Chicago, I met under peculiar circumstances a celebrated half-breed French-Indian, named Henri Dupont,[1] and it was through him I went in myself for a strange gamble in shares, even though I had foretold by his hand that there was no success before him at that period of his life. But Henri Dupont was an extraordinary personality, and though I lost by my gamble, I have nothing but thanks to give him for an unusual experience that taught me a great deal.

I was sitting down to dinner in my own rooms in the Auditorium Hotel one night, when something made me glance up from my evening paper, and I beheld one of the most marked-looking types of humanity I think I have ever seen, standing in the doorway.

This man, though only of medium size, had the head and bearing of a lion, and with a mass of rough, shaggy, black hair, tossed back from his head, he looked, at least at that moment, exactly like " the noble king of beasts." As I glanced up from the head of my table, our eyes met and we quietly looked at one another for a few minutes without speaking.

With an inborn courtesy which there was no mistaking, seeing me sitting waiting for dinner, he evidently hesitated to come in, and yet did not seem to be able to make a graceful retreat.

I got up and said, " Well, you have evidently come to dine with me, have you not ? "

" Yes," he replied, " if you have the goodness to invite me."

" Certainly, my dear sir," I answered, " where there is enough for one, there is always plenty for two. Come in and dine, by all means." And I placed a chair for him on my right.

With every movement speaking of courtesy and refinement, he held out his hand, apologizing for being very roughly dressed ; he sat down at the table as if his dining with me was the most natural thing in the world.

As the light struck his face, I saw at once that he was a half-breed Indian, and as I have always had the greatest admiration for the rapidly dying-out Indian tribes of North America, his having their blood in his veins interested me immensely.

Seeing that my negro waiter was threatened with a fit of apoplexy at seeing me dining with such a wild-looking stranger, I ordered him to place all the dishes on the sideboard and leave us alone. When he had disappeared, I poured out a glass of wine[2] for my unknown guest, and said :

" And now, my dear sir, perhaps you will favour me by telling me who on earth you are."

" Willingly," he replied. " I am Henri Dupont, a half-breed French-

---

[1] This is not the man's real name.　　[2] Many years before Prohibition.

Canadian-Indian, of the Sioux tribe, the companion of Louis Riel, who fought against the English. I was taken prisoner and sentenced to death, but escaped by swimming the St. Lawrence with a bullet in my shoulder that an over-zealous sentry lodged in me. I am outlawed from Canada, but quite content to live the rest of my life under the Stars and Stripes, or to give my life for them if need be. Such is a brief idea of my history, but my desire to come and meet you will take a little longer to explain."

Then this strange individual launched out and told me something of his philosophy—a philosophy of right living, a picture of self-sacrifice and noble ideals that was equalled by nothing I had ever heard of or read before.

He was a rebel against everything that was false; a natural rebel against the hundred and one injustices that Society has consecrated by time and hallowed into the name of Law. His blood boiled at the starving-out of his race, the expropriation of their possessions, the cruelties of the white man against his brother of another colour, and in a few rapid words he sketched out a marvellous redeeming plan of his own, which even embraced his enemies, the white man and the white woman coming equally into his scheme of the fitness of things and the ultimate uplifting of all humanity by the realization that Man was made in "the image and likeness of God," and that all men were brothers.

I listened spellbound until he had finished. "But your plan," I asked, "how can it be carried out?"

"Through the possession of wealth," he answered, "unlimited wealth, but utilized as God has intended wealth to be used."

"But where is this wealth to come from?" I asked, "it increases only in the hands of those who have it—remember a very hard, but true-to-life text, which says: 'Unto him that hath shall be given, but to him that hath not, shall be taken away *even that which he hath.*'"

He answered me by a strange story, but one so wonderful that the mines of the world and the gold of the earth seemed even as nothing before his plan.

Briefly, it was as follows: A young American chemist had discovered how in the womb of Nature metals had been formed, how gold had been born, how precious jewels had been created. Would I come to meet this man? He was no figment of the imagination, no dream of the idealist, he was a real living entity, whose success had already been so great that even at that moment, on the outskirts of that very city, we would find this man with an installation of furnaces and plant which was in itself a marvel, and which had astonished every scientist who had been permitted to see it.

Of course, I agreed to go. Why should not such things be? Has man discovered *all the secrets of Nature?* Every day things are discovered which upset former theories and go to prove that the mysteries of yesterday are no longer mysteries in the light of to-day.

In a few minutes I had a carriage at the hotel door, and away we started for—to me—some unknown place, far out on the fringe of the city.

Three-quarters of an hour's drive with a good pair of horses at last brought us before a large building, half brick and galvanized sheet-iron, that stood by itself in dreary solitude among frozen fields.

My strange guide opened the side-door with a key and led me through several badly lighted passages, until at last we reached a large square room in the centre of the building.

At a long table sat a young man, with microscopes and instruments before him, deeply engaged in examining some samples of a substance that looked like clay.

Dupont introduced me as a friend for whom he would answer with his life, and the young fellow gave me a manly grip of the hand and placed a chair for me at the table.

It was then I realized for the first time what the purpose of Dupont's visit had been in coming to see me. He wanted me to look at this man's hand and see if the success they were hoping for was about to be an accomplished fact.

Again I had found an interesting subject as a study, but, let me say, *en passant*, that America is full of such types. With her mixture of races, her electrical-inspiring climate, her unlimited natural resources, the conditions of life, all help to make her soil the breeding-ground of genius, and the home of invention.

Do not imagine for one moment that the young man before me had one particle of the charlatan or the impostor in his nature. On the contrary, I beheld a man—young, scarcely thirty—if you like, but an earnest student, a scientist in a workman's garb, and a genius in his own particular line of research.

Do not think for a moment that I am indulging in romance—the only romance about this young chemist was the wonder of his work.

Some years before I met him, he had, as a chemist's assistant, saved enough money to enable him to visit and study every well-known volcano in the world; whilst other tourists were seeing Rome or gazing out over the far-famed Bay of Naples, this young scientist was at the same moment risking his life by being let down by a steel rope inside Vesuvius, in order to wrest some of the secrets of Nature from her very heart.

He finally discovered certain laws about the application of heat and the affinities of clays and metals; in the end he had returned to New York and invented a furnace that dissolved clay and sand in such a manner that beautiful white stone in the shape of bricks were produced, which discovery the inventor sold for a considerable sum of money.

He wanted capital, however, for a totally different purpose than the mere manufacture of white bricks, for with this capital he built up the factory I saw outside Chicago, with the express purpose of making gold in a similar manner that Mother Earth did, when as a molten mass of matter she was herself called into being.

It would take far too long to enter into the scientific aspect of his discoveries in these pages; the majority of my readers will probably reject his theories as the dreams of a madman, or deem me a fool for writing about them; or in their superior wisdom (?) they will perhaps shrug their narrow shoulders at his giving up the " brick factory " at New York in search of such a chimera as the manufacture of gold.

Yet, it is to such people as this man represented that the world to-day owes some of its greatest inventions and discoveries. If Monsieur and Madame Curie had not succeeded in their search for radium, they would both have been doomed to end their days in some miserable attic, and, further, would have been scoffed at for their pains. But they succeeded, and to-day their names are honoured ones—the world's pain has been relieved by their toil—Fame has lifted them with her own hands to sit side by side with her on her throne, and those who would have jeered are to-day silent with admiration.

Up to a certain point, the man of whom I write also succeeded.

In the subsequent days on which I visited his " factory," I saw with my own eyes gold extracted from his crucibles, and in such quantities that one day the total reached a little over £2000 paid over to him *by the Government Mint;* and further, the price he got for his gold was as high as any that has ever been given for the precious metal extracted from the famous gold mines of California.

Further, hard-headed men in Chicago bought shares in his little company, these shares rose to treble their value in a few months, and a little later one could not buy these twenty-dollar par value shares from brokers under *four hundred and fifty dollars* each.

His volcanic heat also produced precious stones, and it was quite a common every-day occurrence to find quite a number of rubies, garnets, and sapphires in the hard rock substance found in the crucibles when they were cooled off and broken open.

Was it any wonder then that Henri Dupont had dreamt of untold wealth to carry out his humanitarian plans?

I shall never forget that moment when, to please him, I examined his young friend's hands. Under the strong light in the laboratory, his face looked so white and careworn that I would fain have told him of anything but failure in his hopes.

On every side of him were evidences of success; probably no less than ten glass jars of small rubies stood on the table by my side; a leather bag of very small, but fine, gold nuggets lay under his hands, a kind of cushion, so that I might better examine them, and yet, though I read every possible evidence of his brain power and extraordinary intelligence, I could see nothing of the fortune that they both expected. I told them exactly what I saw, but I am glad to add that my words brought neither of them disappointment or caused a cloud to cross their faces. They were quite accustomed to people doubting that such a thing could be done as the extraction of gold from broken-up stone and powdered clay. I only succeeded in making them doubt me, that was all ; in fact, I doubted myself and before I left asked that I might purchase a few thousand shares in the concern.

Things went on very well with the " factory " for the following six weeks, and many an evening after my work was over, I drove out with Dupont to see what the developments of the day had been.

Then the severest winter that Chicago had known for ages set in rapidly, and with snow so deep that I was for a fortnight practically weather-bound in my hotel.

The shares of the company had about this time reached four hundred and fifty dollars, and I was rather regretting I had not bought a larger quantity, when one evening Dupont rapped on my door.

" Well," I said, " what's the matter ? "

" With this terrible snow and frost," he groaned, " we can't get a load of material to the works ; the land up at Utah, where we get our clay from, is covered twenty feet deep with snow, and even if we could get at it, there is not a railway that could send us a wagon load. We have closed down all the furnaces but one ; *if the newspapers should get to hear of it they will talk about the stoppage and put it down to any cause but the right one."*

" But is there no means of getting the material from any other place but these lands in Utah ? " I asked.

" I fear not," Dupont replied. " We analysed all kinds of earth before we found the particular kind that gives exactly the properties that are needed ; but come out with me to the works to-night."

It was with the greatest difficulty that we got to the " factory." In many of the outlying streets the snow was over three feet deep and frozen solid with the terrible frost.

At last we reached the works. Our young friend was no longer sitting in his brightly lighted laboratory, as before ; we found him upstairs, lying on his bed, utterly prostrated by the load of anxiety he was bearing. In a few minutes we were joined by four other men, who also had interests in the company, and together we sat around a table and held a " council of war."

Every possible plan was discussed ; at last we decided that the only thing to do was to keep the news as long as possible from the newspapers and trust that the frost might break, so that the clay needed could be sent down from Utah.

It was further decided that the one furnace still running should be kept at full blast day and night, so that the outsiders would not notice that anything was amiss, and above all, that no stranger should be admitted on any pretence whatever.

Now let me speak of the loyalty of the men the young inventor had around him. There was not one man among those he employed who did not offer to stand by him and see the siege of winter fought out to the finish. Every man of them volunteered to sleep in the factory, as a safeguard against being approached or questioned by strangers, or offered some bribe that might have tempted some weak brother, who had a wife or children depending on him. It was the finest example of loyalty I have ever seen.

And among those of us who had put our money into the business, the loyalty was just the same; the shares still stood at four hundred and fifty dollars, and during the week of the siege that followed, *not one of us sold as much as a single share.*

Many of us could have made a small fortune by selling out, but we knew if we did, others would follow—the price would come down—questions would be asked in the Press, and the situation discovered.

That we could have sold, there was no question—during that week I alone received no less than five offers from buyers; but as I said before, not one of us who knew the position sold as much as a single share.

At last the week came to an end. There was no sign of the frost breaking, the reports said it was likely to last for the next two months, and with such a prospect we knew there could be no hope.

The inventor decided to call a general meeting of shareholders, and explain the position to them, and notices were sent out for the following Saturday, at eight o'clock in the evening. This extraordinary hour was decided on so as to meet the convenience of many shareholders who were engaged in business during the day.

The night came, but it was so severe that not more than about fifty persons assembled together. The meeting was held in a long room by the side of the works, and the cold was so great that we left the door of the only furnace that was still running open, so that we might get the benefit of its heat.

It was an impressive meeting. Dupont sat on the right of the inventor, I was on his left, at the head of a long table at the top of the room.

The inventor, in a straightforward, businesslike speech, explained the position in a few terse words, and then sat down.

Henri Dupont immediately followed, and in one of the finest fighting speeches I think I have ever listened to, backed up his chairman's remarks, and advocated that a vote of confidence should be passed and funds provided, if necessary, to carry on the works until the frost would break and the wagons came in from Utah.

A howl of dissent prevented any efforts to second the proposal, and in a few moments the meeting was in disorder.

One man, with a yell of rage, sprang at the inventor, but Dupont, quick as a flash, covered him with his body, and whipping out his revolver, faced the crowd and held the situation.

The quietest man in the room was the young man on my right. Pushing Dupont aside, he held up his hand for silence, and then speaking very calmly, said:

"I will prove to you that I am neither a swindler nor a charlatan. I ask you to select six men who will obey my instructions; these men will, before your eyes, fill the crucibles, place them in the furnace, you will control the test for yourselves, and then judge as you like afterwards. Will you accept my proposition?"

"Yes, came from a dozen voices at once.

The six men were selected, I happened to be one of them. We entered the works where the one furnace was still in full blast.

In a few words we were told what to do. In one corner were some pieces of rock that were left over from the last wagon-load from Utah. One man with a machine crushed them into powder; another went into the yard and with a shovel dug up a few buckets full of ordinary common earth from under the snow; two other men attended the furnace; and another with myself filled up the crucibles.

When all was ready, the crucibles were run into the furnace and in dead silence we waited for the result.

Holding his watch in his hand and looking at the thermometer, the inventor stood like a statue near the furnace door. It was one of his own special inventions where by an ingenious system of draught and concentrated heat, he was able to obtain the temperature required in a very short space of time.

At a given moment, he ordered the man in charge of the furnace to withdraw the crucibles. Out they came, a brilliant mass of white heat —so bright that one could not look at them without using smoked glasses.

Again, before our gaze they went through a rapid cooling process—when sufficiently cold they were opened and a solid mass was presented to us. Two analysts, who were shareholders, broke what looked like pieces of solid rock open, and there to the amazement of everyone who crowded round, small clear veins of pure gold could be seen glittering under the rays of the big arc lamp over our heads. One by one, the men examined it, picked the gold out with their penknives, and commented on it.

Half an hour, perhaps, passed; every person there was convinced that we had indeed assisted at something that was almost akin to a miracle. Suddenly, someone said: "Where is he?"

But where was he? That was the question. Through the works they went, yelling his name, up to that simple room with a camp-bed he had called his bedroom, they mounted. *He was nowhere to be found!* Poor Dupont, with a look on his face like a broken-hearted man, searched and searched in every corner of the place, in vain!

. . . .

The night had worn on. One by one, the crowd had slipped away, the furnace was dying out, and the silence of the place was only broken by the footsteps of an old workman who was turning off the lights.

I went up to Dupont and tried to rouse him from a kind of stupor he seemed to have fallen into.

"Come back with me," I said. "It is no use stopping here."

Without saying a word, he assented. After a long dreary drive through the snow, we at last reached my hotel.

"Come in and have something to eat and a rest," I suggested.

With a strange, weary look in his eyes, he shook his head. "No," he said, "I must find my friend." He wrung my hand silently and turned back into the snow and the night, and from that day to this I have never heard of him or of his friend the inventor.

The next day the papers were already full of the story. Some of those who only a few weeks before had nothing but praise for "an American chemist's discovery" were in less than twenty-four hours as equally keen on the mad absurdity of his idea. By Monday morning the shares that had the week before stood at four hundred and fifty dollars were offered without a bid at twenty-five cents apiece.

People need not scoff at the idea that the young inventor I have described in this story did make gold out of earth, stones, and clay— or run away with the idea that he was either a madman or a charlatan. In *The World Magazine* of June 26th, 1916, in an interview with Rudolph M. Hunter, of Philadelphia—a man who ranks third after Edison among the great patentees of the world, a recognized scientist, and an inventor with a world-wide reputation—declared: "I *can* manufacture gold, not only from baser metals, but from *common mineral substances, such as stone.* I can make it at a cost of less than a tenth of the present value, but I have made it so far only as the demonstrated result of scientific research, and not for commercial profit."

Perhaps poor Henri Dupont and his friend, the young chemist, failed in their great plan only because they had lived a little "in advance of the age."

CHAPTER XXXVI

AN INVITATION TO A CHATAUQUA. A METHODIST ASSEMBLY IN FLORIDA
AND SOME CURIOUS EXPERIENCES

AT the height of my season in Chicago I received one day a letter of invitation from the Rev. Dr. Davidson asking me to come and lecture before his Chatauqua in Florida.

The chance of leaving that terribly severe winter of the north to revel under the glorious sun of the southern States and spend some time among the orange groves and flowers of Florida, overcame the practical in my nature, so gladly I decided to stop the niagara of Chicago dollars and accept the invitation.

For the sake of European readers I must explain what a Chatauqua is, otherwise they might perhaps think I was going to teach a Red Indian camp some of the secrets of my art.

Well, a Chatauqua is, I believe, the very cleverest idea that the Methodist body in America ever conceived. Briefly, it is an educational system whereby its members meet at different parts in the States to hear lectures on every subject imaginable, to attend classes, and to live in one great happy community with the brotherly link of their religion as a kind of family tie pervading the whole.

A service of prayer and the heartiest singing imaginable opens the day and closes it at night. These services the members of the Chatauqua can attend or not, just as they please, the same way they can take any course of instruction they like, any set or series of lectures, or if they prefer it they can do nothing, just live in peace and harmony with their fellows and enjoy the beautiful scenery of the country in which the Chatauqua is held.

At the same time, and here is where this plan is so wonderfully intelligent, the whole country for hundreds of miles round is invited to regard this meeting-place as one common centre—special trains and excursions at cheap fares are run daily from all points of the compass, and it is quite an ordinary thing for from four to five thousand people to find themselves gathered together to attend some lecture, concert, or entertainment in the large arena and return home at night both mentally and spiritually improved by their visit.

With such an excellent idea well organized and carried out in various States, it is no wonder that the Methodist body in America is one of the largest and most united of all the religious communities in that "land of many religions."

But to resume, the Chatauqua of which Dr. Davidson was the head was situated in one of the loveliest parts of Florida not far from the beautiful old-world Bay of Pensacola in the Gulf of Mexico. I call it advisedly "an old-world Bay" for I never in all my life experienced the same sensation of rest and peace as we changed trains, and for some hours I wandered through the quaint streets of this old town with its memories of the Spanish Main, or gazed across the tranquil vista of its semi-inland sea, whose blue waters bathed the wounds of the storm-torn ships that came, from—God only knows where, to rest for a while and be at peace.

And such ships! I doubt if in all the world one could find such a quaint collection of types.

Brigs with torn sails with no sound of life on their battered decks, ships that rode silently at anchor like ghosts that had come up in the night from the Saragossa Sea. Farther out rakish-looking low black schooners came in with the dawn and as mysteriously slipped away in the night. Some there were with broken yards or " main mast gone by the board " that looked like old men who had fought the storm of life and after many trials had reached a haven of peace. I felt I wanted to break my journey and rest here—like one of those weary ocean tramps that had carried too many burdens.

After the cold of the northern winter the warmth of the southern skies seemed so good that I did not want to go any farther, but my American manager had already telegraphed our arrival that night, and so with many a regret I went on board an evening train and arrived at the Chatauqua towards midnight.

I would like to go slowly—even that train crawled along—for how could anything animate or inanimate tear through orange groves, forests of pine, and garlands of wild flowers!

At last the station was reached and I found Dr. Davidson himself waiting to bid us welcome. He seemed surprised at my " suite," for I had come down with my American manager, his English wife, my Hindu secretary, and a servant.

We walked from the station up to the Chatauqua Hotel under a starlit night that was indescribable in its beauty.

As we drew near the " Colony " we saw in the distance the enormous building or arena capable of seating four or five thousand people, where the following evening my lecture was to be given. As we passed it, Dr. Davidson made a curious remark. He said, " I am sorry, in a way, you look such a young man.

" I have advertised you far and wide, there are several excursion trains coming, and my only fear is how such an audience is going to take a lecture on the subject of Hands.

" For the first time in my experience of arranging these gatherings I have perhaps made a mistake ; if they should give your strange subject a hostile reception, I fear you are too young to control such an audience."

My reply was perhaps a strange one to give to a Methodist minister : " Doctor," I said, " *don't let us shake hands with the devil till we meet him.*"

Nine o'clock in the morning I strolled out into the grounds and met the Doctor returning from the morning service.

" Well, Doctor," I asked, " how is the devil this morning ? "

" Very bad indeed," he laughed, " and we have not only one to face —but two.

" I have just received a strong protest from some of the members against your being aloud to lecture on our platform on such a tabooed subject as a Study of Hands ; the second trouble is that the concert arranged for three o'clock is doomed, as the train from the north bringing the entertainers is held up by a forest fire which has swept across the track less than fifty miles from here. So now what do you think of our two devils ? "

" I think," I answered, " that you are far too good a Methodist to be afraid of two devils, or even a legion of them, and as far as the concert is concerned I can easily help you out."

He looked at me in surprise. " It happens," I continued, " that my American manager is an excellent pianist, his wife, an Englishwoman, has a most beautiful voice ; she was in fact a celebrated concert singer before she married. I will get her to give her services to-day, and between her songs I will come on and give some recitations. You need not mention the name of ' Cheiro,' just say that owing to the fire the entertainers expected were prevented from getting here, but that another troupe will give an impromptu entertainment in their place. You will find, my dear Doctor, that we have got rid of Devil No. 1, and Devil No. 2 may never even turn up."

So as not to upset my plan, I did not show myself about the hotel or grounds all day, and a little before two o'clock we quietly slipped into the stage entrance at the back of the arena.

Clouds of smoke from the fire were by this time rolling across the sky. Dr. Davidson announced in a brief speech that the advertised concert could not be given, but that he had arranged for another entertainment in its place ; he was greeted with loud applause.

The " celebrated English prima donna " then made her appearance. She was an extremely handsome woman with a superb dramatic soprano voice. She had chosen to sing a series of English songs. The first she opened with was " The Last Rose of Summer." One could have heard a pin drop in that huge audience when the final notes of the old song died away. I think I have never heard such a burst of applause in all my life ; they would not let her off the stage until she had sung it over at least three times.

It was then my turn. Without any announcement as to my name, or who I was, or what I was going to do, I stepped out on the platform. I had intended to give them some serious piece, but as I caught Dr. Davidson's eye our friend the devil came into my mind, and I announced that humorous poem, " The Devil in search of a Wife."

I evidently could not have chosen anything better for a Methodist audience ; they seemed to enjoy themselves thoroughly, and I had to recite it again before they allowed me to escape.

After more songs I was again recalled, and then occurred one of those opportunities that fit in so marvellously with the threads of destiny that design and purpose seemed for a few seconds as if woven together.

A few months previously I had read, like many thousands of others, the stirring story of how an engine driver, racing his train against a forest fire, had stopped and taken on board every person at the village of Hinckley in Minnesota, that was threatened with certain disaster, and in the end not only saved his own passengers, but all the inhabitants of Hinckley as well.

The heroism of this man on the engine had stirred me so much that I had put it into a poem, which some kind critics have been pleased to praise as " a dramatic piece of writing." I had never thought of using this poem in public before, but now the opportunity was about to be given me of testing its power on an audience and with a stage setting that seemed made for the occasion.

All day long, the clouds of smoke from the burning forest that had prevented Dr. Davidson's entertainers from reaching the Chatauqua had been rolling across the sky—the smell of the burning timber was heavy in the air, and now as I stood there facing this large audience, the windows had become darkened with smoke, while great sullen clouds seemed to hang like a pall of destruction over the open roof of the large arena. It was a stage setting made as it were for the poem, " The Burning of Hinckley," and so also it must be my excuse for quoting the verses here.

THE BURNING OF HINCKLEY

An Incident of Western Life

" ' All aboard ! all aboard ! ' the clang of the engine-bell,
An' we stretched our hands thro' the windows, an' bade them a long farewell.
We were going back to the East, sir, for Jack had a vow to keep—
' A wife in bond,' I believe he said, an' he was behind a week.
But that wasn't due to bein' careless, sir, but due to that awful drought
An' the fires about the farmstead that had kept us for weeks in doubt ;
For they rose when we thought them conquered—if you ever have lost your rest
By travellin' across the country, you may know what a blaze is West.

Well, this year it was somethin' awful, for the forests were all on fire,
An' waves of flame for miles and miles rose higher an' ever higher,
An' the oldest in Minnesota could not, in their bygone days,
Remember or even imagine the fierceness of that last blaze.
If you've seen a West'rn fire, sir, you know what I mean when I say
That pictures of the Judgment ain't in it, by a long, long way,
With those forests of pine an' undergrowth, an' grass eight feet in height,
That somehow catch fire and blaze, sir, ay, morn an' noon an' night.

But Jack an' myself had won, sir ; we were safe in the railroad train,
With many a burn on our face an' hands, with many a scar an' stain,
But stains from honest toil, sir, an' 'tis such makes the noblest crest ;
Those are the heraldic signs, sir, that we honour an' love out West.
But we'd soon be back in the East now—we hadn't been home for years—
An' as we talked of the dear old place, I saw in Jack's eyes big tears ;
For he was the kin' o' chap, sir, who'd never say die in a fight,
While the name of home or mother in a moment would queer his sight.

We'd been sittin' still for hours, sir, for the noise an' burr of the train
Had a kind of soothin' calmin' effect after such weeks of strain,
When Jack, he bent over an' roused me, an' pointed away to the right,
Where a bank of smoke rose up to the sky, black as the wings of night ;
With a kin' o' shake in his voice, too, he whispered within my ear :
' Mate, if yon forest takes fire, it will be over with us, I fear.'

I laughed at him for a moment, till I saw that the woods behind
Lay right in the arms of the fire an' straight in the teeth of the wind ;
And before us on either side, sir, they stretched like a great dark wall,
With that cloud of smoke comin' onward, with a shape like a funeral pall ;
An' my heart stood still in my bosom for them childer and women folk
Who were standin' up in the windows, half scared by the blindin' smoke.

On, on, went the train in the darkness, for, tho' it was only noon,
It was black as pitch all around us—ay, dark as the day of doom ;
But away we went tearin' onward, each second increasin' our speed,
For there was a man in that engine, a hero in thought an' in deed—
A man who a few weeks before, sir, was disgraced for aidin' a strike,
But face to face with our danger, he showed what a hero is like ;

For what did he do at Hinckley ?—tho' he hadn't a moment to spare—
He brought that train to a stand, sir, an' took on the few that were there.
For Hinckley was burned to ashes, an' before our nigh sightless eyes
The flames of each cottage an' homestead rose up to the blackened skies,
An' the bodies of men and cattle, escapin' in their mad flight,
Were o'ertaken and burned together—ay, almost before our sight.

But that hero there on the engine, he wouldn't pull off from the place
Till he'd saved full many a hundred—then he entered for that mad race.
An' you should have seen how the wheels flew ; but were they ten times as fast,
Full many of us on the cars, sir, had reckoned that day as our last ;
For the fire had burst through the forest—Oh God ! how it seemed to gain !
As it neared us, an' neared us, an' neared us, till the heat of the flyin' train
Scorched us, as huddled together like cattle we lay on the floor,
Half blind by the smoke an' the flames—half dead by that awful roar ;
For the tongues of fire that followed seemed to hiss with the sparks that fell :
Like the hiss of a million demons let loose from the flames of hell.

. . . .

An' Jack, he suddenly whispered : ' If it should be your fate to get thro'
I want you to tell my old woman that I did just as good as I knew
While struggling to make her a homestead, an' while I was out in the West
I was always honest and upright—I tried to do what was best ;
An' tell her, mate, how I loved her, an' how in this moment of doom——'
But Jack didn't finish his sentence, for he fell at my feet in a swoon.
An' I took him up in my arms, sir, an' I fought to get him some air,
An' I carried him up to the engine, but I laid him down in despair,
For the flames were leapin' around it—ay, leapin' up higher an' higher,
Till the only thing you could see, sir, was a blindin' white sheet of fire.

I'd have lost my head at that moment if I hadn't caught hold of the sight
Of two brave lads on the engine still out in the thick of the fight ;
Their clothes were burnt on their back, sir, the cab of the engine was red,
The flesh of their hands was blistered—still the furnace they rapidly fed
As they urged that engine onwards, for they knew that a swampy creek
Was lyin' not far before them, an' they made for that narrow streak.

I looked back at the train for a second—oh God ! what an awful sight !
For the fire had reached the end, now, an' that car was a blaze of light.
An' the rest were about to follow, when, sickened, I turned away—
But there, just lyin' ahead, sir, was the first faint glimpse of the day ;
An' there lay the creek before us—I tried to call for a cheer,
To tell to the comrades behind us of help and relief so near.
But my heart nigh stopped for dread, sir, for the fire was well in reach,
An' sappin' each post and each pillar, an' lickin' each rod an' rail,
Oh God ! it was awful to see it—ay, awful just then to fail.
But those heroes there on the engine, they thought they'd a moment to spare—
We were out on the bridge in a second—there wasn't e'en time for a prayer—
When away went the blazin' timbers—a crash and a deafenin' roar ;
But we'd crossed, sir—crossed in safety—an' were safe on the other shore."

. . . . . .

An' now for a cheer for those heroes ; if you love to give honour its due,
If you value your country's record of deeds that are great and true,
If you'd like to encourage duty, and actions both brave and right,
Give a ringin' cheer for those heroes, be they far or near to-night.

It was really a great moment of pleasure to hear the applause that followed. I was recalled again and again, I had won the hearts of the audience, and quick as a flash I determined to use my popularity for the advantage of that study that had been so associated with my life.

When at last I could get silence, stepping to the edge of the platform, in a few brief words I told them that I would have the pleasure of meeting them again that evening, when under the name of " Cheiro " I had been engaged to give a lecture on Hands. I made the following bargain and conditions : that if at the end of the first ten minutes they could not pass a unanimous vote that the subject was one that appealed to their reason, and was worthy of their platform, I would stop—and every person in the audience would receive their money back at the doors.

I had the largest audience that night I ever had in my life, and instead of remaining a few days, I remained for three weeks. On the evening before my departure I was given a farewell reception that is one of my happiest memories.

I carried away from this great Florida Chatauqua among many souvenirs two that are very dear to me, one from Dr. Davidson which he wrote in my autograph book :

> " In preparing programmes for my various Chatauqua assemblies, I am constantly on the look out for something new and entertaining. I heard of ' Cheiro,' and with the least bit of mental reservation as to the advisability of my course, I asked him to come to the Florida Chatauqua. I am glad I did. He won instant recognition and made hosts of friends.
>
> He is unaffected and unassuming, and wins not so much by bombastic presentation of great exploits and commendations of the Great who have become his friends, as by the quiet and

logical putting of the facts he has discovered in the study of his science.

He uses exquisite English, and has great power to please and hold an audience whether they agree with him or not. The moral tone of all he says is uplifting and helpful. I may not believe in all he teaches, but I believe *in* ' Cheiro,' and I am so far turned from my scepticism that I am going to study further along these lines of thought.

(Signed) WILBUR L. DAVIDSON."

The other was this little anonymous verse handed to me by a messenger as I was entering my train:

"To 'CHEIRO'
A palmist if you will, yet lay your hand
But for one moment in his own, and he
Whose eyes have felt the touch of spirit-land
Looks through the door that has no key
And in strong subtle fingers takes the scroll
Of your poor life, half writ with tears, and reads
The secret symbols of your earth-bound soul,
Finds wasted days, God's lilies with Life's weeds."

I had no means of thanking the giver, but if these pages should ever meet the eyes of this unknown friend, I trust they will give my thanks and tell the writer that I have tried to live up to the sweet thought embodied in this tribute.

CHAPTER XXXVII

I VISIT WASHINGTON. INTERVIEWS WITH PRESIDENT AND MRS. CLEVELAND, ADMIRAL DEWEY AND MEMBERS OF THE CABINET

IT was a glorious spring day when for the first time I saw Washington, the official capital of the United States. As I drove from the station to my hotel I thought I had never seen a more handsome city or one so beautifully laid out. The capital, set like the centre of a star with wide avenues of white asphalt planted with splendid trees, seemed indeed a worthy setting for the seat of Government of such a prosperous nation.

The "White House," as the President's official residence is appropriately called, is also magnificently situated, and altogether this handsome city, so different from the other large capitals of the various States, cannot help but impress the visitor with its air of luxury and regal magnificence that it possesses.

After staying at the "Arlington" for a few days, I took possession of a complete set of apartments in the late Senator Kay's residence, and there myself and "suite" were quickly installed.

The Press very soon got word of my visit, and in a few days I had the usual round of callers desiring interviews.

Mrs. J. G. Carlisle, the wife of the then Secretary of State, was one of my first visitors. From the commencement, Mrs. Carlisle showed the greatest interest in my work, and a few days later I was invited to meet her husband and dine at their house.

Mr. J. G. Carlisle was a well known political figure in the United States, and as a member of the Cleveland Cabinet he later on played an important role in connection with the Venezuelan troubles which so nearly caused a conflict with England. He was kind and good to me, and the day after our dinner he showed me over the Government Buildings in Washington and left me in the middle of the United States Mint, but in the good company of Mr. D. N. Morgan, the Secretary of the Treasury, whose name in those days appeared on all the dollars bills of the nation.

I was later indebted to Mr. Morgan for having the satisfaction of destroying a million dollar bills which he let me put through the cutting machine—they were old ones, of course, but still it was an unique satisfaction to be able to say that I had once in my life destroyed a million dollars in a minute.

When I was leaving Washington this gentleman presented me with a new bill bearing his signature belonging to the first series signed by his pen, also a copy of the signatures of all the United States Treasurers who had preceded him.

Among the many interesting personalities I met during my visit to Washington was the famous Admiral Dewey, the hero of the Spanish-American War. I was first presented to him at the house of my friends, Commander and Mrs. McCrea, and we met several times during the following fortnight.

The Admiral invited me to come and see him again in the house which had been presented to him as a gift from the nation, and I had the pleasure of taking impressions of his hands to add to my collection.

There were many souvenirs in this house together with presents and decorations from crowned heads, but the one thing the Admiral seemed to prize the most, was a small triangular-shaped flag hanging over the mantelpiece in his dining-room.

He explained to me that it was the " night flag," which had been forgotten on the mast of his ship as she went into action on the famous morning when he entered Santiago Bay and destroyed the Spanish Fleet which was lying there when the war broke out.

The Admiral gave me a signed photograph of himself, which I reproduce in these pages. It is dated December 31st, 1899. He was then at the very height of his fame and popularity, and had been married a few months before to Mrs. McLean Hazen, the widow of General Hazen.

At first they lived very happily in the home given to him by the people of the United States. Later on, finding it too small for the entertainments he was called on to give as Admiral of the Navy, he sold it and bought a much larger house. His disposal of the gift house caused a storm of protest to sweep over the country, especially as he gave the new residence to his wife as a present.

This action was much misunderstood; it dimmed his popularity, from which he never recovered. He died in this new house in 1917. His widow outlived him considerably; she reached the good age of eighty years, passing away on February 21st, 1931. She was a charming, brilliant woman, her only fault being that she failed to grasp the temper of the people in allowing the popular hero to dispose of the house given to him on his return from the Spanish-American War.

Other interesting personalities I met during my visit to Washington were: Nelson A. Miles, Commander-in-Chief of the United States Army; Chief Justice Fuller of the Supreme Court; H. A. Herbert, Secretary to the Naval Board; Senator Frank Hiscock; Senator M. S. Quay; Senator Wolcott; Baron Hengelmuller, the Austrian Ambassador; the Vice-President, H. E. Stevenson; Senator Charles Crisp; Senator W. B. Allison; Senator Allen, of Maryland; and other remarkable men well known in political life.

Another memorable incident of my visit to Washington was my meeting with Mrs. Cleveland, the wife of the then President of the United States. Mrs. Carlisle drove up one afternoon and told me that Mrs. Cleveland had expressed a wish to meet me and would I come at once with her to the White House.

The wish of a President's wife in the States is akin to a Royal Command. I naturally obeyed with pleasure, and giving up my appointments for the rest of the day, we drove over and were admitted at once.

Everyone who has had the honour of meeting Mrs. Cleveland will agree with me that the President's wife was not only a decidedly handsome woman, but still more, she was a woman of such marked personality that one's memory could have no difficulty in recalling such a meeting.

She received me with the utmost cordiality and simplicity; she said: "I have read your books and I have often looked forward to the pleasure of some day meeting you, but you must first have tea and then we shall have a long chat."

Tea was served, English tea I must add, and also English toast, just as if we had been sitting in any London drawing-room.

The President strolled in for a few moments, had me examine his palms, chatted with me about my tour through the States, and with a heart "shake hands" returned to his duties as Chief Executive.

Tea over, I also turned to my duty and told the "Lady of the White House" all I could about the past, present, and future as revealed by her hands.

With all her success in life—there was one thing she wanted, a hungry longing in her heart which had never been realized, a simple mother's wish to have a child—nothing more.

I expect there are wives who may read these lines and who will realize with what joy she received my message *that this desire of her heart would soon be fulfilled.*

Mrs. Carlisle listened with incredulity expressed in every line of her face, and yet when the happy event took place during the following year, she did not hesitate to tell everyone of my prediction and how it had been fulfilled. I have an American newspaper lying before me at this moment which bears out what I say. In any case, Mrs. Cleveland believed—*perhaps belief and realization are twin souls in the mystery of design*, but in any case a year later all America rang with the news that Mrs. Cleveland had become the happiest woman in the world.

As the years rolled onward, two more predictions were equally fulfilled; one the death of Mr. Cleveland, and the other her second marriage.

CHAPTER XXXVIII

THE MAN WITH THE "DOUBLE LINE OF HEAD"

A FEW months ago I read in one of the English papers the story of a man who had lived for fifteen years dressed as a woman, and who might have continued to do so till the time of his death, if a slight accident had not disclosed his real identity.

I can, however, relate in the following chapter an account of a case that came under my own knowledge, of a man who not only lived as a woman, but who at the same time kept up his position as a man, whose double life has never been disclosed except to three persons, one of them myself—but in my case I was privileged to see and hear both sides of the story.

In giving this account to the public, I have for obvious reasons concealed the real names of the parties concerned, but in all other points this strange drama of life is exact.

Science has in recent years in a rather reluctant way admitted that some people have a dual personality, and have been known to lead more or less what is called "double lives." There are, I believe, some persons who deliberately encourage their dual personality, and others again who appear to have no free will in the matter, but who often, even unconsciously to themselves, live or play some double role.

In the case of the person whose history I am about to relate, I have not been able to discover whether he was able to control his dual personality or not ; or whether it was that one side, or the other, controlled at intervals, and compelled him to act as an automaton would do. I can only leave it to my readers to decide the matter according to their way of thinking.

One afternoon, towards the close of my appointments, a very pompous footman brought up a note and said he would wait for an answer. Opening the letter, I read :

GROSVENOR STREET,
LONDON, W.

"DEAR SIR,

I am waiting downstairs and would be glad if you would give me an interview now.

Yours, etc.,
WILLIAM STANDISH."

I replied : "Tell the gentleman yes, I will see him now." The pompous footman went downstairs with my message, and while waiting for my visitor, I turned over in my mind what could Sir William Standish want in consulting me.

Sir William Standish was a well-known man in London in those days, but known in the highest possible way for his great charity, kindness of heart, and liberal subscriptions to societies for the Prevention of Cruelty to Animals, the Protection of Children, Homes for the Aged, and suchlike. What on earth could he want in coming to consult me, I wondered. Besides, I did not like people letting me know their names or who they were in advance.

Just then the gentleman in question entered. He was a man of a most charming personality—quite young, not more than thirty-five, I imagined—clean shaven and faultlessly dressed. Advancing towards me, he held out his hand.

"I am delighted to meet you, 'Cheiro,'" he said. "I have read your many books on your strange study, and as I was free this afternoon, I thought I would come round and see what interpretation you would give of a peculiar mark I have on my hands. You need not trouble to tell me of my past, nor of my future, for I have no ambitions; but I just want you to give me your idea of the two odd lines I have across my palm. I have never noticed similar markings in any other hand. Your books are the only ones that touch on it—and if I am not wrong, you call it 'the double Line of Head.'"

Sitting down at my table, he put two extremely small but finely formed hands before me.

"In your books," he went on, chatting pleasantly, "you say these double head lines indicate a dual personality; a man who would lead a 'Dr. Jekyll and Mr. Hyde' kind of life; but this is what puzzles me—how could it be that this could apply to me, except that I am aware one side of my nature is extremely feminine."

How indeed could it apply to him, I thought, a man who led a clean, simple life, only interested in giving to charities and doing good to others. A man who had, as everyone in London knew, inherited a fortune from a very eccentric father, who had left a curious provision in his will, that his son had to give away in charity a sum not less than £10,000 a year. A man who had married when he came of age a woman who was equally as kind-hearted as himself—a devoted mother to their only child—a son, whose photo was often in the papers as an example of how handsome a boy could be.

In all my experience, I had come across not more than perhaps a dozen cases of what is called "the double Line of Head," and my memory ran back quickly over all these cases, but not one of them seemed in any way to give me a clue to the life of the man before me.

"I have made no attempt to conceal my identity," he went on. "In the first place, subterfuge, somehow, does not seem part of my nature; besides, I have such an admiration for the way you have written about your study that I felt I could not bring myself to ask for an appointment under another name, as I know so many people have done. I hate deceit or double dealing of any kind, and yet, why should I have the mark of 'the double Line of Head' in my hand is what puzzles me, and that is what brings me here."

"You then do believe in this study?" I asked.

"Yes, I admit I do," he replied. "Something in my nature that I cannot explain has always attracted me to books on the subject of character expressed in the face, head, and hands. In reading the Bible, I have often pondered over that verse in Revelation that says: ' I will place my mark in their foreheads and in their hands,' and I do not see anything illogical in thinking that a person who has made such a study as you have of the hand should not be able to interpret what this odd mark means in mine."

" If I had not known who you are," I said, " I might be able to make an attempt at it ; but knowing who you are, I cannot see any reason for these strange double lines, for by reading them as they ought to be read, you should have a dual personality, equally good and equally bad—two distinct mentalities, as it were, each acting independently of the other—compelling you to lead two distinct lives, one not knowing what the other does, or as if two souls or spirits possessed the same body, but if I told you such things you would consider me a lunatic ; and I would feel myself one also."

" In a way you have touched a secret point in my nature, ' Cheiro,' " he said, " for there are times when I confess I feel and *want to live as a woman*. I have to gratify this irresistible desire at times, and then I just as suddenly change, and feel as a person would when waking out of a dream, and trying to remember *what the dream was*.

" I will just give you one example. Only last week I found myself sitting in the early morning in my library, reading a novel in which I was deeply interested, when I chanced to glance at my feet. To my amazement, I noticed that my boots were covered with mud, and such odd, funny-looking boots they were, that I could not believe they could belong to me. Yet why should I be wearing them ? I looked at my clothes ; they were all right, just the usual morning suit I often wear—but those queer, muddy-looking boots ! I could hardly bear the sight of them, yet they seemed part of a dream I had, but try as hard as I could I was unable to get any further."

" Of course, you rang for your valet and asked him where they came from ? " I asked.

With a startled look on his face he seemed to blush, as he said : " I will tell you one thing I can't control, and I may as well confess it, although I do not suppose for a moment you will understand the feeling. I have a dread of appearing ridiculous in the eyes of my servants. I could no more have called my valet and asked him if those muddy boots were mine than I could fly. There are a few men among my acquaintance that I know have also this idea—that they must be absolutely correct before, especially, their butler or their valet ; but with me it is carried to such an extreme that it is absolutely painful."

" Well, what did you do with the boots ? " I asked.

" I would not tell any other man but you," he answered. " Well, I locked them up in a cupboard that I knew was safe, and when night came I stole out of the house by a back way, and feeling exactly like some poor thief that dreaded to meet a policeman, I went by side streets all the way to the Embankment; and when no one was about I dropped them into the river."

"And did you never solve the mystery?" I asked.

"Never, though those muddy boots seem to have haunted me ever since—and I really think they have been the cause of my coming to see you to-day."

The idea seemed so ridiculous I could hardly keep from laughing—to think of this immaculately dressed man before me having discovered himself with muddy boots on his feet; and then stealing down like a thief to the river to get rid of them. It seemed too absurd.

My laughing appeared to do him good. He laughed also, then getting still more confidential, he said:

"There is another thing, 'Cheiro,' that I am awfully sensitive about. I have feet like a woman—in fact, smaller than most women, so I have to wear special boots that are padded out to make them look like a man's size."

"Well, the muddy boots—what size were they?" I asked quickly.

"It makes the whole thing still more queer"—and he looked quite frightened as he said it—"*they were a pair of women's boots—and a small size at that.*"

I was certainly puzzled at this strange individual before me. I had noticed that his hands were unusually small, but in appearance there did not seem anything else very womanly about him, except, perhaps, that extremely sensitive, gentle, feminine side that at times sent flushes of blood into his face. Still, I had seen in my life so many of those half-feminine types of men, that after all, the small hands and feet of the man before me did not seem so very remarkable. Suddenly I thought it might be the answer to the double Line of Head across his hands; so after all I told him it could only mean he had mentally a dual personality of both man and woman—and jokingly, I added: "Sometimes, I suppose, you are strongly tempted to darn things, or see how you would look in a woman's hat."

"Yes," he said, "only I am in such dread of the servants seeing me, *I dare not do that at home.*"

Then in a moment he seemed to think he had said too much. Quick as a flash the confidential tone had vanished. He was again the polished, refined man of the world. A gold cigarette case was slipped from his pocket, and for a few minutes we smoked and talked of the Academy Pictures, and the coming Henley Regatta. At last, when he rose to go, he asked if I were disengaged and would come to dinner the following evening.

"You will enjoy talking to my wife," he said, "she is one of the most interesting women in London. She has studied Occultism, and I know will be happy to meet you."

I accepted with pleasure, and the following evening at eight I found myself very warmly welcomed at the Standish house in Grosvenor Street.

There are few houses in London that could convey that sense of taste and refinement that this home did. It was furnished with exquisite taste. There were not too many pictures, but those that were were rare works of art. In the library, in which we sat before dinner, I noticed some beautiful pieces of bronze, and as for books— there were rows and rows of cases, and most of them in exquisite bindings.

We sat down to dinner, just four of us—Sir William, Lady Standish, and their son, whom they had introduced as Arthur, a manly-looking little fellow with a head and face like a Greek god.

If I had thought on the previous day that the footman was a pompous and splendid person, I wonder how I can find words to describe the butler. He simply radiated " butlerdom " in its most superior sense. He did not walk—*he moved*—the pompous footman followed every gesture, silent signals flashed from their eyes, and in silence we got through the first course. At last came the " thaw," and even though it was only a partial one, still it was very welcome.

Again the Academy pictures cropped up ; again the Henley Regatta. Little Arthur pricked his ears up at the latter and said his greatest wish was to live on the river, so he could punt and splash the pretty girls as they went past. At this the butler nearly dropped the champagne, and had to leave the room for a moment to recover his dignity. We were all grateful to little Arthur, and I encouraged him all I could to give us more of his ideas.

At last the dinner came to an end ; the doors of what I may call " the dining cage " were thrown open. Arthur begged his mother to have the coffee in the library, as his father had promised to let him smoke a cigarette—and with a sigh of relief we entered the more unconventional room. Coffee was served, the servants disappeared, and a sense of home and comfort again reigned supreme.

Lady Standish chatted pleasantly with me about the theatres ; Arthur smoked his cigarette, perched on the back of my chair ; while Sir William actually put some coal on the fire and thoroughly well blackened his small hands in doing so. Before I left, he took me up to his own rooms, in another part of the house. They were so much the rooms of a man that, jokingly, I remarked :

" It certainly does not look as if you did any sewing or darning up here."

A curious change came over his face, as he said : " Yes, but I would like to show you *where I do it*—it is quite another side of my life. Let me call for you to-morrow at six o'clock and I will take you and show you my other rooms."

I agreed, and after saying good-bye to Lady Standish and Arthur, I left.

The next evening, punctually at six, Sir William called. Together we walked up Bond Street, crossed Oxford Street, and reached a block of flats ; entering a side door we went up to the top of the building.

Taking a small Bramah key from his pocket, he opened the door and we went inside. As the blinds were drawn, he turned on the electric light and then went back and closed, and, to my surprise, *bolted the front door.*

The room we had entered was, I saw, a kind of sitting-room, but furnished in a very peculiar way. Every chair and couch was covered in silk of a beautiful " rose du Barry " shade. The curtains and lamp were of the same colour, but the whole effect was that of a lady's boudoir. As if to add to the effect, several small pieces of silk were on the table, and near a rocking-chair a large well-filled basket was lying half turned over on the floor. It was just as if a lady had been sewing, and had left the room for a moment.

Of course, I thought the wrong thing—and stories of men who kept mistresses within a hundred yards of their legitimate home flashed through my mind.

Not noticing the questioning look in my eyes, Sir William said :

" Come with me, and let me show you the rest of the flat."

We went into the next room—a bedroom—and I stood for a moment lost in wonder at the costly decorations and beauty of the place. No Parisien demi-mondaine ever had such a room. The bed was a Louis XV model in gilt, exquisitely carved, while all the other furniture was in keeping with it. The dressing-table had its gold-backed brushes laid out as carefully as if an expert lady's maid was expecting her mistress at any moment. Off this room was a bathroom, equally well done, and then we walked into a tiny kitchen, where I noticed an electric cooker and everything beautifully clean. There was no woman anywhere to be seen—not even a picture of one.

" Do you often come and live here ? " I asked.

As if in a dream, he said : " I wonder why it is I cannot resist the feeling of confessing some parts of my odd life to you—and yet it is such a relief *to be able to tell someone.* I only ask you never to give away my secret until after my death ; but I feel I can trust you. And yet there are some parts of my life that are such an intangible dream, even to me, that I am aware there are at times lapses of weeks, often months, that are like blanks in my mind that I cannot fill up. These pages we will have to leave as blanks, for *what I do during these periods I do not know.* Please do not think I am trying to mislead you if I cannot tell you everything But one thing I am sure of, and that is, that although sometimes I feel I am not responsible for my actions, yet I am certain that ' the double Head Line ' does not mean in my case that I have any cruel or criminal tendencies. I only know that at times I go away and live an entirely different life than I do at Grosvenor Street—*but what that life is, I have not the slightest idea.*"

We had now returned to the sitting-room. Almost instinctively he took the rocking-chair and I dropped into the beautiful brocaded couch opposite.

Without noticing what he was doing, he had stretched out his hand and taken one of the pieces of silk lying on the table, cut some bits like leaves out of it, then, taking a needle and thread, in a few seconds he had formed them into something that looked like a beautiful flower.

"You mean," I said, "that sometimes you go away from Grosvenor Street and come and live here all by yourself?"

Semi-consciously he answered, as if talking to himself: "Oh, yes, I know I come and live here sometimes, and if you could only realize what a pleasure it is for me—the peace and quiet here, no prying eyes of servants to worry one—to be able to take these beautiful silks in my hands and fashion them into all kinds of odd things, and blend and harmonize their colours as a painter would his paints. Yes, I know I live as a woman here, but you will never be able to realize the comfort of being able to do so—to allow that side of my nature, when the craving gets too strong—it's freedom, if only for a few days or a week at a time. And when that is satisfied, to slip back again into ordinary life and take up again my position in the world of men. But it is not these phases that puzzle me—it is some longer lapses that come on when I know I leave this flat and go away—where, I do not know, and what I do I do not know; and as suddenly find myself back here in these rooms, and wake up as if from such strange dream, *and know no more of where I have been or what I have done than a person would who rose from the dead.*"

"But how do you know you have been away from here?" I asked. "Perhaps you may have dropped off to sleep and dreamt you have been gone for some time, for in dreams time is as if it did not exist."

"There is no dream about it," he replied, with a quiet, gentle smile. "You see that clock-calendar on the mantelpiece? That clock wound up goes for 365 days. I never let it run down. Once I was away for as long a spell as three months, and it registered that such a period had passed; but where I was during that time, all I can say is—*I do not know.*"

"Perhaps you were back in Grosvenor Street. But, tell me, what does your wife think of your long absence at times from home?"

"They have grown accustomed to it by now," he said. "Of course, at first I was only away for perhaps a week or ten days at a stretch, and I am seldom absent for more than a month, with the one exception of the three months I have mentioned. Besides, I have trained them to think that I have business interests in Paris and Rome. I have even arranged to have my letters sent on to addresses in either of those cities, and then re-forwarded to me back here. This has gone on now for several years, they are quite happy about it, and ask no questions. Of course, my greatest dread is that some day they will find out. As my son grows up, I often find myself looking across the table and wondering if some day *he will discover my secret.*"

"But Lady Standish?" I asked. "Surely she is not content to allow you to go away to, say, Paris or Rome without her?"

"You are quite wrong," he said, "she is not jealous like other women might be. You see, we married under rather unusual conditions. She always hated the ordinary idea of married life—you know what I mean—and once Arthur was born, we agreed to live together as good comrades and nothing more. But don't think for one moment that I am not happy in my home life. She is the sweetest and truest companion in the world; we never have a cross word, and when I am with her, I am as happy as any man can be. But, alas! *I can't always be with her,* I can't indeed. No, it is utterly impossible—*when the feeling to get away comes over me, there is no will power on earth that can prevent my going.*

"Oh, yes, I have tried. Don't think that; I have tried hard, fought against it; I have walked my room, night after night; yes, fought against it till I have dug my nails deep into my hands with agony, but all to no purpose—*I have to go.*

"I know it is as if I became possessed. Some religious people would explain it that a demon takes possession of my mind. But if it is, it must be a wonderfully clever demon, for in my anxiety that I may not be discovered every point is thought out carefully; everything calculated to such a nicety, that in all these years no slip or error has yet occurred to prevent my plans being carried out. But the only thing I cannot calculate is the length of time I shall be away.

"Don't imagine for a moment that my wife thinks that I have another home or a mistress—she knows I have no passions, that I never had. No, that would be the last thought that would ever come into her mind."

"But when do these strange feelings come over you?" I asked. "Have you noticed if they come at regular intervals?"

"Yes, I have noticed," he replied, "they come with singular regularity *every twenty-eight days*—sometimes the feeling is of the greatest intensity, sometimes so weak that I am able to resist it; but every month I go through the same phase, more or less, as the case may be. I am nearing one of these now, I know, and perhaps that is another reason why I am telling you all this."

I sat silently smoking a cigarette he had given me. I hardly knew what to say or suggest. The piece of silk was nearly finished, and about a dozen really beautiful things, like flowers, or more like orchids, he had made from it. He seemed perfectly happy looking at these things, but as the clock struck seven, he rose, put them away in a drawer, then taking his hat, he said:

"I have just got time to dress for dinner. Will you walk over with me as far as Grosvenor Street?"

The following week I received a note from Lady Standish asking me if I would come around for dinner on Tuesday at eight o'clock. I accepted, and in due course had my coat and hat taken from me by the pompous footman, and was escorted in solemn state up to the drawing-room floor, and ushered into the boudoir.

Lady Standish rose to greet me, saying at the same time :

" I hope you won't mind having only Arthur and myself for dinner to-night, as Sir William had to go rather suddenly to Rome yesterday."

To tell the truth, I was, if anything, very pleased. I thought I might be able to get some information from Lady Standish on what I now considered one of the strangest cases I had ever come across.

" Sir William appeared to have no idea when I saw him a few days ago that he would so soon have to take such a long journey," I said.

" Oh, one can never know with him," she laughed. " I have even known him to leave the dinner table and catch the nine o'clock train for Paris ; and I never know when he is returning until I see him again."

" Rather an uncomfortable kind of husband," I suggested.

" Yes, but then all men have their faults "—she smiled—" and for a man he has really very few."

" I would have imagined you would have loved to run over to Rome also, there is no city I love more to visit at any season of the year."

" I can't say I know it well," she said. " I much prefer Paris. But I never go with Sir William on any of his journeys. He never seemed to care for me to do so, and I have long since given up the idea."

" What a wonderfully well-trained wife," I thought.

" You see," she went on, " we live very independently of one another. He is wrapped up in his various charities, and I am equally absorbed in mine. And then I have my boy to look after. Sir William has his own income and I have mine, so we never even discuss money matters together. It is all for the best, I believe, for we are very contented, and as long as he is happy, that is all I care about."

" But surely you must get anxious at times when he is away, and you do not know when he is coming back ? "

" Well, sometimes I do get anxious. I suppose I would not be human if I did not. But these trips of his to Rome I think I understand, and so would you, if you knew him as well as I do."

" But why Rome ? " I asked.

" Well, you see "—and her whole face changed and looked very grave—" at heart, although he never speaks of it, Sir William is deeply religious, and my idea is that every now and then he gets into a kind of religious ecstasy. He would hate it to be known in London, and so I believe he goes abroad to go into a Retreat or into some Order for a week or a month at a time. With all his family, strict Protestants as they are, he would not dare admit such an idea, for no man is more sensitive to criticism than he is. But I really believe it is this that takes him abroad for a week or so nearly every month ; but, of course, you must never suggest such a thing to him."

Just then Arthur rushed in. " Sorry, Mother, I have kept you waiting dinner for me, but I was scribbling a few lines to father and posting it care of his agent in Rome. I do hope I got the address right."

She looked at the envelope. "Yes, dear, you have written it quite correctly. He has had the same man for the past ten years. I hope you gave him my love?"

"Of course I did, Mother." He laughed. "And I had a double reason for doing so, as I threatened him that if he did not take me with him on one of these trips to Rome, that one of these days I would bolt there after him and make him show me over the place."

"You naughty boy," she said. "Here is James to announce dinner. Don't forget to give him your letter to get it posted at once."

James, more silent and pompous than ever, announced dinner, and together we went downstairs and entered the dining-room.

When the usual formal dinner was over—and this time more formal than ever, because, at heart, I am certain both the butler and the footman agreed in disapproving of their mistress dining with a man, even though Arthur was present. In any case, at the end the doors were flung open with more dignity than ever, and the butler announced that coffee had been served in the library.

"Upstairs," Lady Standish said, in a tone that admitted no dispute, and upstairs we went to the room we had come from. Coffee over, Arthur trotted away to do some lessons, and when we were again alone, Lady Standish said: "I would so long for you to see my hands and tell me in as few words as you like how things will turn out for me in the end."

Hers were easy hands to read. There was nothing in them but goodness and charity, the daily round of kind actions. There was no love but the "mother-love" for her husband and her boy. That other love, that men and women nearly all realize sooner or later, was completely absent—even in the far distant future, there was no love and no re-marriage. One mark, however, stood out strange and threatening, and not so very far away—the sign of some terrible tragedy she would pass through, after which, though she might still live, all emotions and sentiment would be as dead.

Then commenced that parrying of questions—that horrible evasion of straight demands that doctors go through so often from their patients—that covering up of the tragedy that was crying out in her hands to be read. Not much more than a year, and then—that swift sudden blow of some shock that would paralyse her very senses, and after, this woman of the world would never quite see life in the same light as before. But the reason *I did not know*, and *how could I tell her if I did?*

Yes, we all have to tell lies sometimes—perhaps that is why on this earth we have been given speech. Truth in her nakedness can at times become such a monster, that a little paint and powder, or an extra large "fig leaf" becomes absolutely necessary, lest she should send us to a mad-house.

Her woman's quick eyes had, however, caught some of the expressions that passed over my face.

"What is it, 'Cheiro?'" she asked. "What is the tragedy you see in my hands?"

"Only the tragedy of your never having loved," I replied quickly—anything that came into my mind, just to put her off.

Flushing scarlet, "Yes, I suppose it is a tragedy," she said, "but so many married women are like me that such tragedies are commonplace. Perhaps, after all, it is better not to love—better to ask only for contentment, and to thank God if one can get even that. If I were madly in love with my husband, how could I support his going away as he does, leaving me without even a message for weeks or a month at a time? No, love with such a man would be a torment—it is better as it is."

It was fully a month later when I was again invited to dine at Grosvenor Street. Sir William had returned, and things went on as before—the same formal dinner, the same silent butler and footman, coffee in the library, but not one word about his absence.

It was only as I stood at the street door bidding him good-bye, that I summoned up my courage to say: "I suppose you have been in your flat all this time?"

Very calmly he said: "No, I have not been there, at least, not more than a few hours—*I only wish I knew where I had been.*"

. . . .

Months passed. The winter had come and gone; London had thrown off her fogs and furs and the rustling of the new green leaves in the Park was like the whispering of so many lovers in her ears. I had been to America and back, and to me the charm of London after every voyage seemed to grow deeper and more intense. There are other great cities in the world, I know: New York, with its "skyscrapers," making the Tower of Babel a child's toy in comparison, equalling the Bible story in the noise and confusion of its languages; then there are Paris, Rome, Vienna, Cairo, Petrograd—all with their own beauty—all wonderful in their way—but there is no use trying to analyse or explain it, *to the heart that has known London* there is always that strange " home-sickness " to come back.

It must have been somewhere about the middle of May, that I found myself one evening after six sitting under the trees in the Green Park, just having a rest between the day and the night, listening to the song of the streets in the distance, and trying to make up my mind what restaurant would tempt me for dinner.

I had not told the Standishs that I had returned, for I was not in the mood for any formal dinners, and was just thinking of a quaint French place in Soho, when I noticed a man I had not seen for years coming towards me across the grass.

In those days I confess I did like odd people, and certainly this man coming towards me could not be described by any other word.

We had met some years before at a Poets' Club, a weird affair, where everyone brought his own food and drink, and where the rule was to eat everyone else's grub but one's own. Of course, such a club did not last long, but while it did it was decidedly interesting. Many of its members became in the end " quite respectable " ; two of them had been knighted for some extra bad poetry ; the rest have been married—and by now, probably, divorced.

The individual coming towards me had always attracted my interest —not on account of his verses, which were about the maddest things that have ever been written—but on account of his own odd personality. He may not have written good poetry, but he lived as only a good poet should live. He really *did live in the clouds*, and how he kept his feet on earth, and did not have them chopped off in the London traffic, was more than I was ever able to solve.

When I first met him at the Poets' Club, he had given vent to some extraordinary views on the subject of marriage. His idea was that it should be a mental and not a physical association. He would have divided the world into two sects—the breeders and the thinkers—but for the unfortunate " breeders " he had nothing but contempt.

When I pointed out to him that without the " breeders " there would be no population to read his wonderful poems—if they were ever published—he admitted that was a setback to his theory, but immediately got over the difficulty by suggesting that the Creator could institute some kind of cabbage plant incubators, and every back garden in London and the Provinces would then be a truthful example of our usual childhood education.

I had suggested that his hair looked as if he had been found under the proverbial cabbage, but this only led him from the vegetable to the flower kingdom, where he pictured blushing maidens found under rose bushes, and Poets the offspring of orchids.

As this lanky individual came slowly towards me—moving quickly, to him, would have been incompatible with his dignity—it flashed through my mind that if orchids had souls, the most grotesque of them had reincarnated in his body. Still, this man had eyes—wonderful eyes—great violet eyes, with black lashes—eyes that dreamt and thought and held communion with other worlds so that under their spell one forgot the rest of the picture.

" Well, Algy," I said, as he sat down by my side, " have any poems been published yet ? "

" No," he replied calmly, " the publisher has not yet been born who can appreciate my work."

" Publishers are found under cabbages." I laughed. " You remember your theory of years ago ? "

" I do," he replied, " and I have never seen any reason to alter it, except that cabbages are too good for publishers."

*You are wonderful
What more can I say?—
Nellie Melba.
New York 1894*

MADAME MELBA'S WORDS IN "CHEIRO'S" VISITORS' BOOK

"No wonder you have not found one." I laughed. "But, tell me, Algy, how have your theories on marriage progressed during my absence? Have you had any good reason to alter your views on that subject?"

What a transformation! The very thought seemed to have changed the odd being by my side into something that for a moment looked really human.

"My friend," he said, "you will never believe it till you see her. I did find my twin soul after all. I found an odd soul just like my own—a soul wandering in the darkness of loneliness, till we met—and in that meeting to know what heaven means while we still tread this earth."

"Perfectly wonderful," I exclaimed, "I sincerely congratulate you. But tell me, where did you meet this wonderful being?"

"The meeting was a bit strange, I confess. It was not a bit conventional. We were introduced by—by the Dawn."

"Just what I would have thought, Algy," I laughed. "An introduction to you could only be negotiated by the Moon, or the Goddess of Dawn. I wonder one of your Odes to Venus did not bring her down to earth specially for you. But do tell me all about it."

"Well, you know how I hate ridicule; so if you won't ridicule me, I will tell you. But when you know the sequel, you will realize how serious it all is."

I nodded assent, and he went on:

"Well, of course, you know I don't live like anyone else. I never could. I could never earn money at anything, and I must say I have never tried. I have the good fortune to have a retired stockbroker for a father, who, though he never sees me, allows me three hundred a year just to keep me out of the workhouse. With this pittance, I manage to keep along year after year, knowing that some day my talents will be appreciated, and that sooner or later a grateful country will elect me Poet Laureate, Prime Minister, or some odd job that they may have in their giving. Don't forget, my friend, that Beaconsfield was also a writer."

"Yes," I nodded, "but don't forget he was also a Jew."

"Well," he went on, "with my three hundred a year I have discovered one thing that would take more than a Jew to find out. I have solved the economic problem of the world—how to live on the smallest quantity of food."

"The devil you have," I exclaimed, "how have you done it?"

"Oh, very simply, my friend. It is quite an easy problem—merely the elimination of the wear and tear of the tissues of the body."

"Sounds grand," I interrupted, "but explain a bit more."

"You see," he went on, "food and labour are two of the most costly things in life—both have to be paid for by someone. Now, if you don't do any work, you don't need food; and if you don't need food, you are independent of labour. Do you follow?"

P

"Ask the British working-man," I laughed, "he will give you a better answer than I can."

"Then," he went on, delighted to have someone to air his views to, "another fallacy this world has, is the Pagan idea of working during the daytime. The heat of the sun, the brilliancy of the light, all conduce to increased wear and tear of the tissues—result, hunger, the desire for food; consequently, expense in making up the waste and sustaining life. My system is, sleep all day, get up towards evening and wander through the night.

"When one is not jostled by hurrying crowds, one's clothes also last longer; eat when you have something to eat, but you will find that with little wear and tear on the body, you will require very little food. With my system of living, I even save money on my three hundred a year."

"Yes, you look as if you did," I could not help saying; "but suppose now, for a change, you come and have dinner with me and tell me more of this wonderful woman you met—wine and women are good companions, even in your quaint system, I am sure."

"Agreed," he said; "we will have the wine and the woman story together."

After a good dinner and a bottle of wine, the coffee and the cigarettes made their appearance, and my friend Algy went on with his story.

"Yes, I was introduced to her, as I told you, by the Dawn; and it was, indeed, the dawn of another life for me. You see, my friend, with my small allowance I cannot afford to live in London. I live up the river, not far from Richmond.

"One night in June—it is two years ago now—faithful to my system of living while others sleep, I found myself sitting on one of those benches by the river, watching the reflection of the stars in the Thames at my feet. The night had been very dark, but warm with the heat of the summer. As the pink rays of the dawn slowly rose in the East and gently lifted the curtain of night from the valley, to my surprise, I noticed for the first time that I was not alone. Another human being was sitting at the farther end of my bench. Yes, my friend, it was a woman—and the woman of my story.

"At first, she did not notice me—she just sat there with her eyes fixed motionless on the rays of ruby light, breaking and beating, as it were, up there on the far-off shores of heaven. As I sat and watched her, I began to realize that she was like me—a worshipper of Nature, a lonely soul, one who also only lived at night and *whose loneliness was felt less in the night*—yes, a twin soul, with perhaps the same feelings, the same longings, the same ideals.

"No, I won't go into details—why we spoke, or how we spoke, is quite immaterial. It is sufficient to say that it was like the meeting of old friends, who had been parted for a moment and yet not parted; whose minds took up the conversation where they had left off; whose re-meeting was what both expected, a natural thing, and nothing more.

" After some time, as if to avoid the harsh light of the advancing day, by mutual consent we rose and walked by the side of the river—we were the only persons about, we had still the world to ourselves.

" We walked on and on, until at last we came to where I lived—to my very humble little dwelling, half-smothered as it was by roses and virginia creeper. We entered it together, as if it were the most ordinary thing in the world to do.

" She seated herself on the long settee under the window, while I went off to find the only servant I ever had, an old hunchback, whom years ago I had rescued from the workhouse, and who lives with me without wages, but devoted as a dog to his master.

" Poor old Pat was already about. As he had lived in France at some period of his life, he had no equal in the art of making coffee. Soon he appeared with our simple breakfast, and drawing a low table before the settee, he laid it out before us. It was a frugal meal indeed—just some brown bread, fresh watercress, and the coffee.

" With a quick glance he noticed the lady—there was an enquiring look in his eyes as they met mine, but nothing more. Pat was too much of a gentleman to ask questions; besides, his one set law in life was that everything his master did was right, so, closing the door, he left us once more alone.

" My visitor did not speak much; she seemed tired. Walked a long way, perhaps, I thought; so when breakfast was finished, I took her to a room which was always prepared for a guest, but which had never been used, and telling her that it was my custom to sleep all day, and that I would call her for dinner, I left and went to my own room.

" All day I slept, better in fact than I had done for years. It was as if some great peace had come into my heart, as if the lonely brokenness of my life had passed with the night.

" The last rays of red sunset were streaming through the windows. I got up and went into the sitting-room. I could hardly believe my eyes for a moment, as I noticed the transformation that had taken place. The furniture had been arranged in a different way that made the room look much more comfortable and cosy; cushions had been rooted out of holes and corners, and had some kind of order about them; a large vase of roses stood in the centre of the table and another in the window casement.

" Pat was just disappearing as I entered, but he came back, and in a mysterious, half-frightened, half-pleased voice, said:

" ' She did it, sir, she did it, God bless her. I didn't touch a thing. Women are wonderful, sir, it was all done in five minutes. She is out in the garden now, tying up the roses over the porch.'

" Through the open door, I could see her lifting branch after branch and tying them up, so that they would show to the greatest advantage.

Her long, fawn-coloured dust cloak with a hat to match seemed to blend with the pink of the roses and, with the river as a background, made as pretty a picture as any artist could desire.

"Her task finished, she came in. With a woman's critical eye, she took another survey of the room, re-arranged the flowers on the centre table, and then noticed me standing in the shadow of the door.

"'It looks better now, doesn't it?' she said simply. 'I hate disorder. I hope you don't mind, but I can't live in a place that is untidy.'

"Then you are going to live here?" I blurted out in astonishment.

"'Yes, I am,' she answered, 'that is, if you have no objection. You evidently need someone to look after you.'

"'You are indeed right,' I smiled. 'My old Pat is no good at keeping a place tidy.'

"'Of course not,' she answered. 'Men are no use at that sort of thing, but he certainly *can* make coffee.'

"'Yes,' I said, 'but I don't know what he is going to give us for dinner. Hadn't I better see about it—you must be getting hungry by now.'

"'No,' she replied, 'I am never hungry. I can go for days without eating. You had better leave it to him. I think he has been out fishing, for I saw a fish on the kitchen table a few moments ago. Besides, Poets should not think about such things; in fact, I don't believe Poets should eat at all.'

"'It is wonderful how your ideas are so like mine,' I laughed. 'But how could you tell I am a Poet—or, rather, have some pretensions in that direction?'

"'How could I think otherwise?' she said, 'after having dusted that pile of papers on the top of your table?'

"It was now my turn to ask her questions, but the moment I did so, her conversation ceased. She could only remember that she lived somewhere in London. She did not know who she was, or what her name was, or what brought her all the way to the riverside the night before, or how she got there, and very firmly added if I persisted in asking questions she would leave.

"Dinner came in and turned out to be an excellent trout that Pat had caught, by accident, he said. I wondered why such accidents never happened before. I also wondered what a good cook he had suddenly turned out to be. Pat grinned and whispered: 'A lady's influence in the house, sir, they're wonderful things, sir, God bless 'em!'

"After dinner, the lamps were lit; she pulled some sewing out of one of her pockets, I read my poems and marvelled that at last I had found someone who understood what I wrote.

"That night went past, and the next, and the next again; then a week and a month that seemed only moments—we were like two children in a dream, and I prayed that I might never awaken."

"You did wake up, then?" I said.

"Yes," he answered. "It happened like this. One evening she seemed distressed and unhappy. She was continually going to the door, opening it, appearing to listen for something. I was still too much wrapped up in my own selfish happiness to notice details. I slept heavily—the morning came, and when I woke up in the evening, she was gone."

"Gone," I said, "I am so sorry for you. But, tell me, Algy, if it is all really true. How do I know it is not one of your fantastic poems that you are trying on me, to see how it goes?"

"True," he repeated sadly, "I should think it *is* true. But one day you will meet her, and then you will know how true it all is."

"Meet her! Then you met her again?" I asked.

"Oh, yes, I have indeed," he replied. "I was miserable and heart-broken for about a month, then she turned up at the cottage one morning, and walked in, just as if she had never been away."

"What an extraordinary person, Algy. Why don't you give her up?"

"Impossible, my friend, impossible. I would not give her up even if I could. Besides, now that we are married, it would be still more impossible."

"Married!" I cried. "Surely you were not mad enough to marry a woman whom you knew nothing about—and with your queer ideas about marriage, how could you do such a thing?"

"Oh, that part of it was easy." He smiled. "She has just as strong views on marriage as I have. She only believes in the mental side of it, as I do. We were quite agreed on that, and we live like brother and sister together. Yes, we really did marry—all my fault, I expect. Yes, in my selfishness I thought to hold her for ever with me in that way. We were married in a Registry Office, just like ordinary human beings."

"And still she leaves you at times?" I exclaimed, "and you have no idea where she disappears to. Is she away at present?"

"Yes, that is why you found me wandering through the Park. I never come to London when she is with me. She has been away nearly a month now; I am expecting her home at any moment. One of these days I will send you a wire, saying 'I am calling for you.' Will you come then and spend the evening with us?"

"Yes," I said, "you can count on my doing so. I would like to see something of this mysterious lady."

.   .   .   .

A week later the wire came. I sent out to Gunters and had a nice little supper basket prepared; with a couple of bottles of wine I was not going to take any chances with people who could go for weeks without food.

Punctually at six, Algy turned up, and we took the train to Richmond. It was a lovely summer evening, we sauntered up the path by the side of the river, and I thought that after all there was some wisdom in his idea in living away from the dust and heat of London.

The lamps had already been lit in the sitting-room when we arrived; flowers were on the table, on the mantelpiece, and in a large brass bowl in the fireplace. All over the room, one could see the touch of a woman, and a woman of taste at that. In an absent-minded way, she rose to greet me—she had only come back the day before, Algy told me in the train.

There was nothing very remarkable about her beauty, I thought. Her brown hair, with just a glint of gold, was unmistakably like a wig. Of figure, she did not appear to have much, but in any case it was hidden in a straight up-and-down kind of costume. She wore no rings or jewellery of any kind—a bunch of roses at her waist was the only attempt at ornament.

She looked at me in a dreamy kind of way, as if she were not quite awake. I looked at her, perhaps rather boldly, for she seemed to feel it, and shrank back into the corner of the settee where she remained until we took our places at the table.

My supper basket was a welcome addition, otherwise there did not seem to be much to eat. Algy apologized, saying that his wife had been away, and Pat brought in enough watercress to cover the entire table.

The wine I had brought was good; she even sipped a glass, and then played with the tail of a sardine until my cold chicken made its appearance.

Algy was very talkative and happy, he entered into details of the wonderful life they lived—their rambles by the river in the moonlight, the silvery sheen of the dawn when they went to bed, and the golden glory of the sunset when they woke in the evening.

All very beautiful, I thought, but those separate rooms at each side of the house did not quite appeal to my ideas of love, so out of sheer mischief I also painted a picture of children's feet romping through the rooms, and the prattle of children's voices in the early morning.

Of course, I had done the wrong thing; Algy twisted and turned on his chair, like an eel on a hot frying pan, while she glared at me as if I were a wild bull in a china shop. Of course, I *was* in a china shop, *and I knew it*, so I went on with my smashing and had the satisfaction of hearing Pat whisper in my ear: "Keep at it, sir, that's the stuff to give 'em—it will do 'em good, sir, God bless 'em."

Do them good, I thought—could anything do them good?

Algy had choked himself with watercress, and she had shrunk into her corner of the settee where she hugged a huge cushion to her side, as a kind of protector. I had thought to have drawn her and hear her defend her theories, but in that I was mistaken—she simply glared at me as if Algy had brought home the devil himself to their household.

As that would not do, I suggested that we should hear some of Algy's poems, and harmony was at once restored. With the help of a glass of wine, Algy unwound the watercress from his tonsils, and gave us one verse after the other. The one I remember the most is the following :

> "Love the passionless, is Love most pure,
> Love *for Love*, is the Love most sure.
> Love the sexless, alone can be
> The soul of Love for both you and me.
> Love the perfect, is Love sublime,
> Goddess of Fate, and Mistress of Time."

"Wonderful, wonderful," she said slowly, and then in a kind of dreamy way, she fished in her pockets and pulled out one after the other, first a scissors, then a piece of silk, then a thimble, and lastly a spool of thread. Then the silk was cut into curious forms; the needle and thread flew through her fingers, and in a few minutes she had formed two odd-shaped, but beautiful flowers, which fell at her feet, as if she had hardly noticed she had made them.

Before Algy could move I had picked them up, and in handing them to her, our eyes met for a moment. Surely I had seen those eyes before, but yet it could not be, for her eyes looked straight into mine, but with no flash of recognition. I went back to my chair and watched her more closely than ever.

Algy was now reading one of his really exotic poems, in which sunsets were purple, lilies black, the grass blue, and the stars calling one another by pet names.

Another flower fell from her fingers; again I picked it up, but this time I carried it back with me to my chair.

She was so enraptured with Algy's poem, that she had not noticed me.

I turned the flower over in my fingers. Surely I had seen something like it before—but again I dashed the idea from my mind. No, it could not be possible, I thought; it could not be possible.

I had kept very silent for some time—I had not produced any views or ideas to clash with theirs—perfect harmony reigned in the room. They had begun to feel that I was being converted to their own way of thinking; the cushion protector had even dropped from her side; I was no longer the unclean-minded person that she had imagined me to be. I drew my chair closer to her; she did not resent it.

My eyes were full of admiration for those wonderful silk flowers she made so rapidly. A little more admiration and the flattery of it had already reached her feminine heart.

Looking at me quite gently, she gave me one to examine. From it my eyes went to her hands.

"What wonderful hands you have, Madame," I said.

"Do you mean it?" She smiled. "I think they are rather large for a woman."

"Certainly not," I answered, "there are many ladies with much larger hands than yours; and then yours seem so light and quick with the needle. No wonder you can make such wonderful things. May I look at them?"

The flattery had done its work. The needle and thread were quietly laid down, and for a full minute I examined her hands, taking in every line and mark. Suddenly I seemed to realize what it all meant. As I did so, my brain turned icy cold—across both left and right was the "double Line of Head" *that I had seen on a man's hands and not so very long ago.*

With all kinds of ideas racing through my mind, I stumbled back to my chair, hardly knowing what to do or say.

Just then, Algy stopped reading. I took the opportunity of saying that their hours of living were not my hours, and bidding good-bye as quickly as I could, I got out into the coolness of the night.

. . . .

How I got back to my rooms I hardly know; I had walked most of the way, but I believe I found a late cab somewhere near Chiswick.

What should I do? I turned it over and over in my thoughts. Could I have made a mistake? Sometimes I jumped at that idea, and then gave it up again in despair. *There could be no mistake—I had seen those hands in a flat off Oxford Street—that flat furnished only as a woman might have furnished it—also cutting up pieces of silk, and turning them into flowers;* and as proof that I was not out of my mind, here in my possession was *that other flower, made before my eyes in that little cottage by the Thames.*

In one of the half-opened wardrobes in the flat in Oxford Street I had seen women's dresses; he had told me himself that there were lapses in his memory where the calendar clock on the mantelpiece had registered that he had been away for weeks and months at a time —and *without knowing what he did or where he went.*

Then, there was no mistaking that "double Line of Head" across the hands—again I had seen it in that cottage only a few hours ago.

There was no mistaking that sign on the hands I knew only too well.

No, there was no getting away from the fact that Sir William Standish, of Grosvenor Street and of the flat off Oxford Street, *was the same individual that a few hours previously I had been dining with, and who was the supposed wife of that poor crackbrained poet.*

But what should I do? I realized I could not leave things as they were. Yet, if I went and told Lady Standish, two things would most probably happen—the shock would drive her mad, or she would order me from the house. If I went to the police, it might be still worse— there would be one of the greatest scandals in London, and probably one tragedy piled on another.

All day long I paced my rooms—I sent everyone away who called—I could not keep any appointments. At last, towards six o'clock, I wandered out into the usual Bond Street crowd.

Grosvenor Street looked quiet and lonely, and half unconsciously I turned into it.

As I passed the Standishs' house I looked over. Nothing was changed there—it had the same respectable, conventional look that all the other houses had in that most conventional street.

What if I were wrong—what if Sir William were at that moment reading *The Times* in his library—or having tea upstairs with Lady Standish ? The crowds in Bond Street had done me good, they had brought me back to the everyday world of realities. I walked across and rang the bell.

" Is Sir William at home ? " I asked the footman.

Lady Standish saw me from the hall.

" Come in," she said, " I am so glad to see you, it seems ages since you called. Come upstairs and have some tea."

We went upstairs to the drawing-room, where tea had already been served.

" They did keep you a long time in the States," she said. " I suppose you met many interesting people, you must tell me all about it."

" I am so sorry Sir William is not in," she went on. " He had another of his trips to Rome about a month ago—and only last week he went off again. I am at last getting tired of his continual journeys ; they are getting worse than ever ; as for Arthur, he is threatening all sorts of things, he has just gone to the railway to see about trains ; he says he will go to Rome and find out what takes his father there so often."

I had not much heart to talk. I felt the comedy was nearing its end—the footsteps of tragedy had already been set in motion. If Arthur goes to Rome, I thought, he will soon find out his father has not been there—and that in itself will bring about a dénouement.

" You are looking ill and tired," Lady Standish went on, " what is the matter ? "

I had not time to answer. We heard rapid footsteps rushing up the stairs and in another moment Algy was standing before us.

" My wife, my wife," he screamed, " where is my wife ? "

I sprang up. " For God's sake, calm yourself, man," I cried, " what is the matter ? "

Sinking into a chair, he half moaned, " I cannot remember all. After you left last night, I seemed to get half mad with reading my poems aloud. I approached her, took her in my arms, attempted to kiss her for the first time in our married life. She struggled—I succeeded, and kissed her straight on the lips. With a scream of terror, she threw me from her and rushed out into the night.

" I thought she would come back, but hour after hour passed ; then

I determined to follow. After some time I traced her to London—to this street—to my amazement, I saw her with a latchkey enter this very house. I found the door open, and rushed in. My wife is here—I must find her," he screamed, " *I will find her.*"

I stood speechless with horror.

" The man is mad," Lady Standish said. " Ring the bell."

Before anything could be done, steps were heard on the landing outside, steps coming towards the door—strange, shuffling kind of steps, and then a fumbling at the handle.

Lady Standish stood white as death in the centre of the room, every nerve in her body at tension.

Very slowly the door opened, and the figure of the night stood before me.

Lady Standish did not move—she seemed turned into stone.

The Poet, with hands outstretched, leaped towards the figure.

The poor bedraggled-looking creature, with a bunch of roses still at its waist, stood for a moment looking from one to the other; the wide-open, entranced-looking eyes finally fixed themselves on Lady Standish's white face—a pair of trembling hands slowly stretched out towards her; with a broken cry of recognition—" My Wife, my Wife "—Sir William Standish fell dead at her feet.[1]

---

[1] As recently as 1929 a similar example as related in the above story was brought before the Courts in London in the case known as " Colonel Ivor Barker."

It was disclosed in this instance that the person who for six years had lived under this name, and who had occupied important positions in London such as secretary to the National Fascisti Movement, etc., and who actually married a young girl in a church at Brighton and lived with her for several years—was a woman.

Full accounts of this extraordinary case were printed in all the London papers after this person was arrested while filling a position as reception clerk at the Regent Palace Hotel on February 28th, 1929.

CHAPTER XXXIX

SOME GAMBLERS WHO CONSULTED ME AS TO LUCK. LORD CLANRICARDE AND HIS " SHILLING BETS." ARTHUR DE COURCY BOWER—HOW I HELPED HIM TO " BREAK THE BANK " AT MONTE CARLO.

ONE of my most curious visitors was an extremely shabby old gentleman, who called to make an inquiry concerning—Chance. His clothes showed such evidence of poverty that my secretary was loth to admit him; but there was something about the old gentleman that commanded respect, and sorely puzzled by the enigma, he was given entrance. Long experience had taught me that appearances are deceiving, and I was soon convinced that my shabby visitor was a " somebody."

He explained brusquely that he wished to have some information on the subject of " luck."

When he had finished bargaining over the fee with my secretary, I examined his hands and, frankly, they amazed me. They indicated good birth, wealth, and position, and hinted at an alliance in the future that suggested royalty. I told him all this, expecting him to scoff loudly, but he smiled sarcastically and said, " Why not ? "

But racing was his pet subject. He told me in a burst of confidence that he was accustomed to put on an " occasional shilling," but bemoaned the fact that the horses generally lost. " Was there not some system whereby events in racing could be prognosticated with accuracy ? " It was the age-long craving of the covetous to find the short cut to easy money. I assured my caller that his inquiry about luck in this respect was beyond my art.

" My bets are small," he said, " for I am careful with my money, and I don't intend to waste it. But in my young days, ' Cheiro,' I have put my pounds on—yes, and won as well as lost. But it's a fool's game," he added testily and prepared to depart.

" Would you sign my Visitors' Book ? " I inquired. He paused for a moment and then said, " No, I should be giving you a good advertisement and you might benefit by it. I'll tell you who I am, although you may not believe it." He drew himself up and said : " I am Lord Clanricarde, an Irish nobleman, and I live on ten shillings a day," and with this he walked out of the room.

As most people are aware, the late Lord Clanricarde was a miser and, although he lived in his magnificent town mansion, Chesterfield House, he existed as a recluse. All his splendid furniture and pictures were kept covered, while he was often seen eating his lunch from a paper bag in Hyde Park. He died worth a vast fortune, which he left to his nephew, Viscount Lascelles, who later became the husband of Princess Mary.[1]

It was strange how clearly I had seen in that withered old palm the tale of ancient lineage, great wealth, and a more splendid chapter opening out, when, in due course, Lord Lascelles became the son-in-law of the King of England.

[1] Only daughter of the present King and Queen.

About this time I was visited by another inveterate gambler. He came several times to see me, and one day on leaving wrote the following testimony in my Visitors' Book in the outer room :

"I visited 'Cheiro' in his rooms in Bond Street in March last when he told me with the most marvellous accuracy the events of the next three months.

At the time of my visit I was having the most remarkable luck racing. He foretold a great disaster. This came true in the next fortnight when I lost over £4000. At the same time he said I would get this loss back in a most unexpected manner. This I did on the 17th April as I won 84,000 francs at *trente-et-quarante* at Monte Carlo.

On my return I visited him again and he foretold two good wins and then a bad time. The good things came off in Isinglass and Orvieto and now Ascot has brought about the bad time.

Facts go further than empty words of praise.

G. MacCartie."

I am glad to add that I recommended my visitor to go back to Monte Carlo in the following September and play on certain numbers and those only from September 15th until the 25th. This he obeyed to the letter and returned to London with his winnings of over 150,000 francs. He very generously insisted on my accepting a present of a handsome diamond pin, as a souvenir.

One of my remarkable experiences, however, in this line, happened with that "King of Gamblers," Captain Arthur de Courcy Bower. His recent death in London was the means of flooding the papers with all kinds of stories of his adventures at Monte Carlo. I think therefore an account of my experience with this really unusual man may be of interest in these pages.

When I first heard of Bower he was at the height of his fame as a business man and associate of the famous Colonel North who made his fortune in Chilian Nitrate speculations.

As far as I can find out, Colonel North, who was a very uneducated man, owed the foundation of his immense fortune to Arthur de Courcy Bower.

It was owing to him that North first heard of the enormous deposits of Nitrates in Chile. It was Bower who planned his first visit to that country and who, by his fluency in Spanish, together with his charm and diplomacy, opened every door to Colonel North when they visited Chile.

One of Bower's greatest delights was to "pull the strings" and he found in Colonel North an excellent subject for spectacular effects.

On their arrival in Chile, Bower gave out through the channels of the Press and other means, that his friend the Colonel's sole object in life was to develop the resources of unknown parts of the world.

Within a week of their arrival Bower organized that a banquet should be given to welcome the great English capitalist.

This banquet, under the auspices of the Government, was an enormous affair. As Colonel North looked the personification of British solidity and respectability, he only had to make an appearance for Bower to do the rest.

The Colonel had no gift of eloquence. Bower replied to the toasts. North had only to stand up and bow as stiffly and as Britishly as only an Englishman knows how, when he can't speak any other language but his own.

The banquet was a great success. Mines of silver and every possible and impossible concession were offered to the great Englishman. Bower was, however, out for the Nitrate deposits and he got them; before a month passed the two left for London with concessions that were the foundation of one of the greatest trades in the world and have made fortunes for the original buyers of Chilian Nitrate shares.

Colonel North became a millionaire and Bower a very rich man. Then the two quarrelled and each went his own way.

Colonel North stuck to his money and, as the Scripture says, " it multiplied exceedingly." Bower lost his—laughed at Fate and commenced again.

Arthur de Courcy Bower was not built to become a conventional member of Society. He had been at Eton, but had broken every rule of that highly respectable college—that melting-pot of manners where English youth is moulded into models of Aristocracy.

Bower was a gentleman to his finger-tips, but he could not become a cabbage. He had no ambition to have an estate in the country, read the Lessons on Sundays, and have J.P. or M.P. after his name. He wanted to see life in all its forms. He wanted to play " pitch and toss " with Fate, and he cared little which of the two won.

He was one of the most versatile men I ever met; he was a good chemist, an excellent geologist, a mathematician who in figures had no equal, and yet with it all a—wayward child.

In North Africa he won the hearts of the Arabs, and for a year became a kind of Sheik. He returned to England with valuable concessions which he never used; he floated Companies that he never finished, he threw money away as if it were so much dirt.

It was a love affair in the end that drove him to consult me.

And what a riddle the whole thing was! Here was a man, whom the most beautiful women in the world had idolized and thrown themselves at his feet, a man who had married one of the richest women in London, to find, alas! that love and money rarely go well together in double harness.

Then came the love story. I cannot write it all here for it would make a volume in itself. I can only in a book like this give a mere outline.

After a scene of jealousy with his wife—sick to death of trying to live a conventional life—Bower one day walked out of his luxurious surroundings and reached London with the large sum of Two Pounds in his pocket.

He had determined to begin life all over again, but Fate was just as equally determined that her spoiled favourite should first have a severe lesson.

She planned that a bad attack of pneumonia would bring down his pride and strength at the same time and, in the two-roomed flat that he had taken on credit in a back street in Chelsea, left him to get very close to death without food or a friend in the world.

Then it was that Lydia turned up. Do not ask me who Lydia was, or where she came from, for I do not know.

I only know that this wonderful woman loved this broken-down man with a devotion that is almost without equal even among those pages of women's sacrifice to men, that has more than balanced the evil that has been credited to them since the time when Mother Eve nearly choked the first man with an apple.

Night and day for weeks and months Lydia nursed and watched and waited. When her little savings were gone, whatever jewels she had went also, so the fight kept on—until Lydia won.

Fate, also, had not deserted her favourite for ever. She was, perhaps, waiting round the corner of one of Life's turnings to see the effect of her lesson.

Whether this was so or not, Bower, during his convalescence, worked out an extremely clever process to reduce the cost of electric batteries by nearly one-half.

Electricity was in its infancy in those days. Bower's process filled the gap of the moment; within less than a month he had the satisfaction of selling his rights for £10,000 in cash.

Needless to add, Lydia got back her jewels and any others she wanted, while Bower went down to the City, made some extremely lucky gambles on the Stock Exchange, and again became a very rich man.

There was one thing, however, still missing. He wanted to make Lydia his wife—but *that one thing would not come right.*

Thus it was he came to me. Very nervously he put his hands on the cushion on my table. Would he ever have his freedom? Would he ever be able to marry Lydia? Would he ever be able to put her in the position he wanted her to have?

It was one of those cases in which I could give—no hope. The woman to whom he was married would die before she would give him his freedom. Her death was also in the very far off distant future. I could give him no hope whatever.

From this out I saw a good deal of Bower, and before long I met

Lydia. One evening he called for me in a magnificent Rolls-Royce. It had been a hot day towards the end of June. " I will give you some air first," he said, " and then dinner."

During the drive to Hampton Court and back, he explained that our dinner was going to be thoroughly Bohemian.

" Lydia will cook it," he said, " and we will probably have it on the kitchen table."

When we did arrive at the flat—a small, but beautifully furnished one I may add—Lydia joined us in the drawing-room. She had a white silk dress that fitted her perfectly, with a dark blue cook's apron that, tied round her waist, showed off her figure to perfection.

Women *had* figures in those days and were *proud of them*. The age had not arrived when they emulated " drain-pipes " with a waist line round their hips and front and back like flat irons.

No ! Lydia had what was called in those days, " a perfect figure," one in which " bust " and hips had their natural lines and womanly curves. Her hair was also her own, the rich gleam of gold in it setting off the exquisite whiteness of her skin.

She was not only an extremely pretty woman, but she possessed the greatest charm of all, personality and magnetism.

Her devotion to Bower was something really beautiful. There was nothing blatant about it. It did not consist in calling him " darling " every minute, as some women in love irritate every one else by doing. One could simply *feel* it in the atmosphere she created about her, a warm, genial, affectionate something that one may understand, yet not be able to describe.

As for Bower, he simply basked in this eternal sunshine. It brought out all the good in his nature, from a rake he became a lover, from a rank weed—a sun-flower, ever turning towards his giver of light and life.

We followed her out into the kitchen, Bower explaining to me that they got rid of all servants by six o'clock.

He also put on an apron. I laughed to see the man who had at one time two butlers and four footmen to wait on him, engaged in peeling potatoes to help Lydia and as happy as a schoolboy on a holiday.

Love indeed works miracles—what a pity we mortals know so little about it.

Sitting round the snow-white kitchen-table, we had a small but really delightful dinner, accompanied by one of the best bottles of Burgundy one could have.

Then it was " the skeleton " appeared for the first time at the feast. Bower went into the dining-room to fetch a bottle of brandy. It was the one thing in the world he loved most—next to Lydia.

Quick as a flash, she whispered to me——

" His excuse to-night will be that he must have brandy for his guest. For God's sake, refuse it. He would be the greatest man in England if it were not for this curse."

Bower returned holding the bottle more carefully than if it were a baby. Putting it down before me, he said——

"My friend, you must now join me in drinking the finest Cognac in the world. I bought all I could get from the Café Voisin the last time I was in Paris. Lydia hates me to touch it, so I only get a chance when I have a friend like you for dinner."

Of course, I refused.

He had already poured out a large glass for himself. Lydia begged him not to drink it, but it was no use. He held the glass close to his face, fondly warming it in both hands, he smelt it; the whole expression on his face changed, an evil look came into his eyes.

"I must have it, Lydia," he cried. "*I must have it.*"

Lydia did not for one moment lose her head. Very quietly she said, "And to think, Arthur, that I have waited in all the day thinking and looking forward to that drive in the car you promised me for to-night—you would hate yourself if you broke a promise to me."

Bower's face twitched as if he had been struck with a whip. One could see the struggle passing in his mind, a death-like silence seemed to creep in through the windows.

Like a hypnotized man, his eyes slowly turned from the glass in his hands—they met hers—Love won.

Another second the glass went flying through the window to be smashed in a thousand pieces in the garden below.

But Lydia could not always be with him. Temptation waited and watched for him at every corner of the City; men who knew of his weakness called at his office with flasks of brandy in their pockets and faked contracts in their hands.

It did not last long. One mistake followed on the heels of another. Soon gossip got busy that Bower was ruined and the Bankruptcy Court stared him in the face.

One afternoon about three o'clock he called in at my rooms. He was very quiet, very pale, with a horrible hunted look in his eyes.

I had not seen him for over a year. I was shocked at the change that had come over him.

"Great Heavens, Bower," I said. "What's the matter—have you been ill?"

"Yes," he said, "very ill."

"Are you on your way home now?" was my next question.

"No," he answered. "I'm on my way to Monte Carlo if I can get the nine o'clock train."

"But where is Lydia?"

"I do not know," he groaned. "I broke her heart, so she left me."

"Look here," he started off, speaking very rapidly. "Don't let us fence with one another—in the last year I've gone to the dogs—to Hell itself, I've lost everything—even Lydia. I deserve all I've been through and more. You won't preach at me I know. I want your help in a terrible crisis, that's why I've come to you. I must find eighty

> The study of people gifted with occult powers has interested me for several years. I have met and consulted scores, during these studies. In almost every respect I consider Chiero the most highly gifted of all. He helps as well as astonishes.
>
> Ella Wheeler Wilcox
> New York
> Oct. 25th '93.

TESTIMONY FROM ELLA WHEELER WILCOX

thousand pounds within the next fortnight. I must, or there will be a warrant out for me—now do you understand my desperate position."

"But . . ." I began.

"There are no buts," he went on. "I know I can't find eighty thousand pounds for the asking in London, but it is waiting for me at Monte Carlo and you must help me to get there."

Bower had one of those magnetic personalities that it was impossible to resist.

I knew he had studied my system of numbers for years, he had often taunted me that I had not enough courage or belief in myself to apply my ideas in a practical way. He had the most prodigious memory for numbers of any man I had ever come across. He could remember every run of red or black that occurred on a *trente-et-quarante* table in a night's play, and as for roulette he was a veritable master of the various combinations of the game.

"How much money do you require?" I asked.

"Five hundred pounds," was the reply. "We have just time to reach your bank before it closes; bring your cheque book and come with me."

There was such a pathetic look in his eyes I could not refuse.

We went to the bank, got the money, and a few hours later I saw him off on the night train for the Continent.

"Good-bye," he said. "You will have your five hundred back within a week and another five hundred profit."

"I don't want any profit," I answered. "I only want you to get out of your difficulties and win Lydia back to you as well."

He gripped my hand. "Try and find Lydia," he gasped. "Tell her I won't touch a drop of drink till I have redeemed myself."

Two weeks went past, no news of any kind came. On the very last day I found Lydia, a wretched, broken-hearted woman, working as a seamstress in a dressmaker's shop off the Brompton Road.

The next morning, a paragraph in a newspaper caught my eye; it was headed—

"Sensation at Monte Carlo, Arthur de Courcy Bower breaks the bank three times in one night."

A few hours later two telegrams were placed in my hands, one was an order on the Credit Lyonnais to pay me £1000, the other was for Lydia, saying that £5000 was placed to her account at the same bank.

I found Lydia at the dressmaker's place. I showed her the wires, she broke down and sobbed like a child. We went to the bank together and drew the money. The first thing she did was to get back to the dressmaker's as quickly as she could and pay off a writ that had been served on the woman that morning.

Lydia was the best-hearted woman in the world and deserved a better fate than to have loved Bower.

Every day for the following week, telegraphic orders of money came pouring in. He had left me a list of his creditors, his £80,000 of debts vanished like smoke.

Then, one day, came the most welcome wire of all. " Join me with Lydia, Hotel Continental, Paris, end of week."

I will not describe that meeting, no lover's reunion could have equalled it. Like two happy children fresh from school they wandered about Paris together.

Lydia got some beautiful clothes, and Bower could hardly pass a jeweller's window without buying rings or stones for her, to make up for those she had lost during the dark days, before he went to Monte Carlo.

It is in moments like these that one realizes the value of money, and the happiness it can bring. The delight of spending it may not last long it is true, but while it does, it can give the most exquisite pleasure.

After paying all his debts, Bower had still nearly fifty thousand pounds left; with that as capital he returned to London to begin life over again.

Shortly afterwards, I bid the happy pair good-bye and returned again to the States.

When I got back to London, some four years had passed. I had lost touch with Bower, but had casually heard through friends what had in the meantime taken place.

Bower had made money in the City and had lost it again. Once more Lydia's jewels were pawned, once more he had repeated his extraordinary success at Monte Carlo, winning in one night, according to the papers, more than two hundred thousand pounds.

This time, however, he had done it on brandy, sometimes drinking an entire bottle before he faced the tables. Passing through Paris he got robbed of what was left . . . there was no Lydia to meet him on this occasion. Instead, a few brief words on a telegram from a Doctor, to say she was in the London Hospital dying of pneumonia and not expected to live twenty-four hours.

Sobered in an instant by the bad news, he sold even his overcoat to get back to London.

Fate had turned her face on her favourite, those dread words, " too late," were ringing in his ears. A fog in the Channel delayed the boat, a derailed truck held up the train. At last the hospital was reached. Bower rushed past the porter at the gates to meet Lydia's dead body being carried from her ward.

From that day on, Bower never tasted drink of any shape or kind; he was a changed man, but the change had also come " too late."

On Christmas Eve he sent out what he called an S.O.S. to the friends who knew him in his lucky days. He said I was the only one who answered " the Call." I found him in a miserable room below the street level, with the walls reeking with damp. He only asked me one favour, some money to put flowers on Lydia's grave, which he had never failed to do every Christmas morning.

The following week I took an office for him and started him in business in Kingsway House.

Again those awful words, " too late," seemed written on everything he did.

A year went past; Christmas came again. He had been out to Lydia's grave in the morning; he had placed a cross of white lilies where he thought her heart must be—and that same night, Arthur de Courcy Bower passed to his own long rest.

CHAPTER XL

CRIME HAS A PECULIAR FASCINATION OF ITS OWN. HOW WHITTAKER WRIGHT MET HIS WATERLOO

PROFESSOR LOMBROSO, the celebrated criminologist, made the following statement to me after a conversation concerning my Study of Hands.

"There is undoubtedly a criminal, a 'bad' hand. I think it strange that the Study of the Hand has not been cultivated more assiduously by the pathologist and the expert criminologist."

Nature, it certainly appears, imprints its warnings upon the palm of the hand—but few can read, and fewer still—heed the silent witness.

I must confess that there is no department of my art that has fascinated me more strongly than the tracing out of what may be called criminal instincts, as portrayed by the lines of the hand.

Cain, the murderer, was said to have carried his mark on his forehead; I wonder how many people realize that the words of Holy Writ actually say, "I will place a mark upon thy forehead *and on thy hand.*"

Just as there is the suicide's hand, so there is the hand of the murderer, and as if that were not sufficient, there are fatal predominating influences shown by the Planets at birth that seem to mark down many occupants of the murderers' plot in the precincts of the gaol.

On the other hand, criminal instincts may be combated by strength of character and by judicious training. That is why this study should play such a different part in our social scheme. If parents did but know the bias of their offspring, they would be on their guard—but, unhappily, this is rarely done.

In this connection the following may be found of interest.

Right at the beginning of my career, a lady brought her child of ten years of age to me and asked if I would give a characterization of his hand.

I made an examination, and I can write with truth that I was appalled at the lines I saw therein. Not only so, but the abnormal shape, with the talon-like and prehensile fingers indicated the true thief who steals for the love of acquisition. I examined the Line of Head; it was good, showing unusual intelligence; the Heart Line was almost indistinguishable, while the Line of Fate ended abruptly.

After the boy had been removed by his aunt who was with them, the mother told me a story for which I was fully prepared. The boy was untruthful, a thief, callous to an amazing degree, and beyond control. His father was dead; it was indeed a widow's problem.

I explained as tactfully as I could that the only hope was a firm regime, directed with sympathy and intelligence; that a strict school would undoubtedly be best to send him to.

The years passed, and one day I received a visit from a good-looking young man. He had received an important Government position, and was evidently well pleased with the world and himself.

To my surprise, he recalled how his mother had brought him to me as a little lad. I turned up the case in my books. Surely, I thought, this is an instance of how knowledge derived from a study of the hand can combat evil instincts.

I believe it was about two months later that a sensation was caused by a theft of money in a Treasury department of Whitehall. It was alleged that an assailant had attacked a clerk ; he had certainly lost some hundreds of pounds. Eventually the detectives arrested a man ; he was tried at the Old Bailey, and a singular double life was revealed.

He had managed to retain his veneer of outward respectability, but by night he sank into abysmal depths of depravity. It was the young man who seemed to have battled successfully against his bias towards evil. After he came out of prison, I saw him again, but dope had now gripped him ; he descended lower and lower, and died of an overdose of veronal. In this case, the tendencies for crime had evidently been too strong, or the Will had been too weak.

Before giving an account of some of the interesting criminals I have met, it may interest my readers to hear something of the great financiers who came to consult me from time to time.

One evening I was about to sit down to dinner in my apartment in Paris, when the bell rang and my servant announced that a man he took to be English was in the waiting-room and insisted on seeing me at once.

I went out determined to tell him I had finished work for the day and to call some other time.

I found a rather tall heavily built man pacing up and down the room impatiently.

" ' Cheiro '," he said abruptly, " I am sorry to call at this hour, but you *must* see me. There is only one question I want you to answer. I am taking the train to Havre to-night and I was not able to call during the day."

There was something so majestic and compelling about his personality that I could not refuse. There was also an intense yearning, wistful look in his eyes that went straight to my heart.

We entered my consulting-room, he put his hands on the cushion of my table.

" The only question I want to ask," he commenced, at the same time making an effort to appear calm and collected, " is this : I am at this moment at a terrible crisis in my life. Will I get through it ? That is all I want to know.

" I can help you to arrive at your decision by telling you that it all depends on *how long I have got to live*. Look closely at my Line of Life. Is there any indication in it of a sign of any immediate sudden or violent death ? "

It was a startling question for such a well-built, healthy looking man to ask.

Without speaking I examined the main lines of the right hand very closely.

The Line of Mentality or Head was significant; it was long, straight, and clear, the type that is always associated with the man of business or the financier.

I told him so and a sarcastic expression passed over his face.

"You are wrong," he said. "I am the greatest fool that ever lived. If it were not so, I would not be in the crucial position I am in to-day."

"The trouble is," I answered, "your ideas are too large; they have become top-heavy and unmanageable in the last few years, but with such a mentality, you should be able to carry through all your plans to a successful finish."

"That is exactly the point, will I live long enough to do it?"

I pressed the Line of Life. At the part that corresponded to the age he had reached (he told me he was born in Cheshire in 1845 and was consequently in his fifty-eighth year when he visited me in the March of 1903) there was a peculiar sharp red line that appeared to cut into it at this date. It was a sinister mark directly under what is called the Mount of Saturn.

I made a short calculation by Astrology, from his date of birth it was decidedly ominous.

"At this moment," I said, "you are under terribly bad conditions. You cannot help but make errors of judgment in every step you take. This long voyage you are about to take will, I fear, end badly. I see nothing but confusion and failure for you." Then with an effort to soften the effects of my words, I rapidly added—"There is, however, no danger of death for you for about a year, perhaps it is the worry and strain that is killing you. Twelve months is quite a long time to a man of your temperament. Could you not in that time straighten things out?"

For answer, he said very quietly, "Do you think from what you see, that there is a likelihood of death inside of a year?"

"Yes," I replied, "if things do not change for you. I think there is. Your heart is not really sound, there is every indication of sudden death."

He pulled his hands away. "You have told me," he said abruptly, "exactly what I wanted to know. It means that I will not be able to pull things through. I am being hounded to death at the present moment. I am on my way to New York to-night, to see one man who could pull me through and put me in the position to return and face my enemies. From what you say, I am evidently going to take this journey for nothing. If I fail, I have made up my mind to end my life, now you know why there is the indication of sudden death."

"But . . ." I interrupted.

"There are no buts about it," he retorted. "You will read all about me in the papers in the next few days. I must be off now, I have just time to catch my train at St. Lazaire. If I meet my friend in New York and get his help, I will send you a cable. My name is Wright—Whittaker Wright."

The rest of the story is public history. On the arrival of the boat, Whittaker Wright was arrested under an extradition order from England. His friend the banker *did not come to his assistance.*

After considerable delay and legal formalities, he was brought back to London, went through one of the most amazing trials in history before Mr. Justice Bigham, who sentenced him to seven years' penal servitude.

At the end of a long trial that lasted for twelve days, he kept his nerve to the very last. When the sentence was passed, in a silence in which one might have heard a pin drop, he bowed to the Judge and said, " My Lord, all I can say is that I am innocent of any intent to deceive anyone."

Leaving the dock, accompanied by four men, he entered a small room with his lawyer, Sir George Lewis. He discussed the question of an appeal. His solicitors told him that such a thing was hopeless. Very quietly he took a cigar from his pocket, biting the end of it off, he accepted a match from Sir George Lewis, lighted it, and stood for a moment without speaking looking out of the window.

Suddenly he turned, staggered towards a chair, collapsed into it, and died in a few moments.

The end had come within the year.

When a doctor from King's College Hospital arrived, it was discovered that in biting off the end of the cigar he had swallowed a small pilule containing cyanide of potassium which had caused almost instant collapse of the heart.

Such was the end of a man who had controlled some of the biggest financial companies in England, who had financed the now successful Baker Street-Waterloo Tube, which was the forerunner of London's present system of underground railways.

By an extraordinary irony of Fate, it was the backing of this great railway scheme which was later destined to play such a future in London's progress, that had locked up all the money of his group, the London and Globe Financial Corporation, and brought about the failure by which Whittaker Wright met his—Waterloo.

CHAPTER XLI

MATA HARI, THE FAMOUS WOMAN SPY

I MET this extraordinary woman several times. I knew her under her many names of Madame Zelle, Mata Hari, Baroness von Mingen, and in the latter stage of her life when during the War she posed as a neutral under the name of Madame van Hontin.

Of all the remarkable women my profession caused me to meet, I must give an unique place to Mata Hari, and I think if I cannot class her as the most beautiful, I can claim that she was the most bewitching, the most fascinating, and the most dangerous.

The only reason I escaped falling a victim to her toils, as far better and cleverer men had done, was simply and solely because as a beautiful woman—*she had no heart.*

In my unusual career I met many so-called " bad women," but although it may sound an extraordinary thing to say, I believe I can truthfully state that I never met a " bad woman " who had not some redeeming feature *of self-sacrifice, love, or affection that ran like a golden cord through her life.*

Mata Hari was the one exception; she was handsome as a queen, fascinating, intelligent, beautiful.

My curiously constructed nature, however, called for sentiment. To that call there was no answer—*that was the only reason I escaped.*

Perhaps at the time I first met her, her heart was already dead.

All kinds of stories have been circulated about her nationality. After I got to know her well, the tale she told me was that she was a " half-caste." Her father, she said, was a wealthy Dutch planter in Java, her mother a Japanese. Her father had died when she was only a few months old. Her mother took her to Burma and placed her in a Temple where she was trained as a religious dancer.

When only fourteen years of age she fell in love with a distinguished British officer who visited the Temple at a moment of an annual Buddist festival. She escaped from the Temple, found him at the capital, and eventually married him.

This man, from what she told me, held a very distinguished position, representing England in a high official capacity; at the death of his father he became a peer and for many years was a distinguished member of the House of Lords.

Two children were born, a boy and a girl, but the marriage proved to be anything but happy; her explanation was that her husband became cold and indifferent to her, she grew to hate him, and from that *to hate the country he belonged to and everything English.*

Her first tragedy was the death of her little boy. She had reason to suppose that he had been poisoned by a gardener who disliked her. She could not have the man arrested as he had employed a plant poison that had left no trace in the body, but in a moment of folly he had boasted to her maid that he had had his revenge.

As her husband would take no action, she took his revolver, which was always loaded, seized an opportunity of meeting the gardener alone, told him what she intended to do, and shot him through the head as he threw himself on his knees to beg for mercy.

Her husband's high position saved her from being arrested ; but she was compelled to leave Burma.

Her husband refused to accompany her ; taking her little daughter with her she bid him good-bye and never heard from him again.

The little girl died in a convent in Amsterdam a few months later. Free from all ties she turned to Paris to tempt fortune as so many women have done before her.

The few bits of jewellery she had soon went in her fruitless efforts to get work as a dancer among the music halls.

Dancing was the only thing she knew or could do, yet in the early stages of her career she could not get an engagement of any kind whatever.

It was about this time I met her. I was walking home one night from a meeting organized by an English woman for the aid of the badly treated cats and dogs of Paris, when I noticed a few paces ahead an extremely graceful figure of a woman that I could not help but admire.

It was a bitterly cold night, the woman before me had no coat : vanity, I thought—women will do anything for vanity, just because she has such a graceful figure she will risk pneumonia to show it off.

Just then she turned into the Champs Elysées ; twenty yards ahead stood a lighted brazier where some workmen were repairing telephone wires.

She went straight to the fire ; I could see her hold her hands towards it as I passed.

Perhaps she *is* cold, I thought—still, it is no business of mine. I cannot go to the aid of every strange woman I find in the streets of Paris.

I passed on ; I had gone about a hundred feet when some of those sentiments the English woman had used at the meeting about starving cats and homeless dogs twisted and turned in my brain.

Can I go into my house, sit down and read the evening paper at my cheery fireside, and be haunted by the figure of this woman warming her fingers at a street brazier ?

Just then a wisp of sleet struck me in the face.

I turned and went back towards the brazier ; she was still standing there with her hands stretched towards the fire.

I suppose I said the wrong thing. Men always do when they try to be kind.

Like a flash she turned on me. " How dare you speak to me," she snapped. " Do you take me for a woman of the streets ? "

I was too confused to know what I said. I apologized most humbly. Then under those glorious eyes that blazed with scorn, I found myself begging for forgiveness and blurting out something about my sympathy for lost dogs, cats, and the meeting I had attended.

This touched her sense of humour. " So I'm a lost cat, am I ? Oh well, you English are always *gauche;* what can one expect from them ? "

" You can expect sympathy from me," I said rapidly. " I can't leave you here trying to warm yourself at a brazier on such a night as this. Have you no home ? "

" No ! " she said and turned rapidly away.

Yes, I admit I followed her. I talked rapidly as I walked by her side. I did not like to offer her money, yet I did not like to leave her shivering in the streets.

My house was no distance away. Would she come there and warm herself ?

An hour later, after some supper and a good many cigarettes, she curled up on the hearthrug and slept till morning.

It was in this way I made the acquaintance of Mata Hari.

Some few weeks later, one afternoon she called to see me. She looked radiant with hope and excitement. " The turn in the tide has come, as you said it would," she laughed. " I am leaving for Berlin to-morrow. I shall have a thousand marks a week and hotel free. Is it not wonderful ? "

" How did it come about ? " I asked.

" Oh, quite simply and yet in such a funny way. I was giving an exhibition test on the stage of Olympia and had been turned down as they said my dance was too Oriental, too exotic. I was so broken-hearted at my repeated disappointments in trying to get an engagement that I slipped into one of the stalls at the back of the theatre and cried my heart out.

" Two people were sitting near me, a man and a woman. Suddenly the woman came over and, speaking in German, said :

" ' Don't be heart-broken, little Fräulein, the Frenchman is a fool, he does not understand your wonderful art, his mind could never get higher than ballet-skirts. Come with us to Berlin, you will be appreciated there.'

" She introduced me to her husband, Baron von Werthim ; we dined together that night and many times since. Finally, he made me the offer I have mentioned. I accepted. Does my Horoscope say that Berlin will be lucky for me ? "

Some time previously she had given me the date of her birth. She was born in Java on March 31st, 1879. I took it out of my desk and showed it to her.

" Curiously enough," I said, " from your Horoscope, Berlin and Germany, as a nation, will have a great attraction for you and should be fated to play an important role in your life. Under the rules laid down by what is called Mundane Astrology, Germany is governed by

Aries, the House of the Planet Mars, and so are you. At the date of your birth you had what is known as the Sun in Aries, which will influence you all through your life.

"At the same time, owing to some of the aspects in your Horoscope, your life will be a remarkable one, but full of tragedy.

"The cycle you are commencing now will reach its climax about October 1917. There *it will end in some violent death for you.*"

She left for Berlin the following day.

The next time we met was in the Hotel de l'Europe in St. Petersburg. She had the most expensive suite of rooms; she entertained largely, but I noticed the guests were chiefly important heads of the Government or Staff officers in the Russian Army. The name she lived under was Baroness von Mingen; she was considered extremely rich with a weakness for doing charitable and eccentric things.

One night very late I was finishing some writing in my rooms in the hotel, when the handle of the door turned and she entered.

"My dear friend," she said, "I am going to treat myself to having a quiet hour with you—will you mind very much?"

How could any man refuse? I am glad for the reputation of the Catholic Church that St. Anthony died long before Mata Hari was born; he was the only man, it is said, that beauty did not appeal to— *no wonder he was made a Saint.*

She looked exquisitely handsome in the ball dress she was wearing, she was covered with jewels, with a magnificent row of pearls round her shapely throat.

"The German stage seems to be a lucrative profession," I said.

"The World's stage pays still better, my friend."

Then she told me an extraordinary story. On her arrival in Berlin she had found that no theatrical engagement awaited her.

Instead the Baron had installed her in the private hotel run by the International Spy Department of the German Secret Service.

It was gradually instilled into her mind that her beauty, her talents, her knowledge of languages would be lost in an ordinary stage career as a dancer, but that as "a diplomatic investigator" she would have a wonderful career.

For three months she went through every day a systematic training in the general political aims of the leading countries of the world. Naval and military plans were given to her to copy, she was also instructed in deciphering secret codes, also how to make them, and how to send and receive messages by Morse signals.

She was invited by high officials to witness field days, army displays, and many of the important Court ceremonies.

The Kaiser himself had been specially gracious to her on many occasions, the result being that she conceived an admiration for Germany and everything German that became as fanatical as the devotion of any convert to a new religion.

"How did you obtain your title?" I asked.

"I am supposed to be the widow of a rich German Baron," she laughed. " If you should be tempted to make inquiries at the German Legation here, or in any other country, you will find my papers are quite in order ; further, you will get the information that my late husband and myself are only interested in charitable work and in the promotion of International Peace."

" And the end of it all will be," I said sadly, " that if war ever does come, you will be shot somewhere ' At Dawn ' as a German spy."

" Yes," she nodded, " I have never forgotten your prediction for October 1917, but believe me or not, as you wish, the life I have chosen is well worth the risk.

" ' Espionage ' is the greatest game of all," she went on ; " it is the battle of brains on the chess-board of life, a game in which even the humblest spy plays a hand in the destiny of Empires.

" Think of it ye little people content to live in the monotony of ' an eat, drink, and sleep existence.' The end for you may be a marble cross in some village churchyard, a few wreaths, or an obituary notice probably paid for out of the money you left some poor relation.

" Some penny journal, if you were a shareholder, may extol the good you did your country. A year later your ' proud country ' may forget your very name. Think of the mockery of it all !

" For us, spies, life has no illusions. We know the gold we gain is tainted. We have not to delude ourselves that we are honest shop-keepers who have never cheated our neighbour, added water to children's milk, chalk to flour, or damped sugar to gain an extra penny a pound.

" Believe me, the money we make is just as clean—if making money can ever be called clean—we sell our brains for the highest price. If we sometimes sell lives—don't forget we as often sell our own—but in that case ' Shot at Dawn ' cancels the promissory notes.

" For us there is no grassy mound in some village churchyard, no cross of marble—a bed of quick-lime is our shroud—a number in a prison yard—our reward.

" For us there is no brevet of Merit, no Legion d'Honeur, as for the soldier who killed all he could before he fell in glory. The bomb-thrower, or the gas chemist can be honoured by their grateful country. The treacherous mine-maker who burrows under ground, who blows up whole regiments by the press of a button, can be decorated or receive columns of praise for bravery.

" Our Obituary Notice is a propaganda of lies, the country we have served denies having employed us, denies having paid us, denies that they bought us with their gold or tricked us into service.

" For us there is no appeal—no friend to come forward to testify how well we obeyed orders.

" As we have worked in silence—so we must die in silence."

She had made me shudder with the bitterness of her words.

"The picture you paint is terrible," I said. "For God's sake give the whole thing up."

"Spies never give up," she retorted. "No gambling fever, no drug that was ever invented has such a hold.

"No," she interrupted savagely, "don't tell me I can marry and settle down. I tried it once—what did it give me? A husband who used me as a plaything, who gave me two children, and then did not care if we starved or went to hell.

"Marriage is good enough for the cabbage type of woman—all leaves and no heart. In her turn she is fit food for the caterpillars who crawl on her—who eat her—and who desert her when there is nothing left but the stalk.

"Don't preach to me of love—it exists solely in the egotistical brains of fuddled fools. Friendship, camaraderie, passion, between men and women, if you like. Beyond this there is nothing but sex-warfare that knows neither armistice nor peace.

"The one career that women can excel in—is that of the professional spy. In this all her natural qualities can find full scope. Her powers as an actress, her love of intrigue, her desire for wealth, dissimulation, her intuition, her inherent gift of lying, her art of thieving, her innate curiosity, her snake-like body, her beauty, and lastly—her sex.

"One of the maxims of the German Secret Service is 'The only perfect spy is a perfect woman provided she has no heart.'"

"You must be perfection," I could not help saying under my breath.

She had either heard or read my thoughts.

"I am," she frankly admitted, "and yet with the weakness of the woman in me I wanted to unburden my thoughts to someone —to someone I could trust—that is why I have come to you to-night.

"God only knows when we may meet again. I am leaving Russia in the morning, but my good friend, if our paths should cross in the future, I will always come and tell you if I am still successful as a woman spy."

Our paths did not again cross until a few months before the outbreak of the Great War.

The telephone bell rang in my room, the voice of Mata Hari sounded very clear and distinct. Her voice like her face she was able to change at a moment's notice to suit any part she might be playing. Her own natural voice was soft, deep-toned, with a curious cadence of sadness about it that once heard one could never forget.

"'Cheiro,'" the voice said, "I am in London for a few days. Come and dine to-night at the 'Savoy.' There will be one other man, but an interesting study for you."

"A study, in what way?" I asked.

Along the wire came that same low, curious laugh that she used when she was pleased with something she had accomplished.

"A study in love," came the answer. "Surely nothing could be more interesting for you."

"Are you caught at last, Mata?"

"Come and judge for yourself," she purred. "I hardly know what to say. Love is such a wonderful thing, it takes so many forms and shapes."

"Who shall I ask for when I arrive at the 'Savoy?'"

"Baroness von Mingen, of course. Do you think I change my name as often as I do my dresses?"

At eight o'clock I presented myself at her suite of rooms.

As I came down the corridor, I amused myself trying to picture what this wonderful lover of hers would be like. Her remark on the telephone about "many forms and shapes" had decidedly roused my curiosity. I was prepared to meet anything from a dwarf to an elephant, but I was hardly prepared for the surprise that awaited me.

It was midsummer, the blinds had not yet been drawn, the ruby sunset gleaming across the Thames had turned London into a city of gold.

Lost in admiration stood before me one of the most prominent men in French politics. One of those few really great men that France has created in recent years.

He turned round as I crossed the room, he recognized me. We had met several times in Paris when I was running the paper *L'Entente Cordiale* that I have alluded to in a previous chapter.

"Just to think of meeting you here," he said, as he cordially shook my hand. "But of course it is natural that you know our charming hostess on account of her wonderful work for international goodwill among nations.

"What a wonderful woman, is she not?" he rattled on. "Just to think of the good feeling that has sprung up between France and England and also with Germany since that night you and I met at the banquet given to the late King Edward on his visit to Paris in 1903. It is women like our hostess who have done so much to bring all this about. Baroness von Mingen may, it is true, be a German by marriage, but she is an Angel of Peace by birth."

I had no time to answer, I could only look at this remarkable man and wonder—wonder at the metamorphosis that love can make when it touches the heart and brain of men who are supposed to be as hard as stone.

When I had first met this man, he was so French that the very mention of Germany was enough to give him a fit of apoplexy. As for England, she had always been "la perfide Albion" in his eyes, so much so that persons of all shades of politics had asked how much he was bribed to attend the banquet to King Edward.

Just then "the Angel" entered.

If I had thought her handsome that last time I saw her in St. Petersburg, how could I describe her now. I can only say that if ever an

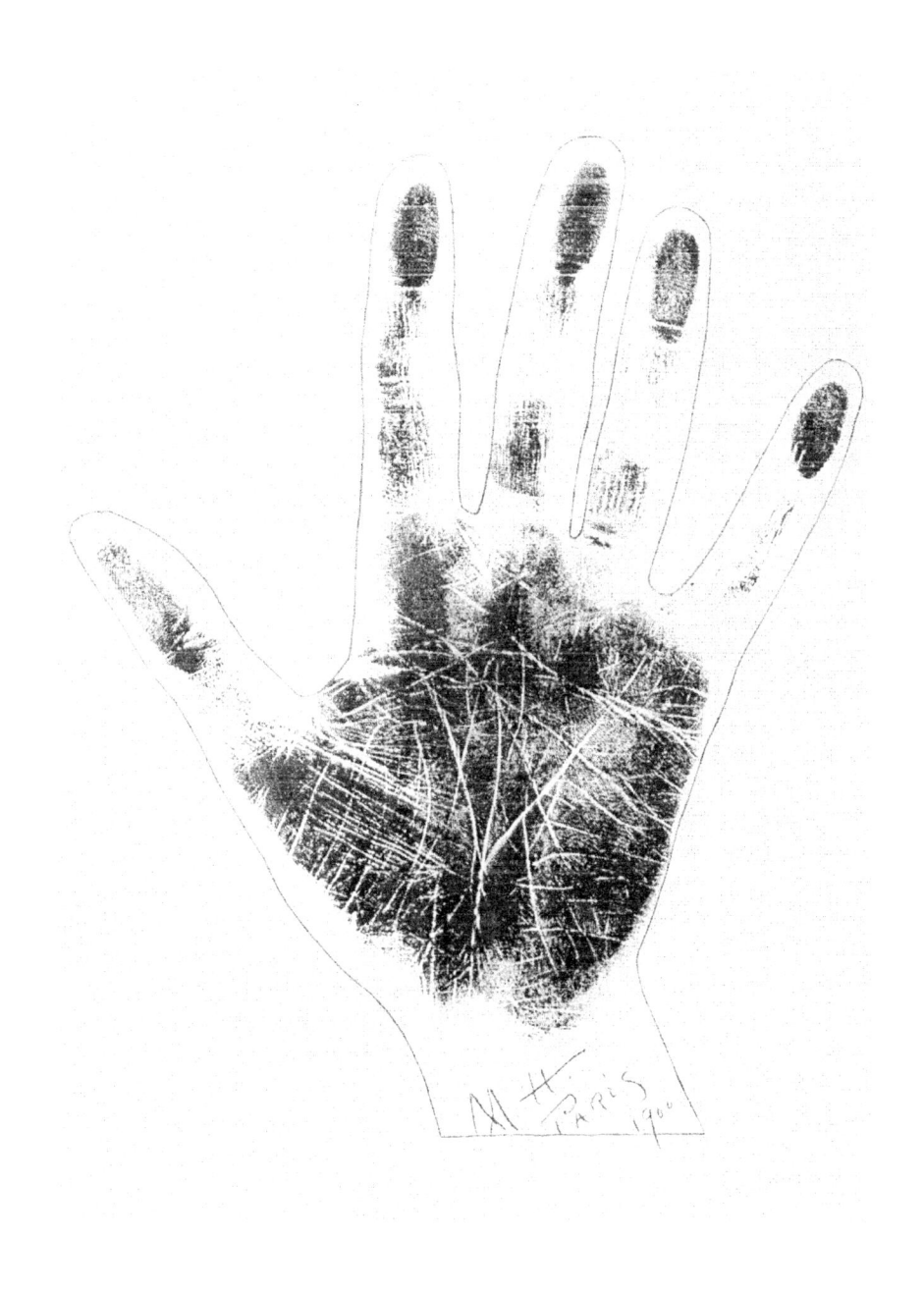

THE RIGHT HAND OF MATA HARI, THE FAMOUS WOMAN SPY

angel had come down to earth and got dressed by Parisian masters of art—it was the woman who entered the room at that moment.

Being nearer to her she greeted me almost affectionately as an old friend, but I was merely a foil, a prelude, a symphony in B Flat for the greeting she gave the French politician.

She did not walk—she glided across the carpet to him. Her glorious eyes—made no doubt more brilliant by an extra drop of belladonna—shone with a radiance almost divine.

She stretched out both hands. He stooped and kissed them as devotedly as he would have done the hands of a saint.

"*Mon cher ami*," was all she said, but those three words vibrated with such apparent emotion and meaning, that the poor Frenchman looked for a moment quite weak about the knees.

Then I learned that in answer to her telegram, he had risked his life by coming in an aeroplane from Paris, and such things *were a risk* in those early days of flying.

She rewarded him by a cocktail of absinthe made by her own hands, and we sat down to dinner.

What a dinner it was! As a compliment to her guest, everything was French; in fact, she told him the frogs' legs—and the snails—had come over by aeroplane—perhaps the very one that had brought him.

"*Mon Dieu*," she sighed. "If all had crashed together—what a mess!

"But why have gloomy thoughts?" she added quickly, seeing his look of horror. "God is so good, life is so beautiful, disaster could not happen to any friend of mine—I bear their names in my prayers each night to the Throne of Grace."

The dinner, like all good things, came to an end. The waiters had disappeared, we lit our cigarettes and moved out to the chairs on the balcony.

The wine, her beautiful words, the scene below us, the Thames sweeping silently out to the sea, the last rays of light touching the dome of St. Paul's, gilding its Cross with gold, all conspired to give one a feeling of peace with oneself and with humanity in general.

If the Frenchman's face looked benign before dinner, it now wore a expression of satisfied beatitude, something like what one sees on a fat priest's face when he breaks his fast after the midday Mass.

"Yes," Mata went on, "I know my dreams of Universal Peace will be realized before long. I know it is coming. As you are such good friends of mine, I will trust you with a secret. Only last week when interviewing the Kaiser for his subscription to the International Red Cross, I found him in his study taking down the picture of Germany's earliest battleship and hanging in its place an illuminated text. What do you imagine were the words?"

We leaned forward breathlessly.

"They were: 'I will turn their swords into ploughshares and their battleships into Noah's Arks.'"

"*Mon Dieu!* how wonderful," the Frenchman said.

Then in his turn he confided that the Minister of War had such a deficit in his Budget that certain stores had run out, that the Army had not enough boots to last three months, that the new rifle had not been supplied, and that famous gas which had been tried on a flock of sheep and killed them in a moment could not be manufactured in any quantity, as it was too dangerous to handle.

"As I said," Mata whispered, "all is making for international peace. What a glorious place this world will be to live in in the next few years."

"It is due to noble women like you, Madame, that all this has come about," the Frenchman said. "The English have a true proverb: 'The hand that rocks the cradle rules the world.'"

As the conversation had now turned to cradles and from that might turn to babies, I thought it was time for me to leave.

She stepped out on the landing to bid me good-bye.

"My Frenchman is very much in love, don't you think so?" she laughed.

"Yes," I replied. "But why did you have me at the dinner?"

"Because," she laughed, "I am an actress at heart and must have an audience. Good-bye—don't forget me in October 1917."

But perhaps the most dramatic experience I had in connection with Mata Hari was a strange encounter with her activities in Ireland towards the end of the War. I had run up to Dublin to pass a few hours there and attend to some business. About seven o'clock one evening I went into a rather third-rate restaurant in the shipping district of the Liffey.

I was just finishing some tea and toast before I started home, when I noticed at the other side of the restaurant a decrepit Irish peasant woman, about to finish her meal. After she had paid her bill she looked across at me in a wistful lonely kind of way, as if she wanted to ask something. Then she got up and came over to my table and said, in a broad Irish brogue—rather that of the South of Ireland: "Sure, sir, an' can you tell me what time o' day it is?" I pulled out my watch and said: "My good woman, it is now seven-thirty." It appeared to distress her. "Sure, sir," she said sharply, "how thin can I get my train for the South that is to be leaving Kingsbridge at eight o'clock?"

I replied: "It'll certainly take you all your time to get there. I suppose the best plan would be for you to walk up to O'Connell Bridge and take a tram from there to Kingsbridge Station." As I was saying the words I realized that she could not possibly get there in time. I felt sorry for the poor old thing, and impulsively decided to help her.

I said quickly: "You'll never be able to get that train in time. Where do you want to go to?"

She replied: "Sure an I must get to Cork some time to-night and from there on to Kinsale, and I *must* do it. Oh God, sir—if you only *knew why I must do it!*"

Touched by the agonized look on her face I said : " My car is at the door. It will not take me far out of my way. Jump in and I'll get you there in time."

" Sure—an' may the good Lord bless you," she said, in her quaint Irish brogue, and picking up her bundle, which was that of an Irish peasant, she and I went out to the car and were quickly racing to Kingsbridge, to the station.

She had a return third class ticket, I put her in a compartment. As I said good-bye and turned away, the woman leaned out of the window, and in a very soft voice called me back. With a sweet smile she said : " ' Cheiro,' my dear, I am so glad you did not recognize me. It gives me implicit confidence in my disguise." For a moment I was dumbfounded. It was none other than Mata Hari.

The next morning she reached Kinsale, and as far as anyone can follow the story, she was taken off by a collapsible boat and picked up by a German submarine waiting off the coast, which took her to Spain. From there she could easily have escaped. She knew the police of all countries were now watching for her. Instead, however, she risked her life by returning to France. She went straight to the trenches near Verdun, where she again took up her role as a dancer.

One night she slipped across the trenches into the German lines, but she had been watched and followed. When she returned she was placed under arrest, transferred to Paris, tried and sentenced to the death of a spy.

One dismal morning in October 1917 she met her fate to the year and the month of my tragic prediction. Actress and soldier of fortune to the last, she refused to be blindfolded, kissed her hands to the soldiers, and met her fate with a smile on her lips.

CHAPTER XLII

I VISIT MONTE CARLO TO PROVE MY SYSTEM OF NUMBERS. ITS ASTROLOGICAL FOUNDATION

AFTER a long journey in Russia, I concluded I would give my nerves a much-needed rest, so being in the south near Odessa, I took the Black Sea route for Europe, stopped a few days off Constantinople, and finally found myself in Genoa.

After a good rest in Italy, I thought I would like to try a new form of excitement, so I let myself drift into that maelstrom of humanity that circles and surges round the tables at Monte Carlo.

There was, however, a method in my madness. I wanted to see for myself if that strange law of numbers that I have so often alluded to in my books would have any practical meaning when applied to the numbers of roulette.

It may surprise some people to hear that it can be amply demonstrated that this extraordinary game, which to many conveys no meaning to their ears, except that of a gambling idea that has no equal, is in reality a wonderfully thought out system, whose base rests on astrological knowledge.

Without going into too much detail which might prove confusing to the majority of my readers, I will just point out a few of the leading peculiarities about roulette which go far to prove my contention.

Why were the 36 numbers and a zero placed round the circumference of the wheel ? Add the zero to the 36 and you will immediately have the answer. *It will then represent the 360 degrees of the earth's Zodiac.*

The four-pointed cross by which the wheel is turned corresponds in its turn to the four cardinal points of the Zodiac, and to the four divisions of the year.

No matter what way one may add the numbers that lie on the green cloth together (which even by its very colour—green—represents vegetation or the earth) one can only get the number 9 as a total, which is in itself *the exact number of the planets of our Solar System.*

In all occult studies the number 7 is regarded as the " sacred " creative, or spiritual number, while the 9 in all cases represents the " material."

It is a curious fact worth remembering that there are seven planets that revolve on their axis through the Zodiac *in one direction*, and two of the farthest planets, Uranus and Neptune, that revolve on the axis in the opposite direction. The seven tones of Music represent their " Spirit of Music " from which all harmony is produced, the seven colours represent the " Spirit of Colour " which manifests itself in all that relates to colour, and in passing it may be remarked that all through the Bible the " seven " wherever mentioned always stands in relation to the mysterious God force influencing humanity.

In the most ancient rules of occult philosophy one can find the law laid down that the number 7 is the only number capable of dividing what is called the " Number of Eternity " and continuing to do so as long as the symbol representing Eternity lasts, and yet at every addition of its division *producing the number 9*, or in other words *it creates the basic number on which all materialistic calculations are built* and on which *all human effort depends. Example.*—Number 1 the first number—represents the First Cause or Creator, while a circle or zero has from time immemorial been given to represent the endless—or in other words, Eternity.

Place the 1 and this symbol of zero side by side as seven figures, divide by the " sacred number," the 7, and one obtains the number 142857, which if added together to the last digit produces the number 9, or in other words, the materialistic or Earth symbol, as :

$$7) 1000000$$
$$142857 = 27 = 9.$$

In the Book of Revelation we read the following cryptic words :

> " Here is Wisdom. Let him that hath understanding count the number of the beast : for it is the number of man ; and his number is 666." (Rev. xiii, v. 18.)

Add this number together, it gives 18, and reducing it to one digit, 1 plus 8, we get the number 9 " *which is the number of man.*"

Looking at the tableau of the roulette table, no matter in what way one may add the numbers on it together, either across the columns or up the columns, the total in every case is the mysterious number of 9, the " number of man " and *the number of the planets that govern man.*

The very colours of the numbers given in roulette as Red and Black convey in the most accurate symbolism the qualities of the planets these numbers represent, namely, masculine and feminine, and fit the following series :

Moon's Number	2, 11, 20, 29	are	Black (feminine)
Mars „	9, 18, 27, 36	„	Red (masculine)
Venus „	6, 15, 24, 33	„	Black (feminine)
Jupiter „	3, 12, 21, 30	„	Red (masculine)
Uranus „	4, 13, 22, 31	„	Black (feminine)
Mercury „	5, 14, 25, 32	„	Red (masculine)
Saturn „	8, 17, 26, 35	„	Black (feminine)
Neptune „	7, 16, 25, 34	„	Red (masculine)
Sun „	1, 19, 28	„	Red (masculine)
The number 10 of the Sun		is	Black (feminine)
And the Zero	. . .	„	Black (feminine)

The numbers given above as belonging to the nine planets are no fantasy of modern times, but have been handed down to man as representative of the various planets.

In those far-off ages, certain sects of men devoted their lives to these studies. Such men were the absolute masters of the occult or hidden meaning of numbers, both in their application to Time and in their relation to human life. We cannot forget that it was the ancient Hindus who discovered what is known as "the procession of the Equinoxes," and in their calculation they worked out that such an occurrence takes place every 25,850 years. Our modern science with all its advantages of mechanical devices has after endless labour only proved that the discovery of this ancient people *was correct in every particular*.

How, or by what means, these wonderful students of the heavens were able to arrive at such a calculation has never been discovered, but their decision as to this remarkable occurrence has been handed down to us from the most remote ages and by our modern appliances been proved correct. It is, therefore, not illogical to accept the idea that they may have been as equally right in the numbers they gave to each planet and in some mysterious way intimately related to them.

It would not be appropriate for me in a book of this nature to set out the arguments that can be raised in favour of the theory that the Sun, Moon, and other planets influence not only the smallest action of our lives, but also the vibrations of the tiniest molecules of matter. It has recently been demonstrated by scientists that electrons in the atom revolve at a speed of 1800 revolutions per second.

As even the greatest sceptic of such things is forced to admit the influence of the Moon on the tides of the ocean and on the brain of lunatics, he is also forced to admit when a conjunction of the Sun and Moon occurs in some particular longitude and latitude that the highest tides must take place. Following this line of argument, it is not illogical to assume that when *the conjunction of planets occurs*, say directly over Monte Carlo, that all things, even the succession of numbers coming from the roulette wheel, may also be affected.

Briefly working on this idea, and calculating the conjunctions and aspects of the planets for an exact period such as one hour at Monte Carlo, I was able after a little time to work out with considerable accuracy the probable run of numbers that would most occur during an hour on a given day when I went to the "tables."

It would take too much space and perhaps be wearying to the majority of my readers if I went more deeply into this subject in such a book of Memoirs. I can, however, state and without fear of contradiction, as I have kept the records, that after considerable practice I was able to gain on an average about 5000 francs (£200) during the hour that I had selected to play.

To do this, however, day after day was no easy matter; the working out of the calculations that were necessary, together with the nervous tension involved, became so great, that I confess I was rather glad when the period of my self-imposed test was ended and I said *au revoir* to that "mile square bit of earthly Paradise" called Monte Carlo.

I have said, I think, sufficient to show the astrological connection that may be found between numbers in themselves and the famous game of roulette—but I specify *as played at Monte Carlo,* for there is no place in the world where this game is played with more fairness or under such good conditions.

It certainly took me a month of real hard work to finally demonstrate with success that one can work out the relation between the numbers given by roulette and Astrology, but I must warn those who think such an idea is an easy way of making money that unless they are armed with an equally well thought out system of progression in connection with the amount they are prepared to stake, there is no system that will enable them to win, for the financial side of the game has been as cleverly thought out as is the game itself.

The real origin of roulette can be traced back to the cousin of Mah Jongg, who invented the famous Chinese game of that name that recently became such a vogue in Europe and America. It is said that he taught roulette to a Jesuit priest in Mongolia, who brought it back with him to France, where it was reconstructed into its present form by a monk who discovered the secret of the game by his knowledge of Astrology as I will set out in the following chapter. France claims that it was invented by her celebrated mathematician, Pascal, who was the originator of the accepted Theory of Probability. I however consider that the story of the monk is the more likely of the two.

CHAPTER XLIII

THE LEGEND OF MONTE CARLO—THE SECRET THAT WAS LOST

I WILL now tell "The Legend of Monte Carlo." I received it from a good old priest who lived no great distance from the Casino, and I have every reason for believing that this story is the correct one.

Long before Monte Carlo was ever heard of, so the story runs, it was an unknown hamlet in the bankrupt Principality of Monaco, and far up in the mountains overlooking it stood an also equally bankrupt monastery.

The good monks prayed the good Lord day after day and night after night for money to carry on their work, but the good Lord, in His wisdom, up to then had only seen fit to augment year by year their flock of impoverished peasants, and the day was not far distant when the monastery would be seized for debt and the good monks turned out to the mercies of a cold and heartless world.

Unable to endure the suspense any longer, one evening after Vespers the monks went in a body to call on the Head of the monastery to impress on him that it was his duty to see that something should be done.

This important personage, who was to them a kind of a semi-god, the oldest of them all, lived apart in the top of one of the towers, as near Heaven as he could possibly get.

All day he studied old manuscripts and books, at night he studied the stars, and between the two he had lost the confidence of his inferiors, for he also, like God, did not seem to listen to their prayers and had also closed his eyes to the rapidly diminishing size of their waists.

The evening they climbed to his uppermost abode, they found him in the best of good humour, playfully turning a curious-looking wheel and jotting down figures on a paper beside him.

The good monks were, of course, terribly shocked—so much so, they could hardly speak. When they did, they all spoke at once, but the old monk turned from them and went on spinning his wheel.

At last, when they had tired themselves out, he heard their story.

He asked how much money they needed by the end of the year.

"One hundred thousand francs," they all gasped with one voice.

"A mere bagatelle," he smiled. "Come to me on the first day of the year and you shall have it."

When they had gone, the old monk, still smiling, packed his wheel in a bag, put his papers in his pocket, and the next day descended from the monastery, took the narrow path down the mountain, and before long might have been seen wending his way towards a small restaurant that lay under the shadow of the castle of Monaco, kept by a man known as Monsieur Blanc.

Monsieur Blanc was not a successful man, but he was enterprising; he had also something of the artist in his composition, for he had built his little café in one of the loveliest spots in Nature, believing with the true artistic spirit that some day Nature would call her worshippers there to revel in her beauty, and when they had fed their eyes, he would feed their stomachs, and then his fortune would be made.

Alas! like many other artists, Monsieur Blanc had been a little too premature in his dreams. Nature's worshippers had not heard her call. No railway had yet gone farther than Nice and the solitary coach that passed only occasionally deposited a visitor at his door.

Up above him in his lonely castle, the Prince of Monaco was nearly as poor as himself, and being poor, perhaps as rarely saw a visitor at his door.

Monsieur Blanc received the old monk rather dubiously: monks generally came to beg, and he was not in a very charitable mood that that day.

Imagine his surprise when the black-robed stranger shook him by the hand and said, "Mon cher Monsieur Blanc, I have come to bring you a fortune, I have come to make you the wealthiest man in the world, I have come to make of this place the Mecca of the earth."

Monsieur Blanc at first thought that his visitor was an escaped lunatic, but as the little restaurant was empty, he perhaps thought he might as well waste his time with a lunatic as to have no one to talk so. They sat down at a little iron-topped table in the window, and over a glass of red wine he let the old man talk.

"Monsieur Blanc," he said, waving his hand towards the window, "look at the beauty of that exquisite scene beneath us, and not a person here to appreciate it but our own two selves."

Monsieur Blanc nodded his head. He had often thought the same thing himself.

"Well," the old monk continued, "what we want here is something that will draw people—a magnet charged with the greatest of all human attractions, a magnet whose lines of force will radiate north, south, east, and west. Yes, a magnet to draw people and to hold them here when they come."

"Yes, mon cher Monsieur Blanc," continued the monk, "you nearly had the same idea when you built your restaurant. You thought you would draw people by their stomachs, but there are too many other restaurants in competition—and you forget, cher Monsieur, that there is another magnet even more strong than the stomach."

"What is it?" Monsieur Blanc asked.

"The pocket," the old man quickly replied.

Monsieur Blanc had, in spite of himself, become interested. There was something in the monk's philosophy that appealed to his reason.

"Go on, Father," he said, "tell me some more about your magnet."

"Ah cher Monsieur," the monk went on, "Nature is a strange goddess. I have had time to study her ways and in return she has told me something of her secrets. She plays with man as a woman plays with her lover. She kisses him one moment and ruins him the next. She brings to life in order to kill. She gives in order to take. Is it not so, cher Monsieur ? "

Monsieur Blanc did not know what to reply, and the old man continued.

" Man is vain, Monsieur Blanc. He thinks he has intelligence, but Nature has only given him enough to illuminate his own stupidity.

" Man pretends he worships God, but it is only to gain something from Him that he goes down upon his knees, he would even steal from his God if he only knew that he would not be found out.

" No, believe me, Monsieur Blanc, man does not worship either Nature or God. If he did this little paradise here would be crowded to its seashore and your little place would be a temple and not a café."

" But I don't want a temple, my good friend," Monsieur Blanc said.

" I know you don't, cher Monsieur, but you shall have one all the same—and your temple will do great good to the world as well. It will humble the rich, it will raise the poor, it will encourage Art ; Music will find her home here among these gardens, Painting will have galleries built for her among these rocks. Thousands who have never seen Nature at her best will one day from here look into her eyes for the first time—and if you never did more than that, Monsieur Blanc, you would even then have done a great deal."

" But how is all this to be done ? " Monsieur Blanc asked.

" Oh, so easily," the old man smiled, " that you would never have guessed it—it is only a game, Monsieur Blanc—only a game. But let us not forget that all life is but a game and men and women but stupid players."

Opening his valise, he drew out his cloth and roulette wheel and explained his invention. He next showed how mathematically he had calculated all the chances, and how all were, in the end, *in favour of the bank*.

" The gambling instinct," he went on to say, " is, in the human family, the strongest of all outside of self-preservation.

" You gambled," he continued, " when you staked your money on this little restaurant. The respectable shopkeeper in London gambles when he chooses Oxford Street instead of Regent Street for his shop. Every man gambles, even when he takes a woman to be his lawful wife. All gamble ! Nations on navies, Kings on armies, it is the one active principle of life and without it there would be stagnation.

" In the case of my invention, cher Monsieur," he continued, " it is the most honest gamble of all. Most people only get ' even chances ' in life, but here you can give a thirty-five to one chance against any one chosen number turning up, and if this should be too much for the player's mind to grasp, or if he should be so religious that he would not like to take such advantage of your generosity, then he can console his conscience on the even chances of black and red, just as he knows he does on the everyday affairs of life.

"Yes, Monsieur, you have the magnet here to draw all classes. You appeal to the strongest instinct of all.

"Lastly, it is only a toy—a plaything—and remember, cher Monsieur, all human beings love toys. When they are young they have them given to them and when they are old *they pay for them themselves.*"

He then spun the roulette wheel. Monsieur Blanc put counters on the different numbers and the other combinations, and as he sometimes won and sometimes lost, he marvelled at the monk's marvellous financial combination which was calculated to such a nicety that, although perfectly fair to the players, resulted in giving a percentage to the bank of, an average, $1\frac{1}{2}$ to 2 per cent on every transaction. Although apparently such a small percentage in the favour of the bank, each hour's play would bring in such a profit that was undreamt of in any other business.

Monsieur Blanc was enchanted with the idea. At last in a hesitating voice he said: "Tell me, Father, what will be your terms if I agree to start this wonderful game?"

"My good Monsieur Blanc," the monk answered, "riches have no meaning in my eyes; it is only for the good of my monastery I have worked out this idea. Every year the claims on my little community become heavier and heavier, and it is only to enable us to carry on our good work that I would give you this plan.

"But I am not going to ask you for commissions or regular percentage on the profits you will make, for that would be a burden I would be placing on you, and it would have the effect of making my community so rich that those who came after me might cease to work, for money too easily got, *breeds laziness, even among the best.*

"No, mon cher Monsieur, my terms will be easier than you think. They will be as follows—at the close of every year when I have the accounts of the monastery brought before me, I will see what the debt is we have to face. I will come down to your casino (dressed as a civilian) and I will have the right to go to your bank and draw the amount of capital I will require (but don't look frightened, cher Monsieur, I will only require it as a loan). With this capital, which again will be only the quarter of the sum we will be in need of at the end of any year, I will play my system, and in one evening I will gain the amount required for our debts, plus the amount I may have borrowed from your bank. Before leaving, I will repay your bank whatever amount it has advanced and I will return to my monastery with the balance.

"When my life comes to a close, as it shortly will, I shall bequeath my system to my successor, he will do the same at the end of every year, and his successor after him, and so on year after year. We will have the satisfaction of looking down from our windows and seeing these barren rocks becoming covered with gardens.

"Beautiful villas will be built along the slopes of these wild mountains, the railway will be brought here and trains will come from all parts of Europe.

"Music will make her home here, and the paintings of great masters will be hung in your galleries. Taxation will be unknown, the lamentations of the poor will not be heard in your streets, pilgrims will come from all parts of the world to your Mecca of gold, but they will be rich pilgrims, Monsieur Blanc—and as pilgrims always leave some souvenirs of their pilgrimage behind them, so will your rich pilgrims leave their wealth and their jewels with you, in return for the new sensation your enterprise will give them.

"Some will be humbled while others will be exalted, some will come in poverty and leave in wealth, some will learn lessons that no other school could teach them, and lastly, though some may lose, Monsieur Blanc *will gain always*. Dost thou like the picture, cher Monsieur?"

. . . .

Within a month Monsieur Blanc had already started with the first table of roulette in his little restaurant under the grey walls of the castle of Monaco.

Carriages and diligences loaded with passengers soon came in daily from Nice, Cannes, Mentone, and Italy; in a few months the P.L.M. Railway asked the Prince of Monaco for a concession to carry their line through; villas sprang up as in a night, and large hotels began laying their foundations.

The then semi-bankrupt Prince of Monaco woke from a nightmare of poverty to a day-dream of wealth. He gave Monsieur Blanc a concession of land for a new casino in Monte Carlo, on the consideration of a royalty to be paid to his family for ever.

Then an alliance was brought about. The princely house of Monaco became joined with the lowly house of Blanc, in "the holy bonds of matrimony." Monte Carlo became the magnet of the world—the old monk's prophetic vision had become a reality.

Meanwhile, the little monastery high up in the mountains had also gone ahead; at the end of every year the old Superior had always the money to meet its debts. The rare flowers in the garden could now be distilled and their perfume sent to all parts of the earth; old monks had no longer to die in poverty or hope for the charity of an ungrateful world.

And when the Angelus tolled at sunset, the prayers that rose from that monastery on the hill, were so full of gratefulness and heartfelt thanks that I can imagine the harps of Heaven grew silent for a moment to let them pass.

Alas! that it should be so in this world of change, this "abiding place" where no happiness can last for long, the days of the old Superior were numbered, the sands in Life's hour glass were running out.

It had been with slow and laboured steps he made at the end of one of his years his last journey to the casino, and when the needed money was won, the weight of the gold was so heavy that dawn was breaking when he at last again reached the monastery.

Looking upward with a prayer of thankfulness on his trembling lips, he read his own approaching end in the fading stars that were extinguished one by one with the approach of another day. " I, too, must appoint another to take my place," he murmured, as he opened the side gate that led him towards his abode.

With a quiet sigh of relief he paid over the money, but as the monks filed away with cheerful faces, he called one back and closed the door.

The one his choice had fallen on was Father Ambrose, a man about middle age, but so handsome that had he not been a monk, the goddess of Fortune herself might have given up her throne to follow his fate.

Father Ambrose had also studied Astrology, he was such a good mathematician that " the stars in their courses " could not err for him in the fraction of a second in a cycle of time. The old Superior had often thought of him in his choice of a successor—and so the moment had come at last for the secret he held so dear to his heart to be given to another.

Up there in the silence of the hills, day after day, and month after month, broken only by the hours of devotion, the old monk taught the younger one his wonderful system.

As he had made the game, based on Astrology, he alone could teach the conjunctions and combinations of the planets that produced certain effects on animate and inanimate things, whose slightest vibration changed the colours of flowers, the thoughts of men, and affected the formation of the hardest rock in the very depths of the earth itself.

One evening, when all had been taught, when error of judgment had been made impossible—the vow was given—*the vow to keep the secret inviolate—to keep it until the footsteps of death came near enough to warn him it was time to pass his trust on to another.*

Father Ambrose, with trembling lips, took the vow.

The last rays of sunset lit the Mediterranean with gold and purple and blue, the approaching night stood still for a moment to watch the light quivering through the windows of the monastery, then the gold and the blue faded away and *the purple majesty of death came into its own.*

.   .   .   .

The year was again coming to a close; the monks had passed their accounts to Father Ambrose, and many an anxious thought went round as to whether the secret had been passed on to him—the secret that paid their debts on the first day of every year.

The new Superior seemed the least worried of all. His duties had always been carried out to the letter of the law, and under his rule the monastery had gained in many ways, even better than when the old monk was at its head.

Towards night, a man in correct evening dress with a dark Inverness cloak thrown across his shoulders, might have been seen leaving the side gate of the monastery and, with long vigorous strides, making his way down the narrow, twisted mountain path towards the casino of Monte Carlo that lay like a glittering jewel far down below.

Being the last night of the old year, light-heartedness and gaiety ruled supreme. The restaurants and hotels, gay with flowers and brilliant with light, vied with one another in their many-sided attractions, music floated through the air and rose and fell as if keeping time to the ripple of the waves of the Mediterranean's tideless sea.

Men in evening dress and women robed like queens, passed and re-passed through the gardens and the streets.

Poets, philosophers, politicians, financiers, Jews, and Gentiles, every description of mankind jostled and joked and were happy together.

Women of all grades and from all parts of the earth—the dark, the fair, the ugly, and the beautiful, wore their jewels as lightly as they did their smiles. Money seemed to have lost its value ; it appeared for a moment—to vanish the next.

The brilliant light of the casino streamed far out to sea ; passing ships caught its rays for a moment, shone like spectres and disappeared. White gulls, like dead gamblers' souls, seemed to whirl and float for ever and ever round its glistening dome. And below—the fluttering of the living moths in and out and round the tables and back again to the glittering piles of gold.

As if he suddenly came out of the night, the tall figure of Father Ambrose passed through the brilliantly lighted streets and the crowds and passed into the casino.

He went to the bank near the door, had a few moments' conversation with the cashier, exchanged a paper for a bag of money, and finding a seat at one of the centre tables, without any hesitation commenced to play.

Putting the limit in gold on a set of numbers, he did the same with the square, the transversal, the dozen, the column, and the colour of the number. "Rien ne va plus," the croupier cried. A moment's silence, then the click of the ivory ball as it fell into the pocket of the number he had chosen. It took some moments for the croupier to pay out the enormous amount of the winnings, and meanwhile, every one's eyes seemed fixed on the strong face of the handsome stranger.

For him the scene seemed to have no interest. There was no smile of pleasure on his lips—his eyes had no gleam of triumph.

On again the wheel spun with again the same result, and again and again without one miss.

Then it was he suddenly stopped and with a pencil quickly totted on a piece of paper the amount he had won. It was the first moment that an expression passed over his face—it was an expression of surprise. He had gained more than he had intended.

For him the play was over. He leaned back in his chair while he filled a chamois-leather bag with the gold he had won.

He had not noticed that by his side sat a fragile, but beautiful-looking girl—one could hardly call her a woman, she looked so fair and sweet and, in her rather simple dress, she appeared strangely out of place in such surroundings.

She also had some system and was so engrossed in her play that she never once looked up at the handsome face beside her.

Piece by piece her money disappeared. She never winced or murmured, but steadily went on to the end.

When she came to her last gold piece, for the first time a mental struggle went on in her mind. She turned it over in her hand and twice made a movement to put it on some number, but each time withdrew the coin.

The stranger at her side had been watching her for a few minutes—she seemed the only thing he saw in the room. He made an effort to leave and then as suddenly leaned forward and told her some number.

She did not hesitate—there was not a moment to lose—the croupier had already begun his " Rien ne va . . ." but she had got it on. A second more, the ball fell—she had won.

For a moment she seemed dazed by the pile of gold that was pushed before her.

The stranger whispered again, and she put all her winnings back on a number, its square, transversal, column, dozen, and colour. One could hear a pin drop in that moment of tension, the veins stood out like cords on her delicate shapely throat; her lips grew as white as her face.

She hardly seemed to hear the click of the ball.

She hardly realized she had won again, and this time, a very large amount.

Her white hands touched the gold, poured it into her bag—a short, quick gasp came from her lips, she slipped from her chair and fell in a swoon by the side of the man that up to then she had but barely noticed.

The stranger lifted her gently and carried her through the long windows into the garden.

. . . .

He had heard her story, he had felt her tears of gratitude fall on his strong hands—her face, as beautiful as that of a Madonna, was lifted up towards his; her eyes were fixed on his. And such eyes—he who had only seen the painted eyes of saints, trembled before the human eyes of this woman.

As in a dream he heard her story. A short confession it was, out there in the garden with the vault of Heaven for a confessional, *the same old human story*—the woman who had lost her way in a dream, and when the awakening came, *Love had gone and everything had gone with it*.

Again it was the same old story—why should I trouble to repeat it—some strange law of affinity had brought these two together, it made of one a Magdalen, and the other an outcast.

The dawn was breaking over the sea as they wandered from the terrace garden and reached the outskirts of the town. At the commencement of the winding path towards the mountains, he bade her good-bye, then he turned again and drew her towards him.

There is something terrible about the love of a strong-willed man—especially a man who has passed middle life, and still more so if he has never loved before. It is the bursting into being of a new heaven and new earth—the breaking up of past ideals—the shattering of the former idols that one thought one worshipped and the placing of the true god on the altar of one's heart.

It is the *birth of the real* that makes the travail and the labour-pains so intense; this *birth of the soul* that sweeps everything into nothingness, that one moment in existence when man can look Ambition, Wealth, Life itself, in the face—and reply to all *that it is only Love that matters*.

As Father Ambrose felt this love I describe sweeping through his veins he made up his mind.

"I will come back to-morrow night," he said. "I will play till I make enough money for us both to live on. You will give up your life. I will give up mine. Together we will know what love means—the love that is jealous of all things, *the love for which we must sacrifice all—* the love *which is in itself all.*"

He never looked back, he felt he dared not.

With new vigour and new life he climbed the mountain path to the monastery gate.

He reached his cell as the dawn was breaking.

The monks were waiting anxiously, impatiently. Changing into his habit, he called them and emptied his leather bag of gold before their eyes. Quickly they counted it, and again the second time, it was more than they wanted or expected to receive.

"Are you satisfied?" Father Ambrose asked.

"More than satisfied," they replied.

"*And so am I*," he said, as they filed out of the room and left him alone.

Night fell; again the side gate of the monastery opened, again a man stood there for a moment, but this time he hesitated and his hands trembled so much he could hardly bring himself to close the gate.

His heart and soul seemed torn in twain, he was surrendering all that he had cherished most, and, as he had been taught to believe, abandoning his hope of salvation.

The struggle was more than he could bear. He sank on his knees, but dared not pray. He attempted to make the sign of the cross, but his arm seemed paralysed; he could not lift it. The words of his vow rang through his ears and froze his brain—that vow to use till death, the secret the old monk had taught him, *not for his own gain, but for his monastery*.

The night had got suddenly dark; a bitter wind from the far-off Alps chilled him to the bone. Snow already had begun to fall.

In another moment a blizzard of ice and hail raged and hissed and blotted the twisting pathway from his view. Again he hesitated and this time he looked back.

The chapel windows of the monastery were aglow with light, a bell tolled softly the call to prayers. Shaking in every limb, he dropped on his knees in the snow. Again he tried to pray, but no prayer would come. Pulling himself to his feet in a moment of agony he cried:

"Even God has forsaken me. I have given up all—for what?"

It may have been an echo—it may have been the delirium of his own brain—but the answer came back from the valley below—*For Love.*

"For Love," he cried, "for Love I have given up all."

Staggering forward with his hands stretched out towards the valley, the storm caught him in its arms—hurled him over the precipice to his doom; and the secret of Monte Carlo was lost for ever.

CHAPTER XLIV

A DEAL IN A SOUTH AFRICAN MINE. A LADY PAYS HER £100 BET.
I AM OUTWITTED BY A FRENCH ADVENTURESS

AS I stated in the Foreword at the commencement of these Confessions, I have no longer any reason to try to persuade my readers of the truth of that strange study which has given me the material on which I write these reminiscences; and they are not written with the object of " converting " the public to any theory or belief of my own.

I have finished " the span " I allotted myself to what I regarded as a kind of mission in life. I have consequently to-day " no axe to grind " in rendering my account of a strange career.

For myself, I will ever be grateful that I was privileged to lead such an unusual life, to meet the interesting personalities I have met, to be allowed to come so closely and so intimately with the human side of so many of those who came to consult me.

Although I have never posed as a philanthropist, I gladly gave my time, and often my money to those I thought I could help; I was always ready to sacrifice personal gain in the interest of my study; and perhaps because I did not make money my sole object, money poured in all the same, and " the bread " that I threw " upon the waters " was returned to me even multiplied a thousandfold.

Apart from my ordinary fees, I got odd chances of making money; but in every case, due to something relating to my strange profession. One or two illustrations may be of interest to my readers.

A DEAL IN A SOUTH AFRICAN MINE

At the close of one of my busy days in London, a peculiar-looking, wild-eyed man insisted on an interview and would not be put off by any excuse.

Perhaps for this reason I could not feel very sympathetic, so I confess I told him what I saw, without much regard as to whether he liked the picture of himself or not.

I told him he had risen from nothing; had no education and very little brains, that Fate had been unusually kind to him and had given him chances that few men get; that he had but one gift, the only one that I could make out, an instinct for speculation in land and mines, which had always brought him money, and which he as rapidly threw away by gambles in Stocks and Shares and things he did not understand.

I also told him he was a drunkard, but with the one redeeming feature, *that he drank only when successful*, but that in a few years he would drink himself to death.

At this remark he looked up for the first time. " Then I will be successful again," he said.

I almost laughed at the longing expression of his eyes. " Yes," I said, " I am sure you will. From what I see, Fate will give you a last chance as you enter your forty-eighth year."

" Are you quite sure that in my forty-eighth year, my luck will turn ? "

" Yes," I said, " absolutely sure."

Speaking slowly and deliberately, he looked me straight in the eyes and went on : " I was forty-eight on the 14th of September—just a month ago from to-day—and things have been worse than ever since then. Do you still hold to what you said ? "

I hesitated a moment and then took another look at a certain line that stood out clear and distinct at the forty-eighth year. I could feel the man trembling; my words perhaps meant life or death to him. Then something seemed to possess me and give me confidence.

" Yes," I answered, " I hold to what I said—as you enter your forty-eighth year you will get your last chance ; you will succeed in whatever your plan is, provided it is in lands or mines."

" Look here, guv'nor," he said. " I will tell you what the position is. I am an Australian, born on the land, reared on it, and as you say, I have made money both with land and mines, and with nothing else. I have now been in London for the past eight months trying to get people interested in an option I have on land near Johannesburg, in which I know there are the best diamonds ever found in South Africa.

" I have no money myself to exercise my option, which will soon run out. I can get no group in the City to join me. I am, in fact, ' broke to the world.' Do you still believe in what you have said ? "

" Yes," I said, " I do."

" Very well, then. Will you back up this study you believe in so much, by handing me over fifty pounds to carry me on for one month more ? "

Without a word I went to my desk and handed him over the money he asked for. I did not even ask for a receipt.

He just said : " Thank you, guv'nor—you're a white man," rammed the notes in his pocket, and walked out.

I admit I felt a fool, but I felt a bigger one when, a month later, he turned up again.

" Well, guv'nor," he said, " the month has gone and things are just as bad as ever. Will you gamble another fifty and give me another month's run ? "

There was a hungry, wistful look in his eyes that was terrible to see. I felt a greater fool than before, and yet I could not refuse. I gave him the second fifty without a word.

He gave my hand a grip that hurt it for a week.

He went to the door, stopped, and said : " Look here, guv'nor— don't think I am going to come down on you every month like this. If I can't pull it off this time, you won't be bothered by seeing me again—but by God if I do pull it off, you won't regret it."

About ten days later he phoned me from the City, asking me to join him at once at an address he gave in Austin Friars.

He had indeed " pulled it off." He had sold his option outright for a very large sum of money—and I returned to my rooms with a good many thousand pounds which, he said, was my share in the deal.

The last I heard of him was that he had returned to South Africa, where he persistently drank himself to death and died without a penny, a few years later.

A LADY PAYS HER £100 BET

Another instance of my getting a " coup " of money in an unexpected way was as equally mysterious.

People are inclined to think that women are not good in paying up bets, but in the case I am about to relate, I certainly met with one woman who was most scrupulous in " settling up."

One morning I received by post some excellent impressions on paper of a man and a woman's hands, asking my opinion as to the prospects if marriage took place, and the likely year when such would occur, if at all. It was also stated that the man's age was twenty-eight and the woman's twenty. I was above all enjoined to state exactly what I saw in these hands, and a fee of twenty guineas was enclosed for my work. The only address given for my reply was: " X, Poste Restante, Charing Cross Post Office."

The woman's hands were particularly well marked: the lines were unusually clear and easy to read. They showed every indication of her being not only rich, but with great promise of success and a distinguished position in life, and a splendid and happy marriage *if she waited until she reached twenty-four.*

The man's hands were the very reverse. They indicated a magnetic but strongly animal nature: a man with no real purpose or ambition except to get money by any means—honest or otherwise.

I answered back that " I had rarely seen the hands of two people more dissimilar in character or temperament, and that if a marriage did occur between such persons, it could only end in separation, scandal, and disaster to the lady." I further added: " If this man is now twenty-eight years of age, there is every indication that he has been married before: there is no indication that this marriage has been terminated; and I believe such a man is not free to marry again in his twenty-eighth year."

In due course, back came a reply, and again in the same lady's writing. It was to the effect that all I had said about herself was correct; but everything I had said about the man was wrong—that he had never been married, had not even been engaged, or ever had a love affair in his life before. And she added: " We shall be married next month, and to show how wrong you are, I will bet you one hundred pounds to ten, that within two years from this date, our marriage, instead of being a disaster, will be happy and successful; and I will consider it *only honourable of you* (and she underlined it) *to acknowledge this challenge and accept my bet.*"

I accepted the bet and sent my answer to " X, Poste Restante, Charing Cross," as before.

The following month, I again went to America, and it was exactly two years later before I found myself back in London.

One afternoon, someone made an appointment by telephone for five o'clock, and punctually at that hour a lady called and claimed the appointment.

Hardly looking at the person who entered, I placed a chair for her at the small consulting-table near the window.

Throwing her veil back, she said : " I have not come to consult you, ' Cheiro ' ; I have only come to pay my bet." Opening her satchel, she laid before me the letter in my own handwriting accepting the bet of two years ago, together with a Bank of England Note for £100.

" I never paid a bet with greater pleasure," she said. " He turned out in every way as you described. He had been married before ; a few months after our marriage he was arrested. He got a heavy sentence for bigamy, but, thank God, I got free and took back my maiden name. Perhaps you know now who I am."

" Yes," I said, " every one read the case in the papers. Even in America it was published, on account of your family ; but I had not thought of associating the scandal with my bet to a Poste Restante address."

" Of course not," she laughed, " but as you were so accurate over it, I am now living in hopes that the happy marriage you predicted for me at twenty-four will take place."

I am glad to say that less than two years later I was one of the many invited guests to her wedding in St. Margaret's, Westminster, which was one of the most distinguished that took place that season.

OUTWITTED BY A FRENCH ADVENTURESS

My readers must not conclude, after reading some of the previous experiences, that my life was always an easy one, or that my profession did not sometimes lead me into dangers that on one or two occasions very nearly cost me my life.

In the middle of my second season in New York, a man attempted to stab me, and did in fact succeed in making a gash just above my heart—the scar of which I will carry to the end of my life, my attacker's object being to put me out of the world before a lady—the subject of his affections—could have her hands read by me the following day. That story I will, however, leave aside as so many papers quoted it, and give a more amusing one, but one in which the principal character swore to have my life if we ever again met—which, thanks to Fate and another visit to the States very kindly prevented, and allowed sufficient time for a beneficent Providence to remove the gentleman to another world.

One evening a distinguished French diplomat called at my rooms in London and insisted on an immediate interview, although he had made no specific appointment in advance.

He carried under his arm a small wooden box and laid it down on the table before me with as much care as if it contained some priceless treasure.

One glance was sufficient to show that he was in a state of great nervous excitement that required all his self-command to control.

Seeing that the easiest way to dispose of the matter was to have the interview over as quickly as possible, I invited my guest to be seated.

He spoke with great impetuosity and mixed his very elegant French with very broken English, explaining his mission in a few words. It was " ze affairs of ze heart," as he put it, " and ze affection is here," he added as he patted the little box in the most tender manner.

According to his statement, he was madly in love with a woman whom all his friends were arrayed against. Their prejudice against the lady was, to his mind, as unaccountable as it was violent. They had told him she was an adventuress of the worst type, whose only object could be some political intrigue, and to accomplish his downfall. He, of course, man-like, believed nothing of such gossip. He was in love with the woman—and *a man in love is a child at play*.

" I believe in ze grand science of ze hand, Monsieur," he rattled on, " so I have brought you my angel's palms here in dis leetle box. I want you to write down what you in them see. I know you will be in one accord with my judgment that she has great enemies that tell ze lies, but that she is pure as one great piece of white snow.

" For many weeks," he went on, " she has modestly refused to my many requests to send me over casts of her leetle hands from Paris, but at last she had given in and ze casts had arrived that morning."

The box he reverently opened contained the precious hands that had been made in plaster, for it was impossible for her to leave Paris at that moment and bring her beautiful hands for me to read.

Very carefully he undid the cotton wool in which they were packed, and then as he laid them before me, he lightly touched them with his lips, as if he were offering adoration to the relics of some saint.

I looked at the casts. They were extremely well made ; every line stood out clear and distinct ; even the nails were of the delicate almond-shaped type. Yes, a pair of hands that seemed made more for prayer than for love. I took them up very carefully—he was trembling for fear I should let them drop. They were wonderful hands, every line and mark indicating innocence, tenderness, constancy, devotion—every virtue that an angel and not a woman is supposed to possess.

I looked over at my visitor. I noticed his waxed moustache, dyed at the ends, his sensual lips, his glittering cruel eyes, and I marvelled at the miracle that love performs.

" Monsieur," I said, " let me sum these hands up in a single sentence.

To Cheiro's encouraging words & prediction I owe my life's success & happiness

Lucile.

London
6th July '96.

What an exceedingly interesting & profitable half-hour this morning!

10/7/96

J. Page Hopps

**LUCILE (LADY DUFF-GORDON), THE FAMOUS COSTUMIÈRE,
AND THE REV. J. PAGE HOPPS**

Whoever the owner of them may be, she is a thousand times too good for you."

"Oui, Oui!" he interrupted, with unrestrained delight. "She is one angel; I knew you would speak ze truth. I am an unworthy pig, but I shall get good ven I get her as my angel vife."

I took a sheet of paper and wrote out my verdict, and as I did so, I got enthusiastic myself. I pointed out to him the good sides in the character as shown by the various marks. I called his attention to the indication of extreme honesty and truthfulness; that duplicity and intrigue would be impossible to the owner of such hands; that they were almost ideal and showed a nature with high spiritual devotion with almost every virtue in the calendar. In response to each statement I made, he smiled with profuse delight, and reaffirmed every moment his belief in and admiration for "my wonderful science."

Some months passed. I had quite forgotten the incident, when one day an extremely beautiful woman, wearing a dazzling array of jewels, called to have her hands read.

Her visit was in the regular order of appointments made in advance by my secretary.

As she crossed the room towards me, I could not help noticing a curious cynical smile on her lips and a defiant look in her eyes.

Without a word, she took the seat I offered her, and at once placed both her hands on the cushion, with the palms turned upward.

If ever I gave a really unflattering reading, it was in this case. My analysis of her character was scathing in the extreme, but fully justified by the pair of hands spread out on the cushion before me.

She did not get angry; she remained perfectly calm until I had finished. Then she leaned back, and indulged for a moment in a subdued laugh, full of cold, heartless triumph.

"How men do change their minds!" she said, with irony. "How different all this is from the verdict you rendered less than a year ago. Then I was 'an angel' a thousand times too good to become the wife of a crafty French diplomat. I was a marvel of spiritual devotion, a being devoid of duplicity, faithful, loving, virtuous—in fact, in your professional opinion, the direct opposite of everything you have just had the goodness to declare I am to-day."

"But," I blurted out in astonishment, "your hands are not those from which the casts were . . ."

"Wait a moment, please," she interrupted. "I have come for the express purpose of having a good laugh at you, and also to express my obligation.

"To the wonderful 'reading' you gave to those self-same casts, I am indebted for the fact that I am now the 'angel wife' of Monsieur So-and-So, and I can assure you I have made good use of my position.

"Yes, I used you and his belief in your 'grand science' for my own purpose.

"He has become aware of this fact, so I thought it was as well to inform you and also to warn you, for the first thing my charming husband will do when he gets up from his bed of sickness will be to shoot you at sight. But," she added, "I somehow doubt that he will get up. Don't look so sad over it. I will solve the mystery for you in a few words. It was simply that there were certain things which I was determined to accomplish in a political way, and the only way was by marriage to the man who brought you the casts.

"His people knew too much, but still, my friend, fortunately for me, Love is blind and a bit deaf as well. I knew he had absolute confidence in your ability to read character from the lines of the hand. I was afraid of you and determined not to gratify his wish that I should have casts made of my hands to be submitted to you.

"He insisted, so I had to give in; but still, I was not too stupid. I went to the nearest convent and persuaded the most devout and angelic little nun, who possessed exquisite hands, to allow me to make casts of them. The rest of the story you know. But don't look so grieved about it. I only used you, Monsieur, as I use all men. Au revoir."

CHAPTER XLV

STRANGE FATALITIES OF THE GREAT WAR. HOW I PREDICTED A VIOLENT DEATH FOR LENA GUILBERT FORD, AUTHORESS OF THE FAMOUS SONG, "KEEP THE HOME FIRES BURNING"

WHAT a strange fatality, people said, "that the gifted authoress of 'Keep the Home Fires Burning' should meet her death in a London air-raid, buried in the burning ruins of her own home."

The following story is still more strange, it indicates how for some persons escape from Fate seems to be impossible.

It was so with Lena Guilbert Ford, a charming, great-hearted woman from the Southern States of North America.

I first met her when she was a hard-working journalist in London, where her name is still revered in Fleet Street, not from any great brilliancy in her work, but for her good-heartedness in never failing to help others in distress or trouble of any kind.

Her reputation in giving every cent she earned away became so well known that editors insisted that she had to be paid by cheques marked "not negotiable," so she could not cash them to get immediate money, but would be compelled to pay them into her bank.

Yet no woman worked harder to earn money than did this "hack writer" of Fleet Street—she had a crippled son and an aged invalid mother to support.

One afternoon she called to interview me for some newspaper, so very naturally I examined her hands.

She had plenty of signs of having brains and mentality, her Line of Head was finely traced; but what struck me most forcibly was that the Line of Heart (the line under the base of the fingers) dominated all other marks and lay like a deep furrow across her palm.

Her thumb also was supple-jointed and bent outwards, another indication of a generous nature, while the fourth finger was so extremely short that it was quite abnormal. The fourth, or as it is called "the little finger," for the benefit of my readers, I must remark *en passant*, is called in symbolism "the croupier's rake." If long, the man or woman has the quality of "raking" money or things toward him or herself; if short, they are deficient in this quality, they also lack acquisitiveness, and especially so with a supple-jointed thumb.

No wonder this clever woman could never keep a cent for herself.

Another mark that stood out clear and distinct was that of danger from fire or explosions.

She laughed when I told her this, saying: "How curious that is, wherever I go fire seems to be attracted to me. I hardly can remember a month when I have not had some accident by fire of one sort or another. But tell me, 'Cheiro,'" she added, "when shall I ever make some—what I would call *real money by my pen*?"

"You would," I answered, "if some war came on, you would be

inspired to write some 'Battle Hymn,' like Julia Ward Howe did in the Civil War." Being an American, she knew at once what I referred to, and just as quickly she made a note of it in a little red book she always carried.

We did not meet again for some years. The Great War came on, hurling doom and destruction across the world. Lena Guilbert Ford wrote "Keep the Home Fires Burning," and, as the papers after her death said, "there was probably never a soldier song so inspiring."

Many a time I had felt proud of knowing this handsome, gifted woman when regiment after regiment marched past singing her famous song.

Then I met her again; it was one evening at the upper end of Baker Street. I was waiting for an opening in the traffic to allow me to cross when I saw Lena Guilbert Ford coming towards me.

She seemed so happy to see me. "You were right, my friend," she laughed, "it took a war to wake me up."

"Well, I hope the song brought you some money?" I asked.

"I sold it for two guineas, but what does that matter?" She shrugged her shoulders. "The soldiers love it, that is recompense enough. But," she added, "curiously enough, it gave me my start. My other songs that followed, 'When God Gave You to Me,' and 'We are Coming, Mother England,' are bringing me in good royalties. I remember so well you told me I would one day make more money writing verses than I ever would as a journalist, but that it would take a war to make me do it—and it certainly has done."

"Come round and have dinner with me," I said. "My house is no distance away."

"Certainly I will," she replied. "I would love to talk with you over that danger from fire you told me was my fate. Lately it *has become worse than ever*."

We had walked on for about five minutes. Suddenly a gun in the far-off distance gave the alarm that a Zeppelin had been signalled. Then another and another boom, people began to rush past us with frightened faces, street lights went out one after the other. London drew over her shoulders a mantle of darkness, waited and hoped for the best.

At the first boom of that far-off cannon, Lena had clutched my arm with a grip like a vice, she was trembling all over. "We are just at my house," I whispered. "We will be safe there till the raid is over."

"No, no," she answered. "I must get home, something is pulling me there. My mother and my boy have already heard the guns—*I must get home*."

"At least I will drive you there." I hailed a passing taxi. We jumped in. "Warrington Crescent, Maida Vale," she called to the driver.

In a very few minutes we had reached the house. It was in

black darkness, as all houses had to be when a Zeppelin raid was signalled.

Lena Guilbert Ford waved her hand to me as she ran up the steps.

It was the last time I ever saw her.

. . . .

Cannon in the nearer barrages to London were already booming incessantly.

Their circle of protecting shrapnel and bursting shells seemed to pierce the sky from all points of vantage. Defending aeroplanes roared over the now silent city. Taxis, omnibuses, carriages, people had run to shelter.

My taxi-driver refused to go further. I had to get out and make my way home as best I could.

I had reached my door, and groped with my latchkey to find the lock. As I entered, I looked upward to the black sky above me. Far away at an enormous height, like the flash of a falling meteor, I caught sight of an aerial torpedo tearing downwards—then the increasing roar that such engines of destruction make. I stood rooted to the spot. Where would it strike? that was the question.

Passing seconds seemed like eternities—the roar of the torpedo seemed now over my very head—then the crash—and an explosion that shook the doors and windows down the street.

The next morning news filtered through. The enemy torpedo had fallen on the centre of Warrington Crescent. The home of Lena Guilbert Ford had been blown to pieces. Her aged mother, her crippled son and herself, were gone for ever, buried under the burning ruins of what she had once called home.

CHAPTER XLVI

HOW CAPTAIN LIONEL BOWLES WON THE VICTORIA CROSS, TO BE KILLED BY A BOMB IN A LONDON STREET

ANOTHER tragedy during the Great War in which I was forced to play a role was in the case of Captain Lionel Bowles. It came about as follows:

At the outbreak of the Boer War in 1899, Lionel Bowles, then a man of between twenty-nine and thirty years of age, was one of my clients. In his right hand was a sinister mark of fatality, indicated for his forty-fourth year. It seemed so far off that we both laughed over it.

Up to that date the lines in his hand promised exceptional success in everything he undertook—a kind of "lucky Jim" one would pronounce him to be.

Although a young man he had already made a name as one of the most fortunate speculators on the Stock Exchange.

Everything he touched turned to gold—even an old crock of a race-horse he had bought in a moment of caprice at a public auction for the small sum of £50, had the year before won four of the big races in England and brought him in a small fortune.

"I am going to 'join up,' 'Cheiro,'" he laughed. "Do you think from my lines I will be as lucky in war as I have been up to now in everything else?"

"Most decidedly," I answered. "You will certainly come back with the Victoria Cross pinned on your breast." And that was exactly what did happen.

Here is the story as I heard it from his own lips shortly after the Boer War was over.

He joined up as a private in that famous battalion called the C.I.V's,[1] and in due course was sent to South Africa. Out there his luck did not for a moment desert him; he had the most wonderful hairbreadth escapes from death that one could possibly imagine, on one occasion being caught in an ambush—he was the only man to get out alive.

His indifference to danger brought him rapid promotion. He was transferred from one detachment to another, and in an engagement where every officer was killed he took command of the regiment and brought his men safely back to camp. For this action he received his commission, and in due course became captain. And now comes into the picture the curious story of how he won the highest award of the British Army—the Victoria Cross.

Curiously enough, after the war was over he wore this much coveted decoration as rarely as possible.

"One would almost think you were ashamed of having it," I said to him one evening when he used my rooms to dress for an important military dinner.

"I have ten minutes to spare," he said, looking at his watch. "I

[1] City Imperial Volunteers.

will tell you the real story about it, only keep it to yourself till after my smash-up in my forty-fourth year."

I nodded assent and he went on.

" I am supposed to be a brave man, one born with supreme indifference to danger, death, and all that sort of clap-trap.

" Well, let me tell you, my friend, it is all bunkum. I was exceptionally lucky, that is all. In the war I knew I was lucky. I knew my hour had not struck, so I took exceptional risks—but it was not due to courage. When the real test came I realized I was the most arrant coward that ever breathed. I will tell you how the test came ; you can think what you like after you hear it. I will tell you the story straight from my very soul—the soul that has despised me ever since."

Lighting a cigarette and pacing up and down the room, he went on :
" In the madness and excitement of war, men hardly know what they do, or can do, but in the silence of the night when one is alone and face to face with death, then it is that a man knows what his true nature really is.

" Under the blazing light of day with my comrades round me, or galloping across the veldt to the attack, where one could see the enemy in the open, the madness of blood-lust came to my rescue and I felt I could go through anything.

" On Spion Kop, however, I went through my first test, and realized what a coward at heart I really was.

" There, exposed for days and nights without shelter, out-manoeuvred by the Boers, unable to see their sharp-shooters firing down from a higher position, it was quite a different story, I assure you.

" My so-called courage oozed from my very finger tips. I lay in a cold sweat of abject fear, wondering if the next bullet would find me as its mark. I got through without a scratch—just luck, pure luck.

" Then came the battle of Modder River.

" Imagine, if you can, a wide stretch of open veldt between us and the water, no sign of any enemy, not a tree or a shrub to give cover, not a shot fired.

" Our orders were to cross the river to occupy the low-lying hills on the opposite bank.

" Orders have to be obeyed, not a man among us shirked the advance, even though the humblest private in the ranks felt in his heart that ' someone had blundered.'

" The river was wide but fordable, our horses plunged in, the men followed holding their rifles and ammunition above their heads to keep them dry.

" We had gone more than half-way—no enemy was to be seen ; that wonderful product, the British soldier, had already recovered his spirits, jokes were cracked from one man to another.

" Suddenly a shot rang out, then another and another—the bank opposite became a livid line of fire, we were virtually looking into the muzzles of rifles, before us, beyond us, and from the hills above.

"Bullets hissed through the air, splashed the water, dead bodies of horses and men floated down the river. We were trapped as British troops had never been trapped before in all their history.

"And still the fight went on, some men scrambled through and fought the enemy hand to hand.

"Field guns thundered up to our assistance, shells ripped Boer trenches, but to no avail; sharpshooters from holes and rocks above us picked off the commanders first, then the non-commissioned officers, then the men.

"Night was coming on, the retreat rang out. But how any of us scrambled back I do not know.

"For hours I lay behind a dead horse for shelter. The Boers had crossed the river; their snipers shot down any figure that moved in the shadowy night.

"I dared not stir. I was paralysed with fear, the dread silence broken only by groans from dying men completely unnerved me.

"Then it was *I knew I was a coward*. I could not face the death that other men had met with a smile.

"It was not so far back to our advanced lines. In the dim light I could see the Red Cross units bringing in the wounded and the dying, but I was too afraid to make the dash across the open veldt.

"Suddenly, I saw not far from me a badly wounded man struggle to his feet. A sniper saw him, too, and answered with a crack of a rifle. The bullet missed; *the man went on*.

"He was so crippled he could only move slowly, but yet *the bullets missed*.

"'I am not wounded,' I thought. 'If he can make the attempt, surely I can do the same.'

"Creeping on my hands and knees, I passed between bodies of dead and dying. My eyes were fixed on the nearest Red Cross Hospital—I thought of nothing else.

"Making a great effort I forced myself to my feet. I had not run ten yards when a sniper's bullet grazed my face, then another went through the sleeve of my tunic. Hardly knowing what I did, I snatched up the body of a man lying on the ground at my feet. It was the work of an instant to throw him across my back. 'He will stop the bullets,' I thought. 'I have still a couple of hundred yards to go.'

"I ran, as fear alone can make a man run. I reached the Red Cross unit, with my heavy burden slipping from my shoulders.

"Luck—I suppose I should call it—I had carried in a badly wounded officer of high rank, and won the Victoria Cross *for bravery on the field*."

Years later we met again. It was in the worst part of the Great War, October 1916. I was lunching alone in the grill room of the Carlton. Bowles saw me and came over to my table. He looked worn, haggard, a shadow of his former self.

"Yes," he said, in answer to my questioning look, " my wonderful luck has deserted me. I can't even get a job to fill shells.

" When war broke out I tried to ' join up,' but it was no use. I could not pass the medical examination. In 1913 I had pneumonia, and doctors said the fogs of London had done the rest.

" I am a ' broken-down crock,' they pronounced. This war calls for only the young, the fit, the best the nation can produce. Cannon-food, they have all agreed, must be the very flower of manhood, the great god Moloch must not be insulted by offerings of the ' unfit.'

" My record in the Boer War does not assist me one atom. My V.C. was won fighting farmers, they sneer, but fighting Germans is quite another thing.

" So here I am, my friend, without a job of any kind. My old business as a broker in bankruptcy, the Stock Exchange in a state of chaos, myself a derelict on account of health, and worse still, I am in my dreaded forty-fourth year.

" The only thing I can do," he went on, " is to meet the trains bringing in the wounded at the various stations and help the men getting back to their different homes."

A few weeks later, he was at Liverpool Street Station, London, in one of the worst of the Zeppelin raids ; a large bomb fell on a house at the corner of a street opposite where he stood, completely demolishing it, and killing a number of people.

Seized with a paroxysm of fear he started to run for his home fully two miles away. Through the now empty streets he raced till he reached it—a basement flat in Grays Inn Road.

Trembling with fear he threw himself into his bed, pulled the blankets over his head—and waited.

The Zeppelin had followed—high up out of sight in the far-off clouds it hovered for a moment—dropped another bomb and disappeared.

After the crash, when the debris was cleared away, firemen found the mangled body of Captain Lionel Bowles lying on his bed.

CHAPTER XLVII

THE STRANGE STORY OF THE DUCHESS D'AVARAY, PRINCESS DE MONTGLYON.

IN an earlier chapter in these Memoirs, I have related how I met the late King Edward VII, then Prince of Wales, in the *salon* of the Princess de Montglyon at the Berkeley Hotel, London.

Some time before, she had come to me as a client. The lines on her hands had told me a strange story, one so extraordinary and so unequalled in fiction, and one in which I personally became involved, that it will, I think, interest my readers if I relate it in these pages.

In my recent work, *You and Your Hand*,[1] I have reproduced an autographed impression of this lady's remarkable right hand, using it as an example for those who want to learn more about this study for themselves. In these Memoirs I can, however, allow myself to go more deeply into details of her life than I could do in a book dealing with the technical side of the study of hands.

This remarkable woman was a " Child of Fate " in every sense of that expression. Born in the lap of luxury, a descendant of one of the most noble families of Europe, from her birth she carried in the lines of her hands forewarnings of a terribly tragic destiny *which apparently had to be fulfilled.*

When I first met her she was a woman of about thirty-five years of age, remarkably handsome, unusually intelligent, endowed with a charm of personality and magnetism that was irresistible as far as most men were concerned—yet a complete failure as worldly success is measured.

Her birth and surroundings had been as equally " out of the ordinary " as her subsequent life proved itself to be.

Her mother, Countess de Mercy Argenteau, in her own right Princess de Montglyon, was one of the most famous of the " Ladies-in-Waiting " at the brilliant Court of Napoleon III.

There is no doubt that this extraordinarily handsome woman played an important role in the life of the Emperor of the French, as he was so proudly designated.

Surrounded as he was by the most fascinating women of the day, married to the beautiful Eugenie of Spain, the " fair sex " undoubtedly had great influence in his career, but no one more so than the proud and imperious Countess de Mercy Argenteau.

And yet this " love affair," or whatever one may call it, has been left unsullied by scandal, which is a remarkable thing in itself.

In all the chronicles of that gay Court of Napoleon III, no breath of calumny has ever scorched the name of the Countess de Mercy Argenteau, even when after the Emperor's fall a secret passage was discovered in Paris leading from her home to his private rooms in the Palace.

---

[1] *You and Your Hand*, published by Doubleday, Doran and Co., New York, and Jarrolds Ltd., London.

Eight years before the Emperor lost his throne, the Countess's only child, the subject of this story, was born. The event was acclaimed with festivities by the entire French Court, *the Emperor himself standing as godfather to the new arrival.*

To the Countess de Mercy Argenteau, however, it had been a bitter disappointment. She wanted a son, and in consequence it is said she almost hated the little one for being a girl.

Fate in this cruel way started the little Princess under unfavourable conditions, which were made still worse by the defeat of France and the fall of the Emperor into the hands of the German Army.

The Countess, her mother, made every effort possible to go to the assistance of Napoleon, now a prisoner in Germany. At the risk of her own life, leaving her child behind her, she escaped from the Siege of Paris, made her way alone and single-handed direct to Bismarck, and in some extraordinary way won over the Man of Iron sufficiently to grant her permission to see the Emperor alone in the château in which he was a prisoner.

By this means she obtained Napoleon's own views and suggestions as to the terms of the treaty that would sooner or later have to be drawn up, on the surrender of Paris.

What tender scenes must have passed between the man fallen from power and the woman who had risked so much for that interview of a few hours, can be better imagined than described.

As the last moments came, before they separated for ever, the ex-Emperor sent only one request to his conqueror, " that the Countess de Mercy Argenteau should be escorted safely back to Paris and spared every indignity *en route.*"

By Bismarck's special orders this was carried out, his soldiers standing to attention wherever her carriage stopped.

On her arrival in Paris, the Countess made one more daring attempt to carry out what she said were the last wishes of Napoleon before the Treaty of Versailles could be drawn up.

Relying on her beauty and extraordinary charm, she forced a personal interview on the King of Prussia and Bismarck in the Palace of Versailles.

At this interview she put forward for over an hour the views of the ex-Emperor for lenient treatment for vanquished France. " All to no purpose," she wrote in the notes she left behind. " Bismarck was absolutely indifferent to my tears or my charms—the brutal Treaty of Versailles was drawn up last night."

Failing completely in her desires to be of assistance to her Emperor, she retired to her estate, the Château d'Argenteau in Belgium, and remained there to her death.

Meanwhile, her daughter, the little Princess of Montglyon, the subject of this Memoir, had grown up to be a most beautiful and talented girl. Alone, surrounded by the historic walls of one of the oldest of Belgium's châteaus, she was cut off from the world, without companions or distractions of any kind.

Her mother had, however, planned for her a "brilliant marriage," and in due course she was married to the Duke d'Avaray, one of the proudest names of France.

Fate now took the reins in her own hands. Paris opened her arms to welcome her. At the age of eighteen she reigned as a queen of beauty among the handsomest women of that time.

Her *salon* was sought after by the most brilliant men and women of the day, the greatest names of Europe attended her receptions. The Prince of Wales, later King Edward VII, became one of her most devoted admirers, and came over from London whenever possible to be present at her fêtes.

Her marriage was, however, unfortunate; the Duke and she drifted apart and they led their own lives independent of one another.

On the outside everything appeared well for some years, then the jealousy and enmity of a woman so embittered her, that one day she just "walked out," leaving everything behind her—even Paris.

She retired to the Château d'Argenteau which she had inherited from her mother, and with her dogs and her wonderful brood of peacocks and peahens, she appeared to live happily for a time.

It was here in that beautiful old château that I saw her to her greatest advantage.

During an unusually severe winter, one December she invited me to make a house party with a few friends and spend Christmas with her. I reached Ostend in such a storm that I was the only passenger who crossed from England that night. By the time the train reached Ghent, snow had begun to fall heavily, and when I reached Liége, the nearest station to the château, the roads had already become wellnigh impassable.

I had, however, made up my mind to reach my destination. I took it all in the spirit of adventure, so a few difficulties more or less did not seem to matter. After some bargaining and considerable loss of time, a sleigh and four very decrepit-looking horses were finally put at my disposal, and in a blinding snow-storm I set out for the Château of Argenteau.

I need not relate this part of my experience; many others have been in snow-storms before, and snow-storms, like people, are very much built on the same monotonous lines. Suffice it to say, the journey took hours, but some time in the afternoon I reached my destination.

The magnificent wrought-iron gates of the Park were not open, no one could be expected in such a storm. The lodge-keeper and his wife had gone to bed, although it was only four o'clock, but lodge-keepers always do things like that on such occasions. The delay, however, gave me an opportunity of admiring the finest specimens of wrough-iron gates that perhaps exist in Europe.

Of a great height, surmounted by gilded spears, they supported in each centre a shield covered with forty-two dagger handles made to represent forty-two fleurs-de-lis on a field of azure. This example of heraldic work I learned later from the Princess's own lips represented forty-two daggers found embedded in the breast of one of her ancestors under the walls of Jerusalem during the first Crusade, and so remained as the coat of arms of the Argenteau family ever since.

At last the lodge-keeper was routed out of his bed, and with the help of shovels and his buxom wife, the gates were opened sufficiently wide for my sleigh to enter.

We reached the portico of the château, the noise of the sleigh-bells had been heard, the heavy oak doors were thrown open, and the Princess herself appeared to welcome me, together with her English companion, the sole occupants of the place, for none of the other guests had braved the weather.

For nearly a week we were snow-bound in the château. Late one afternoon we heard sleigh-bells in the distance. Was it possible that some one was coming to visit us?

A sleigh drawn by two splendid horses drove up to the portico. We rushed down to the entrance hall to see who had braved the snow. To my profound amazement, the King of the Belgians and Princess Clementine, his royal daughter, entered.

His Majesty recognized me at once. In a previous chapter I have related my meeting with him in Paris and in the Palace of Laeken later.

"Just imagine meeting you here," he said cordially, "and in the château of one of my dearest friends." Turning to my hostess, the Princess, he addressed her as "Cousin" and calmly announced that she would have to put up himself and the Princess Clementine for the night as it would be too dark to risk the snow-drifts on the long drive back to Brussels.

Later, we all met for dinner; on this occasion it was served in the principal dining-room of the château. Up to then the Princess, her English companion, and myself had had all our meals in the more cosy dining-room attached to the Princess's own suite.

The larger room was almost regal in its size and furnishings. The walls of crimson velvet were covered with the paintings of ancestors dating back to the time of the first Crusade. The entire service was of gold—no wonder, I thought, that Kings have poor digestions.

His Majesty of Belgium ate little; looking across the table he chaffed me about the Irish stew I had given him in my house in Paris and told the story of how he had given me the same dish when I visited him in the Palace of Laeken, but "Cheiro," he laughed, "had his revenge by predicting for me stomach trouble in the coming years." And he added, "I believe his prediction is already being fulfilled."

Princess Clementine was in equally good spirits as her royal father and told in an amusing way how she had helped to pull the horses out of a deep snow-drift not far from the château.

The dinner went merrily on, but nothing could keep the intense cold from creeping into that immense room. In spite of three huge fireplaces full of blazing logs, we were all glad when our hostess suggested we should have coffee and liqueurs served upstairs in her own cosy suite. Once up there, things seemed better; as well as two large wood fires, there were no less than four charcoal braziers, one in each corner of the room.

His Majesty suggested a game of poker, " to keep our thoughts off the weather," he laughed ; so we played till long past midnight. We might have gone on till morning if His Majesty had not won all our money. He was not disposed to play for " paper," so we stopped and bid one another *au revoir* till luncheon next day.

On my way to my suite of rooms, I had to pass the private chapel where the Father Confessor with two acolytes was saying an early Mass. It was, however, so cold that the priest was wearing a fur coat under his vestments; while his two little boys, also with fur, looked exactly like two little " Teddy Bears."

Poker, religion, and a royal personage, under the same roof; what a mixture, I thought, as I closed my door and went to sleep.

The next morning, snow that had fallen during the night was piled up at the windows and was still falling. We all met at luncheon, but in the warm dining-room of our hostess's own suite, where the conversation was naturally about the weather. It was finally decided that His Majesty and Princess Clementine could not attempt the journey back to Brussels that day. His Majesty accepted being a prisoner with quite a good grace and sent a couple of men on horses to the Palace to let his Government know where he was.

There was no telephone in Belgian châteaux in those days, so he had a good rest and, I believe, slept for the rest of the day.

The next morning an escort arrived from the Palace of Laeken and His Majesty of Belgium and his royal daughter returned home.

As there was no escort for me I had to remain another four days, before the roads became passable enough to reach Liége and take my train for England.

That was the last time I saw Mercy of Argenteau, Princess de Montglyon, surrounded by the magnificence into which she had been born.

The next time we met, her splendour had diminished, her fortune was gone for ever, with creditors assailing her from every side.

During our many years of friendship I had often foretold for her the financial crisis that was coming, and which she seemed strangely helpless to avert. I had shown her on her hands how the Fate and Success Lines were rapidly fading out.

She was a fatalist to the core and took every blow with a smile. Across her private notepaper she had embossed in French the words, " Et ceci aussi il passera " (and this also will pass away). This was the outlook she took on life and it was impossible to get her to regard it in any other way.

One speculation after the other ruined her. Money melted in her hands like so much snow; jewels and precious relics of her family had to be sold to pay her debts. Finally, creditors seized the Château of Argenteau, and by a strange irony of Fate, the last room to be sold, and the last one she slept in before she left the château for ever, was the very room in which she had been born. That night she left for Paris, her only companion being "Shamrock," a beautiful collie dog that she adored.

Destiny was not finished for her even then. I had always predicted for her that when everything had gone that some romantic love affair would come into her life which would cause her to leave her own country and commence a new life in some world such as the United States. This she laughed at, saying such a thing as love was impossible. Yet, curiously enough, I was fated to be present when the curtain rang up on the strangest romance of this strange life.

One evening in Paris she sent me an invitation to be present at the large arena of the old Moulin Rouge. She wanted me, she wrote, to see a daring exhibition of lion taming where Bonavita, the famous American lion-tamer, was to appear for the first time. In fact, she added, "The more I see of men, the more I love brutes."

We had front seats in the orchestra stalls.

The great crimson curtains rolled open. The entire stage was replaced by a steel cage; enormous African lions paced up and down before us, glared and growled at the audience, snapped and snarled at one another, and generally behaved as the "King of Beasts" is supposed to do.

The famous lion-tamer entered, closed the steel gate behind him, and stood for a moment like a statue.

Bonavita was a man of splendid physique; dressed in a kind of semi-military uniform, he made an imposing appearance. The audience gave him a magnificent ovation. He was the one lion-tamer in the world *who never used a whip*.

Unconcernedly he walked into the midst of the lions and put them through their paces. They obeyed his commands like children—*all but one*.

One powerful tawny beast retired sulkily into a corner, lashed his tail, and snarled at Bonavita in a threatening way.

The audience was enchanted. To them it was a duel between a man's pluck and a dangerous animal's temper.

Bonavita ordered the lion out to the centre. For a moment it appeared ready to obey, but it was only for a moment; it slouched to the back of the cage, then crouched, glaring angrily at its tamer.

The man turned. With his back to the audience, he faced the lion. The other animals slunk into various corners, leaving the man and the beast to settle matters between themselves.

The packed theatre grew silent with expectation, so silent one might have heard a pin fall.

The Princess at my side gripped my arm in the intensity of the moment.

Suddenly the great beast gave a roar of defiance that echoed through the theatre.

The moment had come. With another roar he sprang on the defenceless man, knocked him to the floor, and commenced mauling his left shoulder and arm.

Then the unexpected happened. With every one paralysed by fear, the Princess sprang from her seat; in a second she had reached the cage, jabbing and striking the lion's face with the handle of the parasol she carried.

Growling with pain, the beast retreated a few paces from his victim; an attendant opened the steel gate, but too frightened to enter, he stood holding it open while the other lions, now excited, prowled about the cage.

Pushing the man one side, the Princess entered. Kneeling down, she lifted the injured man's head to her lap, then with the attendant's help carried him through the lions and out of the gate into safety.

Bonavita was rushed to a hospital, the Princess going with him in the ambulance. An operation saved his life but failed to save his arm.

And yet Destiny had not played all her cards. Some weeks later the newspapers announced that the great American lion-tamer was sailing the next day for New York.

That evening the Princess called at my house. " I came to say good-bye," she said. " I am leaving for the States in the morning. Bonavita is not strong enough to travel alone."

A month or so later I received a letter from New York. " My dear ' Cheiro '," she wrote, " you can announce to your friends—don't trouble about mine, I have none now—that Princess de Montglyon has married Bonavita the lion-tamer. I may have lost a great deal in my life—but I have in the end found—love."

And still Destiny had not yet finished. Two years later came another letter—the dream of love was over. " Bonavita was the best and noblest man I ever met," she wrote, " but his ways were not my ways, nor my ways his. We have separated for ever. I shall remain in America—but alone. Make whatever use you like of that impression you took of my hand."

CHAPTER XLVIII

HOW I MARRIED—AND WHY

AS I have received so many letters asking point-blank if I was ever married, it will perhaps not be considered out of place if I answer the question in these Memoirs.

I do not know why anyone should be interested in my own private life, but as they evidently are, and not only women but men, I will endeavour to satisfy this curiosity once and for all.

In order to do this, I will have to lay bare my very soul and give my feelings and reasons on this subject, which may not be in accordance with the views or opinions of some of my readers.

Running through my mind as I write is that well-known quotation:

> " To thine ownself be true,
> And it shall follow, as the night the day,
> Thou can'st not then be false to any man."

I will therefore state quite openly that through all my unusual career, *marriage was the last thing that came into my mind.*

I did not approve of it, at least not for myself, for many reasons. In the first place, I loved independence more than anything else in the world. In the second, I had in me that material that makes one a rebel against conventionality. Third, I led an unusual life which would have been painful for any ordinary woman to follow—the life of a rolling stone, ready at a moment's notice to go anywhere in the search of material for my own particular study. Lastly, I did not understand why two persons had to be tied together by law—when love is the only tie that binds—and as that love had never entered my heart, the necessity for marriage in my early years never came into my mind.

It may surprise many people to know that in Europe there are one or more secret societies that exist, with the avowed purpose that none of their members shall marry.

With my peculiar bent for things out of the ordinary, it was not surprising that I joined one of these societies in my early twenties. The one I joined consisted of five hundred members bound under a common oath never to enter the bonds of wedlock.

That word in our ritual, I may add, was written and pronounced "weed-lock," and played an important part in our ceremony of initiation.

Each member paid dues of one hundred pounds per year into a kind of pension fund, which money, with compound interest added, came to a considerable amount when one reached the supposed unmarriageable age of sixty years—called in our ritual, "the age of wisdom."

Do not suppose for one moment that the members of such an association were "women haters"; quite the contrary, they were "women lovers," *but in the highest sense of that term.*

In one part of our ritual we took an oath to help women in every way that was possible; to respect no rank more than another—that *the title woman covered all ranks.* In another part we were admonished to give generously to the fund for women in distress, so that feminine relatives of our members might be assisted in times of trouble. Further, we were most strictly conjured to respect the liberty of women as much as we did our own; to never force our attentions on her when she gave no encouragement; to wait for her to give before we took. In fact, to regard her as a gift from God and *not a slave of man.*

Marriage was regarded as the enemy of such sentiments, and was the only reason we took the oath to keep free from its entanglements.

In my own case, although the lines of my hand distinctly foretold that I was fated to marry late in life, I laughed at such a possibility and felt strong in the fact that I was a member of an anti-marriage society.

The designs of Fate are, however, as irresistible as they are inscrutable. Shortly after I had joined the society, there came one day to my rooms in London as a client, a young girl whose small and beautifully formed hands attracted me even more than she did herself.

Beautiful hands have always been a weakness of mine; as a connoisseur of art almost worships an exquisite painting, so do I regard beautiful hands.

I foretold that this young girl would have a cruel fate before her; she would marry within a year, lose her husband in some mysterious way that would for a long time prevent her remarrying. She would meet again and again the man she would eventually marry, but be prevented from doing so for many years; finally, overcoming all difficulties, she would be successful in the end.

Looking me straight in the eyes, this young girl of sixteen said quite innocently but impulsively:

"You are the only man I would want to marry; if, as you say, I am fated to lose my first husband, can't you try and make the second come off a bit sooner?"

"What do you mean?" I asked.

"Simply that I mean to have you for my second husband, if I cannot have you for my first."

I thanked her for the compliment she had paid me, smiled the smile of a man sure of himself, bowed her out of my door, but I *could not forget her small, beautiful hands.*

Years later, we met in New York. She was in widow's weeds, but as her husband's body had not been found, they being both of English nationality, she would have to wait seven years, she told me, before the courts would allow his death to be presumed.

We met again in China, Cairo, Monte Carlo, and Paris, but as by my oath I could not marry, we remained good friends and nothing more.

In the end, perhaps to forget, she went to Egypt and lived for over four years in her own caravan, travelling on the confines of the Sahara.

One day, back in the South of England, she read the following in the *Daily Mail:* "We regret to announce that 'Cheiro,' the well-

COUNTESS HAMON

known seer, is so seriously ill with double pneumonia that he is not expected to live. If any relatives should see this announcement they should come to him at Devonshire Lodge, London, without delay.

There were no relatives to turn up, but the next day she reached London and took charge of me as if it was the most natural thing in the world to do.

I had a long, hard fight for life; she nursed me night and day. Those little hands proved they could be useful as well as beautiful.

We took a voyage to the Mediterranean to make my recovery complete. One day on the return journey to England I had a good look at the lines of my own hand. I saw I was approaching the date when marriage was *marked for me late in life*. I went down to the writing room and wrote my resignation to the Anti-marriage Society, to which I had belonged for nearly thirty years. For fear I might weaken in my resolution, I gave the letter to my future wife to post and we were married on my return home.

While writing this chapter I cannot help thinking of that well-known poem which is so appropriate to my own case:

> " Two shall be born the whole wide world apart,
> And speak in different tongues, and have no thought
> Each of the other's being, and no heed—
> And these o'er unknown seas to unknown lands
> Shall cross, escaping wreck, defying death,
> And all unconsciously, shape every act
> And bend each wandering step to this one end,
> That one day, out of darkness they shall meet
> And read life's meaning in each other's eyes."

A brief biographical sketch of my wife's career may be of interest.

On her mother's side she is of French and English descent, on her father's of English stock that trace their pedigree back to the " Black Prince," Edward I of England.

She herself has had an eventful and unusual career. With a very decided bent for chemistry, she was the first woman in England who invented enamelled jewelry, designing her own electric furnace for the purpose. As may be remembered, this craze for enamelled jewelry and lacquer work became the vogue in London about twenty years ago. Being an artist by nature, the designs she turned out were very original. At the same time she developed painting by crayons, using the tips of her fingers instead of brushes. In her early years she had an extremely beautiful voice, but unfortunately, her musical career was cut short by an operation on her throat caused by diphtheria. In order to recover her health she travelled in many countries, visited Egypt, Japan and China, also North and South America, and had the unique experience of being kidnapped by bandits in Mexico. The head of the troop of brigands chanced to be an English Peer who had sacrificed his name and fortune in order to shield a woman he was in love with. This story is very beautifully told in a book she has written, called *Outlawed for Love*, which was recently published in London.[1]

Having a decided talent for geology, botany, and chemistry in later years she has devoted her time to the study of pests that injure plant life in various parts of the world. In such research work she has been extraordinarily successful, having been invited by Governments of many countries to assist them in their fight against insect plagues of many kinds. She has recently written an exhaustive treatise on the cause of the widespread destruction of the coca plantations in South America, and has pointed out how this destruction might be prevented and the plants brought back to their original productiveness.

As I have so often called attention in my books to the fact that persons with extremely small hands have a natural desire to attempt large things, she is a remarkable example of this theory. She has the smallest hands of any woman I have ever met, and her present work, not being confined to one country, may in the end extend its influence to every nation of the world to whom the question of the protection of plant life appeals.

[1] *Outlawed for Love*, by Countess Hamon. The London Publishing Company.

CONCLUSION

IN conclusion, I would like to add a brief word of thanks to the Press—British, American, and Colonial—for the generous way they have always treated me, and the encouragement they have given in reviews of my books. Many times the Press has suggested that I should publish a complete volume of Memoirs. I have obeyed in giving this book to the public. In doing so, I have tried to pick out of the Sheaf of Memory the most varied incidents of as wide an interest as possible. I must, however, state that this volume, large as it is, only covers a small part of my many experiences, but should the demand from the public be sufficiently great, I will be happy to continue with another volume.

If some of the stories I have related are so strange as to be almost unbelievable, I can only ask my readers to bear in mind that a life out of the ordinary highways and byways was bound to attract the unusual. I have held back many other histories, fully as sensational as any that appear in these pages; but those I have given I can vouch for as having actually occurred, the only alterations being, in some cases, the suppression of real names lest unnecessary pain be caused, and in the other, the use of the author's privilege of description as an artist uses his brush—not to obscure or deform, but to bring out the lights and shadows of the picture.

FINIS

INDEX

A

Abbé Thurvillier, 129
Abbey, Henry, 152, 162
Abbots, 15, 16
Act of Parliament, 38, 50
Alfonso XIII, 131
Allen, Senator, 211
Allison, Senator W. B., 211
Ambrose, Father, 267
American Register, 43
" Angel of the Revolution," 83
Anne Boleyn, 50
Argenteau, Mercy, 286
Armour, Phillip, 185
Auditorium Hotel, 186
Ayer, Harriet Hubbard, 190

B

Bachmakow, Lydia, 73, 75
Bagneux, 154
Baku, 92
Balancourt, Commandant, 99
Balfour, Arthur James, 38, 125
Barker, Ivor, 234
Bathe, Lady de, 158
Bell, Sir Charles, 26
Bernhardt, Sarah, 147
Bertillon, 26
Bismarck, 287
Bissing, Baron von, 130
Blanc, Monsieur, 262
Boer War, 41
Bombay, 30, 32
Bonavita, 291, 292
" Book of Books," 22
Borghase, Prince, 108
Boston, Mass., 172
Boulogne-sur-Mer, 140
Bower de Courcy, 236
Bowles, Lionel, 282
Bresci, anarchist, 109
Buckingham Palace, 48, 49
Buffalo, 179
Bull, Mrs. Ole, 173
Burma, 248

C

California, 15
Calvé, Emma, 163
Carlisle, Mrs. J. L., 210
Caton, Arthur, 187
Caucasus, 92
Chamberlain, Joseph, 123
Chamberlain, Sir Austen, 124
Champs Elysées, 249

Chanizoff, Olga, 72
Chatauqua, 203
Cheir (hand), 37
Cheiro's World Predictions, 15
Chicago, 184
Chief of Police, 69
Chinese Buddha, 16
Chinese tablets, 15, 17, 18
Churchill, Lord Randolph, 123
Clanricarde, Lord, 235
Clarke, Charles W., 163
Cleveland, Grover, 210
Colonna, Prince Marco, 102
Confucius, 15
Cornwallis, Mrs., 135
Coronation, 48, 49
Covent Garden, 138, 160
Crisp, Senator, 211
Croker, " Boss," 128
Cronstadt, John of, 74
Cross (Major), 19
Curzon, Lord, 170
Czarevich, 71
Czarina, 63
Czar of Russia, 62

D

Daily Telegraph, 27
Davidson, Rev. Dr., 203
Davis, Major Alexander, 136
Dee, Dr. John, 50
Delcassé, 44
Demidoff, Princess, 108
Deslys, Gaby, 59
Detroit, 184
Dewey, Admiral, 210
Dickinson, Don M., 184
Die Kunst Ciromanta, 24
Dimitri, Grand Duke, 78
Dnieper, 90
Dupont, Henri, 195
Duse, Madame, 164

E

Edward VII, 39
Edward the Peacemaker, 47
Egypt, 34
El Karnack, 34
Entente cordiale, 43
Eulalie of Spain, 130

F

Fairbrother, Ellis & Co., 137
Field, Marshall, 185

INDEX

Flammarion, Camille, 133
Fleet Street, 35
Ford, Lena Guilbert, 279
French-Indian, 195
Fuller, Chief Justice, 211

G

George III, 51
Georgia, route of, 93
German Secret Service, 253
Gladstone, 117
Golitizen, Princess, 84
Gonne, Maud, 166
Grand Llarva, 89
Grand Patriach, 89
Grand Vizier, 113
Great Masters, 151
Great Thoughts, 951
Grey, Lady de, 160

H

Hackett, James K., 155
Hague Conference, 1899, 83
Hall, Sir Edward Marshall, 135
Hamon, Countess, 296
Hamon, Robert de, 21
Hamon the Sea-king, 21
Hari, Mata, 248
Harland and Wolff, 127
Hawarden Castle, 117
Hawtrey, Mrs. Charles, 151
Heliodor, 66
Hengelmuller, Baron, 211
Henry VIII, 21, 50
Herbert, H. A., 211
Hermitage, 77
Higginbotham, H. N., 185
High Courts of Justice, 145
Hinckley, 206
Hiscock, Senator, 211
H.M.S. *Hampshire*, 99
Hontin, Van, 248
Hopps, Rev. Page, 278
Houndsditch murders, 27
House of Aries, 42
Howe, Julia Ward, 174
Hunter, Rudolph M., 202

I

"If We Only Knew," 175
Incarnate, 16
Incarnate Abbot, 15
India, 32
Innovator, 76

Irish stew, 54
Irving, Sir Henry, 52
Isvolsky, 62

J

Janotha, 165
Jews, 35
Jitomer, 92
Johanna, 101

K

Kabbala, 36
Karageorgevitch, Prince, 131
Karali, 79, 80
Kaspeck, 93
Kazan, 73
Kieff, 89
King Carlos, 59
King Humbert of Italy, 108
Kitchener, Lord, 97

L

Lacken Palace, 54
Lake Michigan, 186
Lama, 17
Lambert de St. Croix, 130
Langtry, Lillie, 158
Lascelles, Lord, 235
Lavalia, Princess, 129
Leiter, Mary, 170
Leiter, Mrs., 170
Leo XIII, 102
Leopold II, 53, 54, 289
Lewis, Sir George, 52, 247
Light, 173
Logan, John A., 188
Lombroso, 244
Longfellow, Miss, 173
Louis XVI, 104
Louis Phillipe, 129
Lucille, 278

M

Macbeth, 155
Machetta d'Algri, 151
Madame Sund, 70
Mah Jongg, 261
"Mark Twain," 168
Marlborough House, 41
Mata Hari, 248
Meissner, 26
Melba, 159, 160
Methodist body, 203
Metropolitan Opera House, 161
Miles, Nelson A., 211
Mingen, 248
Modern Society, 135

INDEX

Monaco, Prince of, 266
Monastery, 15
Mongolia, 15
Monk, 16
Monson, Sir Edmund, 44
Monte Carlo, 241, 242
Montgylon, Princess of, 41, 287
Morgan, D. N., 210
Moulin Rouge, 291
Moulton, Lady Fletcher, 136
Mount Ararat, 92
Muzaffer-ed-Din, 113
Mystic Cross, 22

N

Napoleon, 110
Napoleon III, 286
Nevsky Prospect, 65
Newcastle, Duke of, 126
Nor, 15
Nordica, 161
Norman descent, 21
North, Colonel, 236

O

Order of Lion and Sun, 116
Oscar Wilde, 152

P

Pagan, 21
Paget, Lady Arthur, 39, 171
Palace of Peterhof, 63
Palmer, Mrs. Walter, 51
Papal Guard, 102
Parnell, 25
Pensacola, 203
Père la Chaise, 154
Perugini, Signor, 161
Phillips, Sir Lionel, 125
Pingree, Mayor, 184
Pirie, Lord, 126
Poets' Club, 224
Pokrovskoie, 73
Porter, General Horace, 53
Pourichkievitch, 78
Pre-natal influence, 120
President Loubet, 45
Prevision, 142
Prince Colonna, 152
Putbus, Prince von, 130

Q

Queen Alexandra, 48
"Queen Bess," 50
Queen Elizabeth, 50
Quirinal Palace, 108

R

Rasputin, 66, 67, 68
Rhodes, Cecil, 123
Richardson, Rev. Dr., 35
Rollo, Duke of Normandy, 21
Roosevelt, Blanche, 151
Roulette wheel, 259
Rudolph of Austria, 109
Russell, Lillian, 161
Russell of Killowen, Lord, 145

S

St. Helier, 21
St. Louis, 104
St. Peter and St. Paul fortress, 86
Salem, 191, 192
Salson, anarchist, 113
Sarto, Cardinal, 106
Scapa Flow, 101
Scotch landlady, 37
Scotland Yard, 26
Selfridge, H. G., 186
Shackleton, Sir Ernest, 132
Shah of Persia, 113
Sioux tribe, 196
Sipido, anarchist, 109
Sirdar, 97
Sloan, Tod, 159
Smith, J. Heber, 174
Spanish-American War, 190
Standish, 213
Stanley, Sir H. M., 117
Staretz, 73
Stead, W. T., 166
Stevenson, Vice-President, 211
Syracuse, 177

T

Teheran, 115
Tewkesbury Cathedral, 21
Thought machine, 119
Tibet, 15
Tiflis, 92
Tilbury Docks, 27
Tod Sloan, 159
Tolstoi, Count, 77
Toussoun Nor, 15
Twain, Mark, 168

U

Utah, 199

V

Vadikaffquas, 92
Vatican, 102
Vaughan, Baroness, 58

Vaughan, Father Bernard, 126
Vetsera, Mary, 109
Victoria Cross, 242
Victoria Station, 49
Vincent, Judge W., 187
Vorontzoff-Daskoff, Viceroy, 92
Vyronbova, Anna, 75

W

Wakefield, Rev. Russell, 126
Wales, Prince of, 39
Walsh, Thomas, 53
War Office, 97
Washington, D. C., 210
Werner, Cecilia, 77
Western Ghats, 33
White House, 210
Whiting, Lillian, 173
Wilcox, Ella Wheeler, 169
Wolcott, Senator, 211
Wright, Whittaker, 246

X

" X," Madame, 69

Y

Yogis of India, 33
Youssoupoff, Prince, 78
Yvesky, Princess, 82

Z

Zaborovsky, 73
Zelle, Madame, 248
Zemstvo, 92
Zeppelin, 280, 285
Zodiac, 36